Practical
Parallel
Rendering

Practical
Parallel
Rendering

Edited by
Alan Chalmers
Timothy Davis
Erik Reinhard

A K Peters
Natick, Massachusetts

Editorial, Sales, and Customer Service Office

A K Peters, Ltd.
63 South Avenue
Natick, MA 01760
www.akpeters.com

Library of Congress Cataloging-in-Publication Data

Practical parallel rendering / edited by Alan Chalmers, Timothy Davis, Erik Reinhard.
    p. cm.
Includes bibliographical references and index.
ISBN 1-56881-179-9
  1. Parallel processing (Electronic computers) 2. Electronic data processing--Distributed processing. I Chalmers, Alan II. Davis, Timothy, 1965- III. Reinhard, Erik, 1968- IV. Title.

QA76.58 .C44 2002
004'.35--dc21

                                                     2002070381

Printed in Canada
06 05 04 03 02   10 9 8 7 6 5 4 3 2 1

Contents

II Case Studies   185

6 Interactive Ray Tracing on a Supercomputer   187
  6.1 System Architecture 188
    6.1.1 Conventional Operation 189
    6.1.2 Frameless Rendering 192
    6.1.3 Performance 193
  6.2 Ray Tracing for Volume Visualization 194
    6.2.1 Background 195
    6.2.2 Traversal Optimizations 197
    6.2.3 Algorithms 201
    6.2.4 Results 205
    6.2.5 Discussion 211
  6.3 Ray Tracing for Terrain Visualization 214
  6.4 Conclusions 215

7 Interactive Ray Tracing on PCs   217
  7.1 Introduction 217
    7.1.1 Previous Work 220
  7.2 An Optimized Ray Tracing Implementation 221
    7.2.1 Code Complexity 221
    7.2.2 Caching 222
    7.2.3 Coherence through Packets of Rays 223
    7.2.4 Parallelism through SIMD Extensions 223
  7.3 Ray Triangle Intersection Computation 223
    7.3.1 Optimized Barycentric Coordinate Test 223
    7.3.2 Evaluating Instruction Level Parallelism 224
    7.3.3 SIMD Barycentric Coordinate Test 224
  7.4 BSP Traversal 226
    7.4.1 Traversal Algorithm 226
    7.4.2 Memory Layout for Better Caching 228
    7.4.3 Traversal Overhead 229
  7.5 SIMD Phong Shading 229
  7.6 Performance of the Ray Tracing Engine 231
    7.6.1 Comparison to Other Ray Tracers 231
    7.6.2 Reflection and Shadow Rays 233
    7.6.3 Comparison with Rasterization Hardware 234
  7.7 Interactive Ray Tracing on PC Clusters 236
    7.7.1 Overview 238

Preface

The ever increasing computational demands associated with rendering has meant that parallel rendering is almost as old as rendering itself. However, the full potential parallel processing has to offer of producing wonderful images in reasonable times has always seemed to allude those striving for this "holy grail."

While parallel processing on a low number of processors is relatively straightforward, the challenge comes when confronting an implementation on a large system. Here the overheads associated with the processors working together can rapidly dominate and lead to the frustration of a solution time of *more* than that which was achievable on a single processor. And yet it is precisely these larger systems which offer the computational performance we seek.

The aim of this book is to describe the problems associated with parallel rendering, provide a methodology as to how these problems can be minimized and demonstrate how, with care, it is indeed possible to achieve efficient parallel rendering.

The book is structured into two parts. The first part is intended to provide textbook material that introduces generic parallel processing issues in Chapters 1 and 2. With this background knowledge, the reader is then introduced to high-end graphics algorithms such as ray tracing, radiosity and particle tracing. The specifics of these algorithms and their implications for parallel processing are discussed in Chapter 3, while Chapter 4 deals with recent developments in hardware. For many of these algorithms it turns out that the proper exploitation of coherence is essential. For this reason, an in-depth analysis of coherence for single images as well as image sequences is presented in Chapter 5.

In the second part of this book, a number of case studies are presented. Each case study uses parallelism to speed up ray tracing, but in the process they all take very different approaches to solving the problems faced in parallel rendering. In Chapter 6 parallel ray tracing on large shared memory computers is shown to produce interactive frame rates for data-sets containing tens of millions of quadrilaterals at screen resolutions of 1024^2 pixels. A second case study shows that clusters of PC's can also be effectively utilized to render very large models. Chapter 7 demonstrates that by very carefully exploiting the caching structure of modern PCs, which effectively amounts to leveraging as much coherence as possible, networks of PCs can render models containing millions of triangles at interactive rates. The third case study in Chapter 8 discusses the Kilauea parallel rendering engine, which was used to create the film "Final Fantasy". The last chapter of this book proposes to implement ray tracing in hardware and as such takes a very different approach to parallel rendering.

Acknowledgements

This book has evolved over many years. A number of the concepts described in Chapter 2 were first introduced in lecture notes at the University of Bristol and later appeared in A.G. Chalmers and J.P. Tidmus, *Practical Parallel Processing: An Introduction to Problem Solving in Parallel.* International Thomson Computer Press, 1996.

In 1998 we gave a course on parallel rendering at SIGGRAPH and things just snowballed from there. I would firstly like to thank all the authors who have contributed to this book. Hopefully our combined experience will help you get to grips with practical parallel rendering.

I would also like to thank the Rendering and Parallel Graphics & Visualization communities around the world for providing such a stimulating environment in which to work. I would encourage anyone who hasn't already done so, to attend one of the Eurographics-ACM SIGGRAPH Workshops in these fields; they are inspiring.

I have been extremely lucky to have been able to interact and share a beer or three with so many wonderful people over the years, all of whom have helped me formulate my ideas: the ACM SIGGRAPH Executive Committee and the wider ACM SIGGRAPH and Eurographics communities, especially Bonnie Mitchell, Judy Brown, Steve Cunningham, Leo Hourvitz, Scott Lang, Erica Johnson, Nan Schaller, Greg Ward and David Arnold to mention only a very few; my colleagues and friends at the University of Bristol, in particular Colin Dalton, Neill Campbell and Majid Mirmehdi and all my current and former PhD students. The list could go on. Finally, thank you to my family and especially Rhona and Maya for their love and support.

Alan Chalmers

I wish to acknowledge my advisor, Dr. Edward W. Davis, at North Carolina State University, for his help and guidance, as well as my family for their continued encouragement and support.

Timothy A. Davis

Several people have contributed to this book in both material and immaterial ways. These include Chuck Hansen and Pete Shirley for giving me the freedom to pursue my own interests. I'm very grateful to them as well as Mike Stark, Bill Martin, Helen Hu, Margarita Bratkova, Kristi Potter, Bruce and Amy Gooch and many others for making living in Utah an almost normal experience. They've also managed to put up with me for two years. How cool is that? Finally, I would like to thank all authors who contributed their precious time and delivered the content that I believe makes this book both useful and beautiful.

Erik Reinhard

I | Parallel Rendering

1

Introduction to
Parallel Processing

Alan Chalmers

Parallel processing is like a dog's walking on its hind legs. It is not done well, but you are surprised to find it done at all.
– Steve Fiddes (Univ. of Bristol) with apologies to Samuel Johnson

Realistic computer graphics is an area of research which develops algorithms and methods to render images of artificial models or worlds as realistically as possible. Such algorithms are known for their unpredictable data accesses and their high computational complexity. Rendering a single high quality image may take several hours, or even days. Parallel processing offers the potential for solving such complex problems in reasonable times.

However, there are a number of fundamental issues: task scheduling, data management and caching techniques, which must be addressed if parallel processing is to achieve the desired performance when computing realistic images. These are applicable for all three rendering techniques presented in this tutorial: ray tracing, radiosity and particle tracing.

This chapter introduces the concepts of parallel processing, describes its development, and considers the difficulties associated with solving problems in parallel.

Parallel processing is an integral part of everyday life. The concept is so ingrained in our existence that we benefit from it without realizing. When faced with a difficult problem, we ask others to help us solve it more easily. This co-operation of more than one worker to facilitate the solution of a particular problem may be termed parallel processing. The goal of parallel processing is thus to solve a given problem more rapidly, or to enable the solution of a problem that would otherwise be impracticable by a single worker.

The concept of parallel processing is not new. More than 2000 years ago, the Greeks used such principles in their computational devices. In the 19th Century, Babbage used parallel processing to improve the performance

3

of his Analytical Engine [189]. Indeed, the first general purpose electronic digital computer, the ENIAC, was conceived as a highly parallel and decentralized machine with 25 independent computing units, co-operating towards the solution of a single problem [112]. Two significant perceived problems with parallel processing restricted its widespread acceptance: the complexity of construction and the seemingly high programming effort required [35]. These perceived obstacles, together with the increasing availability of seemingly simpler sequential machines led to a significant shift in development to optimized sequential algorithms and techniques to the detriment of parallel designs.

The performance of serial computers, however, is limited due to their physical implementation and inherent bottlenecks [18]. As users continue to demand improved performance, computer designers have been looking increasingly at parallel approaches to overcome these limitations. All modern computer architectures incorporate a degree of parallelism. Improved hardware design and manufacture coupled with a growing understanding of how to tackle the difficulties of parallel programming has reestablished parallel processing at the forefront of computer technology.

1.1 Concepts

Parallel processing is the solution of a single problem by dividing it into a number of subproblems, each of which may be solved by a separate worker. Co-operation will always be necessary between workers during problem solution, even if this is a simple agreement on the division of labor. A simple illustration of this is the solution of the problem of filling a swimming pool with water using buckets. The problem may be subdivided into the repeated *task* of adding one bucket of water at a time.

A single person completing all the tasks will complete the job, in a certain time. This process may be sped up by utilizing additional workers. Ideally, two people should be able to fill the pool in half the time. Extending this argument, a large number of workers should be able to complete the job in a small fraction of the original time. However, practically there are physical limitations preventing this hypothetical situation.

Using more than one worker to fill the pool will require a basic level of co-operation between multiple workers. This co-operation is necessary to minimize contention for access to the pool, and thus avoid any collision between the workers. The time required to achieve this co-operation involves inter-worker communication which detracts from the overall solution time, and as such, may be termed an *overhead*.

1.1.1 Dependencies

Dependencies inherent in the problem being tackled may also play a significant role in preventing an ideal parallel solution. Consider the problem of
constructing a house. In simple terms, building the roof can only start after
the walls have been completed. Similarly, the walls can only be erected once
the foundations are laid. The roof is thus dependent upon the walls, which
are, in turn, dependent on the foundations. These dependencies have the
effect of dividing the whole problem into a number of distinct stages. The
parallel solution of each stage must be completed before the subsequent
stage can start.

The dependencies within a problem may be so severe that it is not
amenable to parallel processing. A strictly sequential problem consists
of a number of stages, each comprising a single task, and each dependent
upon the previous stage. For example, in Figure 1.1, building a tower of toy
blocks requires a strictly sequential order of task completion. The situation
is the antithesis of dependency-free problems, such as placing blocks in a
row on the floor. In this case, the order of task completion is unimportant,
but the need for co-operation will still exist.

Pipelining is the classic methodology for minimizing the effects of dependencies. This technique can only be exploited when a process, consisting of a number of distinct stages, needs to be repeated several times. An
automotive assembly line is an example of an efficient pipeline. In a simplistic form, the construction of a car may consist of four linearly dependent
stages: chassis fabrication, body assembly, wheel fitting, and wind-screen
installation. An initial lump of metal is introduced into the pipeline; then,
as the partially completed car passes each stage, a new section is added
until finally the finished car is available outside the factory.

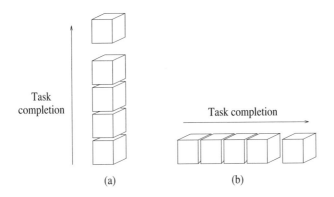

Task
completion

Task completion

(a)   (b)

Figure 1.1. Building with blocks: (a) Strictly sequential, (b) dependency-free.

Consider an implementation of this process consisting of four workers, each performing their task in one time unit. Having completed the task, the worker passes the partially completed car on to the next stage. This worker is now free to repeat its task on a new component fed from the previous stage. The completion of the first car occurs after four time units, but each subsequent car is completed every time unit.

The completion of a car is, of course, sensitive to the time taken by each worker. If one worker were to take longer than one time unit to complete its task, then the workers after this difficult task would stand idle awaiting the next component, while those before the worker with the difficult task would be unable to move their component on to the next stage of the pipeline. The other workers would thus also be unable to do any further work until the difficult task was completed. Should there be any interruption in the input to the pipeline then the pipeline would once more have to be "refilled" before it could operate at maximum efficiency.

1.1.2 Scalability

Every problem contains an upper bound on the number of workers which can be meaningfully employed in its solution. Additional workers beyond this number will not improve solution time, and can indeed be detrimental. This upper bound provides an idea as to how suitable a problem is to parallel implementation: a measure of its *scalability*.

A given problem may only be divided into a finite number of subproblems, corresponding to the smallest tasks. The availability of more workers than there are tasks, will not improve solution time. The problem of clearing a room of 100 chairs may be divided into 100 tasks consisting of removing a single chair. A maximum of 100 workers can be allocated one of these tasks and hence perform useful work.

The optimum solution time for clearing the room may not, in fact, occur when employing 100 workers due to certain aspects of the problem limiting effective worker utilization. This phenomenon can be illustrated by adding a constraint to the problem, in the form of a single doorway providing egress from the room. A *bottleneck* will occur as large numbers of workers attempt to move their chairs through the door simultaneously, as shown in Figure 1.2.

The delays caused by this bottleneck may be so great that the time taken to empty the room of chairs by this large number of workers may, in fact, be *longer* than the original time taken by the single worker. In this case, reducing the number of workers can alleviate the bottleneck and thus reduce solution time.

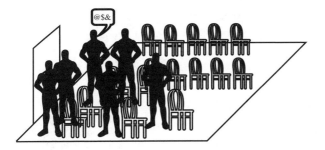

Figure 1.2. Bottleneck caused by doorway.

1.1.3 Control

All parallel solutions of a problem require some form of control. This may be as simple as the control needed to determine what will constitute a task and to ascertain when the problem has been solved satisfactorily. More complex problems may require control at several stages of their solution. For example, solution time could be improved when clearing the room if a controller was placed at the door to schedule its usage. This control would ensure that no time was wasted by two (or more) workers attempting to exit simultaneously and then having to "reverse" to allow a single worker through. An alternative to this explicit *centralized* control would be some form of *distributed* control. Here, the workers themselves could have a way of preventing simultaneous access, for example, if two (or more) workers reach the door at the same time then the biggest worker will always go first while the others wait.

Figure 1.3(a) shows the sequential approach to solving a problem. Computation is applied to the problem domain to produce the desired results. The controlled parallel approach shown in Figure 1.3(b) achieves a parallel implementation of the same problem via three steps. In Step 1, the problem domain is divided into a number of subproblems, in this case four. Parallel processing is introduced in Step 2 to enable each of the subproblems to be computed in parallel to produce subresults. In Step 3, these results must now be collated to achieve the desired final results. Control is necessary in Steps 1 and 3 to divide the problem amongst the workers and then to collect and collate the results that the workers have independently produced.

1.2 Classification of Parallel Systems

A traditional sequential computer is said to conform to the *von Neumann* model. This model typically comprises a processor, an associated mem-

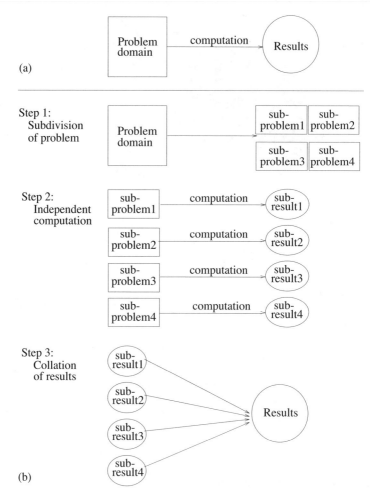

Figure 1.3. Control required in (a) a sequential versus (b) a parallel implementation.

ory, an input/output interface and various busses connecting these devices. The processor in the von Neumann model is the single computational unit responsible for the functions of fetching, decoding, and executing a program's instructions. Parallel processing may be added to this architecture through pipelining using multiple functional units within a single computational unit or by replicating entire computational units (which may contain pipelining). With pipelining, each functional unit repeatedly performs the same operation on data which is received from the preceding functional unit. So in the simplest case, a pipeline for a computational unit could consist of three functional units, one to fetch the instructions from memory, one to decode these instructions and one to execute the decoded instructions. As we saw with the automobile assemblage example, a pipeline is only as effective as its slowest component. Any delay in the pipeline has repercussions for the whole system.

Vector processing provides multiple registers as special vector registers to be used alongside the central processing unit. This type of architecture can achieve efficient execution of loops on large array data structures, producing significant performance improvements over conventional *scalar processing*, as the vector processor is able to perform the *same operation* on *all elements* of a vector simultaneously. However, often problems need to be rewritten to benefit from this form of parallelism. A large number of scientific problems, such as weather forecasting, nuclear research, and seismic data analysis, are well suited to vector processing.

Replication of the entire computational unit, the *processor*, allows individual tasks to be executed on different processors. Tasks are thus sometimes referred to as *virtual processors* which are allocated a physical processor on which to run. The completion of each task contributes to the solution of the problem.

Tasks which are executing on distinct processors at any point in time are said to be running in *parallel*. It may also be possible to execute several tasks on a single processor. Over a period of time, the impression is given that they are running in parallel, when in fact, at any point in time, only *one* task has control of the processor. In this case, we say that the tasks are being performed *concurrently*, that is, their execution is being shared by the same processor. The difference between parallel tasks and concurrent tasks is shown in Figure 1.4.

The workers which perform the computational work and co-operate to facilitate the solution of a problem on a parallel computer are called

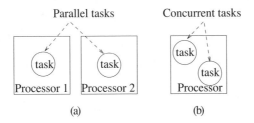

Figure 1.4. (a) Parallel tasks. (b) Concurrent tasks.

processing elements and are often abbreviated as *PEs*. A processing element consists of a processor, one or more tasks, and the software to enable the co-operation with other processing elements. A parallel system comprises of *more than one* processing element.

The wide diversity of computer architectures that have been proposed, and in a large number of cases realized, since the 1940s has led to the desire to classify the designs to facilitate evaluation and comparison. Classification requires a means of identifying distinctive architectural or behavioral features of a machine.

In 1972, Flynn proposed a classification of processors according to a macroscopic view of their principal interaction patterns relating to instruction and data *streams* [75]. The term stream was used by Flynn to refer to the sequence of instructions to be executed, or data to be operated on, by the processor. What has become known as *Flynn's taxonomy* thus categorizes architectures into the four areas shown in Figure 1.5.

Since its inception, Flynn's taxonomy has been criticized as being too broad, and has thus been enlarged by several other authors, for example, Shore in 1973 [267]; Treleaven, Brownbridge and Hopkins in 1982 [296]; Basu in 1984 [24]; and perhaps one of the most detailed classifications was given by Hockney and Jesshope in 1988 [120].

Real architectures are, of course, much more complex than Flynn suggested. For example, an architecture may exhibit properties from more than one of his classes. However, if we are not too worried about the minute details of any individual machine then Flynn's taxonomy serves to separate fundamentally different architectures into four broad categories. The classification scheme is simple (which is one of the main reasons for

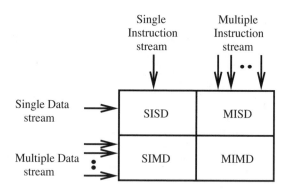

Figure 1.5. Flynn's taxonomy for processors.

its popularity) and thus useful to show an overview of the concepts of
multiprocessor computers.

SISD: Single Instruction Single Data. Single Instruction Single Data
(SISD) embraces the conventional sequential, or von Neumann, processor. The single processing element executes instructions sequentially
on a single data stream. The operations are thus ordered in time
and may be easily traced from start to finish. Modern adaptations of
this uniprocessor use some form of pipelining technique to improve
performance and, as demonstrated by the Cray supercomputers, minimize the length of the component interconnections to reduce signal
propagation times [256].

SIMD: Single Instruction Multiple Data. Single Instruction Multiple
Data machines (SIMD) apply a single instruction to a group of data
items simultaneously. A master instruction is thus acting over a vector of related operands. A number of processors, therefore, obey the
same instruction in the same cycle and may be said to be executing
in strict *lock-step*. Facilities exist to exclude particular processors
from participating in a given instruction cycle. Vector processors, for
example, the Cyber 205, Fujitsu FACOM VP-200 and NEC SX1, and
array processors, such as the DAP [238], Goodyear MPP (Massively
Parallel Processor) [25], or the Connection Machine CM-1 [119], may
be grouped in this category.

MISD: Multiple Instruction Single Data. Although part of Flynn's
taxonomy, no architecture falls obviously into the MISD category.
One of the closest architecture to this concept is a pipelined computer.
Another is systolic array architectures which derives their name from
the medical term "systole" used to describe the rhythmic contraction
of chambers of the heart. Data arrives from different directions at
regular intervals to be combined at the "cells" of the array. The
Intel iWarp system was designed to support systolic computation [11].
Systolic arrays are well suited to specially designed algorithms rather
than general purpose computing [165, 166].

MIMD: Multiple Instruction Multiple Data. The processors within
the MIMD classification autonomously obey their own instruction sequence and apply these instructions to their own data. The processors are, therefore, no longer bound to the synchronous method of
the SIMD processors and may choose to operate *asynchronously*. By
providing these processors with the ability to communicate with each
other, they may interact and therefore, co-operate in the solution of a

single problem. This interaction has led to MIMD systems sometimes being classified as *tightly coupled* if the degree of interaction is high, or *loosely coupled* if the degree of interaction is low. Two methods are available to facilitate this interprocessor communication. *Shared memory* systems allow the processors to communicate by reading and writing to a common address space. Controls are necessary to prevent processors updating the same portion of the shared memory simultaneously. Examples of such shared memory systems are the Sequent Balance [292] and the Alliant FX/8 [61]. In *distributed memory* systems, on the other hand, processors address only their private memory and communicate by passing messages along some form of communication path. Examples of MIMD processors from which such distributed memory systems can be built are the Intel i860 [234], the Inmos transputer, [121] and Analog Devices SHARC processor.

The conceptual difference between shared memory and distributed memory systems of MIMD processors is shown in Figure 1.6. The interconnection method for the shared memory system, Figure 1.6(a), allows all the processors to be connected to the shared memory. If two or more processors wish to access the same portion of this shared memory at the same time, then some arbitration mechanism must be used to ensure only one processor accesses that memory portion at a time. This problem of memory contention may restrict the number of processors that can be interconnected using the shared memory model. The interconnection method of the distributed memory system, Figure 1.6(b), connects the processors in some fashion and if one or more processors wish to access another processor's private memory, it, or they, can only do so by sending a message

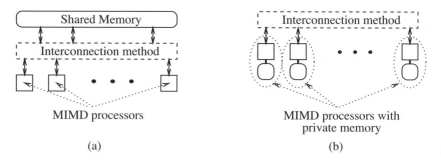

Figure 1.6.   Systems of MIMD processors: (a) shared memory, (b) distributed memory.

to the appropriate processor along this interconnection network. There is thus no memory contention as such. However, the density of the messages that results in distributed memory systems may still limit the number of processors that may be interconnected, although this number is generally larger than that of the shared memory systems.

Busses have been used successfully as an interconnection structure to connect low numbers of processors together. However, if more than one processor wishes to send a message on the bus at the same time, an arbiter must decide which message gets access to the bus first. As the number of processors increases, so the contention for use of the bus grows. Thus, a bus is inappropriate for large multiprocessor systems. An alternative to the bus is to connect processors via dedicated links to form large networks. This removes the bus-contention problem by spreading the communication load across many independent links.

1.2.1   Parallel versus Distributed Systems

Distributed memory MIMD systems consist of autonomous processors together with their own memory which co-operate in the solution of a single complex problem. Such systems may consist of a number of interconnected, dedicated processor and memory nodes, or interconnected "stand-alone" workstations. To distinguish between these two, the former configuration is referred to as a (dedicated) *parallel* system, while the latter is known as a *distributed* system, as shown in Figure 1.7. The main distinguishing features of these two systems are typically the computation-to-communication ratio and the cost. Parallel systems make use of fast, "purpose-built" (and thus expensive) communication infrastructures, while distributed systems rely on existing network facilities such as Ethernet, which are significantly slower and susceptible to other nonrelated traffic.

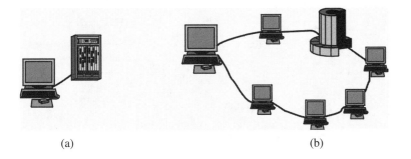

(a)   (b)

Figure 1.7. (a) Parallel system. (b) Distributed system.

The advantage of distributed systems is that they may consist of a cluster of existing workstations which can be used by many (sequential) users when not employed in a parallel capacity. A number of valuable tools have been developed to enable these workstations to act in parallel, such as Parallel Virtual Machine (PVM) [26], and Message Passing Interface (MPI) [193]. These provide an easy framework for coupling heterogeneous computers including workstations, mainframes and even parallel systems. However, while some of the properties of a distributed computing system may be different from those of a parallel system, many of the underlying concepts are equivalent. For example, both systems achieve co-operation between computational units by passing messages, and each computational unit has its own distinct memory. Thus, the ideas presented in this tutorial should prove equally useful to the reader faced with implementing his or her realistic rendering problem on either system.

1.3   The Relationship of Tasks and Data

The implementation of any problem on a computer comprises two components:

- The algorithm chosen to solve the problem

- The domain of the problem which encompasses all the data requirements for that problem.

The algorithm interacts with the domain to produce the result for the problem, as shown diagrammatically in Figure 1.8.

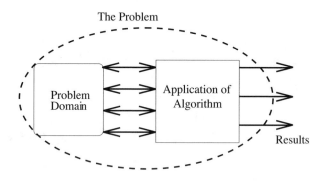

Figure 1.8. The components of a problem.

A sequential implementation of the problem means that the entire algorithm and domain reside on a single processor. To achieve a parallel implementation, it is necessary to divide the problem's components in some manner amongst the parallel processors. Now no longer resident on a single processor, the components will have to interact within the multiprocessor system in order to obtain the same result. This co-operation requirement introduces a number of novel difficulties into any parallel implementation which are not present in the sequential version of the same problem.

1.3.1 Inherent Difficulties

User confidence in any computer implementation of a problem is bolstered by the successful termination of the computation and the fact that the results meet design specifications. The reliability of modern computer architectures and languages is such that any failure of a sequential implementation to complete successfully will point automatically to deficiencies in either the algorithm used or data supplied to the program. In addition to these possibilities of failure, a parallel implementation may also be affected by a number of other factors which arise from the manner of the implementation:

Deadlock. An active parallel processor is said to be deadlocked if it is waiting indefinitely for an event which will never occur. A simple example of deadlock is when two processors, using synchronized communication, attempt to send a message to each other at the same time. Each process will then wait for the other process to perform the corresponding input operation which will never occur.

Data consistency. In a parallel implementation, the problem's data may be distributed across several processors. Care has to be taken to ensure:

- If multiple copies of the same data item exists, that the value of this item is kept consistent.
- Mutual exclusion is maintained to avoid several processors accessing a shared resource simultaneously.
- The data items are fetched from remote locations efficiently in order to avoid processor idle time.

While there is meaningful computation to be performed, a sequential computer is able to devote 100% of its time for this purpose. In a parallel system, it may happen that some of the processors become idle, not because there is no more work to be done, but because current circumstances prevent those processors from being able to perform any computation. Parallel processing introduces communication overheads. The effect of these overheads is to introduce latency into the multiprocessor system. Unless some way is found to minimize communication delays, the percentage of time that a processor can spend on useful computation may be significantly affected. So, as well as the factors affecting the successful termination of the parallel implementation, one of the fundamental considerations also facing parallel programmers is the *computation to communication* ratio.

1.3.2   Tasks

Subdividing a single problem amongst many processors introduces the notion of a task. In its most general sense, a task is a unit of computation which is assigned to a processor within the parallel system. In any parallel implementation, a decision has to be taken as to what exactly constitutes a task. The *task granularity* of a problem is a measure of the amount of computational effort associated with any task. The choice of granularity has a direct bearing on the computation to communication ratio. Selection of too large a granularity may prevent the solution of the problem on a large parallel system, while too fine a granularity may result in significant processor idle time while the system attempts to keep processors supplied with fresh tasks. On completion of a sequential implementation of a problem, any statistics that may have been gathered during the course of the computation may now be displayed in a straightforward manner. Furthermore, the computer is in a state ready to commence the next sequential program. In a multiprocessor system, the statistics would have been gathered at each processor, so after the solution of the problem, the programmer is still faced with the task of collecting and collating these statistics. To ensure that the multiprocessor system is in the correct state for the next parallel program, the programmer must also ensure that all the processors have *terminated gracefully*.

1.3.3   Data

The problem domains of many rendering applications are very large. The size of these domains is typically far more than can be accommodated within the local memory of any processing element (or indeed in the memory of many sequential computers). Yet it is precisely these complex problems that we wish to solve using parallel processing. Consider a multiprocessor system consisting of 64 processing elements, each with 4 MB of local memory. If we were to insist that the entire problem domain were to reside at each processing element then we would be restricted to solving problems with a maximum domain of 4 MB. The total memory within the system is $64 \times 4 = 256$ MB. So, if we were to consider the memory of the multiprocessor system as a whole, then we could contemplate solving problems with domains of up to 256 MB in size; a far more attractive proposition. (If the problem domain was even larger than this, then we could also consider the secondary storage devices as part of the combined memory and that should be sufficient for most problems.) There is a price to pay in treating the combined memory as a single unit. Data management strategies will be necessary to translate between the conceptual single memory unit and the physical distributed implementation. The aims of these strategies will be to keep track of the data items so that an item will always be available at a processing element when required by the task being performed. The distributed nature of the data items will thus be invisible to the application processes performing the computation. However, any delay between the application process requesting an item and this request being satisfied will result in idle time. As we will see, it is the responsibility of data management to avoid this idle time.

1.4   Evaluating Parallel Implementations

The chief reason for opting for a parallel implementation should be: *to obtain answers faster*. The time that the parallel implementation takes to compute results is perhaps the most natural way of determining the benefits of the approach that has been taken. If the parallel solution takes *longer* than any sequential implementation, then the decision to use parallel processing needs to be reexamined. Other measurements, such as speed-up and efficiency, may also provide useful insight on the maximum scalability of the implementation. Of course, there are many issues that need to be considered when comparing parallel and sequential implementations of the same problem, for example:

- Was the same processor used in each case?

- If not, what is the price of the sequential machine compared with that of the multiprocessor system?

- Was the algorithm chosen already optimized for sequential use, that is, did the data dependencies presented preclude an efficient parallel implementation?

1.4.1   Realization Penalties

If we assume that the same processor was used in both the sequential
and parallel implementation, then we should expect that the time to solve
the problem decreases as more processing elements are added. The best
we can reasonably hope for is that two processing elements will solve the
problem twice as quickly, three processing elements three times faster, and
n processing elements, n times faster. If n is sufficiently large, then by
this process, we should expect our large scale parallel implementation to
produce the answer in a tiny fraction of the sequential computation, as
shown by the "optimum time" curve in the graph in Figure 1.9.

However, in reality we are unlikely to achieve these optimized times
as the number of processors is increased. A more realistic scenario is that
shown by the curve "actual time" in Figure 1.9. This curve shows an initial
decrease in time taken to solve the example problem on the parallel system
up to a certain number of processing elements. Beyond this point, adding
more processors actually leads to an *increase* in computation time. Failure
to achieve the optimum solution time means that the parallel solution has
suffered some form of *realization* penalty. A realization penalty can arise
from two sources:

- An *algorithmic* penalty.

- An *implementation* penalty.

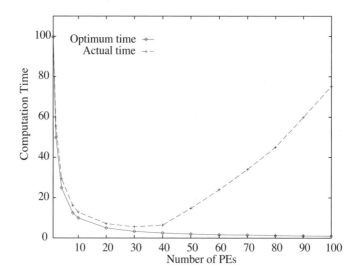

Figure 1.9. Optimum and actual parallel implementation times.

The algorithmic penalty stems from the very nature of the algorithm selected for parallel processing. The more inherently sequential the algorithm, the less likely the algorithm will be a good candidate for parallel processing. **Aside:** It has also been shown, albeit not conclusively, that the more experience the writer of the parallel algorithm has in sequential algorithms, the less parallelism that algorithm is likely to exhibit [42]. This sequential nature of an algorithm and its implicit data dependencies will translate, in the domain decomposition approach, to a requirement to *synchronize* the processing elements at certain points in the algorithm. This can result in processing elements standing idle awaiting messages from other processing elements. A further algorithmic penalty may also come about from the need to reconstruct sequentially the results generated by the individual processors into an overall result for the computation. Solving the same problem twice as fast on two processing elements implies that those two processing elements must spend 100% of their time on computation. We know that a parallel implementation requires some form of communication. The time a processing element is forced to spend on communication will naturally impinge on the time a processor has for computation. Any time that a processor cannot spend doing useful computation is an implementation penalty. Implementation penalties are thus caused by

- **The need to communicate.** As mentioned above, in a multiprocessor system, processing elements need to communicate. This communication may not only be that which is necessary for a processing element's own actions, but in some architectures, a processing element may also have to act as an intermediate for other processing elements' communication.

- **Idle time.** Idle time is any period of time when an application process is available to perform some useful computation, but is unable to do so because either there is no work locally available, or its current task is suspended awaiting a synchronization signal, or a data item which has yet to arrive. It is the job of the local task manager to ensure that an application process is kept supplied with work. The computation to communication ratio within the system will determine how much time a task manager has to fetch a task before the current one is completed. A *load imbalance* is said to exist if some processing elements still have tasks to complete, while the others do not. While synchronization points are introduced by the algorithm, the management of data items for a processing element is the job for the local data manager. The domain decomposition approach means that the problem domain is divided amongst the processing elements in some fashion. If an application process requires a data item that is not available locally, then this must be fetched from some other processing element within the system. If the processing element is unable to perform other useful computation while this fetch is being performed, for example by means of multithreading as discussed in Section 2.5.5, then the processing element is said to be idle

- **Concurrent communication, data management and task management activity.** Implementing each of a processing element's activities as a separate concurrent process on the same processor, means that the physical processor has to be shared. When a process other than the application process is scheduled then the processing element is not performing useful computation even though its current activity is necessary for the parallel implementation.

The fundamental goal of the system software is to minimize the implementation penalty. While this penalty can never be removed, intelligent communication, data management and task scheduling strategies can avoid idle time and significantly reduce the impact of the need to communicate.

1.4.2 Performance Metrics

Solution time provides a simple way of evaluating a parallel implementation. However, if we wish to investigate the relative merits of our implementation, then further insight can be gained by additional metrics. A range of metrics will allow us to compare aspects of different implementations and perhaps provide clues as to how overall system performance may be improved.

Speed-up

A useful measure of any multiprocessor implementation of a problem is *speed-up*. This relates the time taken to solve the problem on a single processor machine to the time taken to solve the same problem using the parallel implementation. We will define the speed-up of a multiprocessor system in terms of the elapsed time that is taken to complete a given problem, as follows:

$$\text{Speed-up} = \frac{\text{elapsed time of a uniprocessor}}{\text{elapsed time of the multiprocessors.}} \tag{1.1}$$

The term *linear speed-up* is used when the solution time on an n processor system is n times faster than the solution time on the uniprocessor.

This linear speed-up is thus equivalent to the optimum time shown in Section 1.4.1. The optimum and actual computation times in Figure 1.9 are represented as a graph of linear and actual speed-ups in Figure 1.10. Note that the actual speed-up curve increases until a certain point and then subsequently decreases. Beyond this point, we say that the parallel implementation has suffered a *speed-down*.

The third curve in Figure 1.10 represents so-called *super-linear speed-up*. In this example, the implementation on 20 processors has achieved a computation time which is approximately 32 times faster than the uniprocessor solution. It has been argued (see [70]) that it is not possible to achieve a speed-up greater than the number of processors used. While in practice it certainly is possible to achieve super-linear speed-up, such implementation may have exploited "unfair" circumstances to obtain such timings. For example, most modern processors have a limited amount of cache memory with an access time significantly faster compared with a standard memory access. Two processors would have double the amount of this cache memory. Given we are investigating a fixed size problem, this means that a larger proportion of the problem domain is in the cache in the parallel implementation than in the sequential implementation. It is not unreasonable, therefore, to imagine a situation where the two processor solution time is more than twice as fast than the uniprocessor time.

Although super-linear speed-up is desirable, in this tutorial we will assume a "fair" comparison between uniprocessor and multiprocessor imple-

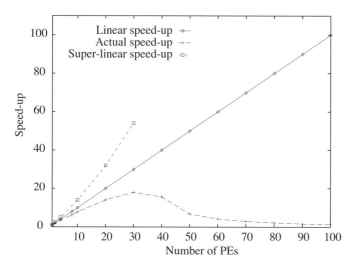

Figure 1.10. Linear and actual speed-ups.

mentations. The results that are presented in the case studies thus make no
attempt to exploit any hardware advantages offered by the increasing number of processors. This will enable the performance improvements offered
by the proposed system software extensions to be highlighted without being
masked by any variations in underlying hardware. In practice, of course,
it would be foolish to ignore these benefits and readers are encouraged to
"squeeze every last ounce of performance" out of their parallel implementation.

Two possibilities exist for determining the elapsed time of a uniprocessor. This could be the time obtained when executing:

- An optimized sequential algorithm on a single processor, T_s, or

- The parallel implementation on *one* processing element, T_1.

The time taken to solve the problem on n processing elements we will
term T_n. The difference between how the two sequential times are obtained is shown in Figure 1.11. There are advantages in acquiring both
these sequential times. Comparing the parallel to the optimized sequential implementation highlights any algorithmic efficiencies that had to be
sacrificed to achieve the parallel version. In addition, none of the parallel implementation penalties are hidden by this comparison and thus the
speed-up is not exaggerated. One of these penalties is the time taken
simply to supply the data to the processing element and collect the results. The comparison of the single processing element with the multiple

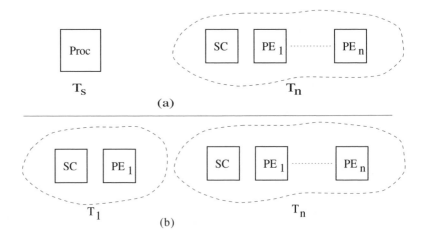

Figure 1.11. Systems used to obtain T_n and (a) T_s (b) T_1.

processing element implementation shows how well the problem is "coping" with an increasing number of processing elements. Speed-up calculated as $\frac{T_1}{T_n}$, therefore, provides the indication as to the *scalability* of the parallel implementation. Unless otherwise stated, we will use this alternative for speed-up in the case studies in this book as it better emphasizes the performance improvements brought about by the system software we shall be introducing. As we can see from the curve for "actual speed-up" in Figure 1.10, the speed-up obtained for that problem increased to a maximum value and then subsequently decreased as more processing elements were added. In 1967, Amdahl presented what has become known as "Amdahl's law" [10]. This law attempts to give a maximum bound for speed-up from the nature of the algorithm chosen for the parallel implementation. We are given an algorithm in which the proportion of time that needs to be spent on the purely sequential parts is s, and the proportion of time that might be done in parallel is p, by definition. The total time for the algorithm on a single processor is $s + p = 1$ (where the 1 is for algebraic simplicity), and the maximum speed-up that can be achieved on n processors is:

$$\text{maximum speed-up} \quad = \quad \frac{(s + p)}{s + \frac{p}{n}}$$

$$= \quad \frac{1}{s + \frac{p}{n}}. \qquad (1.2)$$

Figure 1.12 shows the maximum speed-up predicted by Amdahl's law for a sequential portion of an algorithm requiring 0.1%, 0.5%, 1% and 10% of the total algorithm time, that is $s = 0.001$, 0.005, 0.01, and 0.1, respectively. For 1000 processors, the maximum speed-up that can be achieved for a sequential portion of only 1% is less than 91. This rather depressing forecast puts a serious damper on the possibilities of massive parallel implementations of algorithms and led Gustafson in 1988 to issue a counter claim [107]. Gustafson stated that a problem size is virtually never independent of the number of processors, as it appears in Equation (1.2), but rather:

In practice, the problem size scales with the number of processors.

Gustafson thus derives a maximum speed-up of:

$$\text{maximum speed-up} \quad = \quad \frac{(s + (p \times n))}{s + p}$$

$$= \quad n + (1 - n) \times s. \qquad (1.3)$$

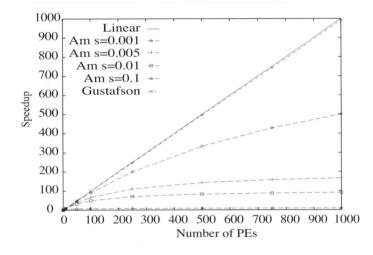

Figure 1.12. Example maximum speed-up from Amdahl and Gustafson's laws.

This maximum speed-up according to Gustafson is also shown in Figure 1.12. As the curve shows, the maximum achievable speed-up is nearly linear when the problem size is increased as more processing elements are added. Despite this optimistic forecast, Gustafson's premise is not applicable in a large number of cases. Most scientists and engineers have a particular problem they want to solve in as short a time as possible. Typically, the application already has a specified size for the problem domain. For example, in parallel radiosity, we will be considering the diffuse lighting within a particular environment subdivided into a necessary number of patches. In this example, it would be inappropriate for us to follow Gustafson's advice and increase the problem size as more processing elements were added to their parallel implementation, because to do so would mean either:

- The physical size of the three-dimensional objects within the environment would have to be increased, which is, of course, not possible, or

- The size of the patches used to approximate the surface would have to be reduced, thereby increasing the number of patches and thus the size of the problem domain.

This latter case is also not an option, because the computational method is sensitive to the size of the patches relative to their distances apart. Artificially significantly decreasing the size of the patches may introduce numerical instabilities into the method. Furthermore, artificially increasing the size of the problem domain may improve speed-up, but it *will not* improve the time taken to solve the problem. For fixed sized problems, it appears that we are left with Amdahl's gloomy prediction of the maximum speed-up that is possible for our parallel implementation. However, all is not lost, as Amdahl's assumption that an algorithm can be separated into a component which has to be executed sequentially and part which can be performed in parallel, may not be totally appropriate for the domain decomposition approach. Remember, in this model, we are retaining the complete sequential algorithm and exploiting the parallelism that exists in the problem domain. So, in this case, an equivalent to Amdahl's law would imply that the data can be divided into two parts, that which must be dealt with in a strictly sequential manner and that which can be executed in parallel. Any data dependencies will certainly imply some form of sequential ordering when dealing with the data, however, for a large number of problems, such data dependencies may not exist. It may also be possible to reduce the effect of dependencies by clever scheduling. The achievable speed-up for a problem using the domain decomposition approach is, however, bounded by the number of tasks that make up the problem. Solving a problem comprising of a maximum of 20 tasks on more than twenty processors makes no sense. In practice, of course, any parallel implementation suffers from realization penalties which increase as more processing elements are added. The actual speed-up obtained will thus be less than the maximum possible speed-up.

1.4.3 Efficiency

A relative efficiency based on the performance of the problem on one processor can be a useful measure as to what percentage of a processor's time is being spent in useful computation. This, therefore, determines what the system overheads are. The relative efficiency we will measure as:

$$\text{Efficiency} = \frac{\text{speed-up}}{\text{number of processors}} \times 100\%. \qquad (1.4)$$

Figure 1.13 shows the optimum and actual computation times given in Figure 1.9 represented as processing element efficiency. The graph shows that optimum computation time, and therefore linear speed-up, equates to an efficiency of 100% for each processing element. This again shows that to achieve this level of efficiency, every processing element must spend 100% of its time performing useful computation. Any implementation penalty would be immediately reflected by a decrease in efficiency. This is clearly shown in the curve for the actual computation times. Here, the efficiency

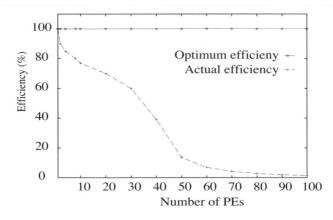

Figure 1.13. Optimum and actual processing element efficiency.

of each processing element decreases steadily as more are added until by
the time 100 processing elements are incorporated, the realization penalties
are so high that each processing element is only able to devote just over
1% of its time to useful computation.

Optimum number of processing elements

Faced with implementing a fixed size problem on a parallel system, it may
be useful to know the optimum number of processing elements on which
this particular problem should be implemented in order to achieve the best
possible performance. We term this optimum number n_{opt}. We shall judge
the *maximum performance* for a particular problem with a fixed problem
domain size, as the shortest possible time required to produce the desired
results for a certain parallel implementation. This optimum number of
processing elements may be derived directly from the "computation time"
graph. In Figure 1.9, the minimum actual computation time occurred when
the problem was implemented on 30 processing elements. As Figure 1.14
shows, this optimum number of processing elements is also the point on
the horizontal axis in Figure 1.10 at which the maximum speed-up was
obtained.

The optimum number of processing elements is also the upper bound for
the scalability of the problem for that parallel implementation. To improve
the scalability of the problem, it is necessary to reexamine the decisions
concerning the algorithm chosen and the make-up of the system software
that has been adopted for supporting the parallel implementation. As we

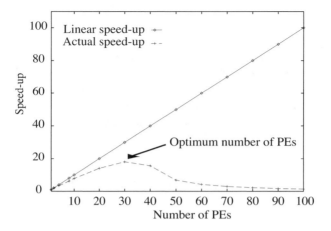

Figure 1.14. Optimum number of processing elements related to speed-up.

will see in the subsequent chapters, the correct choice of system software can
have a significant effect on the performance of a parallel implementation.

Figure 1.15 shows the speed-up graphs for different system software
decisions for the *same* problem. The goal of a parallel implementation
may be restated as:

> *To ensure that the optimum number of processing elements for
> your problem is greater than the number of processing elements
> physically available to solve the problem!*

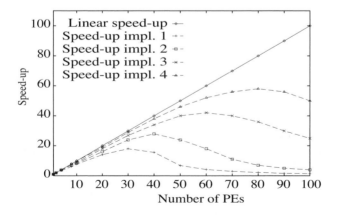

Figure 1.15. Speed-up graphs for different system software for the same problem.

Other metrics

Computation time, speed-up, and efficiency provide insight into how successful a parallel implementation of a problem has been. As Figure 1.15 shows, different implementations of the same algorithm on the same multiprocessor system may produce very different performances. A multitude of other metrics have been proposed over the years as a means of comparing the relative merits of different architectures and to provide a way of assessing their suitability as the chosen multiprocessor machine. The performance of a computer is frequently measured as the rate of some number of events per second. Within a multiuser environment, the elapsed time to solve a problem will comprise the user's CPU time plus the system's CPU time. Assuming that the computer's clock is running at a constant rate, the user's CPU performance may be measured as:

$$\text{CPU time} = \frac{\text{CPU clock cycles for a program}}{\text{clock rate (e.g. 100MHz)}}.$$

The average clock *Cycles per Instruction* (CPI) may be calculated as:

$$\text{CPI} = \frac{\text{CPU clock cycles for a program}}{\text{Instruction count}}.$$

We can also compute the CPU time from the time a program took to run:

$$
\begin{aligned}
\text{CPU time} &= \frac{\text{seconds}}{\text{program}} \\
&= \frac{\text{seconds}}{\text{clock cycle}} \times \frac{\text{clock cycles}}{\text{instructions}} \times \frac{\text{instructions}}{\text{program}}.
\end{aligned}
$$

Such a performance metric is dependent on:

- *Clock rate.* This is determined by the hardware technology and the organization of the architecture;

- *CPI.* A function of the system organization and the instruction set architecture.

- *Instruction count.* This is affected by the instruction set architecture and the compiler technology utilized.

One of the most frequently used performance metrics is the *MIPS* rating of a computer, that is how many Million Instructions Per Second the computer is capable of performing:

$$\text{MIPS} = \frac{\text{instruction count}}{\text{execution time} \times 10^6} = \frac{\text{clock rate}}{\text{CPI} \times 10^6}.$$

However, the MIPS value is dependent on the instruction set used and thus any comparison between computers with different instruction sets is not valid. The MIPS value may even vary between programs running on the same computer. Furthermore, a program which makes use of hardware floating point routines may take *less time* to complete than a similar program which uses a software floating point implementation, but the first program will have a *lower* MIPS rating than the second [117]. These anomalies have led to MIPS sometimes being referred to as *Meaningless Indication of Processor Speed*. Similar to MIPS is the *Mega-FLOPS* (MFLOPS) rating for computers, where MFLOPS represents Million FLoating point OPerations per Second:

$$\text{MFLOPS} = \frac{\text{no. of floating point operations in a program}}{\text{execution time} \times 10^6}.$$

MFLOPS is not universally applicable; for example, a word processor utilizing no floating point operations would register no MFLOPS rating. However, the same program executing on different machines should be comparable, because although the computers may execute a different number of instructions, they should perform the same number of operations, provided the set of floating point operations is consistent across both architectures. The MFLOPS value will vary for programs running on the same computer which have different mixtures of integer and floating point instructions as well as a different blend of "fast" and "slow" floating point instructions. For example, the *add* instruction often executes in less time than a *divide* instruction. A MFLOPS rating for a single program cannot, therefore, be generalized to provide a single performance metric for a computer. A suite of benchmark programs, such as the LINPACK or Livermore Loops routines, has been developed to allow a more meaningful method of comparison between machines. When examining the relative performance of computers using such benchmarks, it is important to discover the *sustained* MFLOPS performance as a more accurate indication of the machines' potential rather than merely the *peak* MFLOPS rating, a figure that *can be guaranteed never to be exceeded"*. Other metrics for comparing computers include:

Dhrystone. A CPU-intensive benchmark used to measure the integer performance especially as it pertains to system programming.

Whetstone. A synthetic benchmark without any vectorizable code for evaluating floating point performance.

TPS. *Transactions Per Second* measure for applications, such as airline reservation systems, which require on-line database transactions.

KLIPS. *Kilo Logic Inferences Per Second* is used to measure the relative inference performance of artificial intelligence machines.

Tables showing the comparison of the results of these metrics for a number of architectures can be found in several books, for example [120, 131]. Cost is seldom an issue that can be ignored when purchasing a high performance computer. The desirability of a particular computer or even the number of processors within a system may be offset by the extraordinarily high costs associated with many high performance architectures. This prompted an early law by Grosch that the speed of a computer is proportional to its cost [104, 103]. Fortunately, although this is no longer completely true, multiprocessor machines are nevertheless typically more expensive than their general purpose counterparts. The parallel computer eventually purchased should provide acceptable computation times for an affordable price, that is, maximize: *the bangs per buck* (performance per unit price).

2

Task Scheduling and Data Management

Alan Chalmers

The efficient solution of a problem on a parallel system requires the computational performance of the processing elements to be fully utilized. Any processing element that is not busy performing useful computations is degrading overall system performance. Task scheduling strategies may be used to minimize these potential performance limitations.

2.1 Problem Decomposition

A problem may be solved on a parallel system by either exploiting the parallelism inherent in the algorithm, known as *algorithmic decomposition,* or by making use of the fact that the algorithm can be applied to different parts of the problem domain in parallel, which is termed *domain decomposition.* These two decomposition methods can be further categorized as shown in Figure 2.1.

Over the years, an abundance of algorithms have been developed to solve a multitude of problems on sequential machines. A great deal of time and effort has been invested in the production of these sequential algorithms. Users are thus loathed to undertake the development of novel parallel algorithms, and yet still demand the performance that multiprocessor machines have to offer.

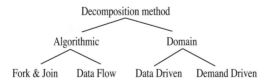

Figure 2.1. Methods of decomposing a problem to exploit parallelism.

31

Algorithmic decomposition approaches to this dilemma have led to the development of compilers, such as those for High Performance Fortran, which attempt to parallelize automatically these existing algorithms. Not only do these compilers have to identify the parallelism hidden in the algorithm, but they also need to decide upon an effective strategy to place the identified segments of code within the multiprocessor system so that they can interact efficiently. This has proved to be an extremely hard goal to accomplish.

The domain decomposition approach, on the other hand, requires little or no modification to the existing sequential algorithm. There is thus no need for sophisticated compiler technology to analyze the algorithm. However, there will be a need for a parallel framework in the form of system software to support the division of the problem domain amongst the parallel processors.

2.1.1 Algorithmic Decomposition

In algorithmic decomposition, the algorithm itself is analyzed to identify which of its features are capable of being executed in parallel. The finest granularity of parallelism is achievable at the operation level. Known as *dataflow*, at this level of parallelism the data "flows" between individual operations which are being executed in parallel [1]. An advantage of this type of decomposition is that little data space is required per processor [118]. However, the communication overheads may be very large due to the very poor computation to communication ratio.

Fork & join parallelism, on the other hand, allocates portions of the algorithm to separate processors as the computation proceeds. These portions are typically several statements or complete procedures. The difference between the two algorithmic forms of decomposition is shown for a simple case in Figure 2.2.

2.1.2 Domain Decomposition

Instead of determining the parallelism inherent in the algorithm, domain decomposition examines the problem domain to ascertain the parallelism that may be exploited by solving the algorithm on distinct data items in parallel. Each parallel processor in this approach will, therefore, have a complete copy of the algorithm and it is the problem domain that is divided amongst the processors. Domain decomposition can be accomplished using either a data driven or demand driven approach.

As we shall see, given this framework, the domain decomposition approach is applicable to a wide range of problems. Adoption of this approach to solve a particular problem in parallel, consists of two steps:

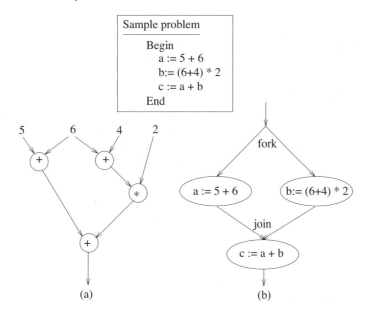

Figure 2.2. Algorithmic decomposition: (a) Dataflow, (b) fork & join.

- **Choosing the appropriate sequential algorithm.** Many algorithms have been honed over a number of years to a high level of efficiency for implementation on sequential machines. The data dependencies that these highly sequential algorithms exhibit may substantially inhibit their use in a parallel system. In this case alternative sequential algorithms which are more suitable to the domain decomposition approach will need to be considered.

- **Analysis of the problem in order to extract the criteria necessary to determine the optimum system software.** The system software provides the framework in which the sequential algorithm can execute. This system software takes care of ensuring each processor is kept busy, the data is correctly managed, and any communication within the parallel system is performed rapidly. To provide maximum efficiency, the system software needs to be tailored to the requirements of the problem. There is thus no *general purpose* parallel solution using the domain decomposition approach, but, as we shall see, a straightforward analysis of any problem's parallel requirements, will determine the correct construction of the system software and lead to an efficient parallel implementation.

Before commencing the detailed description of how we intend to tackle the solution of realistic rendering problems in parallel, it might be useful to clarify some of the terminology we shall be using.

2.1.3   Abstract Definition of a Task

The domain decomposition model solves a single problem in parallel by having multiple processors apply the same sequential algorithm to different data items from the problem domain in parallel. The lowest unit of computation within the parallel system is thus the application of the algorithm to one data item within the problem domain.

The data required to solve this unit of computation consists of two parts:

- The *Principal Data Items* (or PDIs) on which the algorithm is to be applied.

- *Additional Data Items* (or ADIs) that may be needed to complete this computation on the PDIs.

For example, in ray tracing, we are computing the value at each pixel of our image plane. Thus these pixels would form our PDIs, while all the data describing the scene would constitute the ADIs. The problem domain is therefore the pixels *plus* the scene description.

The application of the algorithm to a specified principal data item may be regarded as performing a single *task*. The task forms the elemental unit of computation within the parallel implementation. This is shown diagrammatically in Figure 2.3.

2.1.4   System Architecture

This book is concentrating on implementing realistic rendering techniques on distributed memory systems (either a dedicated parallel machine or a distributed system of workstations). These processors may be connected together in some manner to form a *configuration*. A *process* is a segment of code that runs concurrently with other processes on a single processor. Several processes will be needed at each processor to implement the desired application and provide the necessary system software support. A *Processing Element/* (PE) consists of a single processor together with these application and system processes and is thus the building block of the *multiprocessor system*. When discussing configurations of processing elements, we shall use the term *links* to mean the communication paths between processes.

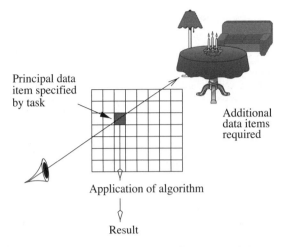

Principal data
item specified
by task

Additional
data items
required

Application of algorithm

Result

Figure 2.3. A task: the processing of a principal data item.

Structure of the System Controller

To provide a useful parallel processing platform, a multiprocessor system must have access to input/output facilities. Most systems achieve this by designating at least one processing element as the *System Controller* (SC) with the responsibilities of providing this input/output interface, as shown in Figure 2.4. If the need for input/output facilities becomes a serious bottleneck, then more than one system controller may be required. Other processing elements perform the actual computation associated with the problem.

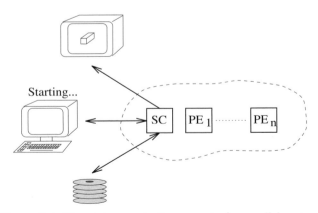

Starting...

SC   PE $_1$ ········· PE $_n$

Figure 2.4. The system controller as part of a parallel system.

In addition to providing the input/output facilities, the system controller may also be used to collect and collate results computed by the processing elements. In this case, the system controller is in the useful position of being able to determine when the computation is complete and gracefully terminate the concurrent processes at every processing element.

2.2 Computational Models

The computational model chosen to solve a particular problem determines the manner in which work is distributed across the processors of the multiprocessor system. In our quest for an efficient parallel implementation, we must maximize the proportion of time the processors spend performing necessary computation. Any imbalance may result in processors standing idle while others struggle to complete their allocated work, thus limiting potential performance. Load balancing techniques aim to provide an even division of computational effort to all processors.

The solution of a problem using the domain decomposition model involves each processing element applying the specified algorithm to a set of principal data items. The computational model ensures that every principal data item is acted upon and determines how the tasks are allocated amongst the processing elements. A choice of computation model exists for each problem. To achieve maximum system performance, the model chosen must see that the total work load is distributed evenly amongst the processing elements. This balances the overheads associated with communicating principal data items to processing elements with the need to avoid processing element idle time. A simplified ray tracing example illustrates the differences between the computational models.

A sequential solution to this problem may be achieved by dividing the image plane into 24 distinct regions, with each region constituting a single principal data item, as shown in Figure 2.5, and then applying the ray tracing algorithm at each of these regions in turn. There are thus 24 tasks to be performed for this problem where each task is to compute the pixel value at one area of the image plane. To understand the computational models, it is not necessary to know the details of the algorithm; suffice it to say that each principal data item represents an area of the image plane on which the algorithm can be applied to determine the value for that position. We will assume that no additional data items are required to complete any task.

2.2.1   Data Driven Model

The data driven model allocates all the principal data items to specific processing elements before computation commences. Each processing ele-

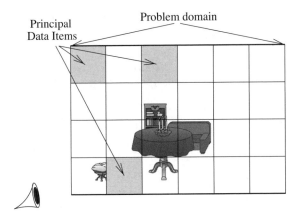

Figure 2.5. Principal data items for calculating the pixels in the image plane.

ment thus knows a priori the principal data items to which they are required to apply the algorithm. Providing there is sufficient memory to hold the allocated set at each processing element, then apart from the initial distribution, there is no further communication of principal data items. If there is insufficient local memory, then the extra items must be *fetched* as soon as memory space allows. This fetching of remote data items will be discussed further when data management is examined in Chapter 2.5.

Balanced data driven

In balanced data driven systems (also known as geometric decompositions), an equal number of principal data items is allocated to each processing element. This portion is determined simply by dividing the total number of principal data items by the number of processing elements:

$$\text{portion at each PE} = \frac{\text{number of principal data items}}{\text{number of PEs.}}$$

If the number of principal data items is not an exact multiple of the number of processing elements, then

$$(number\ of\ principal\ data\ items)\ MOD\ (number\ of\ PEs)$$

will each have one extra principal data item, and thus perform one extra task. The required start task and the number of tasks is communicated by the system controller to each processing element and these can then apply the required algorithm to their allotted principal data items. This is similar to the way in which problems are solved on arrays of SIMD processors.

In this example, consider the simple ray tracing calculation for an empty scene. The principal data items (the pixels) may be allocated equally to three processing elements, labeled PE_1, PE_2 and PE_3, as shown in Figure 2.6. In this case, each processing element is allotted eight principal data items.

As no further principal data item allocation takes place after the initial distribution, a balanced work load is only achieved for the balanced data driven computational model if the computational effort associated with each portion of principal data items is *identical*. If not, some processing elements will have finished their portions while others still have work to do. With the balanced data driven model the division of principal data items amongst processing elements is geometric in nature, that is, each processing element simply may be allocated an equal number of principal data items irrespective of their position within the problem domain. Thus, to ensure a balanced work load, this model should only be used if the computational effort associated with each principal data item is the same, and preferably where the number of principal data items is an exact multiple of the number of processing elements. This implies *a priori* knowledge, but given this, the balanced data driven approach is the simplest of the computational models to implement.

Using Figure 2.6, if the computation of each pixel takes 1 *time unit* to complete, then the sequential solution of this problem would take 24

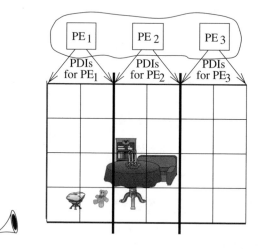

Figure 2.6. Equal allocation of data items to processing elements.

time units. The parallel implementation of this problem using the three processing elements, each allocated eight tasks, should take approximately 8 *time units*, a third of the time required by the sequential implementation. Note, however, that the parallel solution will not be exactly one third of the sequential time as this would ignore the time required to communicate the portions from the system controller to the processing elements. This also ignores time required to receive the results back from the processing elements and for the system controller to collate the solution. A balanced data driven version of this problem on the three processing elements would more accurately take:

$$\text{Solution time} = \text{initial distribution} + \lceil \frac{24}{3} \rceil + \text{result collation}.$$

Assuming low communication times, this model gives the solution in approximately one third of the time of the sequential solution, close to the maximum possible linear speed-up. Solution of the same problem on five processing elements would give:

$$\text{Solution time} = \text{initial distribution} + \lceil \frac{24}{5} \rceil + \text{result collation}.$$

This will be solved in even longer than the expected 4.8 *time units* as, in this case, one processing element is allocated 4 principal data items while the other four have to be apportioned 5. As computation draws to a close, one processing element will be idle while the four others complete their extra work. The solution time will thus be slightly more than 5 *time units*.

Unbalanced data driven

Differences in the computational effort associated with the principal data items will increase the probability of substantial processing element idle time if the simplistic balanced data driven approach is adopted. If the individual computation efforts differ, and are known a priori, then this can be exploited to achieve optimum load balancing.

The unbalanced data driven computational model allocates principal data items to processing elements based on their computational requirements. Rather than just apportioning an equal number of tasks to each processing element, the principal data items are allocated to ensure that each processing element will complete its portion at approximately *the same time*.

For example, the complexity introduced into the ray tracing calculations by placing objects into the scene, as shown in Figure 2.7, will cause an increased computational effort required to solve the portions allocated to

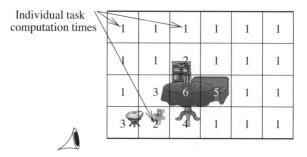

Figure 2.7. Unequal computational effort due to presence of objects in the scene.

PE_1 and PE_2 in the balanced data driven model. This will result in these two processing elements still being busy with their computations long after the other processing element, PE_3, has completed its less computationally complex portion.

Should *a priori* knowledge be available regarding the computational effort associated with each principal data item, then they may be allocated *unequally* amongst the processing elements, as shown in Figure 2.8. The computational effort now required to process each of these unequal por-

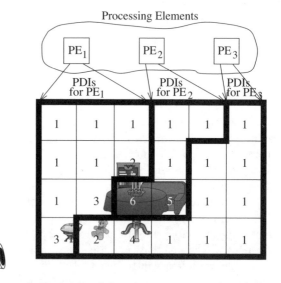

Figure 2.8. Unequal allocation of data items to processing elements to assist with load balancing.

tions will be approximately the same, minimizing any processing element idle time.

The sequential time required to solve the ray tracing with objects in the scene is now 42 *time units*. To balance the work load amongst the three processing elements, each processing element should compute for 14 *time units*. Allocation of the portions to each processing element in the unbalanced data driven model involves a preprocessing step to determine precisely the best way to subdivide the principal data items. The optimum compute time for each processing element can be obtained by simply dividing the total computation time by the number of processing elements. If possible, no processing element should be allocated principal data items whose combined computation time exceeds this optimum amount. Sorting the principal data items in descending computation times can facilitate the subdivision.

The total solution time for a problem using the unbalanced data driven model is thus:

$$\text{Solution time} \quad = \quad \text{preprocessing} + \text{distribution}$$
$$+\text{longest portion time} + \text{result collation}.$$

So comparing the naive balanced distribution from Section 2.2.1:

$$\text{Balanced solution time} \quad = \quad \text{distribution} + 21 + \text{result collation}$$
$$\text{Unbalanced solution time} \quad = \quad \text{preprocessing} + \text{distribution}$$
$$+14 + \text{result collation}.$$

The preprocessing stage is a simple sort requiring far less time than the ray tracing calculations. Thus, in this example, the unbalanced data driven model would be significantly faster than the balanced model due to the large variations in task computational complexity.

The necessity for the preprocessing stage means that this model will take more time to use than the balanced data driven approach should the tasks have the same computation requirement. However, if there are variations in computational complexity and they are known, then the unbalanced data driven model is the most efficient way of implementing the problem in parallel.

2.2.2 Demand Driven Model

The data driven computational models are dependent on the computational requirements of the principal data items being known, or at least being predictable, before actual computation starts. Only with this knowledge can these data items be allocated in the correct manner to ensure an even load balance. Should the computational effort of the principal data items be unknown or unpredictable, then serious load balancing problems can occur if the data driven models are used. In this situation, the demand driven computational model should be adopted to allocate work to processing elements evenly and thus optimize system performance.

In the demand driven computational model, work is allocated to processing elements *dynamically* as they become idle, with processing elements no longer bound to any particular portion of the principal data items. Having produced the result from one principal data item, the processing elements demand the next principal data item from some work supplier process. This is shown diagrammatically in Figure 2.9 for the simple ray tracing calculation.

Unlike the data driven models, there is no initial communication of work to the processing elements, however, there is now the need to send requests for individual principal data items to the supplier and for the supplier to communicate with the processing elements in order to satisfy these requests. To avoid unnecessary communication, it may be possible to combine the return of the results from one computation with the request for the next principal data item.

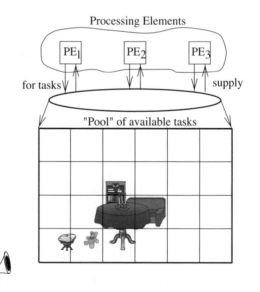

Figure 2.9. A demand driven model for a simple ray tracing calculation.

The optimum time for solving a problem using this simple demand driven model is thus:

Solution time =

$$\frac{2 \times \text{total communication time} + \text{total computation time for all PDIs}}{\text{number of PEs}}.$$

This optimum computation time,

$$\frac{\text{total computation time for all PDIs}}{\text{number of PEs}},$$

will only be possible if the work can be allocated so that all processing elements complete the last of their tasks at exactly the same time. If this is not so, then some processing elements will still be busy with their final task while the others have completed. It may also be possible to reduce the communication overheads of the demand driven model by overlapping the communication with the computation in some manner. This possibility will be discussed later in Section 2.3.

On receipt of a request, if there is still work to be done, the work supplier responds with the next available task for processing. If there are no more tasks which need to be computed, then the work supplier may safely ignore the request. The problem will be solved when all principal data items have been requested and all the results of the computations on these items have been returned and collated. The dynamic allocation of work by the demand driven model will ensure that while some processing elements are busy with more computationally demanding principal data items, other processing elements are available to compute the less complex parts of the problem.

Using the computational times for the presence of objects in the scene as shown in Figure 2.8, Figure 2.10 shows how the principal data items may be allocated by the task supplier to the processing elements using a simple serial allocation scheme. Note that the processing elements do not complete the same number of tasks. So, for example, while processing elements 2 and 3 are busy completing the computationally complex work associated with principal data items 15 and 16, processing element 1 can compute the less computationally taxing tasks of principal data items 17 and 18.

The demand driven computational model facilitates dynamic load balancing when there is no prior knowledge as to the complexity of the different

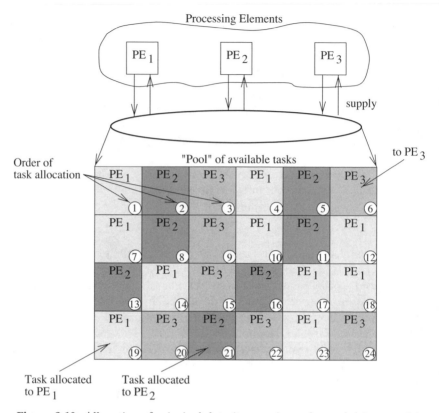

Figure 2.10. Allocation of principal data items using a demand driven model.

parts of the problem domain. Optimum load balancing is still dependent
on all the processing elements completing the last of the work at the same
time. An unbalanced solution may still result if a processing element is allocated a complex part of the domain towards the end of the solution. This
processing element may then still be busy well after the other processing
elements have completed computation on the remainder of the principal
data items and are now idle as there is no further work to do. To reduce
the likelihood of this situation, it is important that the computationally
complex portions of the domain, the so called *hot spots*, are allocated to
processing elements early on in the solution process. Although there is
no *a priori* knowledge as to the exact computational effort associated with
any principal data item (if there were, an unbalanced data driven approach
would have been adopted), nevertheless, any insight as to possible hot spot

areas should be exploited. The task supplier would thus assign principal data items from these areas first.

In the ray tracing example, while the exact computational requirement associated with the principal data items in proximity of the objects in the scene may be unknown, it is highly likely that the solution of the principal items in that area will be more complex than those elsewhere. In this problem, these principal data items should be allocated first.

If no insight is possible, then a simple serial allocation (as shown in Figure 2.10), spiral allocation, or even a random allocation of principal data items will have to suffice. While a random allocation offers perhaps a higher probability of avoiding late allocation of principal data items from hot spots, additional effort is required when choosing the next principal data item to allocate to ensure that no principal data item is allocated more than once.

As with all aspects of parallel processing, extra levels of sophistication can be added in order to exploit any information that becomes available as the parallel solution proceeds. Identifying possible hot spots in the problem domain may be possible from the computation time associated with each principal data item as these become known. If this time is returned along with the result for that principal data item, the work supplier can build a dynamic profile of the computational requirements associated with areas of the domain. This information can be used to adapt the allocation scheme to send principal data items from the possible hot spot regions. There is, of course, a trade off here between the possible benefits to load balancing in the early allocation of principal data items from hot spots, and the overhead that is introduced by the need to:

- Time each computation at the processing elements.

- Return this time to the work supplier.

- Develop the time profile at the work supplier.

- Adapt the allocation strategy to take into account this profile.

The benefits gained by such an adaptive scheme are difficult to predict as they are dependent on the problem being considered and the efficiency of the scheme implementation. The advice in these matters is always: *Implement a simple scheme initially and then add extra sophistication should resultant low system performance justify it.*

2.2.3   Hybrid Computational Model

For most problems, the correct choice of computational model will either be one of the data driven strategies or the demand driven approach. However, for a number of problems, a hybrid computational model, exhibiting properties of both data and demand driven models, can be adopted to achieve improved efficiency. The class of problem that can benefit from the hybrid model is one in which an initial set of principal data items of known computational complexity may spawn an unknown quantity of further work.

In this case, the total number of principal data items required to solve the problem is *unknown* at the start of the computation, however, there are at least a known number of principal data items that must be processed first. If the computational complexity associated with these initial principal data items is unknown then a demand driven model will suffice for the whole problem, but if the computational complexity is known then one of the data driven models, with their lower communication overheads, should at least be used for these initial principal data items. Use of the hybrid model thus requires the computational model to be switched from data driven to demand driven mode as required.

2.3   Task Management

Task management encompasses the following functions:

- The definition of a task.

- Controlling the allocation of tasks.

- Distribution of the tasks to the processing elements.

- Collation of the results, especially in the case of a problem with multiple stages.

2.3.1   Task Definition and Granularity

An *atomic element* may be thought of as a problem's lowest computational element within the sequential algorithm adopted to solve the problem. As introduced in Section 2.1.2, in the domain decomposition model a single task is the application of this sequential algorithm to a principal data item to produce a result for the subparts of the problem domain. The task is thus the smallest element of computation for the problem within the parallel system. The *task granularity* (or *grain size*) of a problem is the number of atomic elements, which are included in one task. Generally, the task granularity remains constant for all tasks, but in some cases, it may be desirable to alter dynamically this granularity as the computation proceeds. A task which includes only one atomic element is said to have the *finest granularity*, while a task which contains many is *coarser grained*, or has a *coarser granularity*. The actual definition of what constitutes a principal data item is determined by the granularity of the tasks.

A parallel system solves a problem by its constituent processing elements executing tasks in parallel. A *task packet* is used to inform a processing element which task, or tasks, to perform. This task packet may simply indicate which tasks require processing by that processing element, thus forming the lowest level of distributed work. The packet may include additional information, such as additional data items, which the tasks require in order to be completed.

To illustrate the differences in this terminology, consider again the simple ray tracing problem. The atomic element of a sequential solution of this problem could be to perform a single ray-object intersection test. The principal data item is the pixel being computed, and the additional data item required will be the object being considered. A sequential solution of this problem would be for a single processing element to consider each ray-object intersection in turn. The help of several processing elements could substantially improve the time taken to perform the ray tracing.

The finest task granularity for the parallel implementation of this problem is for each task to complete one atomic element, that is perform one ray-object intersection. For practical considerations, it is perhaps more appropriate that each task should instead be to trace the complete path of a single ray. The granularity of each task is now the number of ray-object intersections required to trace this single ray and each pixel is a principal data item. A sensible task packet to distribute the work to the processing elements would include details about one or more pixels together with the necessary scene data (if possible, see Chapter 2.5).

To summarize our choices for this problem:

Atomic element. To perform one ray-object intersection.

Task. To trace the complete path of one ray (may consist of a number of atomic elements).

PDI. The pixel location for which we are computing the color.

ADI. The scene data.

Task packet. One or more rays to be computed.

Choosing the task granularity for the parallel implementation of a problem is not straightforward. Although it may be fairly easy to identify the atomic element for the sequential version of the problem, such a fine grain may not be appropriate when using many processing elements. Although the atomic element for ray tracing was specified as computing a single ray-object intersection in the above example, the task granularity for the parallel solution was chosen as computing the complete color contribution at a particular pixel. If one atomic element had been used as the task granularity then additional problems would have introduced for the parallel solution, namely, the need for processors to exchange partial results. This difficulty would have been exacerbated if, instead, the atomic element had been chosen as tracing a ray into a voxel and considering whether it does, in fact, intersect with an object there. Indeed, apart from the higher communication overhead this would have introduced, the issue of dependencies would also have to be checked to ensure, for example, that a ray was not checked against an object more than once.

As well as introducing additional communication and dependency overheads, the incorrect choice of granularity may also increase computational complexity variations and hinder efficient load balancing. The choice of granularity is seldom easy; however, a number of parameters of the parallel system can provide an indication as to the desirable granularity. The computation to communication ratio of the architecture will suggest whether additional communication is acceptable to avoid dependency or load balancing problems. As a general rule, where possible, data dependencies should be avoided in the choice of granularity as these imply unnecessary synchronization points within the parallel solution which can have a significant effect on overall system performance.

2.3.2   Task Distribution and Control

The task management strategy controls the distribution of packets throughout the system. Upon receipt, a processing element performs the tasks specified by a packet. The composition of the task packet is thus an important issue that must be decided before distribution of the tasks can begin. To complete a task, a processing element needs a copy of the algorithm, the principal data item(s), and any additional data items that the algorithm may require for that principal data item. The domain decomposition paradigm provides each processing element with a copy of the algorithm, and so the responsibility of the task packet is to provide the other information.

The principal data items form part of the problem domain. If there is sufficient memory, it may be possible to store the entire problem domain as well as the algorithm at each processing element. In this case, the inclusion of the principal data item as part of the task packet is unnecessary. A better method would be simply to include the identification of the principal data item within the task packet. Typically, the identification of a principal data item is considerably smaller, in terms of actual storage capacity, than the item itself. The communication overheads associated with sending this smaller packet will be significantly less than sending the principal data item with the packet. On receipt of the packet, the processing element could use the identification simply to fetch the principal data item from its local storage. The identification of the principal data item is, of course, also essential to enable the results of the entire parallel computation to be collated.

If the additional data items required by the task are known, then they— or if possible, their identities—may also be included in the task packet. In this case, the task packet would form an integral unit of computation which could be directly handled by a processing element. However, in reality, it may not be possible to store the whole problem domain at every processing element. Similarly, numerous additional data items may be required which would make their inclusion in the task packet impossible. Furthermore, for a large number of problems, the additional data items which are required for a particular principal data item may not be known in advance and will only become apparent as the computation proceeds.

A task packet should contain as a minimum either the identity, or the identity and actual principal data items of the task. The inability to include the other required information in the packet means that the parallel system will have to resort to some form of *data management*. This topic is described fully in Chapter 2.5.

2.3.3   Algorithmic Dependencies

The algorithm of the problem may specify an order in which the work must be undertaken. This implies that certain tasks must be completed before others can commence. These dependencies must be preserved in the parallel implementation. In the worst case, algorithmic dependencies can prevent an efficient parallel implementation, as shown with the tower of toy blocks in Figure 1.1. Amdahl's law, described in Section 1.4, shows the implications to the algorithmic decomposition model of parallel processing of the presence of even a small percentage of purely sequential code. In the domain decomposition approach, algorithmic dependencies may introduce two phenomena which will have to be tackled:

- *Synchronization points*, which have the effect of dividing the parallel implementation into a number of distinct stages.

- *Data dependencies*, which will require careful data management to ensure a consistent view of the data to all processing elements.

Multistage algorithms

Many problems can be solved by a single stage of computation, utilizing known principal data items to produce the desired results. However, the dependencies inherent in other algorithms may divide computation into a number of distinct stages. The *partial results* produced by one stage become the principal data items for the following stage of the algorithm, as shown in Figure 2.11. For example, many scientific problems involve the construction of a set of simultaneous equations, a distinct stage, and the subsequent solution of these equations for the unknowns. The partial

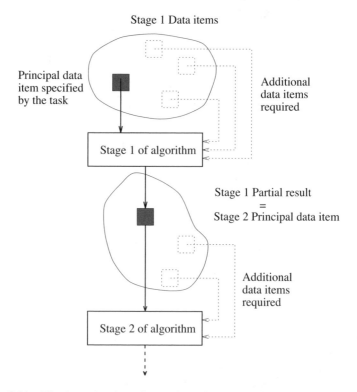

Figure 2.11. The introduction of partial results due to algorithmic dependencies.

results, in this case elements of the simultaneous equations, become the
principal data for the tasks of the next stage.

Even a single stage of a problem may contain a number of distinct
sub-stages which must first be completed before the next sub-stage can
proceed. An example of this is the use of an iterative solver, such as the
Jacobi method [88, 127], to solve a set of simultaneous equations. An iterative method starts with an approximate solution and uses it in a recurrence
formula to provide another approximate solution. By repeatedly applying
this process, a sequence of solutions is obtained which, under suitable conditions, converges towards the exact solution.

Consider the problem of solving a set of six equations for six unknowns,
$\mathbf{A}x = \mathbf{b}$. The Jacobi method will solve this set of equations by calculating,
at each iteration, a new approximation from the values of the previous
iteration. So the value for the x_i's at the nth iteration is calculated as:

$$x_1^n = \frac{b_i - a_{12}x_2^{n-1} - \ldots - a_{16}x_6^{n-1}}{a_{11}}$$

$$x_2^n = \frac{b_i - a_{21}x_1^{n-1} - \ldots - a_{26}x_6^{n-1}}{a_{22}}$$

$$\vdots$$

$$x_6^n = \frac{b_i - a_{61}x_1^{n-1} - \ldots - a_{65}x_6^{n-1}}{a_{66}.}$$

A parallel solution to this problem on two processing elements could
allocate three rows to be solved to each processing element as shown in
Figure 2.12. Now PE_1 can solve the nth iteration values x_1^n, x_2^n and x_3^n in

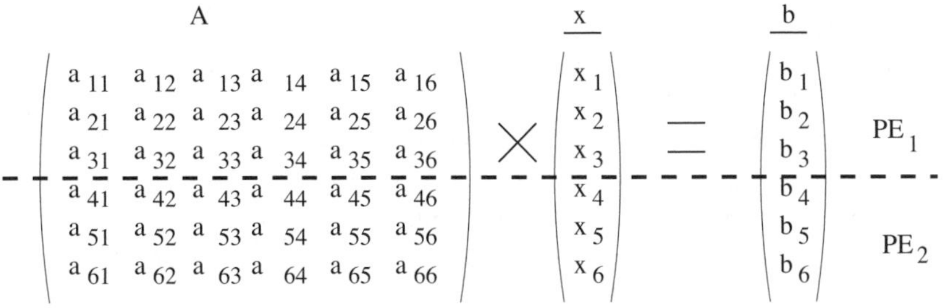

Figure 2.12.   Solving an iterative matrix solution method on two processing
elements.

parallel with PE_2 computing the values of x_4^n, x_5^n, and x_6^n. However, neither processing element can proceed onto the $(n+1)^{st}$ iteration until both have finished the nth iteration and exchanged their new approximations for the x_i^ns. Each iteration is, therefore, a substage which must be completed before the next sub-stage can commence. This point is illustrated by the following code segment from PE_1:

```
PROCEDURE Jacobi() (* Executing on PE 1 *)
    Begin
        Estimate x[1] ... x[6]
        n := 0 (* Iteration number *)
        WHILE solution_not_converged DO
            Begin
                n := n + 1
                Calculate new x[1], x[2] & x[3] using old x[1] ... x[6]
                PARALLEL
                    SEND new x[1], x[2] & x[3] TO PE_2
                    RECEIVE new x[4], x[5] & x[6] FROM PE_2
            End
    End (* Jacobi *)
```

Data dependencies

The concept of dependencies was introduced in Section 1.1.1 when we were unable to construct a tower of blocks in parallel as this required a strictly sequential order of task completion. In the domain decomposition model, data dependencies exist when a task may not be performed on some principal data item until another task has been completed. There is thus an implicit ordering on the way in which the task packets may be allocated to the processing elements. This ordering will prevent certain tasks being allocated, even if there are processing elements idle, until the tasks on which they are dependent have completed.

A linear dependency exists between each of the iterations of the Jacobi method discussed above. However, no dependency exists for the calculation of each x_i^n, for all i, as all the values they require, x_j^{n-1}, $\forall j \neq i$, will already have been exchanged and thus be available at every processing element.

The Gauss-Seidel iterative method has long been preferred in the sequential computing community as an alternative to Jacobi. The Gauss-Seidel method makes use of new approximations for the x_i as soon as they are available rather than waiting for the next iteration. Provided the methods converge, Gauss-Seidel will converge more rapidly than the Jacobi method. So, in the example of six unknowns above, in the nth iteration the value of x_1^n would still be calculated as:

$$x_1^n = \frac{b_i - a_{12}x_2^{n-1} - \ldots - a_{16}x_6^{n-1}}{a_{11}},$$

but the x_2^n value would now be calculated by:

$$x_2^n = \frac{b_i - a_{21}\mathbf{x_1^n} - a_{23}x_3^{n-1} - \ldots - a_{26}x_6^{n-1}}{a_{22}}.$$

Although well-suited to sequential programming, the strong linear dependency that has been introduced makes the Gauss-Seidel method poorly suited for parallel implementation. Now within each iteration no value of x_i^n can be calculated until all the values for x_j^n, $j < i$ are available; a strict sequential ordering of the tasks. The less severe data dependencies within the Jacobi method thus make it a more suitable candidate for parallel processing than the Gauss-Seidel method which is more efficient on a sequential machine.

It is possible to implement a hybrid of these two methods in parallel, the so-called Block Gauss-Seidel - Global Jacobi method. A processing element which is computing several rows of the equations, may use the Gauss-Seidel method for these rows as they will be computed sequentially within the processing element. Any values for x_i^n not computed locally will assume the values of the previous iteration, as in the Jacobi method. All new approximations will be exchanged at each iteration. So, in the example, PE_2 would calculate the values of x_4^n, x_5^n and x_6^n as follows:

$$x_4^n = \frac{b_i - a_{11}x_1^{n-1} - a_{12}x_2^{n-1} - a_{13}x_3^{n-1} - a_{15}x_5^{n-1} - a_{16}x_6^{n-1}}{a_{44}}$$

$$x_5^n = \frac{b_i - a_{11}x_1^{n-1} - a_{12}x_2^{n-1} - a_{13}x_3^{n-1} - a_{14}\mathbf{x_4^n} - a_{16}x_6^{n-1}}{a_{55}}$$

$$x_6^n = \frac{b_i - a_{11}x_1^{n-1} - a_{12}x_2^{n-1} - a_{13}x_3^{n-1} - a_{14}\mathbf{x_4^n} - a_{15}\mathbf{x_5^n}}{a_{66}}.$$

2.4 Task Scheduling Strategies

2.4.1 Data Driven Task Management Strategies

In a data driven approach, the system controller determines the allocation of tasks prior to computation proceeding. With the unbalanced strategy, this may entail an initial sorting stage based on the known computational complexity, as described in Section 2.2.1. A single task-packet detailing the tasks to be performed is sent to each processing element. The application

processes may return the results upon completion of their allocated portion,
or return individual results as each task is performed, as shown in this code
segment:

```
PROCESS Application_Process()
    Begin
        RECEIVE task_packet FROM SC via R
        FOR i = start_task_id TO finish_task_id DO
            Begin
                result[i] := Perform_Algorithm(task[i])
                SEND result[i] TO SC via R
            End
    End (* Application_Process *)
```

In a data driven model of computation a processing element may initially be supplied with as many of its allocated principal data items as
its local memory will allow. Should there be insufficient storage capacity, a simple data management strategy may be necessary to prefetch the
missing principal data items as computation proceeds and local storage allows. This is discussed further when considering the management of data
in Chapter 2.5.

2.4.2   Demand Driven Task Management Strategies

Task management within the demand driven computational model is explicit. The work supplier process, which forms part of the system controller,
is responsible for placing the tasks into packets and sending these packets
to requesting processing elements. To facilitate this process, the system
controller maintains a *pool* of already constituted task packets. On receipt
of a request, the work supplier simply dispatches the next available task
packet from this task pool, as can be seen in Figure 2.13.

The advantage of a task pool is that the packets can be inserted into it
in advance, or concurrently as the solution proceeds, according to the allocation strategy adopted. This is especially useful for problems that create
work dynamically, such as those using the hybrid approach as described in
Section 2.2.3. Another advantage of the task pool is that if a hot spot in
the problem domain is identified, then the ordering within the task pool
can be changed dynamically to reflect this and thus ensure that potentially
computationally complex tasks are allocated first.

More than one task pool may be used to reflect different levels of task
priority. High priority tasks contained in the appropriate task pool will
always be sent to a requesting processing element first. Only once this
high priority task pool is (temporarily) empty will tasks from lower priority

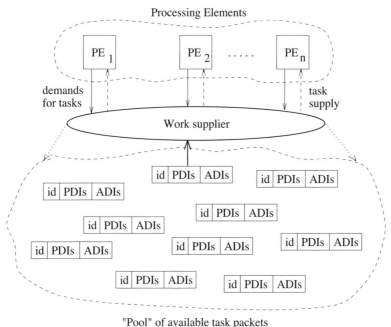

"Pool" of available task packets

Figure 2.13. Supplying task packets from a task pool at the system controller.

pools be sent. The multiple pool approach ensures that high priority tasks are not ignored as other tasks are allocated.

In the demand driven computational model, the processing elements demand the next task as soon as they have completed their current task. This demand is translated into sending a request to the work supplier, and the demand is only satisfied when the work supplier has delivered the next task. There is thus a definite delay period from the time the request is issued until the next task is received. During this period, the processing element will be computationally idle. To avoid this idle time, it may be useful to include a buffer at each processing element capable of holding at least one task packet. This buffer may be considered as the processing element's own private task pool. Now, rather than waiting for a request to be satisfied from the remote system controller, the processing element may proceed with the computation on the task packet already present locally. When the remote request has been satisfied and a new task packet delivered, this can be stored in the buffer waiting for the processing element to complete the current task.

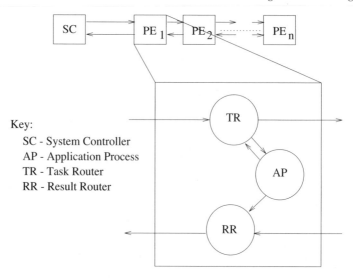

Figure 2.14. A processing element for the processor farm model.

While avoiding delays in fetching tasks from a remote task pool, the use of a buffer at each processing element may have serious implications for load balancing, especially towards the end of the problem solution. We will examine these issues in more detail after we have considered the realization of task management for a simple demand driven system - the processor farm.

A first approach: the processor farm

Simple demand driven models of computation have been implemented and used for a wide range of applications. One realization of such a model, often referred to in the literature, is that implemented by May and Shepherd [188]. This simple demand driven model, which they term a *processor farm*, has been used for solving problems with high computation to communication ratios. The model proposes a single system controller and one or more processing elements connected in a linear configuration, or chain. The structure of a processing element in this model is shown in Figure 2.14.

The application process performs the desired computation, while the communication within the system is dealt with by two router processes, the *Task Router* (TR) and the *Result Router* (RR). As their names suggest, the task router is responsible for distributing the tasks to the application process, while the result router returns the results from the completed tasks back to the system controller. The system controller contains the initial pool of tasks to be performed and collates the results. Such a communication strategy is simple to implement and largely problem independent.

To reduce possible processing element idle time, each task router process contains a single buffer in which to store a task so that a new task can be passed to the application process as soon as it becomes idle. When a task has been completed, the results are sent to the system controller. On receipt of a result, the system controller releases a new task into the system. This synchronized releasing of tasks ensures that there are never more tasks in the system than there is space available.

On receipt of a new task, the task router process either:

- Passes the task directly to the application process if it is waiting for a task,

- Places the task into its buffer if the buffer is empty, or

- Passes the task onto the next processing element in the chain.

The processor farm is initialized by loading sufficient tasks into the system so that the buffer at each task router is full and each application process has a task with which to commence processing. Figure 2.15 shows the manner in which task requests are satisfied within a simple two processing element configured in a chain.

The simplicity of this realization of a demand driven model has contributed largely to its popularity. Note that because of the balance maintained within the system, the only instance at which the last processing element is different from any other processing element in the chain is to ensure the closedown_command does not get passed any further. However, such a model does have disadvantages which may limit its use for more complex problems.

The computation to communication ratio of the desired application is critical in order to ensure an adequate performance of a processor farm. If this ratio is too low, then significant processing element idle time will occur. This idle time occurs because the computation time for the application process to complete its current task and the task buffered at the task router may be lower than the combined communication time required for the results to reach the system controller plus the time for the new tasks released into the system to reach the processing element. This problem may be partially alleviated by the inclusion of several buffers at each task router instead of just one. However, without *a priori* knowledge as to the

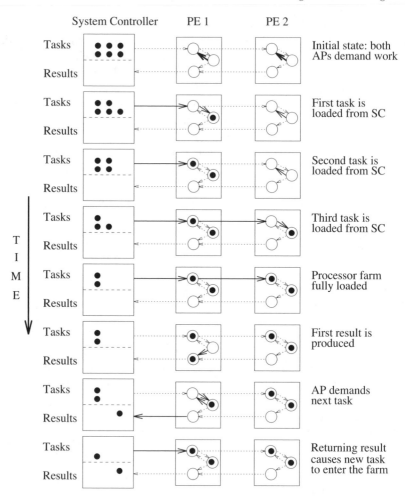

Figure 2.15. Task movement within a two PE processor farm.

computation to communication ratio of the application, it may be impossible to determine precisely what the optimum number of buffers should be. This analysis is particularly difficult if the computational complexity of the tasks vary; precisely the type of problem demand driven models are more apt at solving. The problem independence of the system will also be compromised by the use of any *a priori* knowledge.

If the number of buffers chosen is too small, then the possibility of application process idle time will not be avoided. Provision of too many buffers will certainly remove any immediate application process idle time, but will re-introduce the predicament as the processing draws to a close. This occurs once the system controller has no further tasks to introduce into the system and now processing must only continue until all tasks still buffered at the processing elements have been completed. Obviously, significant idle time may occur as some processing elements struggle to complete their large number of buffered tasks.

The computation to communication ratio of the processor farm is severely exacerbated by the choice of the chain topology. The distance between the furthest processing element in the chain and the system controller grows linearly as more processing elements are added. This means that the combined communication time to return a result and receive a new task also increases. Furthermore, this communication time will also be adversely affected by the message traffic of all the intermediate processing elements which are closer to the system controller.

2.4.3 Task Manager Process

The aim of task management within a parallel system is to ensure the efficient supply of tasks to the processing elements. A *Task Manager process* (TM) is introduced at each processing element to assist in maintaining a continuous supply of tasks to the application process. The application process no longer deals with task requests directly, but rather indirectly, using the facilities of the task manager. The task manager process assumes the responsibility for ensuring that every request for additional tasks from the application process will be satisfied immediately. The task manager attempts to achieve this by maintaining a local task pool.

In the processor farm, the task router process contains a single buffered task in order to satisfy the next local task request. As long as this buffer is full, task supply is immediate as far as the application process is concerned. The buffer is refilled by a new task from the system controller triggered on receipt of a result. The task router acts in a *passive* manner, awaiting replenishment by a new task within the farm. However, if the buffer is empty when the application process requests a task then this process must remain idle until a new task arrives. This idle time is wasted computation time and so to improve system performance, the passive task router should be replaced by an "intelligent" task manager process more capable of ensuring new tasks are always available locally.

The task management strategies implemented by the task manager and outlined in the following sections are *active*, dynamically requesting and acquiring tasks during computation. The task manager thus assumes the responsibility of ensuring local availability of tasks. This means that an application process should *always* have its request for a task satisfied immediately by the task manager unless:

- At the start of the problem, the application processes make a request before the initial tasks have been provided by the system controller,

- There are no more tasks which need to be solved for a particular stage of the parallel implementation, or

- The task manager's replenishment strategy has failed in some way.

A local task pool

To avoid any processing element idle time, it is essential that the task manager has at least one task available locally at the moment the application process issues a task request. This desirable situation was achieved in the processor farm by the provision of a single buffer at each task router. As we saw, the single buffer approach is vulnerable to the computation to communication ratio within the system. Adding more buffers to the task router led to the possibility of serious load imbalances towards the end of the computation.

The task manager process maintains a local task pool of tasks awaiting computation by the application process. This pool is similar to the task pool at the system controller, as shown in Figure 2.13. However, not only will this local pool be much smaller than the system controller's task pool, but also it may be desirable to introduce some form of "status" to the number of available tasks at any point in time.

Satisfying a task request will free some space in the local task pool. A simple replenishment strategy would be for the task manager to immediately request a new task packet from the system controller. This request has obvious communication implications for the system. If the current message densities within the system are high and as long as there are still tasks available in the local task pool, this request will place an unnecessary additional burden on the already overloaded communication network.

As an active process, it is quite possible for the task manager to delay its replenishment request until message densities have diminished. However, this delay must not be so large that subsequent application process demands will deplete the local task pool before any new tasks can be fetched causing processor idle time to occur. There are a number of indicators which the task manager can use to determine a suitable delay. Firstly, this delay is only necessary if current message densities are high. Such information should be available for the router. Given a need for delay, the number of tasks in the task pool, the approximate computation time each of these

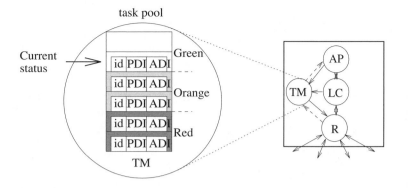

Figure 2.16. Status of task manager's task pool.

tasks requires, and the probable communication latency in replenishing the tasks should all contribute to determining the request delay.

In a demand driven system, the computational complexity variations of the tasks are not known. However, the task manager will be aware of how long previous tasks have taken to compute (the time between application process requests). Assuming some form of preferred biased allocation of tasks in which tasks from similar regions of the problem domain are allocated to the same processing element, as discussed in Section 2.4.5, the task manager will be able to build up a profile of task completion time which can be used to predict approximate completion times for tasks in the task pool. The times required to satisfy previous replenishment requests will provide the task manager with an idea of likely future communication responses. These values are, of course, mere approximations, but they can be used to assist in determining reasonable tolerance levels for the issuing of replenishment requests.

The task manager's task pool is divided into three regions: *green*, *orange*, and *red*. The number of tasks available in the pool will determine the current status level, as shown in Figure 2.16. When faced with the need to replenish the task pool the decision can be taken based on the current status of the pool:

Green. Only issue the replenishment request if current message traffic density is low.

Orange. Issue the replenishment request unless the message density is very high.

Red. Always issue the replenishment request.

The boundaries of these regions may be altered dynamically as the task manager acquires more information. At the start of the computation, the task pool will be all red. The computation to communication ratio is critical in determining the boundaries of the regions of the task pool. The better this ratio, that is when computation times are high relative to the time taken to replenish a task packet, the smaller the red region of the task pool need be. This will provide the task manager with greater flexibility and the opportunity to contribute to minimizing communication densities.

2.4.4   Distributed Task Management

One handicap of the centralized task pool system is that all replenishment task requests from the task managers must reach the system controller before the new tasks can be allocated. The associated communication delay in satisfying these requests can be significant. The communication problems can be exacerbated by the bottleneck arising near the system controller. Distributed task management allows task requests to be handled at a number of locations remote from the system controller. Although all the tasks originate from the system controller, requests from processing elements no longer have to reach there in order to be satisfied.

The closest location for a task manager to replenish a task packet is from the task pool located at the task manager of one of its nearest neighbors. In this case, a replenishment request no longer proceeds directly to the system controller, but simply via the appropriate routers to the neighboring task manager. If this neighboring task manager is able to satisfy the replenishment request, then it does so from its task pool. This task manager may now decide, in turn, to replenish its task pool, depending on its current status and so it will also request another task from one of its neighboring task managers, but obviously not the same neighbor to which it has just supplied the task. One sensible strategy is to propagate these requests in a "chain-like" fashion in the direction towards the main task supplier at the system controller, as shown in Figure 2.17.

This distributed task management strategy is referred to as a *producer-consumer* model. The application process is the initial consumer and its local task manager the producer. If a replenishment request is issued, then this task manager becomes the consumer and the neighboring task manager the producer, and so on. The task supplier process of the system controller is the overall producer for the system. If no further tasks exist at the system controller, then the last requesting task manager may change the direction of the search. This situation may occur towards the end of a stage of processing and facilitates load balancing of any tasks remaining in task manager buffers. As well as reducing the communication distances

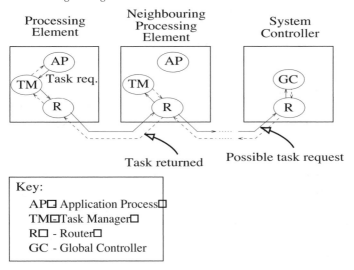

Figure 2.17. Task request propagating towards the system controller.

for task replenishment, an additional advantage of this "chain reaction" strategy is that the number of request messages in the system is reduced. This will play a major rôle in helping maintain a lower overall message density within the system.

If a task manager is unable to satisfy a replenishment request as its task pool is empty, then to avoid "starvation" at the requesting processing element, this task manager must ensure that the request is passed on to another processing element.

A number of variants of the producer-consumer model are also possible:

- Instead of following a path towards the system controller, the "chain reaction" could follow a predetermined Hamiltonian path (the system controller could be one of the processors on this path).

  Aside: A Hamiltonian path is a circuit starting and finishing at one processing element. This circuit passes through each processor in the network once only.

  Such a path would ensure that a processing element would be assured of replenishing a task if there was one available and there would be no need to keep track of the progress of the "chain reaction" to ensure no task manager was queried more than once per chain.

- In the course of its through-routing activities, a router may handle a task packet destined for a distant task manager. If that router's local task manager has an outstanding "red request" for a task, then it is possible for the router to *poach* the "en route task" by diverting it, so satisfying its local task manager immediately. Care must be taken to ensure that the task manager for whom the task was intended is informed that the task has been poached, so it may issue another request. In general, tasks should only be poached from "red replenishment" if to do so would avoid local application process idle time.

2.4.5   Preferred Bias Task Allocation

The preferred bias method of task management is a way of allocating tasks to processing elements which combines the simplicity of the balanced data driven model with the flexibility of the demand driven approach. To reiterate the difference in these two computational models as they pertain to task management:

- Tasks are allocated to processing elements in a predetermined manner in the balanced data driven approach.

- In the demand driven model, tasks are allocated to processing elements on demand. The requesting processing element will be assigned the next available task packet from the task pool, and thus no processing element is bound to any area of the problem domain.

Provided no data dependencies exist, the order of task completion is unimportant. Once all tasks have been computed, the problem is solved. In the preferred bias method, the problem domain is divided into equal regions with each region being assigned to a particular processing element, as is done in the balanced data driven approach. However, in this method, these regions are purely *conceptual* in nature. A demand driven model of computation is still used, but the tasks are not now allocated in an arbitrary fashion to the processing elements. Rather, a task is dispatched to a processing element from its conceptual portion. Once all tasks from a processing element's conceptual portion have been completed, only then will that processing element be allocated its next task from the portion of another processing element which has yet to complete its conceptual portion of tasks. Generally, this task should be allocated from the portion of the processing element that has completed the least number of tasks. So, for example, from Figure 2.18, on completion of the tasks in its own conceptual region, PE_3 may get allocated task number 22 from PE_2's conceptual region. Preferred bias allocation is sometimes also referred to as *conceptual task allocation*.

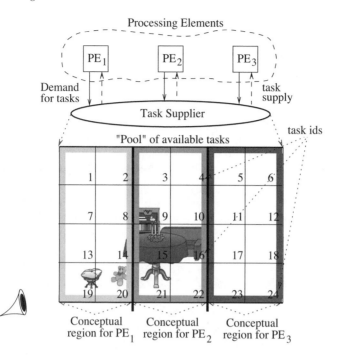

Figure 2.18. Partial result storage balancing by means of conceptual regions.

The implications of preferred bias allocation are substantial. The demand driven model's ability to deal with variations in computational complexity is retained, but now the system controller and the processing elements themselves know to whom a task that they have been allocated conceptually belongs. As we will see in Section 2.5.6, this can greatly facilitate the even distribution of partial results at the end of any stage of a multistage problem.

The exploitation of data coherence is a vital ploy in reducing idle time due to remote data fetches. Preferred bias allocation of tasks can ensure that tasks from the same region of the problem are allocated to the same processing element. This can greatly improve the cache hit ratio at that processing element.

2.5 Data Management

The data requirements of many problems may be far larger than can be accommodated at any individual processing element. Rather than restricting ourselves to only solving those problems that fit completely within every processing element's local memory, we can make use of the combined memory of all processing elements. The large problem domain can now be distributed across the system and even secondary storage devices if necessary. For this class of application, some form of data management will be necessary to ensure that data items are available at the processing elements when required by the computations.

Virtual shared memory regards the whole problem domain as a single unit in which the data items may be individually referenced. This is precisely how the domain could be treated if the problem was implemented on a shared memory multiprocessor system. However, on a distributed memory system, the problem domain is distributed across the system and hence the term **virtual**. Virtual shared memory systems may be implemented at different levels, such as in hardware or at the operating system level. In this chapter, we will see how the introduction of a data manager process at each processing element can provide an elegant virtual shared memory at the system software level of our parallel implementation.

2.5.1   World Model of the Data: No Data Management Required

Not all problems possess very large data domains. If the size of the domain is such that it may be accommodated at every processing element, then we say that the processing elements have a "world model" of the data. A world model may also exist if all the tasks allocated to a processing element only ever require a *subset* of the problem domain and this subset can be accommodated completely. In the world model, all principal and additional data items required by an application process will always be available locally at each processing element and thus there is no need for any data item to be fetched from another remote location within the system. If there is no requirement to fetch data items from remote locations as the solution of the problem proceeds then there is no need for any form of data management.

The processor farm described in Section 2.4.2 is an example of a parallel implementation which assumes a world model. In this approach, tasks are allocated to processing elements in an arbitrary fashion and thus there is no restriction on which tasks may be computed by which processing element. No provision is made for data management and thus to perform any task, the entire domain must reside at each processing element.

Data items do not always have to be present at the processing element from the start of computation to avoid any form of data management. As discussed in Section 2.3.1, both principal and additional data items may be included within a task packet. Provided no further data items are required to complete the tasks specified in the task packet then no data management is required and this situation may also be said to be demonstrating a world data model.

2.5.2 Virtual Shared Memory

Virtual Shared Memory (VSM) provides all processors with the concept of a single memory space. Unlike a traditional shared memory model, this physical memory is distributed amongst the processing elements. Thus, a virtual shared memory environment can be thought of providing each processing element with a *virtual world model* of the problem domain. So, as far as the application process is concerned, there is no difference between requesting a data item that happens to be local, or remote; only the speed of access can be (very) different.

VSM can be implemented at any level in the computer hierarchy. Implementations at the hardware level provide a transparent interface to software developers, but requires a specialized machine, such as the DASH system [171]. There have also been implementations at the operating system and compiler level. However, as we shall see, in the absence of dedicated hardware, virtual shared memory can also be easily provided at the system software level. At this level, a great deal of flexibility is available to provide specialized support to minimize any implementation penalties when undertaking the solution of problems with very large data requirements on multiprocessor systems. Figure 2.19 gives four levels at which VSM can be supported, and examples of systems that implement VSM at that particular level.

Implementing virtual shared memory

At the *hardware level*, VSM intercepts all memory traffic from the processor, and decides which memory accesses are serviced locally, and which memory accesses need to go off-processor. This means that everything

Higher level	System Software	Provided by the Data Manager process
	Compiler	High Performance Fortran[128], ORCA[22]
	Operating System	Coherent Paging[175]
Lower level	Hardware	DDM [314], DASH [171], KSR-1 [163]

Figure 2.19. The levels where virtual shared memory can be implemented.

above the hardware level (machine code, operating system, etc.) sees a virtual shared memory with which it may interact in exactly the same manner as a physically shared memory. Providing this, so called, transparency to the higher levels, means that the size of data is not determined by the hardware level. However, in hardware, a data item becomes a fixed consecutive number of bytes, typically around 16-256. By choosing the size to be a power of 2, and by aligning data items in the memory, the physical memory address can become the concatenation of the "item-identifier" and the "byte selection." This strategy is easier to implement in hardware.

31 ... 6	5 ... 0
Item identifier	byte-selection

In this example, the most significant bits of a memory address locates the data item, and the lower bits address a byte within the item. The choice of using 6 bits as the byte selection in this example is arbitrary.

If a data structure of some higher level language containing two integers of four bytes each happened to be allocated from, say, address ...1100 111100 to ...1101 000100, then item ...1100 will contain the first integer, and item ...1101 will contain the other one. This means that two logically related integers of data are located in two physically separate items (although they could fit in a single data item).

Considered another way, if two unrelated variables, say x and y are allocated at addresses ...1100 110000 and ...1100 110100, then they reside in the same data item. If they are heavily used on separate processors, this can cause inefficiencies when the machine tries to maintain sequentially consistent copies of x and y on both processors. The machine cannot put x on one processor and y on the other, because it does not recognize x and y as different entities; the machine observes it as a single item that is shared between two processors. If sequential consistency has to be maintained, the machine must update every write to x and y on both processors, even though the variables are not shared at all. This phenomenon is known as *false sharing*.

Virtual shared memory implemented at the *operating system level* also uses a fixed size for data items, but these are typically much larger than at the hardware level. By making an item as large as a page of the operating system (around 1-4 KB), data can be managed at the page level. This is cheaper, but slower, than a hardware implementation.

When the *compiler* supports virtual shared memory, a data item can be made exactly as large as any user data structure. In contrast with virtual shared memory implementations at the hardware or operating system level, compiler-based implementations can keep logically connected variables together and distribute others. The detection of logically related variables is in the general case very hard, which means that applications written in existing languages such as C, Modula-2, or Fortran cannot be compiled in this way. However, compilers for specially designed languages can provide some assistance. For example, in High Performance Fortran, the programmer indicates how arrays should be divided and then the compiler provides the appropriate commands to support data transport and data consistency.

Implementing virtual shared memory at the *system software* level provides the greatest flexibility to the programmer. However, this requires explicit development of system features to support the manipulation of the distributed data item. A *data manager* process is introduced at each processing element especially to undertake this job.

2.5.3   The Data Manager

Virtual shared memory is provided at the system software level by a data manager process at each processing element. The aim of data management within the parallel system is to ensure the efficient supply of data items to the processing elements. The data manager process manages data items just as the task manager was responsible for maintaining a continuous supply of tasks. Note that the data items being referred to here are the principal and additional data items as specified by the problem domain and not every variable or constant the application process may invoke for the completion of a task.

The application process now no longer deals with the principal and additional data items directly, but rather indirectly, using the facilities of the data manager. The application process achieves this by issuing a data request to the data manager process every time a data item is required. The data manager process assumes the responsibility for ensuring that every request for a data item from the application process will be satisfied. The data manager attempts to satisfy these requests by maintaining a local data cache.

The data management strategies implemented by the data manager and outlined in the following sections are *active*, dynamically requesting and acquiring data items during computation. This means that an application process should *always* have its request for a data item satisfied immediately by the data manager unless:

- At the start of the problem, the application processes make requests before any initial data items are provided by the system controller.

- The data manager's data fetch strategy has failed in some way.

The local data cache

The concept of *data sharing* may be used to cope with very large data requirements [43, 96]. Data sharing implements virtual shared memory by allocating every data item in the problem domain an unique identifier. This allows a required item to be "located" from somewhere within the system, or from secondary storage if necessary. The size of problem that can now be tackled is, therefore, no longer dictated by the size of the local memory at each processing element, but rather only by the limitations of the combined memory plus the secondary storage.

The principal data item required by an application process is specified by the task it is currently performing. Any additional data item requirements are determined by the task *and* by the algorithm chosen to solve the problem. These additional data items may be known *a priori* by the nature of the problem, or they may only become apparent as the computation of the task proceeds.

To avoid any processing element idle time, it is essential that the data manager has the required data item available locally at the moment the application process issues a request for it. In an attempt to achieve this, the data manager maintains a local cache of data items. The size of this cache, and thus the number of data items it can contain, is determined by the size of a processing element's local memory.

Each data item in the system is a packet containing the unique identifier together with the actual data which makes up the item. The data items may be permanently located at a specific processing element, or they may be free to migrate within the system to where they are required. When a data manager requires a particular data item which is not already available locally, this data item must be fetched from some remote location and placed into the local cache. This must occur before the application process can access the data item. The virtual shared memory of the system is thus the combination of the local caches at all the processing elements plus any secondary storage.

In certain circumstances, as will be seen in the following sections, rather than removing the data item from the local cache in which it was found, it may be sufficient simply to take a copy of the data item and return this to the local cache. This is certainly the case when the data items within the problem domain are *read-only*, that is the values of the data items are not altered during the course of the parallel solution of the problem (and indeed the same would be true of the sequential implementation). This means that it is possible for copies of the same data item to be present in a number of local caches. Note that it is no advantage to have more than one copy of any data item in one local cache.

There is a limited amount of space in any local cache. When the cache is full and another data item is acquired from a remote location, then one of the existing data items in the local cache must be replaced by this new data item. Care must be taken to ensure that no data item is inadvertently completely removed from the system by being replaced in all local caches. If this does happen then, assuming the data item is read-only, a copy of the entire problem domain will reside on secondary storage, from where the data items were initially loaded into the local caches of the parallel system. This means that should a data item be destroyed within the system, another copy can be retrieved from the secondary storage.

If the data items are *read-write*, then their values may be altered as the computation progresses. In this case, the data managers have to beware of consistency issues when procuring a data item. The implications of consistency will be discussed in Section 2.5.4.

As we will now see, the strategies adopted in the parallel implementation for acquiring data items and storing them in the local caches can have a significant effect on minimizing the implementation penalties and thus improving overall system performance. The onus is on the data manager process to ensure these strategies are carried out efficiently.

Requesting data items

The algorithm being executed at the application process will determine the next data item required.

The data item's unique identifier enables the data manager to extract the appropriate item from its local cache. If a data item requested by the application process is available, it is immediately transferred. The only slight delay in the computation of the application process will occur by the need to schedule the concurrent data manager and for this process to send the data item from its local cache. However, if the data item is not available locally, then the data manager must "locate" this item from elsewhere in the system. Having been found, the appropriate item is returned to the requesting data manager's own local cache and then finally a copy of the item is transferred to the application process.

If the communicated request from the application process is asynchronous and this process is able to continue with its task while awaiting the data item, then no idle time occurs. However, if the communication with the data manager is synchronous, or if the data item is essential for the continuation of the task, then idle time will persist until the data item can be fetched from the remote location. Unless otherwise stated, we will assume for the rest of this chapter that an application process is unable to

continue with its current task until its data item request has been satisfied
by the data manager.

Locating data items

When confronted with having to acquire a remote data item, two possibilities exist for the data manager. Either it knows exactly the location of the
data item within the system, or this location is unknown and some form of
search will have to be instigated.

Resident sets. Knowing the precise location of the requested data item
within the system enables the data manager to instruct the router to
send the request for the data item, directly to the appropriate processing
element.

One of the simplest strategies for allocating data items to each processing element's local cache is to divide all the data items of the problem
domain evenly amongst the processing elements before the computation
commences. Providing there is sufficient local memory and assuming there
are n processing elements, this means that each processing element would
be allocated $\frac{1}{n}^{th}$ of the total number of data items. If there isn't enough
memory at each processing element for even this fraction of the total problem domain, then as many as possible could be allocated to the local caches
and the remainder of the data items would be held on secondary storage.
Such a simplistic scheme has its advantages. Provided these data items
remain at their predetermined local cache for the duration of the computation, then the processing element from which any data item may be found
can be computed directly from the identity of the data item.

For example, assume there are 12 data items, given the unique identification numbers $1, \dots, 12$, and three processing elements, PE_1, PE_2,
and PE_3. A predetermined allocation strategy may allocate permanently
data items $1, \dots, 4$ to PE_1, data items $5, \dots, 8$ to PE_2 and $9, \dots, 12$ to
PE_3. Should PE_2 wish to acquire a copy of data item 10, it may do so
directly from the processing element known to have that data item, in this
case PE_3.

It is essential for this simple predetermined allocation strategy that the
data items are not overwritten or moved from the local cache to which they
are assigned initially. However, it may be necessary for a processing element
to also acquire copies of other data items as the computation proceeds,
as we saw with PE_2 above. This implies that the local cache should be
partitioned into two distinct regions:

- A region containing data items which may never be replaced, known as the *resident set*, and

- A region for data items which may be replaced during the parallel computation.

The size of the resident set should be sufficient to accommodate all the pre-allocated data items. The remaining portion of the local cache will be as large as allowed by the local memory of the processing element. Note that this portion needs to have sufficient space to hold a minimum of *one* data item as this is the maximum that the application process can require at any specific point during a task's computation. To complete a task, an application process may require many data items. Each of these data items may, in turn, replace the previously acquired one in the single available space in the local cache.

The balanced data driven model of computation is well suited to a simple predetermined even data item allocation scheme. In this model, the system controller knows prior to the computation commencing precisely which tasks are to be assigned to which processing elements. The same number of tasks is assigned to each processing element and thus the principal data items for each of these tasks may be preallocated evenly amongst the local caches of the appropriate processing elements. Similar knowledge is available to the system controller for the unbalanced data driven model, but in this case, the number of tasks allocated to each processing element is not the same and so different numbers of principal data items will be loaded into each resident set. Note that the algorithm used to solve the problem may be such that, even if a data driven model is used and thus the principal data items are known in advance, the additional data items may not be known *a priori*. In this case, these additional data items will have to be fetched into the local caches by the data managers as the computation proceeds and the data requirements become known.

More sophisticated preallocation strategies, for example, some form of hashing function, are possible to provide resident sets at each processing element. It is also not necessary for each data item to be resident at only one processing element. Should space permit, the same data item may be resident at several local caches.

The preallocation of resident sets allows the location of a data item to be determined from its unique identifier. A preallocated resident set may occupy a significant portion of a local cache and leave little space for other data items which have not been preallocated. The shortage of space would require these other data items to be replaced constantly as the computation proceeds. It is quite possible that one data item may be needed often by the same application process either for the same task or for several tasks. If this data item is not in the resident set for that processing element, then there is the danger that the data item will be replaced during the periods that it is not required and thus will have to be refetched when it is required once more. Furthermore, despite being preallocated, the data items of a resident set may in fact never be required by the processing element to which they were allocated. In the example given earlier, PE_2 has a resident set containing data items $5, \ldots, 8$. Unless there is a priori knowledge about the data requirements of the tasks, there is no guarantee that PE_2 will ever require any of these data items from its resident set. In this case, a portion of PE_2's valuable local cache is being used to store data items which are never required, thus reducing the available storage for data items which are needed. Those processing elements that do require data items $5, \ldots, 8$ are going to have to fetch them from PE_2. Not only will the fetches of these data items imply communication delays for the requesting data managers, but also, the need for PE_2's data manager to service these requests will imply concurrent activity by its data manager which will detract from the computation of the application process.

The solution to this dilemma is not to preallocate resident sets, but to build up such a set as computation proceeds and information is gained by each data manager as to the data items most frequently used by its processing element. Profiling can also assist in establishing these resident sets, as explained in Section 2.5.5. The price to pay for this flexibility is that it may no longer be possible for a data manager to determine precisely where a particular data item may be found within the system.

Searching for data at unknown locations. Acquiring a specific data item from an unknown location will necessitate the data manager requesting the router process to "search" the system for this item. The naive approach would be for the requesting data manager to send the request to the data manager process of each processing element in turn. If the requested data manager has the necessary data item, it will return a copy and then there is no need to request any further processing elements. If the requested data manager does not have the data item, then it must send back a not_found message, whereupon the next processing element may be tried. The advantage of this *one-to-one* scheme is that as soon as the required data item is found, no further requests need be issued and only one copy of the data item will ever be returned. However, the communication implications of such a scheme for a large parallel system are substantial. If by some quirk of fate (or Murphy's law), the last processing element to be asked is the one which has the necessary data item, then one request will have resulted in $2 \times (number\ of\ PEs\ - 1)$ messages, a quite unacceptable number for large systems. Furthermore, the delay before the data item is finally found will be large, resulting in long application process idle time.

An alternative to this communication intensive *one-to-one* approach is for the router process to issue a global broadcast of the request; a *one-to-many* method. A bus used to connect the processing elements is particularly suited to such a communication strategy, although, as discussed in Section 1.2, a bus is not an appropriate interconnection method for large multiprocessor systems. The broadcast strategy may also be used efficiently on a more suitable interconnection method for large systems, such as interconnections between individual processors. In this case, the router issues the request to its directly connected neighboring processing elements. If the data managers at these processing elements have the required data item, then it is returned; if not, then these neighboring processing elements in turn propagate the request to their neighbors (excluding the one from which they received the message). In this way, the request propagates through the system like ripples on a pond. The message density inherent in this approach is significantly less than the *one-to-one* approach, however one disadvantage is that if the requested data item is replicated at several local caches, then several copies of the same data item will be returned to the requesting data manager, when only one is required.

For very large multiprocessor systems, even this *one-to-many* approach to discovering the unknown location of a data item may be too costly in terms of communication latency and its contribution to message density within the system. A compromise of the direct access capabilities of the preallocated resident set approach and the flexibility of the dynamic composition of the local caches is the notion of a *directory* of data item locations.

In this approach, it is not necessary to maintain a particular data item at a fixed processing element. We can introduce the notion of a *home*-processing element that knows where that data item is, while the data item is currently located at the *owner*-processing element. The home-processing element is fixed and its address may be determined from the identifier of the data item. The home processing element knows which processing element is currently owning the data item. Should this data item be subsequently moved and the one at the owner-process removed, then either the home-processing element must be informed as to the new location of the data item or the previous owner-processing element must now maintain a pointer to this new location. The first scheme has the advantage that a request message may be forwarded directly from the home-processing element to the current owner, while the second strategy may be necessary, at least for a while after the data item has been moved from an owner, to cope with any requests forwarded by the home-processing element before it has received the latest location update.

Finally, it is also possible to do away with the notion of a home-processing element, by adding a hierarchy of directories. Each directory on a processing element "knows" which data items are present on the processing element. If the required data item is not present, a directory higher up in the hierarchy might know if it is somewhere nearby. If that directory does not know, yet another directory might if it is further away. This is much like the organization of libraries: You first check the local library for a book; if they do not have it, you ask the central library, and so on until you finally query the national library. With this organization, there is always a directory that knows the whereabouts of the data item, but it is very likely that the location of the data item will be found long before asking the highest directory. (The Data Diffusion Machine [314] and KSR-1 [163] used a similar strategy implemented in hardware).

2.5.4 Consistency

Copies of *read-only* data items may exist in numerous local caches within the system without any need to "keep track" of where all the copies are. However, if copies of *read-write* data items exist then, in a virtual shared memory system, there is the danger that the data items may become *inconsistent*. The example in Figure 2.20 illustrates this problem of inconsistency. Suppose that we have two processing elements, PE_1 and PE_2, and a data item y with a value 0, that is located at processing element PE_1. Processing Element PE_2 needs y, so it requests and gets a copy of y. The data manager on processing element PE_2 decides to keep this copy for possible future reference. When the application at processing element PE_1 updates the value of y, for example, by overwriting it with the value 1; processing element PE_2 will have a *stale* copy of y. This situation is called *inconsistent*: If the application running at processing element PE_1 requests y it will get the new value (1), while the application at processing element PE_2 will still read the old value of y (0). This situation will exist until the data manager at processing element PE_2 decides to evict y from its local memory.

The programming model of a physical shared memory system maintains only one copy of any data item: the copy in the shared memory. Because there is only one copy, the data items cannot become inconsistent. Hence, naive *virtual* shared memory differs from *physical* shared memory in that virtual shared memory can become inconsistent.

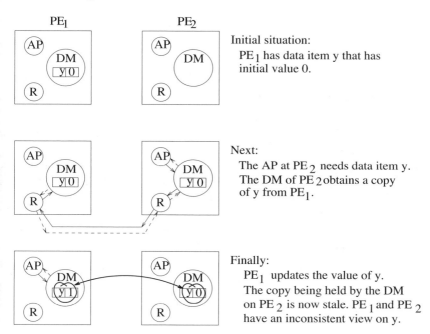

Initial situation:
PE$_1$ has data item y that has initial value 0.

Next:
The AP at PE$_2$ needs data item y. The DM of PE$_2$ obtains a copy of y from PE$_1$.

Finally:
PE$_1$ updates the value of y. The copy being held by the DM on PE$_2$ is now stale. PE$_1$ and PE$_2$ have an inconsistent view on y.

Figure 2.20. An example how an inconsistency arises. There are two processing elements, PE_1 and PE_2, and a data item y. PE_2 keeps a copy of y, while y is updated at PE_1.

To maintain consistency all copies of the data items will have to be "tracked down" at certain times during the parallel computation. Once again one-to-one or many-to-one methods could be used to determine the unknown locations of copies of the data items. If the directory approach is used then it will be necessary to maintain a complete "linked list" through all copies of any data item, where each copy knows where the next copy is, or it knows that there are no more copies. A consistency operation is performed on this list by sending a message to the first copy on the list, which then ripples through the list. These operations thus take a time linear in the number of copies. This is expensive if there are many copies, so it can be more efficient to use a tree structure (where the operation needs logarithmic time). (A combination of a software and hardware tree directory of this form is used in the LimitLESS directory [40].)

There are several ways to deal with this inconsistency problem. We will discuss three options: data items are kept consistent at all times (known as sequential consistency); the actual problem somehow copes with the inconsistencies (known as weak consistency); and finally, inconsistent data items are allowed to live for a well defined period (the particular scheme discussed here is known as release consistency).

Keeping the data items consistent

The first option is that the data manager will keep the data items consistent at all times. To see how the data items can be kept consistent, observe first that there are two conditions that must be met before a data item can become inconsistent. Firstly, the data item must be duplicated; as long as there is only a single copy of the data item, it cannot be inconsistent. Secondly, some processing element must update one of the copies, without updating the other copies. This observation leads to two protocols that the data manager can observe to enforce consistency, while still allowing copies to be made:

1. Ensure that there is not more than a single copy of the data item when it is updated. This means that before a write, all but one of the copies must be deleted. This solution is known as an *invalidating protocol*.

2. Ensure that all copies of the data item are replaced when it is updated. This solution is known as an *updating protocol*.

It is relatively straightforward to check that the invalidating option will always work: All copies are always identical, because a write only occurs when there is only a single copy. In the example, the copy of y at processing element PE_2 will be destroyed before y is updated on processing element PE_1.

For the updating protocol to be correct, the protocol must ensure that all copies are replaced "at the same time." Suppose that this is not the case: In the example, the value on processing element PE_1 might be updated, while processing element PE_2 still has an old value for y. If the data managers running on processing elements PE_1 and PE_2 communicate, they can find out about this inconsistency. In order for the update protocol to work, the updating data manager must either ensure that no other data manager is accessing the data item while it is being updated, or that it is impossible for any communication (or other update) to overtake this update.

It is not easy to decide in general whether an invalidating or an updating protocol is better. Below are two examples that show that invalidating and updating protocols both have advantages and disadvantages. In both cases, we assume that the problem is running on a large number of processing elements, and that there is a single shared data item that is initially replicated over all processing elements.

1. A task, or tasks, being performed by an application process at one processing element might require that the data item be updated at this data manager many times, without any of the other processing elements using it. An updating protocol will update all copies on all processing elements during every update, even though the copies are not being used on any of the other processing elements.

   An invalidating protocol is more efficient, because it will invalidate all outstanding copies once, whereupon the application process can continue updating the data item without extra communication.

2. Suppose that instead of ignoring the data item, all other processing elements do need the updated value. An invalidating protocol will invalidate all copies and update the data item, whereupon all other processing elements have to fetch the value again. This fetch is on-demand, which means that they will have to wait on the data item.

   An updating protocol does a better job since it distributes the new value, avoiding the need for the other processing elements to wait for it.

There is a case for (and against) both protocols. It is for this reason that these two protocols are sometimes combined. This gives a protocol that, for example, invalidates all copies that have not been used since the last update, and updates the copies that were used since the last update. Although these hybrid protocols are potentially more efficient, they are unfortunately often more complex than a pure invalidating or updating protocol.

Weak consistency: repair consistency on request

The option to maintain sequential consistency is an expensive one. In general, an application process is allowed to proceed with its computation only after the invalidate or update has been completed. In the example of the invalidating protocol, all outstanding copies must have been erased and the local copy must have been updated before the application process can proceed. This idle time may be an unacceptable overhead. One of the ways to reduce this overhead is to forget about maintaining consistency automatically. Instead, the local cache will stay inconsistent until the application process orders the data manager to repair the inconsistency.

There are two important advantages of weak consistency. Firstly, the local cache is made consistent at certain points in the task execution only, reducing the overhead. Secondly, local caches can be made consistent in parallel. Recall for example, the updating protocol of the previous section. In a weakly consistent system we can envisage that every write to a data item is asynchronously broadcasted to all remote copies. Asynchronously means that the processing element performing the write continues whether the update has been completed or not. Only when a consistency-command is executed must the application process wait until all outstanding updates are completed. In the same way, a weakly consistent invalidating protocol can invalidate remote copies in parallel. These optimizations lead to further performance improvement. The disadvantage of weak consistency is the need for the explicit commands within the algorithm at each application process so that when a task is being executed, at the appropriate point, the data manager can be instructed to make the local cache consistent.

Repair consistency on synchronization: release consistency

A weak consistency model as sketched above requires the algorithm programmer to ensure consistency at any moment in time. Release consistency is based on the observation that algorithms do not go from one phase to the other without first synchronizing. So it suffices to make the local caches consistent during the synchronization operation. This means that immediately after each synchronization, the local caches are guaranteed to be consistent. This is, in general, slightly more often than strictly necessary, but it is far less often than would be the case when using sequential consistency. More importantly, the application process itself does not have to make the local caches consistent anymore; it is done "invisibly."

Note that although invisible, consistency is only restored during an explicit synchronization operation; release consistency behaves still very differently from sequential consistency. As an example, an application process at PE_1 can poll a data item in a loop, waiting for the data item to be changed by the application process at PE_2. Under sequential consistency, any update to the data item will be propagated, and cause the application process at PE_1 to exit the loop. Under release consistency, updates do not need to be propagated until a synchronization point, and because it does not recognize that the polling loop is actually a synchronization point, the application process at PE_1 might be looping forever.

2.5.5 Minimizing the Impact of Remote Data Requests

Failure to find a required data item locally means that the data manager has to acquire this data item from elsewhere within the system. The time to fetch this data item and, therefore, the application process idle time, can be significant. This *latency* is difficult to predict and may not be repeatable due to other factors, such as current message densities within the system. The overall aim of data management is to maximize effective processing element computation by minimizing the occurrence and effects of remote data fetches. A number of techniques may be used to reduce this latency by:

Hiding the latency. Overlapping the communication with the computation, by:

> **Prefetching.** Anticipating data items that will be required.

> **Multithreading.** Keeping the processing element busy with other useful computation during the remote fetch.

Minimizing the latency. Reducing the time associated with a remote fetch by:

> **Caching & profiling.** Exploiting any coherence that may exist in the problem domain

Prefetching

If it is known at the start of the computation which data items will be required by each task, then these data items can be *prefetched* by the data manager so that they are available locally when required. The data manager thus issues the requests for the data items *before* they are actually required, and in this way overlaps the communication required for the remote fetches with the ongoing computation of the application process. This is in contrast with the simple fetch-upon-demand strategy where the data manager only issues the external request for a data item at the moment it is requested by the application process and it is not found in the local cache.

By treating its local cache as a "circular buffer" the data manager can be loading prefetched data items into one end of the buffer while the application process is requesting the data items from the other end, as shown in Figure 2.21. The "speed" at which the data manager can prefetch the data items will be determined by the size of the local cache and the rate at which the application process is "using" the data items.

This knowledge about the data items may be known *a priori* by the nature of problem. For example, in a parallel solution of the hemi-cube radiosity method, the data manager knows that each task, that is the computation of a single row of the matrix of form factors, requires all the environment's patch data. The order in which these data items are considered is unimportant, as long as all data items are considered. The

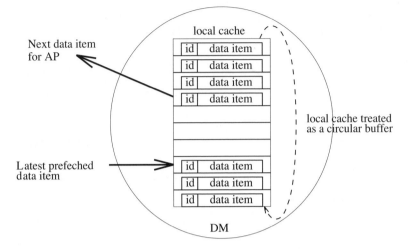

Figure 2.21. Storing the prefetched data items in the local cache.

data manager can thus continually prefetch those data items which have yet to be considered by the current task. Note that in this problem, because all the data items are required by every task and the order is unimportant (we are assuming that the local cache is not sufficiently big to hold all these data items), those data items which remain in the local cache at the end of one task are also required by the subsequent task. Thus, at the start of the next task, the first data item in the local cache can be forwarded to the application process and prefetching can commence once more as soon as this has happened.

The choice of computation model adopted can also provide the information required by the data manager in order to prefetch. The principal data items for both the balanced and unbalanced data driven models will be known by the system controller before the computation commences. Giving this information to the data manager will enable it to prefetch these data items. A prefetch strategy can also be used for principal data items within the preferred bias task allocation strategy for the demand driven computation model, as described in section 2.4.5. Knowledge of its processing element's conceptual region can be exploited by the data manager to prefetch the principal data items within this region of the problem domain.

Multithreading

Any failure by the data manager to have the requested data item available locally for the application process will result in idle time unless the processing element can be kept busy doing some other useful computation.

One possibility is for the application process to save the current state of a task and commence a new task whenever a requested data item is not available locally. When the requested data item is finally forthcoming, either this new task could be suspended and the original task resumed, or processing of the new task could be continued until it is completed. This new task may be suspended awaiting a data fetch and so the original task may be resumed. Saving the state of a task may require a large amount of memory and indeed, several states may need to be saved before one requested data item finally arrives. Should the nature of the problem allow these stored tasks to in turn be considered as task packets, then this method has the additional advantage that these task packets could potentially be completed by another processing element in the course of load balancing, as explained in the section 2.4.4 on distributed task management.

Another possible option is multithreading. In this method, there is not only one, but several application processes on each processing element. Each application process is known as a separate *thread* of computation. Now, although one thread may be suspended awaiting a remote data item, the other threads may still be able to continue. It may not be feasible to determine just how many of these application processes will be necessary to avoid the case where all of them are suspended awaiting data. However, if there are sufficient *threads* (and, of course, sufficient tasks), then the processing element should always be performing useful computation. Note that multithreading is similar to the Bulk Synchronous Parallel paradigm [300].

One disadvantage of this approach is the overhead incurred by the additional context switching that will be required between all the processes that are now resident on the same processor. A variation of multiple active threads is to have several application processes existing on each processing element, but to only have *one* of them active at any time and have managed scheduling of these processes explicitly from information provided by the data manager. When an application process' data item request cannot be satisfied locally, that process will remain descheduled until the data item is forthcoming. The data manager is thus in a position to inform this explicit scheduler to activate another application process, and only reactivate the original application process once the required data has been obtained.

Both forms of multithreading have other limitations. The first of these is the extra memory requirements each thread places on the processing elements' local memory. The more memory that each thread will require (for local constants and variables, etc.), the less memory there will be available for the local cache and thus fewer data items will be able to be kept locally by the data manager. A "catch 22" (or is that "cache 22"?)

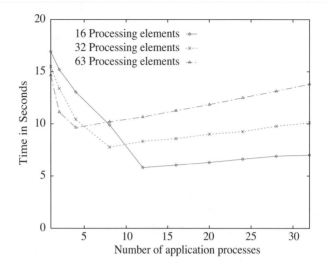

Figure 2.22. Problem solution time in seconds.

situation now arises as fewer local data items implies more remote data fetches and thus the possible need for yet more threads to hide this increase in latency. The second difficulty of a large number of threads running on the same processing element is the unacceptably heavy overhead that may be placed on the data manager when maintaining the local cache. For example, a dilemma may exist as to whether a recently fetched data item for one thread should be overwritten before it has been used if its "slot" in the local cache is required by the currently active thread.

Figure 2.22 shows results for a multithreaded application. The graph shows the time in seconds to solve a complex parallel ray tracing problem with large data requirements using more than one application process per processing element. As can be seen, increasing the number of application processes per processing element produces a performance improvement until a certain number of threads have been added. Beyond this point, the overheads of having the additional threads are greater than the benefit gained, and thus the times to solve the problem once more increase. The number of threads at which the overheads outweigh the benefits gained is lower for larger numbers of processing elements. This is because the more application processes there are per processing element, the larger the message output from each processing element will be (assuming an average number of remote fetches per thread). As the average distances the remote data fetches have to travel in larger systems is greater, the impact of increasing numbers of messages on the overall system density is more significant and thus the request latency will be higher. Adding more threads now no longer helps overcome communication delays, but in fact, the increasing number of messages actually exacerbates the communication difficulties. Ways must be found of dynamically scheduling the optimum number of application processes at each processing element depending on the current system message densities.

Despite these shortcomings, multithreading does work well, especially for low numbers of threads and is a useful technique for avoiding idle time in the face of unpredictable data item requirements. Remember that multiple threads are only needed at a processing element if a prefetch strategy is not possible and the data item required by one thread was not available locally. If ways can be found to try and guess which data items are likely to be required next, and then if the data manager is right at least some of the time, the number of remote fetches-on-demand will be reduced. Caching and profiling assist the data manager with these predictions.

Profiling

Although primarily a task management technique, profiling is used explicitly to assist with data management, and so is discussed here. At the start of the solution of many problems, no knowledge exists as to the data requirements of any of the tasks. (If this knowledge did exist, then a prefetching strategy would be applicable). Monitoring the solution of a single task provides a list of all the data items required by that task. If the same monitoring action is carried for all tasks, then at the completion of the problem, a complete "picture" of the data requirements of all tasks would be known. Profiling attempts to predict the data requirements of future tasks from the list of data requirements of completed tasks.

Any spatial coherence in the problem domain will provide the profiling technique with a good estimate of the future data requirements of those tasks from a similar region of the problem domain. The data manager can now use this profiling information to *prefetch* those data items which are *likely* to be used by subsequent tasks being performed at that processing element. If the data manager is always correct with its prediction, then profiling provides an equivalent situation to prefetching in which the application process is never delayed awaiting a remote fetch. Note that in this case, there is no need for multithreading.

2.5.6   Data Management for Multistage Problems

In Section 2.3.3, we discussed the algorithmic and data dependencies that can arise in problems which exhibit more than one distinct stage. In such

problems, the results from one stage become the principal data items for
the subsequent stage as was shown in Figure 2.11. So, in addition to
ensuring the application processes are kept supplied with data items during
one stage, the data manager also needs to be aware as to how the partial
results from one stage of the computation are stored at each processing
element in anticipation of the following stage.

This balancing of partial result storage could be achieved statically by
all the results of a stage being returned to the system controller. At the end
of that current stage, the system controller is in a position to distribute this
data evenly as the principal and additional data items for the next stage
of the problem. The communication of these potentially large data packets
twice, once during the previous stage to the system controller and again
from the system controller to specific processing elements, obviously may
impose an enormous communication overhead. A better static distribution
strategy might be to leave the results in place at the processing elements
for the duration of the stage and then have them distributed from the
processing elements in a manner prescribed by the system controller. Note
that in such a scheme, the local cache of each processing element must
be able to hold not only the principal and additional data items for the
current stage, but also have space in which to store these partial results
in anticipation of the forthcoming stage. It is important that these partial
results are kept separate so that they are not inadvertently overwritten by
data items during the current stage.

In a demand driven model of computation, the uneven computational
complexity may result in a few processing elements completing many more
tasks than others. This produces a flaw in the second static storage strategy. The individual processing elements may simply not have sufficient
space in their local cache to store more than their fair share of the partial
results until the end of the stage.

Two dynamic methods of balancing this partial result data may also
be considered. Adoption of the preferred bias task management strategy,
as discussed in Section 2.4.5, can greatly facilitate the correct distribution
of any partial results. Any results produced by one processing element
from another's conceptual portion, due to task load balancing, may be sent
directly to this other processing element. The initial conceptual allocation
of tasks ensures that the destination processing element will have sufficient
storage for the partial result.

If this conceptual allocation is not possible, or not desirable, then balancing the partial results dynamically requires each processing element to
be kept informed of the progress of all other processing elements. This may
be achieved by each processing element broadcasting a short message on

completion of every task to all other processing elements. To ensure that this information is as up to date as possible, it is advisable that these messages have a special high priority so that they may be handled immediately by the router processes, by-passing the normal queue of messages. Once a data manager's local cache reaches its capacity, the results from the next task are sent in the direction of the processing element that is known to have completed the least number of tasks and, therefore, the one which will have the most available space. To further reduce the possible time that this data packet may exist in the system, any processing element on its path which has storage capacity available may absorb the packet and thus not route it further.

3

Parallel Global
Illumination
Erik Reinhard # Algorithms

Many methods and techniques exist that aim to render images of artificial models or worlds: Some are able to create these images interactively, or even in real-time. Others produce images with high fidelity, but do so at the cost of a much higher computational complexity. The quality of the rendered imagery and the speed of computation are related, and for many applications a trade-off must be sought to render the highest quality images within the time allowed. This is the reason that such a large number of algorithms exists. With many of these techniques well established and their implementations highly optimized, further speed up of the computations can only be accomplished in one of two ways.

First, one may opt to wait for faster hardware to become available. This would be a valid approach if it is assumed that the demands on the rendering algorithms do not change, i.e., the visual effects one wishes to render do not alter over time, and the size of the images and scenes also remains the same. Using Moore's law, one could then compute how many months or years one would have to wait before the latest hardware can render images at the desired speed. Unfortunately, this approach is thwarted because the demands on rendering algorithms do change over time. Currently, few people are willing to accept image resolutions of 512^2 pixels or less, a size that was common only a short time ago. Recent advances in display technology will result in much higher display resolutions becoming commonplace.

Also, with the advent of advanced data acquisition techniques, the size of the models is steadily increasing. Combine this with the fact that shading and reflection models are becoming more realistic and therefore computationally more expensive, and it is clear that waiting for the right hardware to come along is not a viable approach.

A second and more proactive option would be to beat computational complexity by employing parallelism. It is intuitively clear that if a rendering problem is divided into a number of smaller problems, each of which is rendered on a separate computer, the time required to solve the full problem is reduced. In practice this is true also, although many issues arise from distributing such rendering problems. The question of how to distribute the computations needs to be answered in tandem with the question of if and how to distribute the input data. In this book, many ideas about these and other issues are presented. To prepare the reader and provide a gentle introduction to parallel rendering, this chapter gives a high level overview of some of the rendering algorithms that are discussed elsewhere in the book. We also attempt to show for each of these algorithms what the potential pitfalls are when attempting to parallelize them.

This chapter is structured as follows. We first discuss rendering and parallel processing in Sections 3.1 and 3.2. In Section 3.3, ray tracing and its parallel variants are explained, while spatial subdivisions are discussed in Section 3.4. Radiosity is described in Sections 3.5 through 3.8, while stochastic rendering is presented in Section 3.9. Issues pertaining to preserving and exploiting coherence and data locality are discussed in Section 3.10. Finally, this chapter is concluded with a discussion in Section 3.11.

3.1   Rendering

Rendering algorithms generally take a model or scene as input and produce an image or a sequence of images as output. In the process, various aspects of light behavior may be included. Simple and fast algorithms may choose to ignore most lighting effects and for example perform local shading and compute shadows at best. Such methods are normally classified as local illumination algorithms, since many light paths that involve illumination off other reflective or transmissive surfaces are ignored.

More complete lighting simulations involve global illumination and may include effects such as diffuse inter-reflection and caustics (for example, the light patterns cast on the bottom of a swimming pool). Global illumination algorithms are known for their unpredictable data accesses and their high computational complexity. Rendering a single high quality image may take several hours, or even days, and for this reason, parallel processing should be considered as a viable option to speed image generation. The nature of data access patterns and often the sheer size of the scene, means that a straightforward parallelization, if one exists, may not always lead to good performance. This holds for all three rendering techniques considered in this chapter: ray tracing, radiosity, and particle tracing. However, later chapters will show that if the right algorithm is matched with a clever choice of hardware, some of these problems may be overcome. In particular, with current shared memory technology, interactive ray tracing has become feasible (Chapter 6).

Physically correct rendering of artificial scenes requires the simulation of light behavior. Such simulations are computationally very expensive and may take between a couple of hours to several days. The trend towards faster general purpose hardware continues to be offset by increased scene complexity, as well as image size and shader complexity. To gain additional computational speed, one might consider the use of dedicated global illumination hardware, as discussed in Chapter 9 of this book.

The best lighting simulation algorithms to date are ray tracing [318], radiosity [93], and particle tracing [223]. These algorithms differ in the way the light paths are approximated. This means that each algorithm offers a different subset of lighting effects. However, as pointed out by Kajiya [149], all rendering algorithms aim to model the same lighting behavior, i.e., light scattering off various types of surfaces, and hence try to solve the same equation, termed the rendering equation. Following the notation adopted by Shirley [263], the rendering equation is formulated as:

$$L_o(x, \Theta_o) = L_e(x, \Theta_o) \tag{3.1}$$
$$+ \int_{allx'} v(x, x') f_r(x, \Theta'_o, \Theta_o) L_o(x', \Theta'_o) \cos \Theta_i \frac{\cos \Theta'_o dA'}{\|x' - x\|^2}.$$

This equation simply states that the outgoing radiance L_o at surface point x in direction Θ_o is equal to the emitted radiance L_e plus the incoming radiance from all points x' reflected into direction Θ_o. In this equation, $v(x, x')$ is a visibility term, being 1 if x' is visible from surface point x and 0 otherwise. The material properties of surface point x are represented in the *Bidirectional Reflection Distribution Function* (BRDF) $f_r(x, \Theta'_o, \Theta_o)$, which returns the amount of radiance reflected into direction Θ_o as function of incident radiance from direction Θ'_o. The cosine terms translate surface points in the scene into projected solid angles.

The rendering equation is an approximation to Maxwell's equation for electro-magnetics [149], and therefore does not model all optical phenomena. For example, it does not include diffraction and it also assumes that the media in between surfaces do not scatter light. Participating media, such as smoke, clouds, mist, and fire are therefore not accounted for without extending the above formulation.

There are two reasons for the complexity of physically correct rendering algorithms. One stems from the fact that the quantity to be computed, L_o is part of the integral in Equation 3.1, turning the rendering equation into a recursive integral equation. The other is that, although generally fixed, the integration domain can be arbitrarily complex. Recursive integral equations with fixed integration domains are called Fredholm equations of the second kind and have to be solved numerically [66]. Ray tracing (Section 3.3), radiosity (Sections 3.5 to 3.8), and particle tracing (Section 3.9) are examples of such numerical methods that approximate the rendering equation. Ray tracing approximates the rendering equation by means of (Monte Carlo) sampling from the eye point whereas particle tracing samples from the light sources. Radiosity is a finite element method for approximating energy exchange between surfaces in a scene.

3.2   Parallel Processing

To speed up high fidelity algorithms such as ray tracing, radiosity, or particle tracing, many different schemes have been proposed. Parallel processing is one of them. To successfully implement a rendering algorithm in parallel, a number of issues must be addressed. First of all, one must decide whether the algorithm will be decomposed into separate functional parts (algorithmic decomposition), or if identical programs will be executed on different parts of the data (domain decomposition). The latter tends to be more suitable for parallel rendering purposes and is certainly the method that is used most frequently nowadays. This chapter therefore concentrates mainly on domain decomposition methods.

Second, different types of parallel hardware must be considered. Dedicated parallel graphics hardware may be used, as well as clusters of workstations (distributed processing). If available, general purpose multiprocessors with either shared or distributed memory can be successfully employed. Shared memory systems have the advantage of simplicity of programming, as all processors address the same pool of data. On the other hand, this is also a disadvantage, because memory access may become a bottleneck when a large number of processors are connected together. Although algorithms running on shared memory architectures do not necessarily have to be optimized for memory access patterns, their performance may certainly benefit from doing so (Chapter 6).

Distributed memory systems are theoretically more scalable, but in practice, moving data and tasks from processor to processor is costly, and tends to limit the scalability of the system. Most parallel rendering algorithms are implemented on distributed memory systems, with a few notable exceptions. Since distributed memory machines are much more widespread than shared memory systems, a large part of this book focuses on networked clusters of computers. Whether or not these computers are physically located within a single box, or distributed over an office or a whole country, is largely irrelevant.

A third decision involves scheduling strategies. Tasks need to be identified and the appropriate data has to be selected for each. Managing which tasks are executed by which processors and if and how data is going to be moved between various processors are important design decisions which directly affect performance of the resulting parallel system. Improper task and data management may lead to idle time, for example, because the workload is unevenly distributed between processors (load imbalance), or because data fetches from remote processors cause extra delays. Excessive data or task communication between processors is another common performance degrading effect. Choreographing tasks and data such that all processors have sufficient work all the time, while ensuring that the data needed to complete all tasks is available at the right moments in time, are generally the main issues in parallel processing.

Three different types of task scheduling are distinguished: data parallel, data driven, and demand driven scheduling. If data is distributed over a number of processors, then data parallel scheduling implies that tasks are executed with the processors that hold the data required for those tasks. If some data items are unavailable at one processor, the task is migrated to the processor that holds these data items. Very large data sets can be processed in this way, because the problem size does not depend on the size of a single processor's memory.

In data driven scheduling, all tasks are distributed over the processors before the computations start. Scheduling is extremely simple, but data management is more involved. Data is either replicated across all processors, or data is fetched on demand, thereby penalizing performance. Another disadvantage is that the workload associated with each task is unknown. Data driven scheduling therefore tends to cause load imbalances.

Demand driven scheduling is generally more successful in avoiding load imbalances, because work is distributed on demand. Whenever a processor finishes a task, it requests a new task from a master processor. Data management is usually similar to that used for data driven scheduling, which means that best performance is attained if the data is replicated over all processors.

Demand driven and data parallel types of scheduling can be combined into a hybrid scheduling algorithm. Each processor then stores part of the data, allowing scene size to be independent of each processor's individual memory. Whenever data accesses are unpredictable, or a large amount of data is required to complete a task, these tasks are handled in data parallel fashion. If a task requires only a relatively small amount of data, which can be determined before it is executed, then demand driven scheduling is chosen for that task. Load balancing can be achieved by scheduling such tasks with processors that have a low workload.

For highly complex scenes, the above scheduling approaches may lose efficiency due to lack of data and cache coherence. Recently, several techniques have been developed to improve data locality, either by replacing complex objects by simpler approximations or by reordering computations. Similar data management strategies have been proposed to reduce the amount of task communication in data parallel approaches. These issues are discussed further in Section 3.10.

3.3   Ray Tracing

One of the most popular rendering techniques, ray tracing [91, 264, 318], is explained in some detail in this section. In addition, we examine some strategies for parallelizing this algorithm.

For each pixel of the image, the basic ray tracing algorithm follows one or more rays into the scene [318]. If such a primary ray hits an object, the light intensity of that object is assigned to the corresponding pixel. From the intersection point of the ray and the object, new rays are spawned towards each of the light sources (Figure 3.1). When these shadow rays intersect other objects between the intersection point and the light sources, the intersection point is in shadow. If the light sources are the first objects hit by the shadow rays, it is concluded that the intersection point was directly lit.

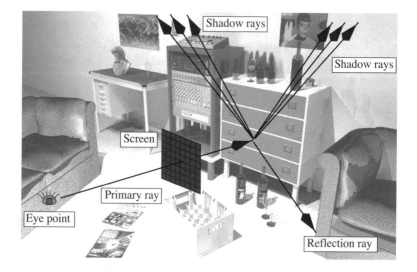

Figure 3.1. Modeling reflection and shadowing.

Specular reflection and transparency may be modeled similarly by shooting new rays into the reflected and/or transmitted directions (Figure 3.1). These reflection and transparency rays are treated in exactly the same way as primary rays, making ray tracing a recursive algorithm.

In terms of the rendering equation, ray tracing can be defined as [161]:

$$L_o(x, \Theta_o) = L_e(x, \Theta_o)$$

$$+ \sum_L \int_{all x_i \in L} v(x, x_l) f_{r,d}(x) L_e(x_l, \Theta_o') \cos \Theta_l d\omega_l$$

$$+ \int_{\Theta_s \in \Omega_s} f_{r,s}(x, \Theta_s, \Theta_o) L(x_s, \Theta_s) \cos \Theta_s d\omega_s + \rho_d L_a(x).$$

Here, the first term on the right-hand side is the emitted radiance. The second term computes the direct contribution of the light sources L. Visibility for this term is evaluated by casting shadow rays towards the light sources. The specular contribution is computed by evaluating the third term. If rays evaluated for the specular and transparency components intersect a surface, this equation is evaluated recursively. As normally no diffuse inter-reflection is computed in ray tracing, the ambient component is approximated by a constant, the fourth term. A notable exception is the Radiance lighting simulation package [313, 312] which replaces the constant ambient term with an accurate, but costly evaluation of diffuse inter-reflection. It achieves this by shooting a large number of undirected rays from the intersection point into the scene. As these diffuse rays are distributed over a hemisphere placed over the intersection point, some rays may accidentally hit a light emitting surface. Light sources are normally evaluated separately by shadow rays, and therefore, other secondary rays hitting light sources ought to be discounted. Sampling diffuse inter-reflection and transmission is also performed recursively.

The recursive ray tracing process has to be carried out for each individual pixel separately. A typical image therefore takes at least a million primary rays and a multiple of that for shadow, reflection, and transparency rays. If more than one ray is traced per pixel (super-sampling), aliasing artifacts can be overcome by taking a weighted average of all the shading results obtained for that pixel.

The most expensive part of the algorithm is normally the visibility calculations. For each ray, the object that intersected the ray first, must be determined. To do this, a potentially large number of objects need to be intersected with each ray. In fact, without any special optimization, one would have to intersect all objects in the scene with each ray, thus limiting the usefulness of ray tracing to very small scenes.

One of the first and arguably one of the most obvious optimizations is to spatially sort the objects as a preprocess, so that for each ray instead of intersecting all the objects in the scene, only a small subset of the objects needs to be tested. Sorting techniques of this kind are commonly known as spatial subdivision techniques [91, 264]. All rendering algorithms that rely on ray casting to test visibility, benefit from spatial subdivisions.

3.4   Spatial Subdivisions

For ray tracing-based algorithms to be efficient, a number of optimizations are commonly applied to the basic algorithm. These usually fall in one of three classes:

- Limit the number of rays shot. By shooting fewer rays, the cost of rendering an image will go down. However, this also means that the quality of the rendering will be reduced, e.g., by rendering a smaller image, ignoring specular and diffuse reflection, or limiting the number of light sources. Sometimes, only a sparse subset of pixels is rendered and the remaining pixels are computed by interpolation, possibly employing additional data structures [313, 248, 272, 309].

- Limit the length of the rays. For certain applications, it is permissible to not trace rays until an intersection is found, but to limit the extent of each ray. For example, when secondary rays exceed a certain length, a shading solution may be approximated by table look-up. The look-up table may be constructed during a preprocessing step; environment mapping may be a suitable solution [30, 100]. Alternatively, look-up tables can be constructed on the fly [139].

- Reduce the cost of each ray. Instead of intersecting each ray with all objects in the scene, the scene may be presorted, allowing each ray to be intersected with only a small proportion of the objects in the scene. This is a very common and necessary optimization that has become part of any ray-tracing based algorithm. However, a large number of spatial sorting algorithms have been proposed [113]. Some of these spatial subdivisions are discussed in this section.

The simplest of all spatial subdivisions is the grid, which subdivides the scene into a number cells (or voxels—we use these terms interchangeably) of equal size [79]. Tracing a ray is now performed in two steps. First, each

ray intersects a number of cells, and these must be determined. This is
called ray traversal. Because these cells are adjacent and all have the same
size, grid traversal can be highly efficient. It is usually implemented as a
3DDDA algorithm, which resembles a 3D equivalent of Bresenham's line
drawing algorithm [51]. In the second step, objects contained within these
cells are intersected. Once an intersection in one cell is found, subsequent
cells are not traversed any further. The objects in the cells that are not
traversed are therefore not tested at all. On the other hand, double testing
of objects that cross voxel boundaries can be avoided by employing a mail
box system [14].

Although the grid is simple to implement and cheap to traverse, it does
not adapt very well to the quirks of the particular model being rendered.
For a grid structure to work well, the bounding box of the scene needs to
fit tightly around the objects. Unfortunately, complex models usually concentrate a large number of objects in a few relatively small areas, whereas
the rest of the scene is almost empty. Figure 3.1 shows one such example
of a complex scene in which a large number of small objects are located
close together to form the musical equipment and the sofas. The floor and
the walls, however, consist of just a few polygons.

Adaptive spatial subdivisions, such as the octree [90] and the bintree [137] are better suited for complex scenes. Being tree structures, space
is recursively subdivided into two (bintree) or eight (octree) cells whenever
the number of objects in a cell is above a given threshold and the maximum
tree depth is not yet reached. The cells are smaller in areas of high object
concentration, but the number of objects in each cell should be more or
less the same. The cost of intersecting a ray with the objects in a cell is
therefore nearly the same for all cells in the tree.

Experiments have shown that as a rule of thumb, the number of cells in
a spatial subdivision structure should be of the same order as the number
of objects N in the scene [244]. Given this assumption, an upper bound for
the time taken to trace a single ray through the scene for the above three
spatial subdivision structures may be derived as follows [247]:

Grid. The number of grid cells is N, so that in each of the orthogonal
directions x, y and z, the number of cells will be $\sqrt[3]{N}$. A ray traveling
linearly through the structure will therefore cost:

$$T = \sqrt[3]{N}(T_{cell} + T_{int})$$
$$= O(\sqrt[3]{N})$$

In this and the following equations, T_{cell} is the time it takes to traverse a single cell and T_{int} is the time it takes on average to intersect
a single object.

Bintree. Considering a balanced bintree with N leaf cells, the height of the tree will be h, where $2^h = N$. The number of cells traversed by a single ray is then $O(2^{\frac{h}{3}})$, giving:

$$
\begin{aligned}
T &= 2^{\frac{h}{3}}(T_{cell} + T_{int}) \\
  &= \sqrt[3]{N}(T_{cell} + T_{int}) \\
  &= O(\sqrt[3]{N})
\end{aligned}
$$

For bintrees that are not balanced, the same upper-bound on time complexity may be used under the assumption that the maximum height of the tree is h.

Octree. In a balanced octree with N leaf cells, the height is h, where $8^h = N$. A ray traversing such an octree intersects $O(2^h)$ cells:

$$
\begin{aligned}
T &= 2^h(T_{cell} + T_{int}) \\
  &= \sqrt[3]{N}(T_{cell} + T_{int}) \\
  &= O(\sqrt[3]{N})
\end{aligned}
$$

Although the asymptotic behavior of these three spatial subdivision techniques are the same, in practice, differences may occur between the grid and the tree structures due to the grid's inability to adapt to the distribution of data in the scene. Also, the time complexity may be of the same order, but the constants incorporated in the order symbol may be very different.

Spatial subdivision techniques have reduced the number of intersection tests dramatically from $O(N)$ to $O(\sqrt[3]{N})$, but a very large number of intersection tests is still required due to the sheer number of rays being traced and to the complexity of the scenes that has only increased over the years.

Other sorting mechanisms that improve the speed of rendering, such as bounding box strategies, exist, but differ only in the fact that objects are now bounded by simple shapes that need not be in a regular structure. Hence, bounding spheres or bounding boxes may overlap and may be of arbitrary size. The optimization is due to the fact that intersecting a ray with such a simple shape is often much cheaper than intersecting with the more complex geometry it encapsulates. Bounding spheres or boxes may be ordered in a hierarchy as well, leading to a tree structure that removes the need to test all the bounding shapes for each ray.

Because bounding boxes (and spheres) are quite similar to spatial subdivision techniques, their improved adaptability to the scene and their possibly more expensive ray traversal cost being the differences, these techniques are not considered any further. The reduction in intersection tests is of the same order as for spatial subdivision techniques, however. We believe that other optimizations to significantly reduce the time complexity of ray tracing are not imminent. Hence, the most viable route to reduce execution times is to exploit parallel processing.

3.4.1 Parallel Ray Tracing

The object of parallel processing is to find a number of preferably independent tasks and to execute these tasks on different processors. Because in ray tracing the computation of one pixel is completely independent of any other pixel, this algorithm lends itself very well to parallel processing. As the data used during the computation is read, but not modified, the data could easily be duplicated over the available processors. This would thus lead to the simplest possible parallel implementation of a ray tracing algorithm. One remaining issue is that of load balancing, which may be achieved by reducing task sizes towards the end of the computation (Chapter 6). Thus, ray tracing does not appear to present a grand challenge for parallel processing. However, in massively parallel applications running on distributed memory computers, duplicating data over the available processors is extremely wasteful and limits the problem size to that of the memory available with each processor.

When the scene does not fit into a single processor's memory, the problem of parallelizing ray tracing becomes more complicated. The following sections address the issues involved. Three different types of task scheduling have been applied to ray tracing: demand driven, data parallel, and hybrid scheduling approaches. They are discussed in Sections 3.4.2 through 3.4.4.

Finally, it should be noted that if a shared memory machine is available, the scene does not have to be distributed over a number of processors, nor does data have to be duplicated. As such, parallel ray tracing on shared memory architectures is most certainly a viable approach and has led to implementations that may render complex scenery at interactive rates [219, 220]. Successes and complications of interactive ray tracing on a shared memory computer are discussed in detail in Chapter 6.

3.4.2 Demand Driven Ray Tracing

In this and the following sections, it is assumed that the parallel computer on which ray tracing is to run, has its memory distributed over the available processors. The most obvious parallel implementation of ray tracing would then simply replicate all the data with each processor and subdivide the screen into a number of disjunct regions [37, 97, 98, 99, 192, 217, 230,

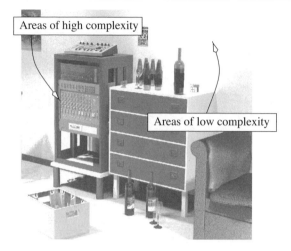

Figure 3.2. Different areas of the scene may have different complexities.

301, 132] or adaptively subdivide the screen and workload [213, 214]. Each processor then renders a number of regions using the unaltered sequential version of the ray tracing algorithm, until the whole image is completed.

In a data driven approach, tasks are distributed before the computation begins [132]. Communication is minimal, as only completed subimages need to be collated by transferring them to file or screen. However, load imbalances may occur due to differing complexities associated with different areas of the image (Figure 3.2).

To actively balance the workload, tasks may be distributed at run-time by a master processor. Whenever a processor finishes a subimage, it requests a new task from the master processor (Figure 3.3). In terms of parallel processing, this is called the demand driven approach. In computer graphics terms, this would be called a screen space subdivision. The speed-ups to be expected with this type of parallelism are near linear, as the overhead introduced is minimal. Because the algorithm itself is sequential as well, this algorithm belongs in the class of embarrassingly parallel algorithms.

Communication is not generally a major issue with demand driven ray tracing. After finishing a task, a processor may request a new task from a master processor. This involves sending a message to the master, which in turn, will send a new task back. The other communication that will occur is that of writing the partial images to either the frame buffer or to a mass storage device.

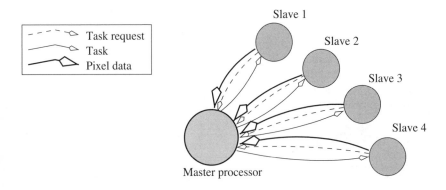

Figure 3.3. Demand driven ray tracing. Each processor requests a task from the master processor. When the master receives a request, it sends a task to the requesting processor. After this processor finishes its task, the resulting pixel data is sent to the master for collation.

Load balancing is achieved dynamically by only sending new tasks to processors that have just become idle. The biggest problems occur at the beginning of the computation, where all processors are waiting for their first tasks, and at the end of the computation, when some processors are still executing their tasks while others have already finished. Load imbalances near the end of the computation could be minimized by employing task stealing, which is a mechanism whereby tasks are migrated from overloaded processors to ones that have just become idle [20].

To facilitate load balancing, each task should take approximately the same number of computer cycles. In a ray tracer based on a screen space subdivision, the complexity of a task depends strongly on the number of objects that are visible in its region (Figure 3.2). For example, objects that have many holes in them, such as plants, cause a relatively large number of intersection tests that may or may not result in a successful intersection. Hence, the depth complexity for image regions containing such objects is high, thereby increasing the cost for rays shot towards these objects. Various methods exist to balance an uneven workload caused by variations in depth complexity.

The left image in Figure 3.4 shows a single task per processor approach. This is likely to suffer from load imbalances as the complexity for each of the tasks is clearly different. The middle image shows a good practical solution by having multiple smaller regions per processor. This is likely to give smaller, but still significant, load imbalances at the end of the computation. Finally, the right image in Figure 3.4 shows how each region

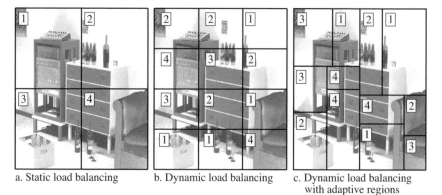

a. Static load balancing   b. Dynamic load balancing   c. Dynamic load balancing
                                                          with adaptive regions

Figure 3.4. Image space subdivision for four processors. (a) One subregion per processor. (b) Multiple regions per processor. (c) Multiple regions per processor, but each region should bring about approximately the same workload.

may be adapted in size to create a roughly similar workload for each of the regions. Profiling by subsampling the image to determine the relative workloads of different areas of the image would be necessary (and may also be used to create a suitable spatial subdivision, should the scene be distributed over the processors [232]).

Unfortunately, parallel implementations based on image space subdivisions normally assume that the local memory of each processor is large enough to hold the entire scene. If this is the case, then this is also the best possible way to parallelize a ray tracing algorithm. Shared memory (or virtual shared memory) architectures would best adopt this strategy too, because good speed-ups can be obtained using highly optimized ray tracers [153, 168, 219, 220, 273]. It has the additional advantage that the parallel implementation is very similar to the sequential implementation.

However, if very large models need to be rendered on distributed memory machines or on clusters of workstations, or if the complexity of the lighting model increases, the storage requirements will increase accordingly. It may then become impossible to run such embarrassingly parallel algorithms efficiently and other strategies need to be found.

An important consequence is that the scene data will have to be distributed. Data access will then incur different costs depending on whether the data is stored locally or with a remote processor. It is therefore very important to store frequently accessed data locally, while less frequently used data may be kept at remote processors. If the above screen space subdivision is to be maintained, caching techniques may be helpful to re-

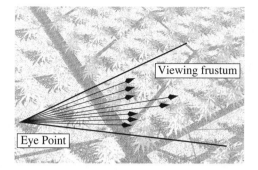

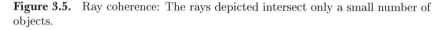

Figure 3.5. Ray coherence: The rays depicted intersect only a small number of objects.

duce the number of remote data accesses. The unpredictable nature of data access patterns that ray tracing exhibits makes cache design a nontrivial task [97, 99]. A study of data access patterns is presented in Chapter 5.

However, for certain classes of rays, cache design can be simplified by exploiting coherence (also called data locality). This is accomplished by observing that the order in which data is accessed, may not always be completely random, but can be somewhat predictable. Different kinds of coherence are distinguished in parallel rendering, the most important of which are:

Object coherence. Objects consist of separate connected pieces bounded in space and distinct objects are disjoint in space [287]. Spatial subdivision techniques, such as grids, octrees and bintrees directly exploit this form of coherence.

Image coherence. When a coherent model is projected onto a screen, the resulting image should exhibit local constancy between neighboring pixels as well. This was effectively exploited in [315].

Ray coherence. Rays that start at the same point and travel in similar directions, are likely to intersect the same objects. An example of ray coherence is given in Figure 3.5, where many plants do not intersect the viewing frustum. Only a small percentage of the plants in this scene are required to intersect all of the primary rays.

For ray tracing, ray coherence is easily exploited for bundles of primary rays and bundles of shadow rays (assuming that area light sources are used). It is possible to select the data necessary for all of these rays by intersecting a shape bounding these rays with a spatial subdivision structure [329]. The resulting list of voxels can then be communicated to the processor requesting the data.

One particularly successful system which carefully exploits cache coherence was recently presented by Wald et al. [307, 306, 305]. Their implementation exploits SIMD instructions on modern PCs to evaluate multiple rays against the same data, thereby gaining significant speed-ups. They also use cache coherence to minimize data traffic in their system, while having the scene data distributed over a number of processors. This allows them to render very large scenes at multiple frames per second. Different forms of coherence are further discussed in detail in Chapter 5, while the Wald et al. system for interactive ray tracing on a cluster of PCs is discussed further in Chapter 7.

3.4.3 Data Parallel Ray Tracing

Data parallel rendering constitutes a different approach to rendering scenes that do not fit into a single processor's memory. Here, the object data is distributed over the processors. Each processor owns only a subset of the scene database and they trace rays only when they pass through their own subspaces [32, 49, 97, 135, 156, 158, 159, 227, 232, 245, 278, 303, 304]. If a processor detects an intersection in its own subspace, it will spawn secondary rays as usual. Shading is normally performed by the processor that spawned the ray. In the example in Figure 3.6, all primary rays are spawned by processor 7. The primary ray drawn in this image intersects a chair, which is detected by processor 2 and a secondary reflection ray, as well as a number of shadow rays are traced. These rays are terminated respectively by processors 1, 3 and 5. The shading results of these processors are then returned to processor 2, which will assemble the results and shade the primary ray. This shading result is subsequently sent back to processor 7, which will eventually write the pixel to screen or file.

In order to exploit coherence between data accesses as much as possible, usually some spatial subdivision is used to decide which parts of the scene are stored with which processor. In its simplest form, the data is distributed according to a uniform distribution (Figure 3.7 left). Each processor will hold one or more equal sized voxels [49, 227, 245, 303, 304]. Having just one voxel per processor allows the data decomposition to be mapped onto a two-dimensional or three-dimensional grid topology in a straightforward manner. However, since the number of objects may vary dramatically from voxel to voxel, the cost of tracing a ray through each of these voxels may vary and therefore, this approach may lead to severe load imbalances.

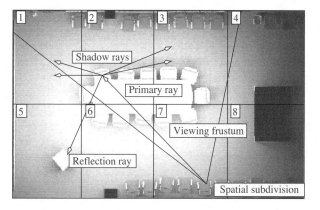

Figure 3.6. Tracing and shading in a data parallel configuration.

A second, and more difficult problem, is that the number of rays passing through each voxel is likely to be variable. Certain parts of the scene attract more rays than other parts. Hot spots are mainly caused by the view point and the locations of the light sources. Both variations in cost per ray and the number of rays passing through each voxel indicate that having multiple voxels per processor may be a good option. It is likely to balance the workload, albeit at the cost of extra communication.

Another approach is to use a hierarchical spatial subdivision, such as an octree (Figure 3.7, right) [97, 158, 159, 240], bintree or hierarchical grid [278] and subdivide the scene according to some cost criterion. Three cost criteria are discussed by Salmon and Goldsmith [259]:

- The data should be distributed over the processors such that the computational load generated at each processor is roughly equal.

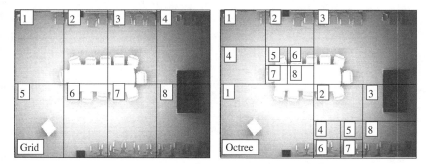

Figure 3.7. Example data distributions for data parallel ray tracing.

- The memory requirements should be similar for all processors.

- The communication cost should be minimized.

In practice, it is very difficult to meet all three criteria. Therefore, a much simpler criterion is normally used, such as splitting off subtrees from a hierarchical spatial subdivision such that the number of objects in each subtree is roughly the equal. This way, at least the cost for tracing a single ray will be roughly the same for all processors. At the same time, storage requirements are evenly spread across all processors. Methods for estimating the cost per ray on a per voxel basis are known [247, 246] and these could potentially be used to produce better data distributions.

Memory permitting, a certain degree of data duplication may be useful to reduce load imbalances. For example, data residing near light sources may be duplicated with some or all processors [245]. Alternatively, data distributions may be partially overlapping by locally storing copies of data from directly neighboring processors [278].

To address the second problem, such that each processor handles roughly the same number of ray tasks, profiling may be used to achieve static load balancing [135, 232]. This method attempts to equalize both the cost per ray and the number of rays over all processors. It is expected to outperform other static load balancing techniques at the cost of an extra preprocessing step.

If such a preprocessing step is to be avoided, the load in a data parallel system could be balanced dynamically. This involves dynamic redistribution of data [62]. Data is moved from heavily loaded processors to their neighbors, provided that these have a lighter workload. This could, for example, be accomplished by shifting the voxel boundaries.

An alternative approach to load balancing is to randomly distribute the objects, thereby ignoring the coherence that exists between objects [156]. A ray will then have to be passed from processor to processor until it has visited all the processors. In ring-based network topologies, pipelined communication could be used, thus avoiding global communication. Load balancing can be achieved by simply moving some objects along the pipeline from a heavily loaded processor to a less busy processor.

A general issue with data redistribution is that data accesses are highly irregular, both in space and in time. Tuning such a system is therefore very difficult. If data is redistributed too often, data communication between processors dominates the computation. On the other hand, if data is not redistributed often enough, a suboptimal load balance is achieved.

In summary, data parallel ray tracing systems allow large scenes to be distributed over the processors' local memories. However, they tend to suffer from load imbalances: A problem which is difficult to solve either with static or dynamic load balancing schemes. Efficiency thus tends to be low in such systems.

3.4.4 Hybrid Scheduling

The challenge in parallel ray tracing is to find algorithms which allow large scenes to be distributed without losing too much efficiency due to load imbalances (data parallel rendering) or communication (data parallel and demand driven ray tracing). Combining data parallel and demand driven aspects into a single algorithm may lead to implementations with a reasonably small amount of communication and an acceptable load balance.

Hybrid scheduling algorithms have both demand driven and data parallel components running on the same set of processors, with each processor being capable of handling both types of task [138, 148, 239, 242, 245, 260]. The data parallel part of the algorithm then creates a basic, albeit uneven, load. Tasks that are not computationally intensive, but require access to a large amount of data are ideally suited for data parallel execution. When it is difficult to predict in advance which data items are required for a given task, then this task is also best scheduled in data parallel fashion.

On the other hand, tasks that require a relatively small amount of data could be handled as demand driven tasks. By assigning demand driven tasks to processors that attract only a few data parallel tasks, the uneven basic load can be balanced. Because it is assumed that these demand driven tasks do not access much data, the communication involved in the assignment of such tasks can be kept under control.

An object subdivision similar to Green and Paddon's [97] is presented by Scherson and Caspary [260]: The algorithm has a preprocessing stage in which a hierarchical data structure is built. The objects and the bounding boxes are subdivided over the processors, whereas the hierarchical data structure is replicated over all processors. During the rendering phase, two tasks are discerned: demand driven ray traversal and data parallel ray-object intersections. Demand driven processes, which compute the intersection of rays with the hierarchical data structure, can therefore be executed on any processor. Data driven processes, which intersect rays with objects, can only be executed with the processor holding the specified object.

Another hybrid approach is presented by Jevans [148]. Again, each processor runs two processes, the intersection process operates in demand driven mode and the ray generator process works in data driven mode. Each ray generator is assigned a number of screen pixels. The environment is subdivided into subspaces (voxels) and all objects within a voxel are stored with the same processor. However, the voxels are distributed over the processors in random fashion. Also, each processor holds the entire subdivision structure. The ray generator that runs on each processor is assigned a number of screen pixels. For each pixel, rays are generated and intersected with the spatial subdivision structure. For all the voxels that the ray intersects, a message is dispatched to the processor holding the object data of that voxel.

The intersection process receives these messages which contain the ray data and intersects them with the objects it locally holds. It also performs shading calculations. After a successful intersection, a message is sent back to the ray generator. The algorithm is optimistic in the sense that the generator process assumes that the intersection process concludes that no object is intersected. Therefore, the generator process does not wait for the intersection process to finish, but continues to intersect the ray with the subdivision structure. Many messages may therefore be sent in vain. To be able to identify and destroy the unwanted intersection requests, all messages carry a time stamp.

The ability of demand driven tasks to effectively balance the load depends strongly on the amount of work involved with each task. If the task is too light, then the load may remain unbalanced. As the cost of ray traversal is generally deemed cheap compared with ray-object intersections, the effectiveness of the above split of the algorithm into data parallel and demand driven tasks needs to be questioned.

Another hybrid algorithm was proposed by Jansen and Chalmers [138], and Reinhard and Jansen [242, 243, 245]. Rays are classified according to the amount of coherence that they exhibit. If much coherence is present, for example, in bundles of primary or shadow rays, these bundles are traced in demand driven mode, one bundle per task. Because the number of rays in each bundle can be controlled, task granularity can be increased or decreased when necessary. Normally, it is advantageous to have as many rays in as narrow a bundle as possible. In this case, the work load associated with the bundle of rays is high, while the number of objects intersected by the bundle is limited. Task and data communication associated with such a bundle is then limited as well.

Finally, the main data distribution can be according to a grid or octree, where the spatial subdivision structure is replicated over the processors. The spatial subdivision either holds the objects themselves in its voxels, or contains identification tags indicating which remote processor stores the data for those voxels. If a processor needs access to a part of the spatial subdivision that is not locally available, it reads the identification tag; and in the case of data parallel tasks, migrates the task at hand to that processor; or in the case of demand driven tasks, sends a request for data to that processor.

3.5 Radiosity

The rendering equation (Equation 3.1) provides a general expression for the interaction of light between surfaces. No assumptions are made about the characteristics of the environment, such as surface and reflectance properties. Whereas ray tracing focuses mainly on specular effects, because sampling diffuse inter-reflection is quite costly, radiosity is better suited for diffusely lit scenes. If the surfaces are assumed to be perfectly diffuse reflectors or emitters, then the rendering equation can be simplified. A Lambertian surface [169] has the property that it reflects light in all directions in equal amounts. Radiance is then independent of outgoing direction and only a function of position:

$$L_{out}(x, \Theta_{out}) = L(x). \tag{3.2}$$

In addition, the relation between a diffuse reflector and its bi-directional reflection distribution function is given by $f_r = \frac{\rho_d}{\pi}$ [161], so that the rendering equation can be simplified to yield the radiosity equation [54]:

$$L(x) = L^e(x) +$$
$$\rho^d(x) \int_{all \ x'} L(x') \frac{\cos \Theta_i \cos \Theta'_o}{\pi \parallel x' - x \parallel^2} v(x, x') dA'.$$

Here, the radiance $L(x)$ for a point x on a surface is the sum of the self-emitted radiance $L^e(x)$ plus the reflected energy that was received from all other points x' in the environment.

It is not practically possible to solve this equation for all points in the scene. Therefore the surfaces in a scene are normally subdivided into sufficiently small patches (Figure 3.8), where the radiance is assumed to be constant over each patch. If x is a point on patch i and x' a point on patch j, the radiance L_i for patch i is given by:

$$L_i = L_i^e +$$
$$\rho^d_{\ i} \sum_j \frac{L_j}{A_i} \int_{A_i} \int_{A_j} \frac{\cos \Theta_i \cos \Theta_j}{\pi r^2} \delta_{ij} dA_j dA_i.$$

In this equation, r is the distance between patches i and j and δ_{ij} gives the mutual visibility between the delta areas of the patches i and j. This equation can be rewritten as:

Figure 3.8. Subdivision of a polygon into smaller patches.

$$L_i = L_i^e + \rho^d_{\ i} \sum_j L_j f_{i \to j} \tag{3.3}$$

$$f_{i \to j} = \frac{1}{A_i} \int_{A_i} \int_{A_j} \frac{\cos \Theta_i \cos \Theta_j}{\pi r^2} \delta_{ij} dA_j dA_i. \tag{3.4}$$

Here, the form factor $f_{i \to j}$ is the fraction of power leaving patch i that arrives at patch j. Form factors depend solely on the geometry of the environment, i.e., the size and the shape of the elements and their orientation relative to each other. Therefore, the radiosity method is inherently view-independent. It is normally used as a preprocessing step that computes the diffuse light distribution over a scene and is followed by a rendering step which produces the final image (or sequence of images).

3.5.1 Form Factors

The most expensive part of radiosity algorithms is generally the computation of the form factors. Visibility computations are required to determine which elements are closest to the target element. This is often accomplished using ray tracing [308].

First, a hemisphere of unit radius is placed over the element (Figure 3.9(a)). The surface of this hemisphere is subdivided (regularly or adaptively) into a number of cells. From the center point of the element, rays are shot through the cells into the environment, yielding a delta form factor for every cell. Summing the delta form factors then gives the form factor for the element. As rays are shot into all directions, this method is called hemisphere shooting, but it is also known as Monte Carlo sampling, or undirected shooting.

More sophisticated hemisphere methods direct more rays towards interesting regions, for example, by explicitly shooting towards patches (directed

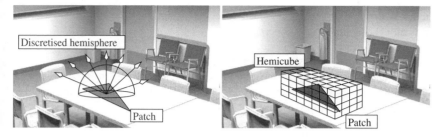

Figure 3.9. Form factor computation by hemisphere and hemicube methods.

shooting) or by adaptive shooting. In the adaptive variation, the delta form factors are compared to each other to see which directions cause large gradients. For these directions, the cells on the hemisphere are subdivided and new delta form factors are computed recursively. Both directed shooting and adaptive refinement are more efficient than undirected shooting.

Instead of placing half a sphere above a patch to determine ray directions, by Nusselt's analogue half a cube could also be used (Figure 3.9b). The five sides of this hemicube are (possibly adaptively) subdivided and for every grid cell on the surface of the hemicube, a delta form factor is computed. Because the sides of the cube can be viewed as image planes, Z-buffer algorithms are applicable to compute the delta form factors. The only extension to a standard Z-buffer algorithm is that with every z value an ID of a patch is stored instead of a color value. In this context the Z-buffer is called an item buffer. The advantage of the hemicube method is that standard Z-buffering hardware may be used.

The computational complexity of the form factor calculations depends on the method of computation. It ranges from full analytical procedures to avoid inaccuracies, to approximations using the hemicube technique, and from incremental evaluations using previously calculated values via the reciprocity relationship to the simplest case in which the form factor is known to be zero when the two patches concerned face away from each other. For parallel radiosity implementations this may well lead to load imbalances.

3.5.2 Parallel Radiosity

In contrast to ray tracing, where load balancing is likely to be the bottleneck, parallel radiosity algorithms tend to suffer from both communication and load balancing problems. This is due to the fact that to compute a patch's radiosity value, visibility calculations involving all other patches are required. In particular, the following issues need to be addressed for parallel radiosity:

- The form factor computations tend to be the most expensive aspect of radiosity. They involve visibility calculations between each pair of elements. If these elements are stored on different processors, inter-processor communication will occur.

- Energy information is stored with each patch. If the environment is replicated with each processor (memory permitting), the energy computed for a certain patch must be broadcast to all other processors. This may lead to a communication bottleneck, even if each processor stores the whole scene data base. The scene data being both read and written is an important difference between ray tracing and radiosity algorithms, leading to different parallelizations.

- Caching of object data may give rise to cache consistency issues, because a processor may compute updated radiosity values for elements that have cached copies elsewhere in the system.

- If the scene is highly segmented, such as a house consisting of a set of rooms, there will not be much energy exchange between the rooms. If some of the rooms do not contain any light sources, the processors storing those rooms may suffer from a lack of work. On the other hand, if all rooms represent a similar amount of work, partitioning the scene across the processors according to the layout of the scene may lead to highly independent calculations. Without paying proper attention to load balancing issues, distributing scenes over a number of processors may or may not lead to severe load imbalances.

- Dependent on the geometric relationships between patches, variations in the computational complexity of calculating form factors may cause further load imbalances.

In the following sections, three different radiosity algorithms and their parallel counterparts are introduced. These are full matrix radiosity (Section 3.6), progressive refinement (Section 3.7), and hierarchical radiosity (Section 3.8).

3.6 Full Matrix Radiosity

Equations 3.3 and 3.4 form the basis of the radiosity method and describe how the radiance of a patch is computed by gathering incoming radiance from all other patches in the scene [93]. For a full radiosity solution, also known as gathering, equations 3.3 and 3.4 must be solved for each pair of patches i and j. Therefore, if the scene consists of N patches, a system of N equations must be solved:

$$
\begin{pmatrix}
1 - \rho^d_1 f_{1 \to 1} & -\rho^d_1 f_{1 \to 2} & \cdots & -\rho^d_1 f_{1 \to N} \\
-\rho^d_2 f_{2 \to 1} & 1 - \rho^d_2 f_{2 \to 2} & \cdots & -\rho^d_2 f_{2 \to N} \\
\vdots & \vdots & \ddots & \vdots \\
-\rho^d_N f_{N \to 1} & -\rho^d_N f_{N \to 2} & \cdots & 1 - \rho^d_N f_{N \to N}
\end{pmatrix}
\begin{pmatrix}
L_1 \\
L_2 \\
\vdots \\
L_N
\end{pmatrix}
=
\begin{pmatrix}
L^e_1 \\
L^e_2 \\
\vdots \\
L^e_N
\end{pmatrix} .
$$

This system of equations tends to be diagonally dominant, so that Gauss-Seidel iterative solutions are appropriate [53]. It requires computing all the form factors beforehand to construct the full matrix and is therefore known as Full Matrix radiosity. The storage requirements of this radiosity approach are $O(N^2)$, as between any two elements a form factor is computed and stored. This may restrict the size of the model that can be rendered. Both the computation of form factors as well as solving the matrix of form factors are discussed in the following subsections.

3.6.1 Setting Up the Matrix of Form Factors

The calculation of a single form factor only requires geometry information and may thus proceed in parallel with all other form factor calculations [218]. This parallel computation may proceed either as a data driven model or as a demand driven model.

In the data driven approach, each processor is initially allotted a certain number of patches. A processor is then responsible for calculating the necessary form factors for its patches. Acting upon the information of a single projecting patch, a processor is able to calculate the form factors for all its allocated patches, thereby producing a partial column of the full form factor matrix. For example, if a processor is allocated $p + 1$ patches, $k, k + 1, \ldots, k + p$, then from the data for the projecting patch j the form factors $F_{k,j}, F_{k+1,j}, \ldots, F_{k+p,j}$ may be calculated:

$$
\begin{pmatrix}
F_{1,2} \cdots\cdots\cdots\cdots\cdots F_{1,N} \\
\quad F_{k,j} \\
\quad F_{k+1,j} \\
\quad F_{k+2,j} \\
\quad F_{k+p,j} \\
F_{N,1} \cdots\cdots\cdots\cdots\cdots F_{N,N}
\end{pmatrix} .
$$

The processor may now process the next projecting patch, and so on until all patches have been acted upon, by which stage the rows of the matrix of form factors corresponding to the allocated patches have been computed. Once all rows have been calculated, the matrix is ready to be solved.

The advantage of data driven approaches is that the data of each projecting patch is only processed once per processing element [233]. The obvious disadvantage is that load balancing difficulties may occur due to the variations in computational complexity of the form factor calculations. These computational variations may result in those processors which have been allocated patches with computationally simple form factor calculations standing idle while the others struggle with their complex form factor calculations. This imbalance may be addressed by sensible allocation of patches to processors, but this typically requires *a priori* knowledge regarding the complexities of the environment. This information may not be available.

An alternative strategy to reduce load imbalances may be to dynamically distribute the work from the processors that are still busy to those that have completed their tasks. This may require the communication of a potentially large, partially completed, row of form factors to the recipient processor. A preferable technique would be to simply inform the recipient processor which projecting patches have already been examined. The recipient processor then only needs to perform the form factor calculations for yet unprocessed projecting patches. Once calculated, the form factors may be returned to the donor processor for storage.

In a demand driven approach, no initial allocation of patches to processors occurs. Instead, a processor requests the next task to be performed from a master processor. Each task requires the processor to calculate all the form factors associated with the receiving patch. The granularity of the task is usually a single receiving patch, but may be increased to include several receiving patches. A processor thus calculates a single row (or several rows) of the matrix of form factors per task. For example, if a processor receives patch k, then the row of form factors for patch k will be produced before the next task is requested:

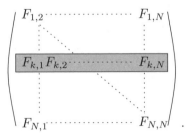

The demand driven approach reduces the imbalance that may result from the data driven model by no longer binding any patches to particular processors. Processor idle time may still result when the final few tasks are completed and this idle time may be exacerbated if a larger task granularity is chosen. The disadvantage of the demand driven approach is that the data required for the projecting patches may have to be refetched for every task. On the other hand, data fetching may be interleaved with the computation.

3.6.2   Solving the Matrix of Form Factors

Using the form factors calculated in the first stage of the gather method, a matrix is produced which must be solved in the second stage of the method. This produces the radiosities of every patch. Parallel iterative solvers may be used because this matrix is diagonally dominant. As the computational effort associated with each row of the matrix does not vary significantly, a data driven approach could be used. This is particularly appropriate if the rows of form factors remain stored with the processors that produced the form factors in the first stage of the method. Each processor may therefore be responsible for a number of rows of the matrix.

Initially, each processor sets the solution vector to the emission values of the patches for which it is responsible. During each iteration, the processors update their solution vector and these updated solution vectors are then exchanged. If each iteration is synchronized, then at the end of an iteration, the master processor can determine if the partial results have converged to the desired level of tolerance and an image may be generated and displayed.

The Jacobi method is most often used in parallel gathering, because it is directly applicable and inherently parallel. Unfortunately, it has a slow convergence rate of $O(N^2)$ [218]. However, it is possible to transform the original coefficient matrix into a suitable form that allows different iterative solution methods to be applied, such as the preconditioned Jacobi method [194] or the scaled conjugate gradient method [167].

3.6.3   Group Iterative Methods

Alternative radiosity solvers include group iterative methods. Here, radiosities are partitioned into groups and instead of relaxing just one variable at a time, whole groups are relaxed within a single iteration. Gauss-Seidel group iteration relaxes each group using current estimates for radiosities in other groups, while Jacobi group iteration uses radiosity estimates from other groups that were updated at the end of the previous iteration.

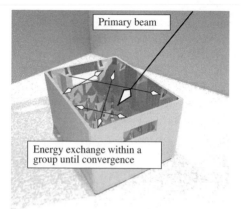

Figure 3.10. Group iterative method. All the patches making up the crate form a single group. These patches exchange energy until convergence is reached. After that, energy is exchanged between other groups and the next iteration starts.

Jacobi group iteration is therefore suitable for a coarse grained parallel implementation [80]. The radiosity mesh is subdivided into groups. During a single iteration, energy is bounced around between the patches within a group until convergence is reached, although no interaction with other groups occurs. After all processors complete an iteration for all the groups under their control, radiosities are exchanged between processors (see Figure 3.10).

An advantage of this method is that for each iteration, each processor may use sophisticated radiosity solvers to relax the group subproblems, for example, by using hierarchical radiosity, which is more efficient [80].

3.7 Progressive Refinement

To avoid the $O(N^2)$ storage requirement of the full radiosity method, a different approach for calculating the radiances L_i exists. It is called progressive radiosity or the shooting method and it reduces storage requirements to $O(N)$. The name "shooting method" stems from its physical interpretation, which is that for each iteration, the element with the highest unshot energy is selected. This element shoots its energy into the environment, instead of gathering energy from the environment. This process is repeated until the total amount of unshot energy drops below a specified threshold. As most patches tend to receive most of their energy after only a few iterations, this method gives a quick initial approximation of the global illumination with subsequent refinements resulting in incremental improvements of the radiosity solution [54].

All patches are initialized to have a radiance equal to the amount of light L_e that they emit, with only the light sources initially emitting light. In progressive radiosity terminology, the light sources are said to have the most unshot radiance. For each iteration, the patch with the largest unshot radiance is selected. This patch shoots its radiance to all other elements. The elements which are visible to the shooting patch therefore gain unshot radiance. Finally, the shooting element's unshot radiance is set to zero, since there is no unshot radiance left. This completes a single iteration. Thus, after each iteration, the total amount of radiance is redistributed over all elements in the environment and an image of the result could be generated before a new iteration commences.

By selecting the element with the largest amount of unshot radiance at the beginning of each iteration, the largest contributions to the final result are added first. This greatly improves the convergence rate in the early stages of the algorithm. Moreover, fewer iterations are needed to have the residual error in the solution drop below a specified threshold [52]. However, if the final solution is required without cutting off the computation after some threshold is reached, the progressive refinement method takes more iterations than gather methods. This is due to the fact that a patch may gain unshot energy after it has been selected for shooting. Such a patch will eventually be selected a second (or third...) time to shoot its energy into the environment.

When intermediary results have to be displayed, an ambient term can be added to the solution vector. This is comparable to the over-relaxation technique for classical radiosity methods in the sense that the estimation of the solution is exaggerated. However, the ambient term in progressive radiosity is only added for display purposes. It is not used to improve the solution vector for the next iteration, as is done in the over-relaxation technique. The ambient radiosity term is derived from the amount of unshot energy in the environment. As the solution vector converges, the ambient term decreases. This way, the sequence of intermediary images gracefully converges to the final image.

Form factors are not stored in progressive radiosity, as this would once more lead to a storage requirement of $O(N^2)$. However, radiances and unshot radiances are stored for every element, resulting in an $O(N)$ storage requirement. The downside of this approach is that visibility between elements occasionally needs to be recomputed. This disadvantage is compensated by the number of iterations necessary to arrive at a good approximation [52]. However, if the full solution is required, the convergence rate of the gathering method is higher [44].

3.7.1   Parallel Shooting

In parallel progressive refinement methods, each shooting patch may update most, if not all, of the remaining patches in the scene. This causes all the geometry data as well as all patch and element data to be accessed during each iteration. If data is to be replicated with each processor, then updates for each element must be broadcast to all other processors. If the data is distributed, then data will have to be fetched from other processors. A number of parallel implementations therefore duplicate the geometry data so that visibility tests can be carried out in parallel. The patch and element information could then be distributed to avoid data consistency problems and to allow larger scenes to be rendered [71, 323].

Most parallel progressive refinement approaches tend to use ray tracing to compute form factors [71, 145, 282, 283, 284, 323], with only a few exceptions that either use a hemicube algorithm [44, 237] or analytic form factors [44].

As with parallel gathering algorithms, progressive refinement methods can be solved both in data parallel and demand driven modes. Data parallel processing requires the patches to be initially distributed over the processors. Each processor may now assume responsibility for selecting the next shooting patch from its allocated patches [31, 33, 44, 105, 106, 284, 323]. The energy of that patch is then shot to all patches that are visible from the source patch. For remote patches, this involves communication of energy to neighboring processors.

One data parallel technique which allows the scene data to be distributed over the processors is the virtual walls method [322]. Here, the scene is distributed according to a grid. When shot energy leaves a processor's subspace, it is temporarily stored at one or more of the grid walls, which are subdivided into small patches. The original virtual walls technique (Figure 3.11(a)) does not store directional information, thus losing some accuracy every time energy is transferred between processors. Later refinements of the virtual walls technique do retain directional information (Figure 3.11(b)) [16, 212, 192, 322]. After a number of iterations, the energy stored at a processor's walls is transferred to neighboring processors and from there shot into the next subscene. Moreover, the computation and communication stages may be overlapping, i.e., each processor communicates energy to neighboring processors while at the same time running its local progressive refinement algorithm.

More recently, the virtual walls technique has been augmented with visibility masks and has been renamed virtual interfaces [15, 250, 251, 252, 289]. When a source shoots its energy, it records which parts of its hemisphere project onto the boundaries of its subenvironment. This in-

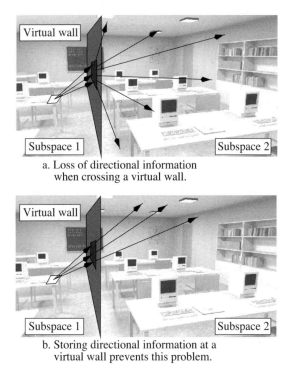

a. Loss of directional information
when crossing a virtual wall.

b. Storing directional information at a
virtual wall prevents this problem.

Figure 3.11. Virtual walls with and without storing direction vectors.

formation is stored in a visibility mask which allows directional energy to
be transferred to neighboring processors. This is accomplished without
accumulating energy for multiple iterations of the shooting algorithm.

In data parallel approaches, careful attention must be paid to the way
in which light sources are distributed over the processors. If one or more
processors do not have a light source patch in their subset of the scene,
then these processors may remain idle for a number of iterations. Also,
during the computations, a processor may run out of patches with unshot
energy. Without a proper mechanism for task redistribution, this would
lead to load imbalances.

In data parallel shooting each processor locally selects its patch with
the most unshot energy, whereas in demand driven approaches, a master
processor would select the shooting patch with globally the most unshot
energy and send it to a processor that requests more work [72, 95, 194, 237,
281, 282, 283]. The issue of load balancing can then be addressed either by

poaching tasks from busy neighboring processors [284] or by dynamically redistributing data [283]. A master processor selects a number of patches to shoot, which are communicated to the slave processors. Communication between slave processors will occur if the geometry is distributed over the processors, because shooting energy from a patch requires access to the entire scene database.

After shooting, either the results are communicated back to the master processor, or the results are broadcast directly to all other processors. In the former case, the master processor usually keeps track of patches and elements, while the surface data is distributed. In the latter case, both geometry and patches are distributed.

Demand driven master-slave configurations tend to have only a single processor controlling the entire computation. This puts a limit on scalability as this processor is bound to become the bottleneck if the number of slave processors is increased. If, in addition, the master controls all the patch and element data, then there may be a memory bottleneck as well. For this reason, master-slave configurations do not seem to be appropriate for parallel shooting methods.

3.8   Hierarchical Radiosity

To minimize the number of insignificant energy exchanges between patches, hierarchical variants of the radiosity algorithm were derived. Instead of computing form factors between individual patches, radiosity exchanges are computed between groups of patches at various levels in the hierarchy [109, 110, 111, 269]. It is therefore possible to perform a minimal amount of work to obtain the best result within a specified error bound. This is accomplished by selecting the coarsest subdivision in the hierarchy for the desired level of precision.

As an example, Figure 3.12 shows a reference patch on the floor which interacts with a number of other patches in the scene. Several different situations may occur, based on the distance between a patch and the reference patch:

- For patches that are close together, such as the reference patch and patch 1 in Figure 3.12, a subdivision into smaller patches may be appropriate.

- For more distant patches, such as patch 2 and the reference patch in the same figure, the form factor can be approximated with no additional subdivision of the reference patch.

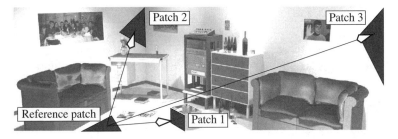

Figure 3.12. Radiosity exchanges between a reference patch and different surfaces in the scene.

- Finally, for very distant patches (patch 3 and the reference patch), the reference patch may be merged with its surrounding patches without affecting precision much.

In effect, the form factor matrix is subdivided into a number of blocks, where each of the blocks represents an interaction between groups of patches. The total number of blocks is $O(N)$, which is a vast improvement over the $O(N^2)$ complexity of the regular form factor matrix.

An extension of hierarchical radiosity comes in the form of wavelet radiosity [94]. It has the same time complexity as the hierarchical radiosity algorithm described above, but allows very high physical accuracy due to the use of higher order basis functions.

3.8.1   Parallel Hierarchical Radiosity

In hierarchical radiosity, the surface geometry is subdivided as the need arises. This leads to clusters of patches in interesting areas, whereas the subdivision remains coarse in other areas. If the environment is subdivided over a number of processors, there is a realistic chance that some processors find their local geometry far further subdivided than the geometry stored at other processors. For hierarchical radiosity, the main issue therefore appears to be load balancing.

As opposed to progressive refinement algorithms, only a few parallel hierarchical radiosity algorithms have been implemented to date. Both shared memory implementations [253, 268, 273, 274] as well as distributed memory implementations exist [28, 73, 84, 85, 326].

Virtual shared memory implementations are attractive in the sense that the algorithm itself needs hardly any modifications because there is an extra software layer which transparently takes care of all communication. Each processor runs a hierarchical radiosity algorithm and whenever a patch is selected for subdivision, it is locked first. Such a locking mechanism is necessary to avoid two processors updating the same patch concurrently. Other than that, there are no changes to the algorithm. A task is defined to be either a patch plus its interactions or a single patch-patch interaction. Each processor has a task queue, which is initialized with a number of initial polygon-polygon interactions. If a patch is subdivided, the tasks associated with its subpatches are enqueued on the task queue of the processor that generated these subpatches. A processor takes new tasks from its task queue until no more tasks remain. When a processor is left with an empty queue, it attempts to steal tasks from other processors' queues. This is a simple mechanism that achieves load balancing.

If no (virtual) shared memory machine is available, the scene data needs to be distributed over the available processors. Load balancing by means of task stealing then involves communication between two processors [28, 73, 84, 85, 326]. Communication will also occur if energy is to be exchanged between patches stored at different processors. Hence, the behavior of a parallel hierarchical radiosity algorithm is likely to be similar to parallel implementations of progressive refinement radiosity.

The wavelet radiosity method [94] is also extended to operate in parallel environments. Versions are implemented to run on shared memory architectures [8, 38] and shared memory architectures with graphics hardware acceleration [39]. The graphics hardware is used to perform visibility computations. Both implementations are capable of rendering highly complex scenes.

3.9   Particle Tracing

Particle tracing [66, 223] is a method in which Monte Carlo simulations are applied to solve the rendering equation directly. In this model, light is viewed as particles being sent out from light emitting surfaces. These particles are traced from the light source and followed through the scene bouncing at the surfaces, until they are absorbed by a surface (Figure 3.13). The direction in which a particle leaves the light emitter, the wavelength of the particle, and its position on the emitter are determined stochastically according to the point spread functions that describe the behavior of the light emitters. A powerful light source is said to have a higher probability than weaker light sources, and has therefore more particles assigned. The same link exists between the wavelength of the particles; the direction in which the particle travels; and the position on the light source and their associated point spread functions. More important wavelengths, for example, are chosen more often because of their higher probability of occurring.

Figure 3.13. Particle tracing.

After a particle is emitted from a light source, it travels in a straight path until it hits a surface. If the particle encounters participating media on its way, the direction of the particle may be altered. This process is called scattering and occurs when light is reflected, refracted, or diffracted due to the presence of the medium.

When particles hit a surface, they may be reflected or refracted. First, it is determined whether the particle is absorbed, reflected, or refracted according to a distribution function. If the particle is reflected, a new direction of the particle is determined using a point spread function which describes the surface properties. If the particle is refracted, the angle of refraction is computed using a different distribution function.

The number of particles a patch receives determines its radiance. In particle tracing, a very large number of particles are required before a reasonable approximation to the actual solution of the rendering equation is reached. This is due to the law of large numbers, which states that the larger the number of samples or traced particles, the better the agreement of the estimator with the actual value.

3.9.1   Parallel Particle Tracing

First impressions of the particle tracing algorithm suggest that it allows an embarrassingly parallel implementation. The path of each particle may be computed independently of all other particles. If each processor stores the entire scene description in its local memory, then particle tracing is completely parallelizable [115, 327]. Each processor traces a large number of particles independently of all other processors. After the computation finishes, the partial results of each processor are collated to determine the final irradiance of each patch.

If a scene is too large to fit into a single processor's memory, the solution is considerably more difficult. First, the data structure that keeps track of where particles have hit surfaces has to be distributed over the processors.

Updating this data structure may therefore involve data communication, similar to radiosity updates.

Second, whereas in ray tracing certain types of rays exhibit coherence that may be exploited, the random nature of the Monte Carlo method restricts similar approaches based on the coherence of particle paths. However, precomputational analysis using the position and intensity of light sources may provide some indication as to which voxels are likely to be requested by particle paths leaving the light sources. The subsequent path of the particle is determined by the nature of the environment as well as the luck of the draw.

To a certain extent, these problems can be solved using standard parallel processing techniques such as prefetching and profiling [294, 295]. This, however, implies an extra preprocessing step.

3.9.2 Density Estimation

Density estimation [265] is a technique in which particle tracing is used to compute a mesh, which is then fit for display. The algorithm is composed of three phases. First, a particle tracing pass is performed to detect where particles intersect surfaces (Figure 3.14(a)). These intersections (hit points, see Figure 3.14(b)) are stored in a list. Second, for each receiving surface, an approximate irradiance function $H(u, v)$ is constructed based on these hit points (Figure 3.14(c)). Finally, this function is further approximated to a more compact form $\bar{H}(u, v)$ (Figure 3.14(d)) which is suitable for hardware rendering or ray tracing and subsequent display.

All three steps can be parallelized, with synchronization only occurring in between consecutive steps. The implementation in [327] uses files for communication between steps. The first step is straightforward, as it is assumed that the scene description can be replicated. Each processor creates as output a file containing the hit points that were generated.

A master processor then takes the hit points created by all processors and reorders them so that each hit point is matched with its surface. In the second parallel step, the density estimation and meshing is performed. Each processor receives an initial number of surfaces to act upon and when this initial set of tasks is finished, the remainder of the work is distributed on demand. When a surface is completely meshed, it is written to file. The algorithm terminates when all processors have finished their work.

For relatively small numbers of processors, this algorithm performs reasonably well. However, it is assumed that the environment fits into a single processor's memory and it therefore precludes the rendering of very complex scenes, unless a shared memory architecture is chosen. It does allow larger scenes to be rendered than radiosity approaches that replicate

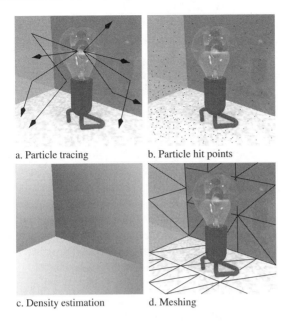

a. Particle tracing   b. Particle hit points

c. Density estimation   d. Meshing

Figure 3.14. Density estimation.

their data, since only the surface geometry needs to be replicated while the
meshing step does not require replication.

3.10 Data Distribution and Data Locality

As can be deduced from the previous section, global illumination algorithms have certain characteristics that make them difficult to parallelize.
First, the sheer amount of data often involved in rendering requires the
database to be distributed over the processors. Scene complexity is continuously increasing, for example, because three-dimensional data acquisition
techniques are becoming more sophisticated and are more widely available.
Such algorithms tend to generate huge amounts of polygonal surfaces. Unfortunately, a distributed scene implies that processors either have to migrate tasks or fetch data. This incurs overheads that prevent algorithms to
scale beyond a fairly small number of processors.

Second, data access patterns are often unpredictable and changing
rapidly over time (even within a single frame) so that for large scenes,
caching strategies may be less effective. The nature of data access patterns
is analyzed within a ray tracing application in Chapter 5.

Third, load patterns may vary significantly over time, which may render profiling and other cost estimations of less value as they only account for the expected average load.

Fourth, near the end of the computation, there usually is insufficient work left in the system to keep all processors busy. The termination phase can therefore take a substantial amount of time, thus reducing efficiency and scalability. Keeping processors busy during the last phase of the computation is largely an unsolved problem, since standard task stealing strategies may introduce a substantial amount of data communication and processing overhead to match the data and the newly stolen tasks.

To some extent, the above problems may be addressed by localizing computations: When it is possible to partition the computations or the data in subtasks in such a way that the interaction with other subtasks is minimal, then data communication may be reduced and cache trashing can be prevented. We will first discuss data distribution strategies and then return to issues of data locality and cache coherence.

3.10.1   Data Distribution

The way data is distributed can have a strong impact on how well the system performs. The more even the workload associated with a particular data distribution, the less idle time is to be expected. To be able to distribute a part of the scene, for instance, a cell of an octree spatial subdivision, first the expected cost per voxel should be computed. In a second step, the voxels can be distributed such that data locality is as preserved as possible, while at the same time attempting to equalize the cost per processor.

Initial research has shown that the cost of a single ray traversing an octree structure can be estimated [246, 247]. The number of intersection tests for each node in the octree is computed by averaging the depth of the leaf cells of the octree and then weighting these depths by the surface area of the cells. For each leaf node, the probability that a ray traversing that voxel intersects one of the objects contained within the voxel is computed as well. The ray traversal cost is then estimated using the average tree depth and the average blocking factor by summing the probabilities that a ray is blocked in the ith voxel, but not in the $i - 1$ preceding voxels. Repeating this algorithm for each internal voxel produces the estimated cost per subtree. Alternatively, the cost per voxel could be predicted by estimating the number of rays that would traverse each voxel during rendering [182, 246]. Such an algorithm would take into account the distribution of objects over the scene, as well as the view point and the position of light sources. The data distribution would therefore be tailored to the chosen view point. It may therefore well outperform other data distribution algorithms.

The second step in such data distribution algorithms would take the estimated cost per voxel as a basis for distributing the voxels over the processors. Such an algorithm has two conflicting goals for achieving a good data distribution. First, the cost of the voxels assigned to each processor should be roughly equal. During rendering, this should simplify the scheduler's job, because now the scheduler may assume that if equal numbers of ray tasks are handed to each processor, then the workload of each processor should be roughly the same as well. A better load balance could therefore be obtained.

The second goal is to maintain coherence as much as possible. If an octree is arbitrarily split up and distributed over a number of processors, tasks may have to be migrated more often than necessary. This is especially true for data parallel ray tasks. It also inhibits the possibility of preferred bias scheduling. Additionally, data fetches are likely to involve many different processors. Maintaining coherence, on the other hand, solves most of these problems, but may require the cost function of the voxels to be ignored occasionally. This may, in turn, lead to a less balanced workload.

The distribution of octree branches over processors may be achieved by splitting the octree into separate branches as near the root of the tree as possible. In that case, the emphasis is on coherence, so that rays traversing the octree will not have to be communicated too often. The cost function assigned to each processor may thus fluctuate between processors.

An alternative algorithm may utilize region growing [293]. Here, a number of seed voxels are chosen and each seed voxel is subsequently assigned to a processor. If a voxel neighbor is already assigned, then this voxel is assigned to the same processor. In this way, whole regions are assigned to the same processor and thus coherence can be maximized.

Octrees and grids are regular subdivisions that do not always segment a model optimally. Better data coherence may be obtained with a space partitioning that is aligned with the internal structure of the model. BSP-trees, for example, use planar surfaces of the model to derive a binary space partition. Several strategies have been developed to choose the most suitable faces as primary dividing planes and to optimize the data coherence within the resulting space partitions, while keeping the number of split surfaces as low as possible [77, 199]. For example, Meneveaux [191] applies a clustering algorithm to the surfaces in a scene to improve the alignment of the partitioning and the structure of the floor plan.

3.10.2 Visibility Preprocessing

A fruitful approach to scene partitioning is to base it on inter-visibility [291]. Energy transfer can only take place between surfaces that are mutually visible. A visibility preprocessing step can be used to create local clusters and to calculate visibility between these clusters. This information can be stored in a visibility graph with the clusters as nodes. The graph can then be segmented in groups to perform, for instance, the group iterative methods that were already discussed in Section 3.6.3. For clustering, the importance of the energy transfer between surfaces may also be taken into account. Two surfaces with a high "form-factor" interaction are then likely to end up in the same cluster [80].

3.10.3   Environment Mapping

Even with a suitable data partitioning, interaction between data partitions may not be completely avoided, leading to either data or task communication. Reducing communication by applying local "place holders" to represent remote objects and space partitions is a recent development. One of the first applications of this idea is the virtual walls technique (Section 3.7.1). A similar strategy can be applied with environment mapping [30, 100]. A data distribution can be created in such a way that each processor stores part of the scene and this geometry is surrounded by an environment map. Instead of fetching data from remote processors, or migrating tasks to other processors, a simple table lookup can be performed to approximate a shading value which would otherwise be very costly to compute [249].

3.10.4   Geometric Simplification

Geometric simplification [48, 122, 123] can be regarded as another successful strategy to minimize data communication. The basic idea is that if a complex object or a densely populated part of the scene is at some distance, then without sacrificing accuracy, the complex geometry can be replaced with a simplified geometry carrying the same energy and having similar reflection and emission properties. In addition, under certain circumstances, the use of simplified geometry may increase the quality of sampling as well [160].

An example where geometric data is not always required at full resolution is presented in Figure 3.15. Assuming that the plants in this figure are distributed over a number of processors, the processor responsible for the volume at the viewpoint may occasionally need to access data that is far away. The plants at the back of the greenhouse could be fetched at a far lower resolution without impacting the quality of the sampling.

There are many different ways in which geometry can be simplified or stored at different resolutions. The methods that should be considered are

Figure 3.15. The plants close-by need to be sampled at full resolution, whereas the plants far away can be sampled at a far lower resolution.

ones where geometry is replaced with simpler geometry (geometric simplification and level of detail techniques), and techniques where geometry is augmented with an extra data structure (impostors, grouping of patches).

Geometric simplification algorithms attempt to reduce the polygon count of objects by replacing large groups of small surfaces by a small group of larger surfaces [83, 124]. Such algorithms usually do not replace different surface reflectance properties by an average BRDF. However, preserving average material properties is important for geometric simplification algorithms to be useful in realistic rendering algorithms. This issue is addressed by Rushmeier et al. [255].

Levels of detail algorithms [48, 81] build a hierarchy of models in different resolutions by repeatedly applying some geometric simplification algorithm. In parallel rendering, building this data structure would be performed as a preprocessing step. During rendering, the distance between the origin of a ray (whether in ray tracing, particle tracing, or radiosity) and the data requested should be used to determine the level in the hierarchy. The further the distance between two processors, the coarser the model and therefore the smaller the amount of data sent.

A locally dense occupation of small polygons, such as a plant, can be grouped or clustered and replaced by an enclosing volume that inherits the same reflection, emission, absorption, or transparency properties as the original. Methods may differ in the way they represent these properties, for example as transfer functions [160], volume rendering [269], or blocking and reflection estimation [255].

Impostors [81, 183] work in much the same way as environment maps, the difference being that rather than replacing the surroundings of an object with a box plus texture map, the object itself is replaced with a simple cube plus texture map. Therefore, impostors borrow from both environment mapping in construction and geometric simplification in usage.

3.10.5 Directional Caching

The disadvantage of the above techniques is that they all require a pre-processing stage, and sometimes even require user intervention, which makes them potentially awkward to use. One could overcome this disadvantage by building a data structure on the fly. If a processor manages a part of the scene, then local sampling proceeds as normal. However, for rays that leave a processor's local subspace, this new data structure is queried. If there is sufficient information present in the data structure, this is used as if it were an environment map. If not, the ray task is migrated to another processor and when a shading result is returned, it is used for both shading the ray and updating the data structure. The further the computation proceeds, the less communication between processors will be necessary, as each processor will build up an image of what surrounds it. We term such methods "directional caching" [139].

3.10.6 Reordering Computations

All the methods discussed above can be used to reduce the amount of data that needs to be fetched from remote processors and so reduce the communication overhead and prevent local caches from thrashing. A further technique to reduce communication may be applied: Reordering the computations to improve cache performance. A request for remote data can be suppressed at the cost of storing some extra state information. There is a possible penalty for not maintaining the optimal order of computations. For instance, in progressive radiosity, some shooting operations may be deferred, possibly leading to a slower convergence. This penalty may be accepted as it will lead to a much higher efficiency in the use of remote data [190].

In Pharr et al [226] and Nakamaru and Ohno [207], rays are processed in voxel order. A voxel with object data is only loaded when enough work is available or when its contribution to the final rendering wins over processing other data voxels. These implementations were originally intended to allow out-of-core rendering, or loading scene data from disk only when this data is needed. The penalty for accessing a hard disk is similar to the penalty of having to fetch data from a remote processor. As such, rendering in voxel order would be an interesting technique in the context of parallel processing.

To enable ray tracing on a per voxel basis, the order of the computations needs to be modified [226]. Normally, a primary ray is shot first, then secondary rays are computed, followed by a shading operation which uses the results of those secondary rays. Ray trees are terminated when a particular ray tree depth is reached. Then only shadow rays are shot. Effectively, this ensures that ray trees are always terminated at the light sources. Rather than shading intersection points after all secondary rays have been traced, one could compute a weight for each secondary ray. At each intersection point, the weight of secondary rays is multiplied by the weight of the parent ray. Once a light source is hit, the weight of its associated shadow ray is multiplied by the emissive properties of the light source. The contribution of that branch of the ray tree may then be directly added as a color value to the pixel which spawned the ray tree.

Shading intersection points after the computation of a number of secondary rays is therefore not necessary. In a data parallel ray tracing solution, where rays are passed from processor to processor, this would have the advantage of a reduction in bookkeeping, since intersection points do not have to be stored. Also, the communication of shading results between processors can be largely avoided. Instead, partial pixel values can be sent directly from the processor that produces a value to the processor which holds the associated pixel. If the level of recursion for a particular ray tree is deep, for example, because there is a large amount of specularity in a scene, the amount of communication of shading results can be reduced substantially.

3.11 Discussion

Photorealistic rendering of large models remains an open research issue. Model sizes are rapidly increasing, for example, due to new data capturing methods. Utilizing the computing and memory resources of a distributed set of processors is very attractive, although task and data distribution strategies generate their own problems. Unfortunately, these are not trivial to solve.

In this chapter, we started with load balancing and load scheduling strategies and we ended with data distribution and data locality methods. This order in itself illustrates the shift from simple to more complex models. The larger the models are, the more emphasis will have to be put on methods that improve cache-coherence. The methods that were discussed in the previous section are only a few of a large number of possible ways to proceed. Other possible solutions are presented in later chapters.

Acknowledgements

This chapter is an expanded and updated version of an older report [241], which had been shaped and formed with the considerable help from both Frederik

Jansen and Alan Chalmers. All images were rendered using the Radiance lighting simulation package [311]. Thanks to Arjan Kok and Jan Eek for their models. Finally, this work was sponsored by NSF grants 97-96136, 97-31859, 98-18344, 99-77218, 99-78099 and by the DOE AVTC/VIEWS.

4

Overview of Parallel
Graphics Hardware

Kadi Bouatouch

Technological advances have dramatically improved the graphics capabilities of personal computers. Reduced prices have also made three-dimensional technology more accessible to consumers. This has been possible thanks to the competitive graphics card market which has considerably increased the power of graphics chips. One can buy a graphics card for a few hundred dollars offering performance equivalent to very expensive workstations.

The new graphics cards (NVIDIA, ATI, 3DLABS, etc.) are in charge of the geometric and photometric calculations while the CPU is free for handling other tasks. The performance of these cards continuously improves in terms of speed and rendering effects. Although the illumination model implemented on graphics cards, is only local, the rendering performed is of high quality due to the application of different kinds of texturing such as: environment maps, light maps, bump maps, shadow maps and displacement maps. Moreover vertex and pixel shading are also powerful operations which enhance the realism of rendering. The implementation of these different effects is facilitated by existing shading languages.

The increasing performance of new graphics chips is due to specialized pipelines which can perform multiple operations in parallel, and also to parallel algorithms. In this chapter, we describe the different stages of a rendering pipeline and the parallel strategies used to make rendering faster. The next section describes in detail the rendering pipeline embedded in graphics chips. Section 4.2 shows how parallel strategies are implemented in graphics accelerators and presents a few examples of graphics cards.

4.1 Pipelining

Rendering can be decomposed into two functional stages called the Geometry Engine (GE) and the Rasterization Unit (RU) (Figure 4.1 (left)), or into a multistage pipeline as shown in Figure 4.1 (right). Further details can be found in Möller and Haines' book [201].

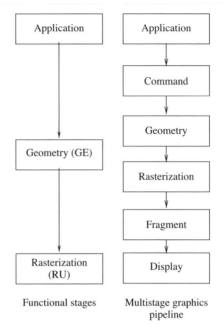

Functional stages   Multistage graphics
                                        pipeline

Figure 4.1. Graphics pipelines.

The application stage is executed on the host processor. It generates graphics primitives (using OpenGL or DirectX), controls the overall display parameters, and handles input events. The roles of the other pipeline stages are described hereafter.

Once the application (using OpenGL or DirectX) has been compiled and executed, the host sends commands to the graphics card which buffers and interprets them. These commands may concern geometric primitives or textures. The geometry stage handles different geometric primitives such as lines, polygons, triangles, t-strips, etc. It also performs model and world transformations, clipping, face culling, shading, perspective and view-port projections, and texture coordinate calculations. Next, the rasterization stage first performs setup calculations which amount to a conversion of data from floating-point to fixed-point representation and to compute gradients (for example, slopes of triangle edges). Then it scan-converts the basic primitives such as points, lines, and triangles and interpolates attributes such as intensities, depth values, and texture coordinates. The fragment stage performs read and write operations to the graphics memory, as well as Z-buffering, texture combination, alpha blending, compositing and fogging.

A fragment is no more than data associated with a pixel covered by a geometric primitive. The display stage performs gamma correction and scans the image from the frame buffer for final display.

Figure 4.2 shows how a graphics card is connected to the CPU. Note that the AGP bus accelerates graphics performance by providing a dedicated high-speed port for the movement of large blocks of three-dimensional texture data between the PC's system memory and the graphics card. The AGP interface, positioned between the PC's chip-set and the graphics card, significantly increases the bandwidth available to a graphics accelerator (current peak bandwidth is over 1 GB/s). AGP lays a scalable foundation for high-performance graphics in future systems, with support for a peak bandwidth of over 2.1 GB/s.

Current three-dimensional applications require a huge memory bandwidth. By providing a high memory bandwidth "fast lane" for graphics data, AGP enables the hardware-accelerated graphics card to access texture maps directly from system memory, instead of sending decoded video from the CPU to the graphics controller.

The on-board graphics memory is used to save the color buffer, the depth buffer, the accumulator buffer, and the stencil buffer as well as texture maps. The memory of three-dimensional graphics cards has a very high impact on the overall three-dimensional performance. 16 MB is sufficient to run three-dimensional applications at up to 1024×768 in 32-bit color depth. Realistic three-dimensional scenes at 1280×1024×32 bit color require 64 MB, which represents current state-of-the-art technology. Graphics memory bandwidth is another important factor that determines three-dimensional performance: Vendors who sell graphics cards that can safely handle highest memory clocks appear to be well prepared for future developments.

It is well-known that textures are numerous in a scene, thereby requiring a huge amount of memory. To make the movement of textures from the PC's system memory to the three-dimensional graphics card faster, texture objects are used (in the sense of OpenGL). When using OpenGL, a working set maintains a part of all the textures in the graphics memory. These textures are called resident. The portion of the graphics memory where these resident textures are stored, acts as a hardware cache. A replacement strategy such as Least Recently Used (LRU) is used to manage this cache. Managing textures in a finite amount of graphics memory is a difficult problem: While fragmentation wastes memory space, garbage collection can result in texture thrashing (some textures can be thrown out before they are required). 3DLABS [297] uses paginated textures in its graphics memory. The graphics card contains a virtual texture memory management unit.

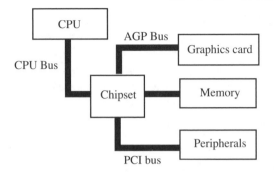

Figure 4.2. Architecture of a graphics workstation.

4.2 Parallelism in Graphics Cards

As mentioned above, rendering can be decomposed into two functional
stages, each being a pipeline of several hardware stages. To speed up
rendering, it is common to use several GEs and RUs working in parallel [197, 201]. In Molnar et al. [197], a classification of three parallel
rendering algorithms is made: sort-first, sort-middle, and sort-last. This
classification is based on where in the graphics pipeline primitives are distributed over multiple processing units. In sort-first systems, objects are
distributed during geometry processing. Sort-middle algorithms redistrib-
ute primitives in the middle of the graphics pipeline between geometry
processing and rasterization, while in sort-last processing, sorting occurs
after rasterization.

In graphics hardware, geometry processing is parallelized by arbitrarily
assigning each GE a subset of the object primitives in the scene. Rasterization is parallelized by assigning each RU a portion of the image (scan-lines,
interleaved subset of scan-lines, tiles, etc.). The objects must be sorted from
object space to image space. Most of the parallel rendering systems are
therefore sort-middle. In the following, some examples of three-dimensional
graphics cards are presented.

4.2.1 3DLABS Products

Wildcat graphics chip-set from 3DLABS [129]. The Wildcat family of
three-dimensional graphics accelerators, which is based on Wildcat's Para-
Scale architecture, utilizes the Wildcat three-dimensional graphics chip-set.
It is the first truly scalable three-dimensional graphics architecture for Windows NT. One major aspect of the architecture is the extremely high level

AGP/PCI

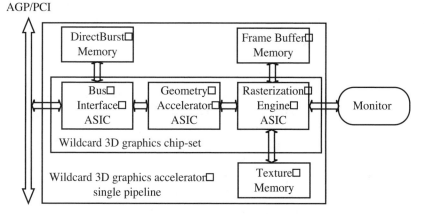

Figure 4.3. Wildcat ParaScale architecture from 3DLABS [129].

of integration that has been achieved at the chip level, which results in faster, more affordable three-dimensional graphics that can accelerate any three-dimensional application (Figure 4.3). The following description of the Wildcat's architecture is taken from [129].

The Wildcat three-dimensional graphics chip-set features three custom ASIC devices, which are specifically designed to provide optimal performance for three-dimensional graphics applications:

- Bus Interface: A single chip utilizing Wildcat's DirectBurst^{TM} technology interfaces the three-dimensional graphics subsystem to the host system via either AGP or PCI busses.

- Geometry Accelerator: A single-chip geometry accelerator provides 3.2 GFLOPS (3.2 billion floating-point operations per second).

- Rasterization Engine: A single chip performs triangle setup, texture processing, and all the pixel operations involved in rasterization. In addition to numerous other functions, this device also contains video lookup tables and digital to analog converters (DACs), so the output from this chip can be used to directly drive the monitor.

Also note that the frame buffer memory is distinct from the texture memory. Some three-dimensional graphics subsystems use a unified memory structure, which means that the same physical memory is used to satisfy both frame buffer and texture requirements. One problem with this scheme is that if the system is uploading or downloading textures, then it cannot be accessing the frame buffer at the same time, slowing the graphics throughput. By comparison, the rasterization engine in the Wildcat three-dimensional graphics chip-set employs wide independent busses for the frame buffer and the texture memory, which significantly increases the performance of the system.

Typical three-dimensional graphics architectures are based on the use of a single three-dimensional graphics pipeline. This pipeline takes data from a three-dimensional graphics application and displays that data on the screen. A key feature of Wildcat's ParaScale architecture is its extremely high level of parallelism. This allows the power of multiple three-dimensional graphics pipelines to be combined, which means that the task of drawing an image is split between pipelines and each pipeline processes only a portion of the application's data (Figures 4.4 and 4.5).

Using multiple pipelines to drive a single display in this manner results in a linearly scaled performance increase. That is, two pipelines provide 2x the performance and four pipelines provide 4x the performance of a single pipeline. It is important to note that the Wildcat graphics driver and hardware handle this capability; it is totally transparent to the application and the user.

In addition to using multiple pipelines to drive a single display, Wildcat's ParaScale architecture also allows each pipeline to drive its own display. Each screen can display a unique image, including multiple views from the same application or from different applications.

Each rasterization engine has its own frame buffer and texture memory. Furthermore, each of the Wildcat rasterization engines is capable of supporting up to 64 MB of frame buffer, which equates to a total frame buffer of up to 256 MB on a quad pipeline system. Similarly, the Wildcat three-dimensional graphics chip-set can support up to 256 MB of texture memory per rasterization engine, yielding a total texture capability of 1 GB for a quad pipeline system.

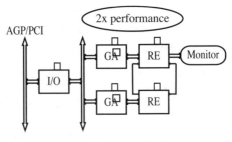

Dual pipeline, single display

Figure 4.4. Parallel architecture from 3DLABS [129].

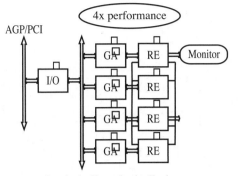

AGP/PCI

Quad pipeline, single display

Figure 4.5. Parallel architecture from 3DLABS [129].

The Jetstream architecture. The Jetstream architecture from 3DLABS allows standard low-cost parts to be used in parallel for high-end performance. Jetstream scales both geometry and rasterization through parallelism. Scalability is made possible by using several GEs and RUs. The geometry engine is called Gamma2 or Gamma3 while the rasterization unit is called GlintR3 or GlintR4. The 3DLABS OXYGEN GVX graphics cards use the Jetstream architecture.

The Jetstream parallel architecture is presented in Figure 4.6. The GLINT rasterizers process interleaved stripes on the screen (Figure 4.7) while the Gamma3 geometry engines are in charge of a subset of the primitives. The OXYGEN GVX420 graphics accelerator uses two GLINT R4 rasterizers and two Gamma2 geometry processors. Each GLINT R4 rasterizer handles virtual texturing through a memory management unit.

4.2.2 Hewlett-Packard Products

HP has developed a family of graphics hardware accelerators called VISU-ALIZE fx [262]. The block diagram of VISUALIZE is shown in Figure 4.8. The graphics hardware accelerator may contain three to eight geometry engines and four rasterization units. HP has implemented a technology called occlusion culling as an extension to OpenGL and implemented it in the VISUALIZE fx graphics hardware. The role of the interface chip is to separate the streams of data that arrive from the host CPU into three paths (three-dimensional, unbuffered, and two-dimensional), as explained next.

Data following a three-dimensional path is routed to the geometry chips. The geometry chips process the data and return the results to the interface

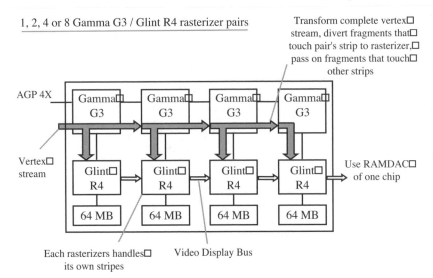

Figure 4.6. Parallel Jetstream architecture. (Courtesy of N. Trevett [297].)

chip. These results are then sent on to the texture chips or directly to the raster chips in case the texture mapping subsystem is not installed. The unbuffered path passes data directly through the interface chip to the texture and raster chips. The two-dimensional path runs directly through the interface chip to the texture and raster chips. The two-dimensional

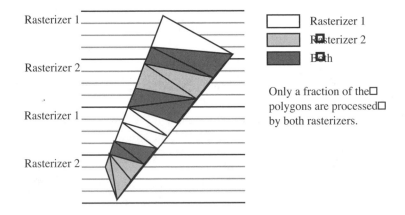

Figure 4.7. Distributing stripes to rasterizers. (Courtesy of N. Trevett [297].)

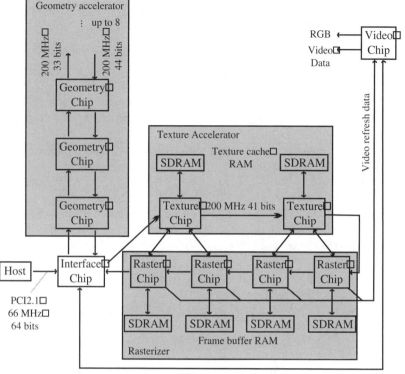

Figure 4.8. Chip-level diagram of the VISUALIZE fx product. (Courtesy of D. Scott et al. [262].)

path differs from the unbuffered path in the way its priority is handled. The interface chip manages priority among the three paths as they all converge on the same set of wires between the interface chip and the first texture chip.

The VISUALIZE fx graphics hardware has three primary busses running at 200 MHz, allowing sustainable transfer rates of more than 800 Mbytes per second. To control the loading on the interconnections for these busses, they are configured as point-to-point connections from one chip to the next.

The first of these three busses distributes work to the geometry chips. This bus starts at the interface chip and runs through all the geometry chips in the system. Each geometry chip monitors the data stream as it flows through the bus and picks off work in a least-busy fashion. The second of these busses starts at the last geometry chip and passes through the others back to the interface chip. The results of the work done by the geometry chips are placed on this bus in the same sequence as was sent along the first bus. The third bus ties the interface chip to the texture and frame buffer subsystems. It is wired in a loop that goes back to the interface chip from the last chip in the chain. Three-dimensional operations typically flow from the interface chip to the chips along this bus, and when they eventually get back to the end of the loop, they are eliminated.

The geometry engine performs different operations: model and view transformation, vertex lighting, texture mapping, clipping, and setup calculations.

The texture chip is responsible for accelerating texture mapping operations. It maintains a cache of texture data and manages it as a Virtual Texture. It then generates perspective corrected texture coordinates from plane equations representing triangles, points, or lines. It also fetches and filters the texture data (as specified by the application based on whether the texture needs to be magnified or minimized) to fit the geometry it is being mapped to and passes the result to the raster chips.

The raster chip rasterizes the geometry into the frame buffer. It determines which pixels are to be potentially modified and, if so, whether they should be modified based on various current state values (including the contents of the Z-buffer). The raster chip also controls access to the various buffers that make up the frame buffer. This includes the image buffer for storing the image displayed on the screen (potentially two buffers if double buffering is in effect), an overlay buffer that contains images that overlay the image buffer, the depth buffer, the stencil buffer, and an alpha buffer. The raster chip rasterizes primitives described as points, lines, or triangles; performs operations as defined by OpenGL (such as blending and raster operations); controls and accesses buffers; and finally refreshes the data stream for the video chip.

Finally, the video chip controls the data flow from the frame buffer to the display and maps data from values to color.

4.2.3   SGI Products (Silicon Graphics, Inc.)

The InfiniteReality system [198] is a sort-middle architecture and is depicted in Figure 4.9. The system contains three distinct board types: the Geometry, Raster Memory, and Display Generator boards. The Geometry board comprises a host computer interface, as well as command interpretation and geometry distribution logic, and four Geometry Engine processors in a MIMD arrangement. Each Raster Memory board comprises a single fragment generator with a single copy of texture memory, 80 image engines, and enough framebuffer memory to allocate 512 bits per pixel to a 1280x1024 framebuffer. The display generator board contains hardware to drive up to eight display output channels, each with its own video timing generator, video resize hardware, gamma correction, and digital-to-analog conversion hardware. Systems can be configured with one, two, or four raster memory boards, resulting in one, two, or four fragment generators and 80, 160, or 320 image engines. Figure 4.9 shows a block diagram of the maximum configuration with four Geometry Engines, four Raster Memory boards, and a Display Generator board with eight output channels.

Display lists. Display list processing is handled in two ways. First, compiled display list objects are stored in the host memory in such a way that leaf display objects can be "pulled" into the graphics subsystem using DMA transfers set up by the Host Interface Processor. A memory of 16 MB is attached to the Host Interface Processor, approximately 15 MB of which is available to cache leaf display list objects. Locally stored display lists are traversed and processed according to a priority specified using an OpenGL extension and the size of the display list object. The OpenGL display list manager determines whether or not a display list object should be cached locally on the Geometry board. Locally cached display lists are read and consumed by the remainder of the InfiniteReality pipeline. Note that if the total size of leaf display list objects exceeds the resident 15 MB limit, then some number of objects will be fetched from host memory at a reduced rate.

Geometry engines. The Geometry Distributor unit passes data and commands from the Host Interface Processor to individual Geometry Engines for further processing. The hardware supports both round-robin and least-busy distribution schemes. Since geometric processing requirements can vary from one vertex to another, a least-busy distribution scheme has a slight performance advantage over round-robin. With each command, an identifier is included which the Geometry-Raster FIFO uses to recreate the original order of incoming primitives.

The Geometry Engine Processor is a semi-custom *Application Specific Integrated Circuit* (ASIC). The heart of the Geometry Engine is a SIMD arrangement of three floating point cores allowing the three vertices of a triangle to be processed in parallel. Each of these three floating point cores comprises an ALU and a multiplier plus a 32-word register file with two read and two write ports. A 2,560 word on-chip memory holds elements of OpenGL state and provides scratch storage for intermediate calculations.

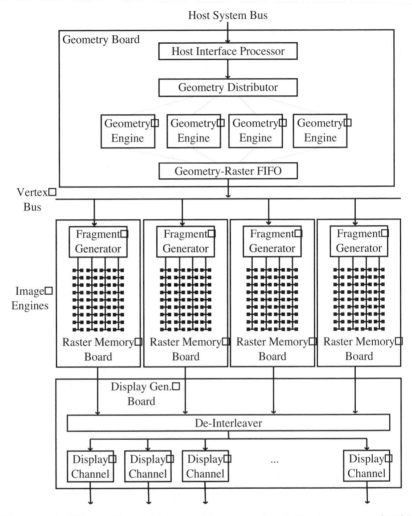

Figure 4.9. SGI graphics architecture (Courtesy of J. S. Montrym et al. [198].)

A portion of the working memory is used as a queue for incoming vertex data. Accordingly, each of the three cores can perform two reads and one write per instruction to working memory. Note that working memory allows data to be shared easily among cores.

Geometry-Raster FIFO. The output streams from the four Geometry Engines are merged into a single stream by the Geometry-Raster FIFO. This

FIFO may hold 65,536 vertices. The merged geometry engine output is written, through the FIFO, to the Vertex Bus. The Geometry-Raster FIFO contains a 256-word shadow RAM which keeps a copy of the latest values of the Fragment Generator and Image Engine control registers. By eliminating the need for the Geometry Engines to retain shadowed raster state in their local RAMs, the shadow RAM permits raster mode changes to be processed by only one of the Geometry Engines.

Vertex bus. The InfiniteReality system employs a Vertex Bus to transfer only screen space vertex information. Vertex Bus data is broadcast to all Fragment Generators. The Vertex Bus protocol supports the OpenGL triangle strip and triangle fan constructs, so the Vertex Bus load corresponds closely to the load on the host-to-graphics bus. The Geometry Engine triangle strip workload is reduced by around 60 percent by not calculating triangle setup information. However, hardware to assemble screen space primitives and compute parameter slopes is incorporated into the Fragment Generators.

Fragment generators. In order to provide increased user-accessible physical texture memory capacity at an acceptable cost, there is only one copy of texture memory per Raster Memory board. As a result, there is also only one fragment generator per raster board. Connected vertex streams are received and assembled into triangle primitives. The Scan Converter unit and the Texel Address Calculator module are ASICs which perform scan conversion, color and depth interpolation, perspective correct texture coordinate interpolation, and level-of-detail computation. Up to four fragments, corresponding to 2x2 pixel regions are produced every clock. Scan conversion is performed by directly evaluating the parameter plane equations at each pixel. Compared to a DDA, direct evaluation requires less setup time per triangle at the expense of more computation per pixel.

Image engines. Fragments output by a single Fragment Generator are distributed equally among the 80 Image Engines associated with that generator. Each Image Engine controls a single 256K x 32 SDRAM memory that comprises its portion of the framebuffer. A single raster board system supports eight sample antialiasing at 1280 x 1024 or four sample antialiasing at 1920 x 1200 resolution.

Image tiling. The Fragment Generator scan-conversion completes all pixels in a two-pixel-wide vertical strip before proceeding to the next strip for every primitive. To keep the Image Engines from limiting fill rate on large area primitives, all Image Engines must be responsible for part of every vertical strip owned by their Fragment Generator. Conversely, for best display request load balancing, all Image Engines must occur equally on every horizontal line. For a maximum system, the Image Engine frame-buffer tiling repeat pattern is a rectangle 320 pixels wide by 80 pixels tall (320 is the number of Image Engines in the system and 80 is the number of Image Engines per Raster Memory board).

4.2.4 UNC Products

The UNC (University of North Carolina) computer graphics group has developed several graphics architectures, including Pixel-Plane5 [78] and PixelFlow Pixel-Plane [136]. Pixel-Plane5 is a sort-middle architecture while PixelFlow relies on sort-last parallelism. In this section, only the PixelFlow will be presented.

PixelFlow (Figures 4.10 and 4.11) uses an object-parallel approach called image-composition to achieve its high speed. Display primitives are distributed over an array of identical renderers, each of which computes a full-screen image using its subset of all primitives. A dedicated, high-speed communication network called the Image Composition Network merges these images in real time, based on visibility information, to produce an image of the entire scene.

A PixelFlow system consists of one or more chassis, each containing up to nine Flow Units (the PixelFlow name for renderers). Each Flow Unit consists of a *Geometry Processor board* (GP), a conventional floating-point microprocessor with DRAM memory, a *Rasterizer Board* (RB), and a SIMD array of eight 192 byte-serial processing elements, each with 384 bytes of local memory.

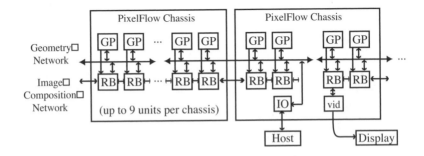

Figure 4.10. The PixelFlow architecture [136].

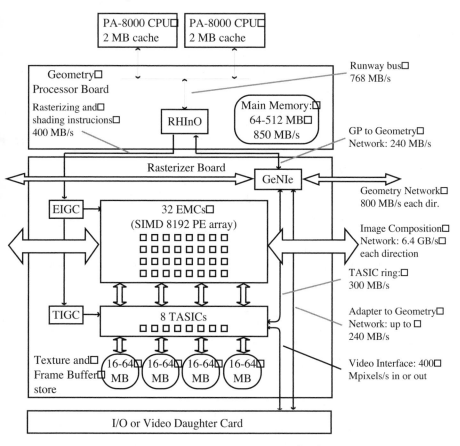

Figure 4.11. The PixelFlow unit [136].

The Image-Composition Network is implemented as a daisy-chained connection between Rasterizer Boards of neighboring Flow Units. A second communication network, the Geometry Network, uses packet-routing to connect Geometry Processor Boards.

System operation. Individual Flow Units can be designated, by software, as one of three types: Renderer, Shader, or Frame Buffer.

The Renderers process a portion of the database to generate regions of pixel data ready for shading. The Geometry Processor Board (Figure 4.11) transforms primitives to screen-space and sorts them into bins according to screen region. The Rasterizer Board rasterizes primitives one region at a time. After all renderers have processed a given region, the region is composited across the Image-Composition Network and the composited pixel values are deposited onto one or more shaders.

The Shaders apply texture and lighting models to regions of raw pixel data, producing RGB color values that are forwarded to the frame buffer. The Frame Buffers send or receive video data via an attached video adapter card.

To compute a frame, the GPs on each renderer first transform their fraction of the primitives into screen coordinates and sort them into bins corresponding to regions of the screen. The renderers then process the regions one at a time, rasterizing all of the primitives that affect the current region before moving on to the next. Once a given region has been rasterized on all of the renderers, the composition network merges the pixel data together and loads the region of composited pixel data onto a shader. Regions are assigned to shaders in round-robin fashion, with each shader processing every region. Shaders operate on entire regions in parallel, converting raw pixel attributes into final RGB values, blending multiple samples together for antialiasing, and forwarding final color values to the frame buffer for display.

PixelFlow renderers operate by sequentially processing small regions of the screen. The region size is determined by the number of samples per pixel and ranges from 32x32 to 64x128 pixels. After each renderer rasterizes a given region, the renderers scan out that region's rasterized pixels over the Image-Composition Network synchronous with the other renderers.

Deferred shading. PixelFlow uses deferred shading, an approach that reduces the calculations required for complex shading models by factoring them out of the rasterization step. PixelFlow rasterizers do not compute pixel colors directly; instead, they compute geometric and intrinsic pixel attributes, such as surface normal vectors and surface color. These attributes, not pixel colors, are then composited. The composited pixels (or samples) containing these shading attributes, are deposited onto designated renderer boards called Shaders (Pixel Flow units). The Shaders look up texture values for the pixels and compute final pixel color values based on surface normal, light sources, etc. Shading information is shared between subpixel samples that hit the same surface, up to a maximum of three surfaces per pixel. For ultimate quality rendering, every subpixel sample can be shaded independently. After shading, regions of shaded pixels are forwarded to a frame buffer for display. The advantage of this approach is that a bounded number of shading calculations are performed per pixel, no matter what the depth complexity of the scene is or how many renderers are in the system.

4.2.5   Pomegranate Graphics Chip

Currently, the entire graphics pipeline can be placed on a single chip. The architecture of the Pomegranate [186] graphics chip provides a way to scale the base unit of a single graphics pipeline to increase rendering performance.

Pomegranate is composed of n graphics pipelines interconnected by a scalable point-to-point network (Figure 4.12). Each pipeline accepts standard, immediate mode OpenGL commands from a single context as well as parallel API commands for ordering the drawing commands of the context with the drawing commands of other contexts. Distributing and balancing this workload in a dynamic fashion while minimizing work replication is a key innovation of the Pomegranate architecture and directly contributes to its scalability. A novel serial ordering mechanism is used to maintain the order specified by the OpenGL command stream, and a novel parallel ordering mechanism is used to interleave the work of multiple graphics contexts. Because the use of broadcast communication is minimized in both the data distribution and the ordering, Pomegranate is able to scale to a high degree of parallelism.

Architecture   The Pomegranate architecture is composed of several graphics pipelines and a high-speed network which connects them. The pipeline is composed of five stages: geometry, rasterization, texture, frag-

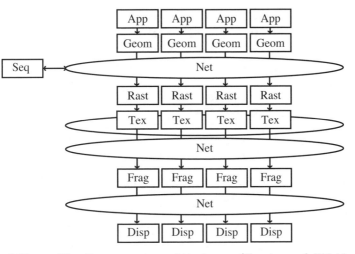

Figure 4.12.   The Pomegranate architecture.   (Courtesy of Eldridge and Igehy [186].)

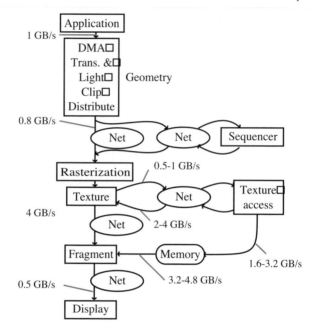

Figure 4.13. The Pomegranate architecture pipeline. (Courtesy of Eldridge and Igehy [186].)

ment, and display (Figure 4.13). The geometry stage receives commands from an application (transforming, lighting, and clipping the primitives) and sends screen-space primitives to the rasterizer. The rasterizer performs rasterization setup on these primitives, and scan converts them into untextured fragments. The texturer applies texture to the resultant fragments. The fragment processor receives textured fragments from the texturer and merges them with the framebuffer. The display processor reads pixels from the fragment processor and sends them to a display. The network allows each pipeline of the architecture to communicate with all the other pipelines at every stage.

Each geometry unit has a host interface that may receive graphics commands simultaneously and independently. Ordering constraints between different graphics contexts may be specified by parallel API commands. A virtual network port allows each geometry unit to transmit screen-space primitives to any rasterizer. There are no constraints on this mapping, thus allowing the geometry units to load balance triangle work among rasterizers.

The sequencer, shared among all pipelines, determines the interleaving of the execution of the primitives emitted by each geometry unit. It allows multiple contexts to simultaneously submit commands to the hardware and to have their order of execution described by the parallel API.

Each rasterizer scan converts screen-space triangles into untextured fragments, and then passes them to the texturer where they are textured. Textures are distributed in a shared fashion among the pipeline memories, and each texture processor has a network port for reading and writing of remote textures.

Additionally, each texture processor's network port enables it to route its resultant fragments to the appropriate fragment processor according to screen-space location. This sorting stage performs the object-space to image-space sort, and allows the unconstrained distribution of triangles between the geometry and rasterization stages that balances object-space parallelism. Fine interleaving of the fragment processors provide load balancing for screen-space parallelism.

Finally, each display unit has a network port that allows it to read pixels from all of the fragment processors and output them for display.

Simulation. The Pomegranate hardware has been modeled under an event-driven simulator. This simulator is composed of multiple threads which communicate with each other via events. The result of this simulation has shown that a 64-pipeline Pomegranate circuit operates with an efficiency of more than 87% for a simulated performance of up to 1.1 billion triangles per second and 21.8 billion pixels per second.

4.3 Conclusion

The performance of graphics chips and graphics boards is impressive. Graphics cards perform increasingly complex calculations and are getting ever faster, while their price is continuously dropping. The architectures of the graphics chips are very complex and may contain several rendering pipelines. Currently, graphics cards can render tens of millions of triangles per second and handle texturing very efficiently through virtual texturing. In the near future, a single graphics chip will be capable of rendering hundreds of millions of triangles per second and manage very large texture memories. The use of several of such future graphics chips (working in parallel) will provide the capability to render billions of triangles per second. Such graphics chips are likely to resemble the Pomegranate chip devised and simulated by the Stanford graphics group.

5

Coherence in Ray Tracing

Timothy Davis
Erik Reinhard

Most meaningful graphics images have regular, nonchaotic characteristics. That is, images depict regular objects colored uniformly or with a pattern. In an animation, successive frames often contain the same objects with the same texturing. Otherwise, our images and animations would be collections of random pixels that change completely from frame to frame, relaying little to no meaning.

Accordingly, when rendering images with such characteristics, the underlying scene geometry will be accessed in coherent, nonrandom patterns. In computer graphics terms, coherence refers to the property of a rendering process in which data accesses (to scene geometry) are closely spaced in time and/or space. For instance, if an object in a scene is accessed to color a particular pixel, the probability that it will be accessed to color the next pixel is very high.

Some of the earliest work in identifying coherence patterns in graphics was reported in [286]. These patterns include many types of coherence that are still used today (e.g., object coherence, scan-line coherence, and frame coherence). Since that time, at least 15 other forms of coherence have been identified and used in rendering acceleration techniques [59], though many of these coherence properties overlap or are closely related in some way.

In rendering algorithms which employ some type of ray tracing or ray casting, a variety of coherence properties can be exploited. One such property is ray coherence, which occurs when a number of rays have similar ray origins and directions. These rays will all travel in roughly the same direction and are likely to intersect the same objects.

Another coherence property, found in the temporal domain, is frame coherence, in which pixels across successive frames of an animation retain their color values. Processes such as MPEG encoding take advantage of frame coherence, but only on images that have already been created either through rendering or video/film capture. Later in this chapter, we will explain how to exploit frame coherence during the image generation, or rendering, process.

For parallel processing, these types of coherence are all important when a scheduling algorithm must decide how to match a given task with a set of data items. Coherence may be used to decide if data should be fetched for the task or if the task will be executed in data parallel fashion. Further, we may be able to take advantage of values that have already been computed to save time in processing coherent aspects of the rendering task.

Different rendering algorithms present different opportunities to exploit coherence. For projective algorithms, all objects (usually polygons) are sent through the graphics pipeline where they are culled, clipped, projected, and rasterized. Each polygon undergoes this treatment once and therefore all data will be required. As such, object or data coherence is difficult to exploit in any significant manner.

Algorithms which rely heavily on stochastic processes to compute an image also exhibit little coherence between data accesses. Examples include path tracing and particle tracing, where rays are traced through the scene and whenever an object is hit, one or more secondary rays are traced in random directions. The randomness of these ray directions makes, a priori, a prediction of objects that will be required for intersection for each given ray difficult, if not impossible.

Yet, we still argue that for many currently popular rendering algorithms, forms of coherence are crucially important. Deterministic ray tracing approaches are one such class of algorithm which can greatly benefit from the exploitation of coherence. Radiosity algorithms, which may use ray tracing to compute form factors, is another class of algorithm which is expected to show coherent data access patterns.

In the following section, we analyze a number of static scenes in the context of deterministic ray tracing to show the level of coherence that is present. We then demonstrate how coherence may be exploited in the temporal domain to speed up the computation of animated sequences.

5.1   Scene Analysis

For ray tracing , it is a priori unknown which scene data is going to be accessed, or when and how often. This has profound implications on any strategies aiming to solve for rendering distributed data sets.

In the following sections, the extent of this issue is assessed by gathering statistics from a sequential ray tracer [243]. This should provide insight into which algorithms may be able to cope with highly complex scenes and irregular data access patterns and which algorithms are likely to perform less adequately.

5.1.1   Distribution of Data Accesses

Given an understanding of the algorithms involved in ray tracing, an intuitive idea may be obtained of the spatial distribution of object accesses. For example, it is to be expected that light sources, and those objects directly in front of light sources, will be queried for intersections much more often than objects located in remote or dark corners. According to similar arguments, the objects that lie within the viewing frustum can be expected to be intersected more often than those outside the viewing frustum. For indirect reflection, it is to be expected that object accesses are less coherent, as this involves sampling a hemisphere, rather than a narrow bundle of rays.

However, it remains difficult to predict the irregularity of data accesses over time and how much more often the most used objects are required compared with the least necessary objects. Nonetheless, these are important notions that may have a direct impact on the efficiency of parallel algorithms. For example, for caching of object data to be useful, it would be advantageous to have a relatively small subset of the scene geometry to be accessed a very large number of times, while the large majority of objects would be required only a couple of times.

In order to determine if there is a small selection of objects that are intersected significantly more often than the other objects, a number of images were rendered while at the same time counting the number of intersection tests per object. The test scenes are the color cube model in both diffuse and transparent versions and the studio model (Figure 5.1). These scenes differ in the distribution of their objects over space. The objects in the color cube model are quite evenly spread over space, leading to a high level of occlusion. The studio model has many objects located in a small

Figure 5.1. Test scenes used for this section's experiments.

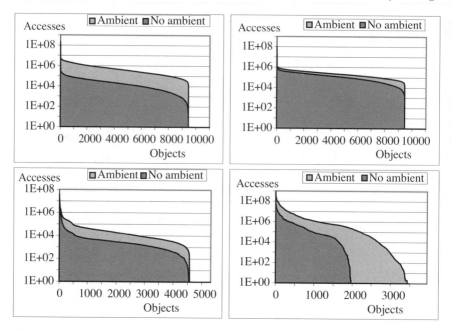

Figure 5.2. Data accesses sorted by frequency. Top left: color cube model. Top right: transparent color cube. Bottom left: studio model. Bottom right: conference room.

part of the scene, with much less occlusion. Images were rendered with and without diffuse inter-reflection.

The results of these renderings can be viewed in Figure 5.2. In these graphs, the objects are sorted according to frequency of access with the most often accessed objects on the left. The more uneven the distribution of data accesses over the objects, the steeper the average slope of the graph. It appears that there is indeed a large difference between the most often intersected object and a selection of objects that is not queried for intersections at all (eight orders of magnitude, in fact). This is according to expectation.

However, it should be noted that for the color cube model, more than half of the objects form a middle category. These are still intersected more than 10^4 (no indirect sampling) and 10^5 times (with indirect sampling). The impact of indirect sampling on the distribution of object intersections is fairly small. Object accesses are distributed slightly more evenly, which in Figure 5.2 shows up as a graph that trails off less than the graph for rendering without indirect sampling.

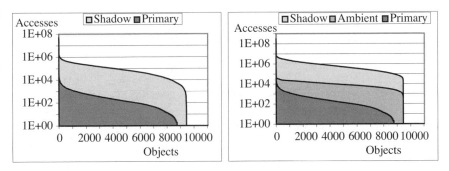

Figure 5.3. Data accesses for the color cube model split according to ray type. The objects are sorted by number of accesses. Renderings were made without diffuse sampling (left) and with diffuse sampling (right).

The following experiments are repetitions of the above ones, but now for different ray types. Doing so should reveal whether object accesses are more unevenly distributed for certain types of rays. For renderings without diffuse inter-reflection or specular reflection, effectively shooting only primary rays and shadow rays, the slopes for shadow and primary rays are similar, indicating that the distribution of data accesses over the objects is similar (Figure 5.3, left). For a nonspecular scene with sampling of diffuse inter-reflection, the slope for rays that sample indirect reflection is less steep than for shadow rays and primary rays (Figure 5.3, right). This indicates a more even distribution for object intersections caused by indirect reflection rays. This is a direct result of the lack of coherence between ambient rays and again confirms expectations.

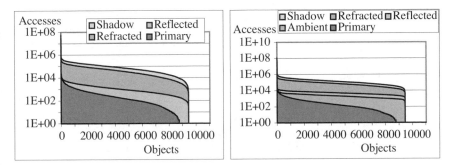

Figure 5.4. Data accesses for the transparent colour cube model split according to ray type. Results of a rendering without diffuse sampling is on the left and with diffuse sampling on the right.

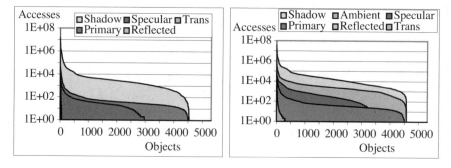

Figure 5.5.   Data accesses for the studio model split according to ray type. Results are presented of a rendering without diffuse sampling (left) and with diffuse sampling (right).

When a significant amount of transparency and reflection is added to the same scene, the results do not alter drastically (Figure 5.4). The object intersections for primary rays are completely unchanged, which is due to the unchanged geometry and view point. The total number of rays is reduced, because diffuse inter-reflection is not sampled for glass objects. However, the pattern of object accesses seems to be largely unaffected. The reflection and refraction rays seem to access most of the objects in a manner similar to shadow and ambient rays.

However, for a more realistic scene, such as the studio model, the results are somewhat different (Figure 5.5). Here, the amount of reflection and refraction in the scene is relatively small, but a fair amount of specularity is present due to some of the materials used.[1] The fact that for specular reflection significantly fewer objects are accessed is probably due to the orientation of most objects in the scene and hence can be attributed to a particularity of the scene chosen. However, for shadow, diffuse inter-reflection and primary rays, the sampling pattern is similar to the other scenes.

5.1.2   Temporal Characteristics

The previous section has shown that most objects will be accessed during rendering, but it does not show how these accesses are distributed over time. Temporal behavior is an important issue, as together with the issues discussed in the previous section, it determines the suitability of caching

---

[1]In radiance, a distinction is made between reflection and specularity. Reflection is sampled with a single ray, whereas specular reflection is meant to sample glossy (Gaussian) reflection with a number of rays scattered around the direction of reflection. The same distinction exists between refraction and transparency.

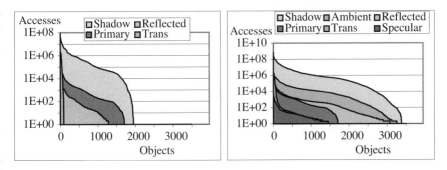

Figure 5.6. Data accesses for the conference room split according to ray type. Results are presented of a rendering without diffuse sampling (left) and with diffuse sampling (right).

schemes. The more concentrated over time data accesses are, the more successful caching algorithms can be. Note that although in this section we discuss temporal behavior, this is with respect to the data access patterns as they evolve over time *within a single frame*. Frame-to-frame behavior is discussed in Section 5.2.

This section assesses the temporal behavior of object accesses. The same test scenes as in the previous section were used. For each of the renderings in the previous section, the objects were sorted according to frequency of access. Here, the ten median objects are chosen which belong to neither the group of most accessed objects nor the group of least accessed objects. The number of ray-object intersections per second was recorded and a selection of graphs are shown in Figures 5.7 to 5.11.

These graphs show that the time between the first and the last data access for a single object is always at least 20% of the total rendering time, and often as much as 60%, even without diffuse inter-reflection. As the ten median objects were chosen for these tests, which can be thought of as representative for most objects in the scene, we deduce that this result extends to the majority of objects in the scene.

Adding diffuse inter-reflection tends to destroy temporal coherence for both the color cube and transparent color cube models. The studio model shows different behavior. Here, the number of data accesses for the median objects is very small and temporally coherent (Figure 5.11). Adding diffuse inter-reflection, does not significantly alter this behaviour (Figure 5.12). The reason appears to be that for this model, the scene is densely populated with objects in a relatively small area, while the rest of the room is empty, except for the walls and the light sources. As the majority of these small

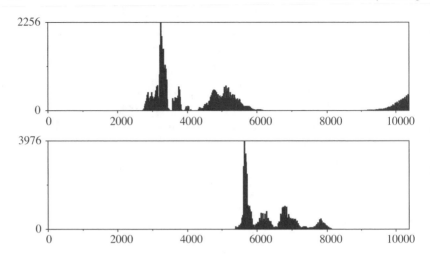

Figure 5.7. Data accesses per second for two objects of the color cube model. Of the ten median objects chosen, the top graph shows the most widespread and the bottom graph shows the most concentrated set of accesses. No diffuse inter-reflection was calculated. The total number of object accesses was 58,555 for the top graph and 58,737 for the bottom graph.

objects do not occlude one another, a relatively small number of objects is accessed during rendering. When adding diffuse inter-reflection, the walls, floor, and ceiling are most likely to be hit by diffuse inter-reflection rays. All other objects may receive an occasional diffuse inter-reflection ray.

For the conference room, the median objects do not record any intersections: Less than half the scene is used for the rendering shown in Figure 5.1. This unexpected behavior is possibly due to the fact that most of these ob-

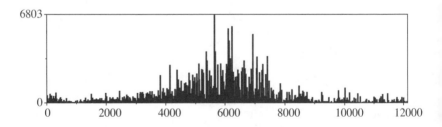

Figure 5.8. This graph shows the temporal behaviour for the colour cube model including diffuse inter-reflection. Otherwise, similar to Figure 5.7.

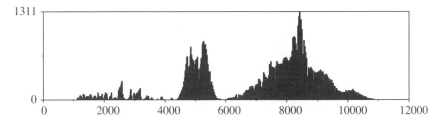

Figure 5.9. Data accesses per second for a characteristic object of the transparent colour cube model.

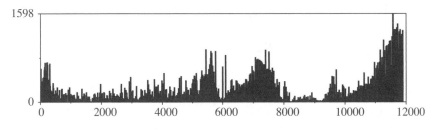

Figure 5.10. This graph shows the temporal behaviour for a characteristic object of the transparent color cube model including diffuse inter-reflection. Compare with Figure 5.9 to see the impact of adding diffuse inter-reflection.

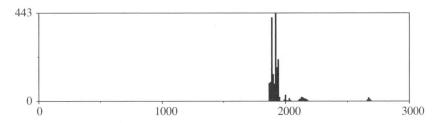

Figure 5.11. Data accesses per second for a characteristic object of the studio model.

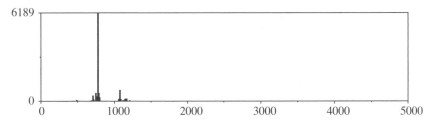

Figure 5.12. This graph shows the temporal behaviour for the studio model including diffuse inter-reflection. Otherwise, similar to Figure 5.11.

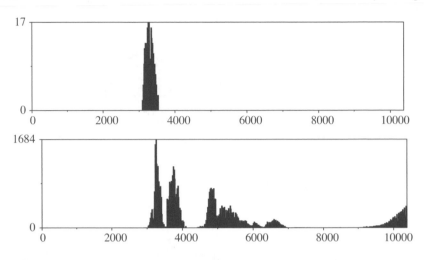

Figure 5.13.   Data accesses per second for primary (top) and shadow rays (bottom). These graphs are for the same object and rendering as the top graph in figure 5.7. The primary rays account for 244 intersections with this object while shadow rays account for 58311 intersections.

jects are instanced (most notably the chairs), leading to a large amount of visible detail caused by a small number of objects. The geometry which is situated near the walls is not within the viewing frustum and therefore does not tend to be intersected either. Adding diffuse inter-reflection to this scene, increases the number of accessed objects substantially, although the number of intersections for a large number of objects is still relatively small.

In summary, the amount of temporal coherence depends on geometry and the chosen view point. In scenes where the geometry is evenly distributed over space, coherence is least, whereas an uneven spread of objects over the scenes, such as seen in the studio and conference room models, gives rise to much more coherent accesses. Adding diffuse inter-reflection is always detrimental to preserving temporal coherence. For this reason, the next section explores to what extent different ray types (such as primary rays, shadow rays, and the like) exhibit coherent object access patterns.

5.1.3   Temporal Behaviour per Ray Type

Although the ray-object intersections per unit of time are spread out, this is not necessarily true for all ray types. Looking, for example, at primary rays only, the time between first and last access is much shorter (see Figure 5.13, where the top graph of Figure 5.7 is split into primary and shadow rays).

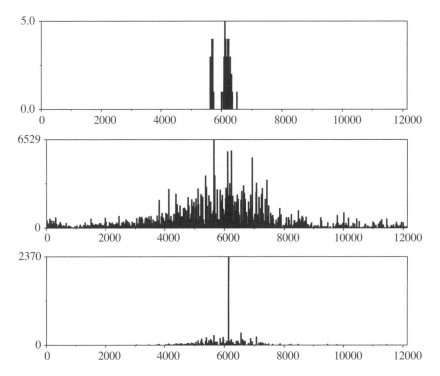

Figure 5.14.   The graph of Figure 5.8 (color cube model including diffuse sampling) split by ray type. From top to bottom: primary rays, shadow, and diffuse inter-reflection.

Much of the spread in this rendering is due to shadow rays. This can be attributed to the fact that shadow rays originate from many different intersection points which are located in different places in the scene.

By sampling diffuse inter-reflection, temporal coherence is lost (as argued in the previous section). Splitting object accesses per ray type reveals that shadow rays, instead of diffuse rays, account for most of the loss of coherence (Figure 5.14). This is attributed to the fact that for every diffuse inter-reflection ray, a number of shadow rays is shot towards the light sources. The diffuse sampling causes the origins of the shadow rays to be spread over the scene.

The transparent color cube model shows behavior similar to the color cube model. As the previous section has already shown that temporal coherence for the studio model is fairly well preserved, this will also be true for the individual ray types. The same argument holds for the conference room scene.

5.1.4   Conclusions

The tests presented in this chapter are set up to show a number of issues in parallel rendering. First of all, regardless of the amount of occlusion in a scene, most objects will be intersected at some stage during rendering. Most objects, typically more than half, are accessed fairly often. This has profound implications for parallel rendering. Assuming that these scenes are to be distributed over a number of processors, different scheduling approaches can be expected to perform in different ways.

Demand driven rendering, for instance, relies normally on the replication of all objects with each processor. In the case that the scene is too large for this, objects will have to be distributed and caching schemes will have to be employed. As Figure 5.2 in the previous section shows, caching would only be partially successful. There is a (small) number of objects in each scene which is intersected by most rays. These would end up in the cache of most processors. However, it is the large number of objects that are still intersected quite often that will cause caches to thrash. It is therefore our opinion that general caching schemes applied to demand driven ray tracing will generally lead to reduced performance.

However, it should also be noted that for specialized applications, these issues may be less severe. For example, in iso-surface rendering applications, one might only be interested in tracing primary and shadow rays. In that case, the amount of data touched during rendering may be substantially smaller than the total amount of data that constitutes the object. For such applications, a demand driven approach may be a viable alternative. Similarly, such applications could benefit from out-of-core rendering, where only parts of the model are loaded from disk.

On the other hand, data parallel approaches, whereby data is distributed from the start, would cope with an even distribution of data accesses very well, since a simple object distribution could lead to an even workload. However, the presence of a small group of objects that is accessed a couple of orders of magnitude more often than the other objects, will almost inevitably lead to load imbalances, unless these objects can be identified, for example, during a preprocessing step, and are replicated with each processor. Also, one could, for example, predict that the light sources will be the most important objects in the scene. Unfortunately, it is likely that there are many other objects that will be touched very frequently during rendering, and automatically identifying those is difficult and for now remains an unsolved problem.

When sampling of indirect illumination is required, a measurable difference can be observed in coherence between indirect rays and, for example, shadow and primary rays. For parallel rendering, this means that data parallel approaches are more appropriate for indirect sampling, while demand driven approaches are more suitable for more coherent tasks such as bundles of primary and shadow rays.

For caching to be most successful, the time between first and last access should be as short as possible. However, the temporal behaviour of object accesses seems to indicate that, for most objects in the scene, the time between first and last access is substantial. This means that if a caching scheme needs to be employed for these objects, the time such objects need to remain in the cache is long. If the cache is not large enough, then these objects will be repeatedly cleared from the cache only to be fetched again later.

For different ray types, the temporal behavior is somewhat different. For example, for primary rays, the number of ray-object intersections largely depends on the size of the projection of the object on the image. Small objects therefore tend to be accessed during a short period of time. This suggests that caching would be effective for primary rays.

Although shadow rays may originate from any part of the scene, and will do so when diffuse inter-reflection is sampled, coherence between bundles of shadow rays is still preserved. In the case of sampling an area light source, a single intersection point generates a bundle of rays. The number of rays will typically depend on the size of the light source and the distance to the intersection point. The amount of data required to complete sampling such a bundle of rays depends on these parameters. However, it is to be expected that such a bundle would require only a small subset of the scene data.

In summary, bundles of primary rays and bundles of shadow rays show more coherence than divergent rays caused by diffuse reflection and to a lesser extent by specular reflection and transmission. This difference in coherence according to ray type suggests that a different scheduling solution may be employed for each of these types of ray. In the absense of coherence, one might resort to a data parallel approach with the data distributed over the processors' memories. On the other hand, data may be actively fetched and cached for coherent ray tasks. For large rendering jobs that exceed the memory capacity of a single processor, these approaches have been pursued with some succes [242, 239].

5.2 Animation Analysis

In the previous section, exploiting coherence within a single graphics image was addressed. In this section, we will look at ways to determine and take advantage of temporal coherence across sequential frames in a computer animation. This discussion follows that reported in [59] and [60].

The motivation for this work should be obvious to anyone who has rendered nontrivial animations. For short animations, lasting only several seconds, rendering can take hours or even days. For full feature productions such as *Toy Story*, rendering time is on the order of tens of years for a single processor [116]. Such demands have been met with collections of inter-networked machines (PCs or Unix workstations) working together as a render farm to get the job done and are now ubiquitous wherever large animations are produced.

While this brute force method has been successful in the past, redundant processing still occurs in the form of rendering the same pixel value from rays following the same ray paths. Taking advantage of frame coherence and previously computed pixel values allows us to avoid this redundancy. For many animations, in which sequential frames do not differ markedly, the number of pixel values that can be re-used is significantly large. Further, the flexible nature of ray tracing calculations allows us to exploit both the parallelism and coherence inherent in an animation, and thus achieve substantial reductions in rendering times. These savings make some animations, which previously had intractable generation time, realizable without costly, special-purpose hardware.

We begin with a brief background and an explanation of the serial temporal coherence algorithm. Next, we describe the parallelization scheme for this algorithm, given its unique constraints. Performance results on sample animations follow this discussion.

5.2.1   Background

Frame coherence denotes the continuity, or lack of change, of pixel data from one frame to the next. When discussing this type of coherence with regard to ray tracing, however, we should note that frame coherence actually results from the temporal and object coherence present in the animation. That is, the same objects remain in roughly the same positions from frame to frame.

To exploit frame coherence effectively, we use an algorithm that predicts which pixels will remain unchanged from frame to frame, given the image information from the current frame and the properties and locations for objects in the next. With this technique, a high percentage of pixel calculations can be avoided and rendering time substantially reduced.

Several high-level goals have driven the current work. These goals are listed below and are referenced throughout the section:

- to reduce computation and to speed rendering, but not at the expense of approximation or compromise.

- to render the exact same set of frames as the standard ray tracer.

- to apply the parallel frame coherence algorithm in conjunction with other ray tracing optimization techniques to achieve the best performance.

- to make the user aware that the new methods are active, but without requiring any special assistance from the user.

In this work, the parallel algorithm is designed to run within a distributed computing environment (i.e., a network of commodity machines working together to solve a problem); however, no technical barrier exists that precludes the algorithm from running on a traditional multiprocessor machine. We have chosen this type of parallel environment for practical purposes; that is, such platforms are widely available and therefore do not require significant start-up costs. Additionally, all of the software we use is freely available on the internet: the POV-Ray renderer and PVM (*Parallel Virtual Machine*) [87]. Both are powerful, widely used systems that run on a variety of machine architectures, including Unix workstations and PCs.

5.2.2   Related Work

Frame coherence was first described by Sutherland, et al. [286], along with other types of coherence that can be exploited in graphics rendering. Few efforts, however, have applied parallel processing to their coherence algorithms. Several related research efforts, however, are included below to provide some context for the current work.

In the area of polygon-based rendering, Hubschman and Zucker [130] introduced an early algorithm which used frame coherence to reduce image generation time in scenes with a moving camera and fixed objects. By carefully tracking camera movement and retaining information on object visibility, local areas of change can be identified and recomputed. The remaining pixel values are copied from the previous frame.

Frame coherence can also be used for generating stereoscopic views. That is, by using the information from say, the left-eye view, the right-eye view can be easily computed. Adelson and Hodges [2] explore this problem further by computing stereoscopic pairs in a ray-tracing environment. They report that up to 95% of the pixels computed for the left-eye view can be used for an approximation of the ray-traced image for the right-eye view. The remaining 5% must be rendered to determine their values. While these results reflect a savings of nearly 50% in terms of time, the algorithm works within a single frame only and does not exploit coherence along the time dimension of successive frames.

Methods for exploiting coherence have also been applied to ray tracing. Both Nimeroff et al. [211] and Zeghers et al. [328] rely on rendering keyframes and using interpolation to generate the frames in between. In a similar manner, Badt [21] and Chapman et al. [45] sample each pixel value across the frames of an animation. If the pixel intensity is the same between two temporally separated samples, that pixel value is used to temporally flood fill the intermediate frames.

In contrast to the approximated frames that result from interpolation and flood-filling, other techniques have been employed to render exact frames for ray-traced animations. The concept of four-dimensional bounding volumes [90, 187, 102] uses temporal coherence by bounding the objects in a scene not only spatially in three dimensions, but also temporally, by constructing a volume based on the full range of space an object sweeps during animation. Intersection tests between rays and this volume can then be performed for all frames simultaneously. While this technique reduces intersection test time, it does not actually reduce the number of rays cast for an animation.

Several other techniques do actually reduce the number of rays cast as well as render exact frame images. Reprojection [3] stores information about every ray so that each frame need only update those rays actually affected by object or camera movement. Similarly, incremental ray tracing [202] retains the entire ray tree for each pixel as well as its interaction with a voxel subdivision of object space. When an update occurs within a particular voxel, updates can be performed on portions of the ray trees to quickly compute new pixel intensities. The problem with these methods, however, is their enormous overhead, in terms of both memory and computation since each grows rapidly with increasing resolution.

The work by Jevans [146] and the work contained here also propose methods for exploiting coherence based on voxel subdivision and ray tracking, but on the pixel level rather than the pixel ray tree level. Although [146] uses an adaptively subdivided space, the algorithm does not handle the non-trivial task of recombining subdivided voxels when detailed objects move out of the space. Further, [146] works best on large blocks of pixels, while the algorithm herein focuses on the individual pixel scale. Additionally, the initial object space for adaptive subdivision in [146] encompasses static objects and light sources which need not be included.

Of these efforts, very few have been implemented in a parallel environment. A parallel version of the incremental ray tracing algorithm is presented by Horiguchi et al. [126]; however, the generality of the algorithm is undetermined since it runs only on TOP-1, a specialized multiprocessor workstation, and results focus on fairly simple animations of low resolution (11 frames of 160×160 images with 122 spheres).

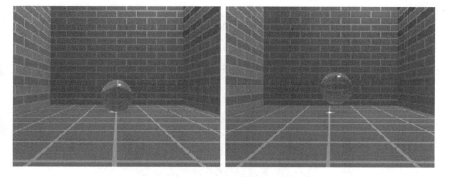

Figure 5.15. First two frames of Glass Bounce.

5.2.3 Frame Coherence Algorithm

Frame coherence, as described previously, denotes the continuity, or lack of change, across successive frames of an animation. As an example, consider the first two frames of a ray-traced animation shown in Figure 5.15. This simple animation consists of a glass ball bouncing around a brick room. A pixel-by-pixel comparison between these two frames results in the image in Figure 5.16, where white pixels denote change from the previous frame. A noticeable feature of this figure is the large number of pixels that do not change—such pixels will not require recomputation for the next frame. One exception is depicted by a few colored dots in the white region of change. Here, some pixels experience incidental frame coherence—that is, the pixel remains the same color even though the rays traced to produce that color may have taken entirely different paths. For our purposes, we do not consider incidental coherence to be frame coherence as applied to ray tracing since the pixel value was generated differently.

To achieve any performance improvements, the animation being rendered must have some amount of frame coherence as defined above; otherwise, no speed-up can be achieved. Such animations usually involve a fixed camera. If the majority of pixel values change between frames due to camera or massive object movement, little frame coherence may be extracted. The algorithm may therefore disengage frame coherence computation for portions or all of certain animation sequences. This decision can be made in a prerendering step that records camera movement and the number and size of objects that experience change.

Camera movement, however, does not have to result in poor frame coherence. Consider a fly-over animation from the viewpoint of the cockpit of an airplane. While the exterior shots through the windows may change dra-

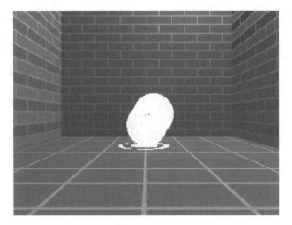

Figure 5.16. Pixel differences between the first two frames of Glass Bounce.

matically each frame, the foreground, which could include cockpit framing and detailed aeronautical instruments, will remain the same. These areas may comprise a large portion of the screen, but even if they do not, vast amounts of time may be saved if such detailed areas do not have to be recomputed for each frame. Our basic concern, then, is not that the camera remain stationary, but that it remain stationary with respect to at least some objects in the scene. The higher the number of objects and their complexity, the more frame coherence can be exploited. Unfortunately, the number of situations in which this type of coherence can be exploited is few.

Main ideas

Figures 5.17 and 5.18 provide insight into the ideas underlying the frame coherence algorithm. Figure 5.17 shows the side view of a ray starting at the eyepoint, traveling through the image plane and into the scene, reflecting off two objects and eventually exiting. By taking into account all the possible contributions from the ray intersection points and the light sources, a color value can be computed for the pixel on the viewing plane associated with this ray.

Note that a spherical object (denoted by the bold circle) is a also present, but does not play a part in determining the color of the specified pixel because there are no intersections between the pixel's associated rays, original or reflected, and the sphere. Furthermore, if the sphere were to move in the next frame to any of the positions represented by the lighter

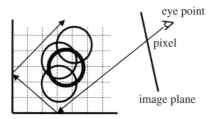

Figure 5.17. Missing an object in ray tracing. Note that the spherical object (shown with a bold circle) can move to any of several positions (shown in lighter circles) and still make no contribution to the pixel's final color.

circles, the pixel's color would remain unaffected by this object. If the sphere is the only object that has moved since the last frame, we do not need to recompute that pixel's value.

If, however, the sphere does intersect the ray in the next frame, as shown in Figure 5.18, we will need to retrace the ray and update the pixel's color value. The same holds true for pixels whose rays no longer intersect an object because that object has moved out of the area. The problem is how to determine which pixels need to recomputed due to changed subareas of the object space.

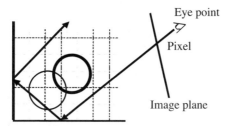

Figure 5.18. Hitting an object in ray tracing. Here, the new position of the sphere intersects one of the rays associated with the pixel; therefore, the pixel must be recomputed.

Subdividing object space

Before any rays are cast, we divide the object space (i.e., the complete three-dimensional volume where the graphics objects reside and move) into cubes, or voxels. The volume occupied by the voxels should be at least large enough to encompass all of the graphics objects that move, along with the volume swept by their full range of motion. Static objects need not be contained in the voxel space. All voxels are the same size; hence, we are employing uniform spatial subdivision.

The extents of the encompassing voxel volume are determined by making a coarse run through the animation and keeping min./max. information in the three dimensions of object movement. All objects are approximated by bounding boxes to keep preprocessing costs low. Due to the rectangular shape of the resulting volume, we may potentially receive an overestimation of the actual space that will be traversed during the animation. To produce a better approximation of the voxel space, we retain a small amount of extra information associated with each bounding box during preprocessing and mark extraneous voxels as inactive.

Tracking rays

As rays are generated during rendering, the algorithm tracks their paths through the voxel space, recording the current pixel in the lists of voxels as they are traversed. The initial camera ray, reflected rays, refracted rays, and shadow rays are all tracked through a modified 3D-DDA algorithm to determine which voxels are hit. Even if a ray only glances the edge of a voxel, that voxel is considered traversed.

After each full frame is rendered, the renderer updates its internal data structures to reflect object movement and changes, such as shape and color. If an object moves, its bounding box is used to determine which voxels the object occupied in the current frame and which will be occupied in the next. All of the pixels contained on the affected voxels lists must be recomputed.

Implementation

The frame coherence algorithm was implemented in C as an enhancement to the Persistence of View ray tracer (POV-Ray), version 3.0, a very popular, freely available package which contains many advanced ray tracing features.

Figure 5.19 shows the result of extracting frame coherence using the frame coherence algorithm on the two animation frames in Figure 5.17. The boxiness of the white area depicting change is a direct result of the sphere's bounding box and the cubical voxels used in subdividing the object space. The algorithm overestimates the area of pixels to recompute, a result also stemming from the bounding box and voxel approximation of the volume occupied by the sphere. This approximation may be tightened by using a larger number of voxels in the subdivision; however, a trade-off exists between the accuracy of the subdivision and the corresponding overhead involved in tracking and storing ray information.

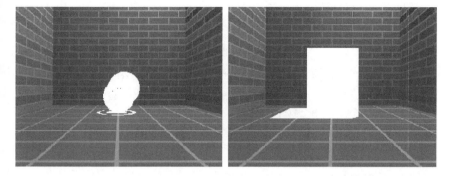

Figure 5.19. Pixel differences: actual (left) and computed (right).

Remarks on shadows and antialiasing

Shadows pose an interesting challenge for finding areas of change from frame to frame. If an object moves very close to a light source, the entire scene may be placed in shadow, causing nearly every pixel to be recomputed, even though the brightness reduction could be applied to the current value of the pixels without recomputing them. By our somewhat strict definition of frame coherence in a ray tracing environment, however, we would recompute many pixels. The situation changes, however, when an object just merely glances a voxel that happens to be close to a light source, or that may even contain the light source. Now we have a situation in which the actual shadow cast by the object may be rather small, but the number of pixels marked for recomputing rather large. Such situations may lead us to treat shadow and light rays differently from others.

Another area of consideration is antialiasing. Several antialiasing techniques are used in POV-Ray, including jitter and supersampling. Antialiasing through jitter, however, is not currently possible. Since we copy frame-coherent pixels directly from the previous frame, we cannot introduce the random noise that jitter produces to reduce aliasing effects. And obviously, we do not want to employ jitter in only the isolated portions of each frame where change occurs. Thus, we can turn to other forms of antialiasing, such as supersampling.

Supersampling is not a problem for the algorithm per se, but its use does invoke consequences. The frame coherence algorithm does not distinguish between the multiple rays fired for a single pixel; therefore, all of the rays pass through the 3D-DDA routine to determine their intersections, if any, with the object space voxels. Much of this processing is redundant since the rays vary only slightly from one another, but once in a while one of the rays will pick up an extra voxel, which, when modified, may cause the pixel color to change, and thus preserve antialiasing.

5.2.4 Parallel Frame Coherence Algorithm

The distributed computing implementation of the frame coherence algorithm is a substantially enhanced version of *povpvm*, a PVM version of POV-Ray written by Andreas Dilger and Cameron MacKinnon. Load balancing, while critical to the overall performance of the algorithm, must be performed carefully. We have two diametrically opposed goals to contend with to handle load balancing correctly.

First, to take advantage of as much parallelism as possible, we want to be able to break up the processing into relatively small chunks in a dynamic and flexible manner. We have the additional goal, however, of keeping work together in tasks spanning the entire sequence to take advantage of frame coherence. Our load balancing algorithm combines image subdivision and temporal (or frame) subdivision in an attempt to satisfy both of these goals.

The master process begins by dividing the image space uniformly into at least as many subregions as processors participating in the rendering (Figure 5.20). Each processor is then assigned a subregion (or block) to render for the entire range of the animation. This process effectively exploits the parallelism of the rendering since each slave receives a sizable chunk of work to perform, while allowing the rendering process on each machine to take advantage of frame coherence by rendering contiguous frames.

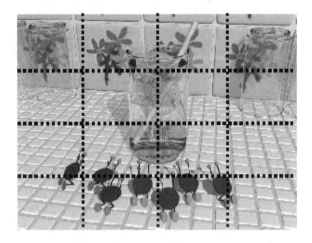

Figure 5.20. A uniformly subdivided frame of Soda Worship.

Slave processors return subregions of pixel values to the master as they are rendered. The master then writes these values to the appropriate frame file. To reduce message traffic, a slave returns a subregion of pixels along with a starting frame and ending frame designation. In this way, if a block of pixels does not change for, say frames 1 through 10, only one message is sent. The master keeps track of all uncomputed blocks and slave/block assignments.

Due to the nature of animations in general, some blocks may be much easier to compute than others. In the extreme case, a block of pixels will remain constant for the entire duration of the animation and may therefore be computed rather quickly. When a slave completes its assigned task, it requests another block for rendering. The master first checks if any blocks remain for initial assignment. If so, the slave is assigned that block for the full length of the animation; otherwise, the master must look for a previously assigned block to reassign.

The reassignment process is rather complex (in explanation, not execution) and relies on a coarse form of bin packing to achieve load balancing. Blocks with the fewest frames rendered are considered first as candidates for reassignment. The algorithm then looks for the first contiguous sequence of unrendered frames (or hole) associated with that block that is large enough for reassignment.

Statistics on rendering times (initial and coherent) are kept for each block to help determine the starting and ending frame numbers for the reassignment. We give slaves already working on this block priority over new requesting slaves so that the algorithm does not continually reassign the same work. The extents of the reassignment takes into consideration the amount of time it will take the new slave to render the first frame, as well as the remaining frames in the subsequence, as compared to the other slave working on the frames directly before the hole. Another factor to consider is the relative processing speed of each slave working on this block.

Using this approach usually results in many processors being assigned to the most difficult blocks early in the reassignment process. This situation is beneficial since we do not want to have complex blocks to render towards the end of the run. Once no holes remain that are large enough to warrant reassignment, a slave is free to terminate. The entire rendering task ends when all blocks have been rendered for all frames.

As an example, consider a four-processor system rendering 120 320×240 frames of animation (Figure 5.21). For this sequence, each processor would initially be assigned a 160×120 block of pixels to render for the entire 120 frames. Undoubtedly, one processor would finish before the others and would be assigned a subsequence of frames from the remaining three blocks.

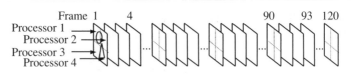

Figure 5.21. Frame subdivision.

5.2.5   Results

We include execution results based on experiments for a POV-Ray animation rendered using the parallel frame coherence algorithm. Experiments were run on 16 Sun Sparc-5 machines using the PVM message-passing software. Animation frames were generated by POV-Ray with 160x120 resolution in 24-bit color targa format. Pixel supersampling was used for antialiasing with image quality set to high and a maximum ray depth of 12. All times are reported in minutes.

Information about the three test animations is shown in Table 5.1. In the Glass Bounce animation, a glass ball bounces around a brick room. While this animation is relatively simple, it does demonstrate the refraction capabilities of ray tracing in producing images that are physically accurate. Images from the Glass Bounce animation were shown in Figure 5.15.

The Newton-Left animation consists of a set of suspended chrome marbles, which when set into motion by raising the marble on either end, illustrates the law of the conservation of energy. To produce this animation, two separate rendering runs are performed: one for the left marble movement and one for the right. Figure 5.22 shows a single frame of the Newton-Left animation. Note in the frame images the highly reflective floor, which must be updated for reflections and shadows when movement occurs. Also, due to the checkerboard pattern placed on a visible infinite plane, antialiasing is required.

Soda Worship is a modified version of an image created by Timothy Eyring for the International Ray Tracing Competition (IRTC). The image is based on an advertising concept in which the product's trademark red

Scene	Resolution	Frames	Objects	Credits
Glass Bounce	320x240	60	5	Joel Newkirk
Newton-Left	320x240	45	23	Chris Gulka
Soda Worship	160x120	60	839	Timothy Eyring and Timothy Davis

Table 5.1. Animation information.

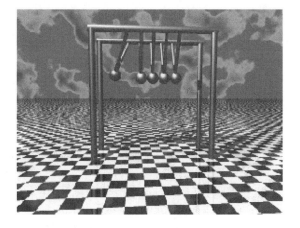

Figure 5.22. A single frame of Newton-Left.

dots come to life. In the 60-frame animated version, we see several of these dots bowing to the soft drink product (Figure 5.20). The original image had to be simplified for these experiments. In full resolution (640×480) and with all three original light sources and objects, a single image takes about 17 hours to render. To reduce rendering time, the resolution was decreased substantially, the number of light sources was reduced to one, an extra glass was removed from the background, and the number of dots was reduced to approximately one-fourth of the original. Dot movement is computed with a sine wave to produce a more natural bowing motion. Note that the image still retains a good deal of complexity, especially with the many reflections and refractions produced by the glasses.

The test results given in Table 5.2 were obtained from the original POV-Ray renderer executing on a single Sun Sparc5 workstation running at 100 MHz with 16 MB of RAM. Pixel supersampling was used for antialiasing in all of the test runs. Image quality was set to high. All times are reported in hours:minutes:seconds format, with the hours and minutes fields appearing only where necessary.

Scene	First frame rendering time	Average frame rendering time	Total number of rays	Total time
Glass Bounce	2:39	2:42	15,731,252	2:42:26
Newton-Left	5:01	5:00	21,970,900	3:45:26
Soda Worship	27:14	28:10	44,454,548	28:10:10

Table 5.2. Execution times on original renderer.

Procs	Total number of rays	Ratio to 1 proc.	Average frame rendering time	Total time	Speed-up
1	15,731,252	1.00	2:42	2:42:26	1.00
2	15,894,604	1.01	1:18	1:18:31	2.06
4	15,910,302	1.01	0:40	40:32	3.98
8	15,965,316	1.01	0:21	22:00	7.82
12	15,998,876	1.02	0:17	17:40	9.35
16	16,003,908	1.02	0:14	14:50	11.38

Table 5.3. Execution results for Glass Bounce with parallel processing only.

The first column shows the amount of time required to render the first frame of each animation. This figure will be important later when we measure the overhead associated with the frame coherence algorithm. The next column lists the average rendering time per frame, while the last two columns report the total number of rays generated and total time required (including parse time for the scene description file) for rendering the entire sequence.

For the parallel results given in Tables 5.3 to 5.5, all experiments were run on a dedicated cluster of 16 Sun Sparc-5 machines using PVM as the message-passing system. The cluster is interconnected by a standard Ethernet LAN. For uniprocessor comparisons, a single machine was used to gather results, as presented above.

Note that in all of the test cases, we achieve fairly good speed-up. In some cases (e.g., two processors for Glass Bounce and Newton-Left), we achieve superlinear speed-up. This phenomenon can be attributed to the fact that the master process performs the file writing, therefore, ray tracing can be performed in parallel with this task, while in the single processor case, the process has to wait each time pixels are written to a file before it can continue. This situation occurs with larger numbers of processors as

Procs	Total number of rays	Ratio to 1 proc.	Average frame rendering time	Total time	Speed-up
1	21,970,900	1.00	5:00	3:45:26	1.00
2	22,209,281	1.01	2:29	1:52:03	2.01
4	22,248,725	1.01	1:15	56:23	4.00
8	22,314,737	1.02	0:38	28:16	7.97
12	22,530,232	1.03	0:26	19:19	11.67
16	22,487,971	1.02	0:19	14:25	15.64

Table 5.4. Execution results for Newton-Left with parallel processing only.

Color Plate 1. Left: A portion of a 600 by 400 pixel image from our system running at approximately fifteen frames per second (Figure 6.2). Right: A model with splines, glass, image textures, and procedural solid textures (Figure 6.5).

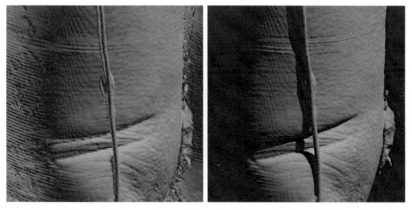

Color Plate 2. Ray tracing with and without shadows (Figure 6.18).

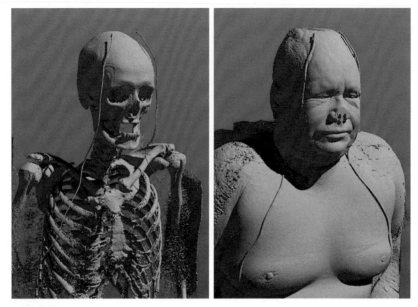

Color Plate 3. Ray tracings of the bone and skin iso-surfaces of the Visible Woman (Figure 6.17).

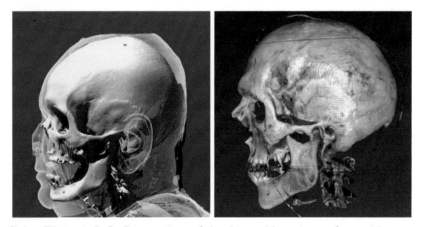

Color Plate 4. Left: Ray tracings of the skin and bone iso-surfaces with transparency (Figure 6.19). Right: A 3D texture applied to an iso-surface from the Visible Man dataset (Figure 6.20).

Color Plate 5. Terrain visualization using the real-time ray tracer (Figure 6.24).

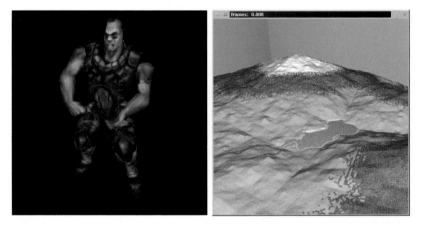

Color Plate 6. For a complex scene with incoherent texture access, texturing only slightly reduces the frame rate, rendering even a scene of one million triangles interactively (Figure 7.3).

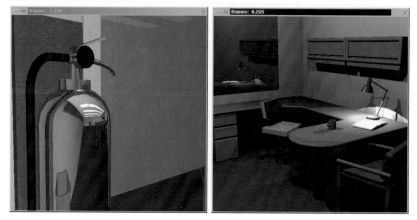

Color Plate 7. Frames from a video showing the entire conference room being reflected in the fire extinguisher (left). The office has been rendered with many reflective materials (window, lamp, mug, and others) and three point light sources (Figure 7.4).

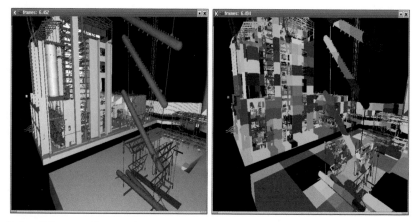

Color Plate 8. Two images showing the structure of the high-level BSP tree by color coding geometry to each voxel in the image at the bottom (Figure 7.8).

Color Plate 9. Two complex views of the power-plant. Both render at about 8 to 10 frames per second (Figure 7.9).

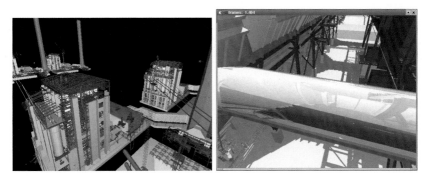

Color Plate 10. Left: Four copies of the UNC power-plant (Figure 7.6). Right: Shadow and reflection effects using one light source (Figure 7.11).

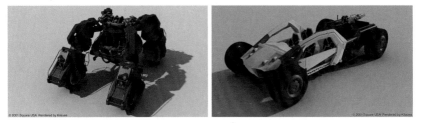

Color Plate 11. Left: Quatro (Figure 8.50). Right: Jeep1 (Figure 8.52).

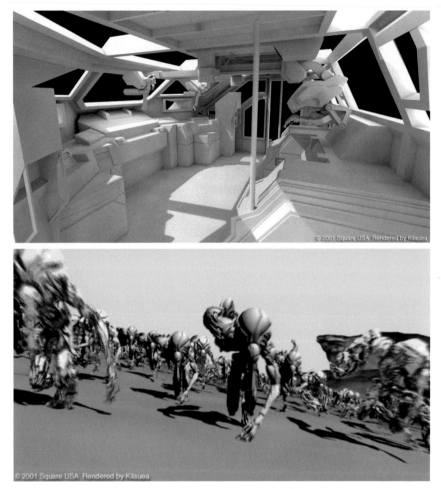

Color Plate 12. Example images from the Kilauea renderer, as discussed in Section 8.7.4 (Figure 8.56).

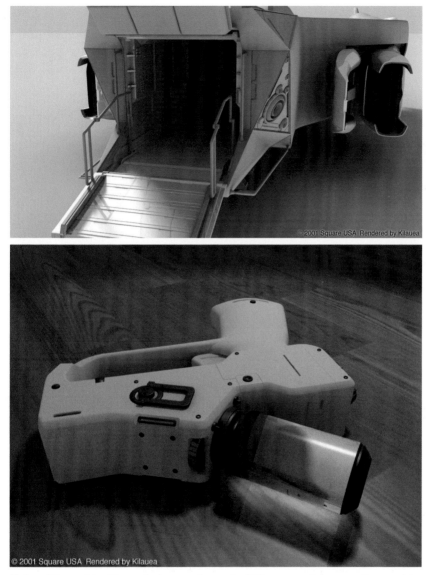

Color Plate 13. Example images from the Kilauea renderer, as discussed in Section 8.7.4 (Figure 8.58).

Color Plate 14. Example image from the Kilauea renderer, as discussed in Section 8.7.4 (Figure 8.58).

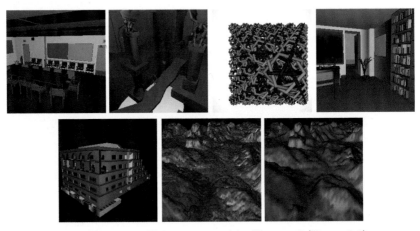

Color Plate 15. Test scenes used in Chapter 9 (Figure 9.5).

Procs	Total number of rays	Ratio to 1 proc.	Average frame rendering time	Total time	Speed-up
1	44,454,548	1.00	28:10	28:10:10	1.00
2	44,618,796	1.00	15:11	15:10:43	1.86
4	44,968,409	1.01	7:45	7:45:02	3.63
8	45,364,887	1.02	3:58	3:57:12	7.13
12	45,642,017	1.03	2:38	2:38:35	10.66
16	45,974,072	1.03	2:02	2:02:11	13.83

Table 5.5. Execution results for Soda Worship with parallel processing only.

well, but the savings are masked by additional overhead.

In the Glass Bounce animation, also note that with an increasing number of processors, speed-up begins to deviate from the ideal speed-up. This effect is due to speed-up limitations as dictated by Amdahl's Law. That is, we begin to reach a point where no more parallelism can be extracted from the processing. The smallest unit of work that slave processors perform is the image subregion. Once we reach a point where work cannot be broken down further, any idle processors will remain idle, awaiting the working processors to finish their tasks.

Execution results for running our frame coherence algorithm on the test animations are shown in Tables 5.6 to 5.8. A new statistic, total parse time, represents the amount of time spent on reading the scene description file for the standard algorithm. For the frame coherence algorithm, this figure also includes the time spent for automatically determining the voxel volume. In most cases, the increased parse time seems dramatic; however, its effect on the overall rendering time is usually insignificant.

The first frame rendering time is provided to show the overhead associated with the algorithm. For the test animations, overhead constitutes anywhere from 7% to 25% for the first frame. In later frames, this overhead is masked by other savings.

	Standard algorithm	Frame coh. algorithm	Ratio of frame coh. to std	Speed-up
Total rays	15,731,252	6,386,883	0.41	–
Parse time	0:11	0:19	1.73	–
First frame time	2:39	3:19	1.25	0.80
Av. frame time	2:42	1:39	0.61	1.64
Total time	2:42:26	1:39:02	0.61	1.64

Table 5.6. Execution results for Glass Bounce with frame coherence only.

	Standard algorithm	Frame coh. algorithm	Ratio of frame coh. to std	Speed-up
Total rays	21,970,900	2,390,960	0.11	–
Parse time	0:26	1:20	3.07	–
First frame time	5.01	6.07	1.22	0.82
Av. frame time	5:00	1:02	0.21	4.84
Total time	3:45:26	48:22	0.21	4.66

Table 5.7. Execution results for Newton-Left with frame coherence only.

Speed-up for the test animations varied from 1.64 to 4.66. Several factors affect these figures, including the amount of inherent coherence exhibited between the frames of each sequence. The number of affected pixels, however, is not always a good indicator of the algorithm's performance.

Consider the Glass Bounce sequence. The area of pixels requiring recalculation, as shown in Figure 5.18, covers much less than half of the image space, yet the algorithm required 61% of the original time to render the animation. In this case, the pixels that require recalculation are the most difficult to compute, since the rays they spawn undergo complex interactions with the glass sphere, which has numerous reflection, refraction, and shadow rays associated with it. During normal rendering, a large portion of the execution time is spent on that object. Conversely, the pixels that remain the same were fairly easy to compute originally; therefore, the work saved in subsequent frames is not as great, yet enough to achieve a marked performance improvement.

The total number of rays gives a better indication of possible speed-up; however, similar problems exist. First, the amount of work required to process a ray varies widely across rays, and depends greatly on the space traversed. Second, the number of rays produced for a particular animation, either for the standard or frame coherence algorithm, is not known until after the rendering is complete.

	Standard algorithm	Frame coh. algorithm	Ratio of frame coh. to std	Speed-up
Total rays	44,454,548	19,944,939	0.45	–
Parse time	3:06	3:47	1.04	–
First frame time	27:54	29:14	1.07	0.94
Av. frame time	28:07	15:07	0.54	1.86
Total time	28:10:10	15:11:27	0.54	1.85

Table 5.8. Execution results for Soda Worship with frame coherence only.

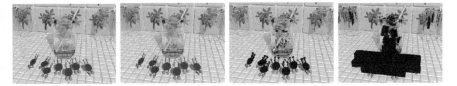

Figure 5.23. Left to right: First two frames of Soda Worship, pixel- by-pixel comparison and estimate from algorithm.

For the Newton-Left sequence, the frame coherence algorithm performed much better, resulting in speed-up of 4.66. The enhanced performance is primarily due to the localized movement in the animation, although reflections and shadows do produce some nonlocalized pixel modifications across image space. The results of Soda Worship provide additional insight into the complex interaction between frame coherence and speed-up. Only very slight movement is occurring between frames, yet as demonstrated in the pixel-by-pixel comparison of Figure 5.23, the effects of that movement are global, due to the many reflective, transparent surfaces of the glasses. Additionally, the bounding boxes of the dots fall directly in front of the most complex region in object space to render (the bottom of the main glass); thus, additional time-consuming pixels are tagged for recalculation through the over-estimate of the modified region produced by the bounding box approximation, as shown in the right-most image of Figure 5.23. As in the Glass Bounce animation, the pixels that remain constant (such as the tile countertop) are relatively easy to compute. Consequently, the algorithm achieves a speed-up of less than 2, even though the number of pixels affected comprise less than one-fourth of the image. (One additional note: For this sequence, the extents of the voxel volume were specified in the scene description file; therefore, the total parse time is roughly the same as that for the standard algorithm.)

Tables 5.9 to 5.11 show results for rendering the test animations on 1–16 processors using the distributed computing frame coherence algorithm. For each test case (2, 4, 8, 12, and 16 processors), figures are given for the total number of rays, average frame rendering time, and total rendering time, as above. These figures are compared to the single processor nonframe coherence algorithm to show the total contribution of the parallel frame coherence approach.

From the tables, we see that with 16 machines, the algorithm renders the animations 13 to 27 times faster than the serial program. These figures reflect substantial time savings for each of the sequences. Some additional ways to improve performance are discussed below.

Procs	Total number of rays	Ratio to 1 proc	Average frame rendering time	Total time	Speed-up
1	15,731,252	1.00	2:42	2:42:26	1.00
2	6.388,095	0.41	0:58	57:51	2.79
4	6,393,240	0.41	0:32	33.07	5.06
8	6,426,667	0.41	0:19	18:47	8.52
12	6,458,917	0.41	0:15	15:23	10.80
16	6,480,988	0.41	0:12	12:06	13.50

Table 5.9.   Execution results for Glass Bounce with both parallel processing and frame coherence.

Procs	Total number of rays	Ratio to 1 proc	Average frame rendering time	Total time	Speed-up
1	21,970,900	1.00	5:00	3:45:26	1.00
2	2,581,218	0.12	0:31	23:06	9.75
4	2,840,097	0.13	0:18	13:08	17.16
8	2,893,176	0.13	0:13	10:01	22.51
12	3,323,674	0.15	0:12	9:45	23.12
16	3,612,717	0.16	0:11	8:18	27.16

Table 5.10.   Execution results for Newton-Left with both parallel processing and frame coherence.

Procs	Total number of rays	Ratio to 1 proc	Average frame rendering time	Total time	Speed-up
1	44,454,548	1.00	28:10	28:10:10	1.00
2	22,163,526	0.50	15:11	11:48:11	2.39
4	22,286,422	0.50	7:45	4:27:26	6.32
8	22,409,023	0.50	3:58	2:16:34	12.38
12	23,125,140	0.52	2:38	1:31:05	18.56
16	23,180,741	0.52	2:02	1:12:15	23.39

Table 5.11.   Execution results for Soda Worship with both parallel processing and frame coherence.

While the speed-ups achieved are substantial, the results could actually be better. Figure 5.24 shows a graph for each of the animations plotting speed-up versus the number of processors. Here, the ideal line is the best possible performance given the speed-up from the frame coherence algorithm, as reported above; thus, the ideal line is the product of the frame coherence speed-up and the number of processors. Accordingly, each animation has a different ideal line based on inherent coherence.

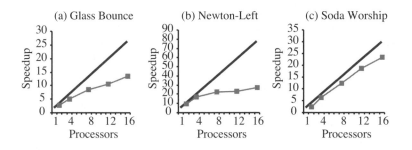

Figure 5.24. Number of processors versus speed-up.

In many ways, the results in Figure 5.24 are a lesson in Amdahl's law. The rendering tasks for the test animations are fairly time-consuming when run on a single machine. When run with multiple machines and the frame coherence algorithm, however, these tasks consume substantially less time. Factors such as the serial voxel volume determination and slight load imbalance become more significant as the time required for the parallel work decreases. Additionally, we must consider the smallest unit of work assigned to processors. Obviously, overall rendering time cannot be shorter than the time it takes to process the most complex single block in the sequence.

Due to these factors, most of the speed-ups level off after four to eight processors, with the notable exception of Soda Worship. This animation, by far, is the most complex and time-consuming sequence to render, requiring over 28 hours on a single machine. With the distributed frame coherence algorithm, the speed-up follows the ideal line fairly closely. If we were to render the frames at a higher resolution, the results would be even better.

This last point holds true for all of the animations. What we need in most instances is more work to divide up among processors. For some animations, in nearly the same amount of time reported above for the 16-processor case, we could probably render the same sequence at twice the resolution.

In general, this method of increasing work while keeping the overall processing time constant follows as Gustafson's law. For the animations tested, increasing the image resolution is desirable anyway since the frames we produce are of small to medium size. We predict that animations at higher resolution will benefit more from our algorithm. This prediction is based partly on empirical result and partly on performance modeling methods.

5.2.6 Summary

In this section, we have presented a parallel frame coherence algorithm that performs well while incurring only a reasonable amount of overhead. Both the frame coherence and distributed computing techniques provide significant improvement on their own, but when combined, achieve substantially improved levels of performance. Such improvements will prove highly beneficial as the demand for large rendering tasks rises.

One feature of the algorithm is that the user does not even need to be aware that it is running. The frame coherence algorithm can be implemented to turn itself on and off as needed after extracting the necessary information from its preprocessing phase. Furthermore, it needs no special parameters from the user since it computes all of the values it needs from the scene description file. Another beneficial feature of this work is its accessibility to a wide range of users. Anyone with a set of workstations can perform parallel rendering without having to buy an expensive multi-processor. Larger rendering environments with many workstations could potentially provide some of the most powerful renderers in the world. These systems will undoubtedly bring new issues of speed-up and load balancing to the forefront.

Acknowledgements

The work in Section 5.1 was sponsored by NSF grants 97-96136, 97-31859, 98-18344, 99-77218, 99-78099 and by the DOE AVTC/VIEWS.

II

Case Studies

6 | Interactive Ray Tracing on a Supercomputer

Steve Parker

This chapter describes our explorations of an interactive ray tracing system designed for current multiprocessor machines. This system was initially developed to examine ray tracing's performance on a modern architecture. We were surprised at just how responsive the resulting system turned out to be. Although the system takes careful advantage of system resources, the basic system is essentially a brute force implementation (Figure 6.1). We intentionally take the simple path at each step believing that neither simplifying assumptions nor complex algorithms are needed for performance.

The ray tracing system is interactive in part because it runs on a high-end machine (SGI Origin 2000) with fast frame buffer, CPU set, and interconnect. The key advantages of ray tracing are

- Ray tracing scales well on tens to hundreds of processors.

- Ray tracing's frame rendering time is sublinear in the number of primitives for static scenes.

- Ray tracing allows a wide range of primitives and user-programmable shading effects.

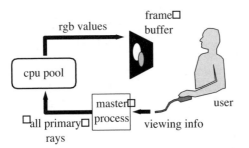

Figure 6.1. The ray tracing system discussed in this chapter explicitly traces all rays on a pool of processors for a viewpoint interactively selected by the viewer.

Figure 6.2. A portion of a 600 x 400 pixel image from our system running at approximately 15 frames per second. See also Color Plate 1.

The first item allows our implementation be interactive, the second allows this interactivity to extend to relatively large (e.g., gigabyte) scenes, and the third allows the familiar ray traced look with shadows and specular reflection. Figure 6.2 shows the type of imagery that can be produced interactively.

6.1   System Architecture

It is well understood that ray tracing can be accelerated through two main techniques [241]: accelerating or eliminating ray/object intersection tests and parallelization (see also Chapter 3). We employ both techniques in our system. We use a hybrid spatial subdivision which combines a grid-based subdivision of the scene [79] with bounding volumes [152]. For a given scene, we can empirically test both methods to arrive at the "best" combination where "best" is dependent upon the scene geometry and the particular application. The beauty of the interactive system is the ability to rapidly explore tradeoffs such as different spatial subdivision techniques.

Ray tracing naturally lends itself towards parallel implementations. The computation for each pixel is independent of all other pixels, and the data structures used for casting rays are usually read-only. These properties have resulted in many parallel ray tracers, as discussed in Section 3.4.2.

The simplest parallel shared memory implementation with reasonable performance uses Master/Slave demand driven scheduling as follows:

- **Master task:** The ray tracing slaves are simple programs that grab primary rays from the queue and compute pixel RGB values.

- **Slave task:** This implementation would work, but it would have excessive synchronization overhead because each pixel is an independent task. The actual implementation uses a larger basic task size and runs in conventional or frameless mode as discussed in the next two sections.

6.1.1   Conventional Operation

To reduce synchronization overhead, we would like to assign groups of rays to each processor. The larger these groups are, the less synchronization is required. However, as they become larger, more time is potentially lost due to poor load balancing because all processors must wait for the last job of the frame to finish before starting the next frame. We address this through a load balancing scheme that uses a static set of variable size jobs that are dispatched in a queue where jobs linearly decrease in size. This is shown in Figure 6.3.

Figure 6.3 has several exaggerations in scale to make it more obvious. First, the time between job runs for a processor is smaller than is shown in the form of gaps between boxes. Second, the actual jobs are multiples of the finest tile granularity which is a 128-pixel tile (32 x 4). We chose this size for two reasons: cache coherency for the pixels and data cache coherency for the scene. The first reason is dictated by the machine architecture which uses 128 byte cache lines (32 4-byte pixels). With a minimum task granularity of a cache line, false sharing between image tiles is eliminated. A further advantage of using a tile is data cache reuse for the scene geometry. Since

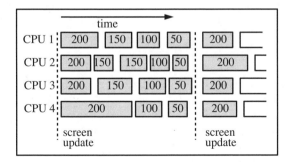

Figure 6.3.   Operation of ray tracer in synchronous mode. Numbers in boxes represent number of pixels in a block being processed. All pixels are traced before the screen swaps buffers.

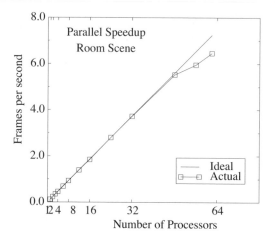

Figure 6.4. Performance results for varying numbers of processors for a single view of the scene shown in Figure 6.5.

primary rays exhibit good spatial coherence, our system takes advantage of this with the 32 x 4-pixel tile.

The implementation of the work queue assignment uses the hardware fetch and op counters on the Origin architecture. This allows efficient access to the central work queue resource. This approach to dividing the work between processors seems to scale very well. In Figure 6.4, we show the scalability for the room scene shown in Figure 6.5. We used up to 64 processors (all that are available locally) and found that up through about 48 we achieved almost ideal performance. Above 48, there is a slight drop off. We also show performance data for interactively ray tracing the iso-surfaces of the visible female dataset in Figure 6.6. For this data, we had access to a 128 processor machine and found nearly ideal speed-ups for up to 128 processors.

Since most scenes fit within the secondary cache of the processor (4 MB), the memory bandwidth used is very small. The room scene, shown in Figure 6.4 uses an average of 9.4 MB/s of main memory bandwidth per processor. Ironically, rendering a scene with a much larger memory foot-print (rendering of iso-surfaces from the visible female dataset [221]) uses only 2.1 to 8.4 MB/s of main memory bandwidth. These statistics were gathered using the SGI perfex utility, benchmarked with 60 processors.

Since ray tracing is an inherently parallel algorithm, efficient scaling is limited by only two factors: load balance and synchronization. The dynamic work assignment scheme described earlier is used to limit the

Figure 6.5. A model with splines, glass, image textures, and procedural solid textures. At 512 by 512 pixels this image is generated at approximately 4 frames per second on 60 CPUs (195 Mhz R10000, SGI Origin 2000). See also Color Plate 1.

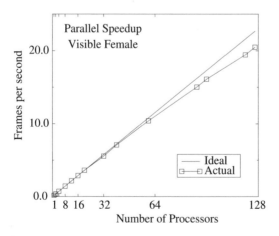

Figure 6.6. Performance results for the visible female dataset, shown in Figure 6.17.

effect of load imbalance. Synchronization for each frame can limit scaling due to the overhead of the barrier. The standard barrier provided in Irix requires an average of 5 milliseconds to synchronize 64 processors, which limits the scaling at high frame-rates. An efficient barrier was implemented using the "fetchop" atomic fetch-and-op facilities in the Origin. A barrier operation consumes 61 microseconds on average, which is an insignificant percentage of the frame time.

6.1.2   Frameless Rendering

For frameless rendering [29, 57, 325] the viewpoint and screen are updated synchronously, but the pixels are updated according to an asynchronous quasi-random pattern. Our implementation is summarized in Figure 6.7.

The implementation assigns a static pixel distribution to the rendering threads—every processor has a list of pixels that it will update, requiring minimal synchronization between threads. The rendering thread handles user input and draws the buffer to the screen at regular intervals. This is done asynchronously to the rendering threads. The rendering threads periodically update their camera—this is done at a specified rate expressed as a percentage of the pixels that each thread owns. The display thread is modified so that it updates the screen at some user defined frame rate.

When creating a "static" pixel distribution (partitioning the screen between processors), there are two conflicting goals: 1) maintain coherent memory access; and 2) have a more random distribution (incoherent memory) of pixels. The first is important for raw system efficiency, and the second is important to avoid visually distracting structure during updates.

In the current system, we partition the image plane using a Hilbert curve (this maps the image to a one-dimensional line), and then break this line into "chunks." These chunks are distributed to the processors

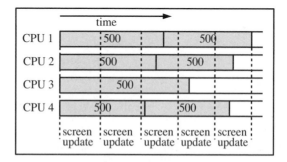

Figure 6.7. Operation of ray tracer in asynchronous (frameless) mode. Screen is constantly updating and each processor is repeatedly tracing its set of pixels.

in a round robin fashion (processors interleaved with chunk granularity along the one-dimensional domain of the Hilbert curve). Each thread then randomly permutes its chunks so that the update doesn't always exactly track the Hilbert curve.

When updating the image, pixels can be blended instead of just stored into the frame buffer. This causes samples to have an exponential decay and effectively creates a smoother image in space and time. This implements the "frameless antialiasing" concept of Scher Zagier [324]. We also use jittered sampling for this where there are four potential sample locations per pixel and two of them are updated when the pixel is updated, so the pixel is only fully updated after two passes.

One nice property of a static pixel distribution is the ease of keeping extra information around (each thread just stores it—and no other threads will access this memory). This can be used for computing a running average, subpixel offsets for jittered sampling, a running variance computation or other information about the scene associated with that pixel (velocity, object ids, etc.).

6.1.3   Performance

Figure 6.8 shows the performance of the system for the picture in Figure 6.9. Lower image resolutions achieve higher frame rates. However, higher image

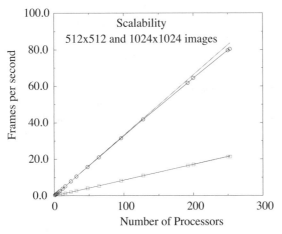

Figure 6.8.   The performance of the parallel ray tracing system, showing frame-rates for two different image resolutions. The 512x512 image renders over 80 frames/second and a 96% parallel efficiency on 256 processors. The 1024x1024 image attains 99% efficiency at approximately 21 frames/second.

Figure 6.9. A typical scene used by the performance benchmarks.

resolutions achieve higher parallel efficiency. These tests were performed on an SGI Origin 3800 with 256 processors (400 MHz R12000).

6.2   Ray Tracing for Volume Visualization

Many applications generate scalar fields $\rho(x, y, z)$ which can be visualized by a variety of methods. These fields are often defined by a set of point samples and an interpolation rule. The point samples are typically in either a rectilinear grid, a curvilinear grid, or an unstructured grid (simplicial complex). The two main visualization techniques used on such fields are to display *iso-surfaces* where $\rho(x, y, z) = \rho_{\text{iso}}$, and *direct volume rendering,* where there is some type of opacity/emission integration along the line of sight. The key difference between these techniques is that iso-surfacing displays actual surfaces, while direct volume rendering displays some function of all the values seen along a ray throughout the pixel. Ideally, the display parameters for each technique are interactively controlled by the user. In this section, we present interactive volume visualization schemes that use ray tracing as their basic computation method.

The basic ray-volume traversal method used in this section is shown in Figure 6.10. This framework allows us to implement volume visualization methods that find exactly one value along a ray. Two such methods are iso-surfacing [221] and maximum-intensity projection. Maximum-intensity projection is a direct volume rendering technique where the opacity is a

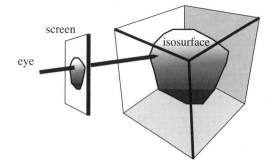

Figure 6.10. A ray traverses a volume looking for a specific or maximum value. No explicit surface or volume is computed.

function of the maximum intensity seen along a ray. More general forms of direct volume rendering are not discussed here.

The methods are implemented in a parallel ray tracing system that runs on an SGI Reality Monster, which is a conventional (distributed) shared-memory multiprocessor machine [219]. The only graphics hardware that is used is the high-speed framebuffer. Conventional wisdom holds that ray tracing is too slow to be competitive with hardware z-buffers. However, when rendering a sufficiently large dataset, ray tracing should be competitive because its low time complexity ultimately overcomes its large time constant [150]. This crossover will happen sooner on a multiple CPU computer because of ray tracing's high degree of intrinsic parallelism. The same arguments apply to the volume traversal problem.

In Section 6.2.1, we review previous work, describe several volume visualization techniques, and give an overview of the parallel ray tracing code that provides the backbone of our system. Section 6.2.2 describes the data organizational optimizations that allow us to achieve interactivity. In Section 6.2.3, we describe our memory optimizations for various types of volume visualization. In Section 6.2.4, we show our methods applied to several datasets. We also discuss the implications of our results in Section 6.2.5.

6.2.1 Background

Ray tracing has been used for volume visualization in many works (e.g., [172, 257, 299]). Typically, the ray tracing of a pixel is a kernel operation that could take place within any conventional ray tracing system. In this section we review how ray tracers are used in visualization, and how they are implemented efficiently at a systems level.

Efficient ray tracing

It is well understood that ray tracing is accelerated through two main techniques [241]: accelerating or eliminating ray/voxel intersection tests and parallelization. Acceleration is usually accomplished by a combination of spatial subdivision and early ray termination [172, 151, 277].

Ray tracing for volume visualization naturally lends itself towards parallel implementations [181, 203]. The computation for each pixel is independent of all other pixels, and the data structures used for casting rays are usually read-only. These properties have resulted in many parallel implementations. A variety of techniques have been used to make such systems parallel, and many successful systems have been built (e.g., [181, 302, 261, 204]). These techniques are surveyed by Whitman [317].

Methods of volume visualization

There are several ways that scalar volumes can be made into images. The most popular simple volume visualization techniques that are not based on cutting planes are *iso-surfacing*, *maximum-intensity projection*, and *direct volume rendering*.

In iso-surfacing, a surface is displayed that is the locus of points where the scalar field equals a certain value. There are several methods for computing images of such surfaces including constructive approaches such as marching cubes [82, 180] and ray tracing [176, 185, 280].

In *Maximum-Intensity Projection* (MIP), each value in the scalar field is associated with an intensity and the maximum intensity seen through a pixel is projected onto that pixel [258]. This is a "winner-takes-all" algorithm, and thus looks more like a search algorithm than a traditional volume color/opacity accumulation algorithm.

More traditional direct volume rendering algorithms accumulate color and opacity along a line of sight [172, 257, 299, 151, 64]. This requires more intrinsic computation than MIP, and we will not deal with it in this chapter.

Traversals of volume data

Traversal algorithms for volume data are usually customized to the details of the volume data characteristics. The three most common types of volume data used in applications are shown in Figure 6.11 [279].

To traverse a line through rectilinear data some type of incremental traversal is used (e.g., [9, 79]). Because there are many cells, a hierarchy can be used that skips "uninteresting" parameter intervals, which increases performance [58, 173, 320, 321].

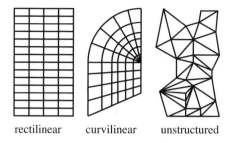

rectilinear   curvilinear   unstructured

Figure 6.11. The three most common types of point-sampled volume data.

For curvilinear volumes, the ray can be intersected against a polygonal approximation to the boundary, and then a more complex cell-to-cell traversal can be used [319].

For unstructured volumes a similar technique can be used [86, 270]. Once the ray is intersected with a volume, it can be tracked from cell-to-cell using the connectivity information present in the mesh.

Another possibility for both curvilinear and unstructured grids is to resample to a rectilinear grid [231], although resampling artifacts and data explosion are both issues.

6.2.2   Traversal Optimizations

Our system organizes the data into a shallow rectilinear hierarchy for ray tracing. For unstructured or curvilinear grids, a rectilinear hierarchy is imposed over the data domain. Within a given level of the hierarchy, we use the incremental method described by Amanatides and Woo [9].

Memory bricking

The first optimization is to improve data locality by organizing the volume into "bricks" that are analogous to the use of image tiles in image-processing software and other volume rendering programs [258, 56] (Figure 6.12). Our use of lookup tables is particularly similar to that of Sakas et al. [258].

Effectively utilizing the cache hierarchy is a crucial task in designing algorithms for modern architectures. Bricking, or three-dimensional tiling, has been a popular method for increasing locality for ray cast volume rendering. The dataset is reordered into $n \times n \times n$ cells which then fill the entire

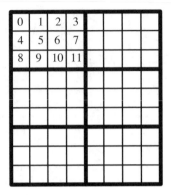

Figure 6.12.   Cells can be organized into "tiles" or "bricks" in memory to improve locality. The numbers in the first brick represent layout in memory. Neither the number of atomic voxels nor the number of bricks need be a power of two.

volume. On a machine with 128-byte cache lines, using 16-bit data values, n is exactly 4. However, using float (32-bit) datasets, n is closer to 3.

Effective *Translation Look-aside Buffer* (TLB) utilization is also becoming a crucial factor in algorithm performance. The same technique can be used to improve TLB hit rates by creating $m \times m \times m$ bricks of $n \times n \times n$ cells. For example, a $40 \times 20 \times 19$ volume could be decomposed into $4 \times 2 \times 2$ macro-bricks of $2 \times 2 \times 2$ bricks of $5 \times 5 \times 5$ cells. This corresponds to $m = 2$ and $n = 5$. Because 19 cannot be factored by $mn = 10$, one level of padding is needed. We use $m = 5$ for 16 bit datasets, and $m = 6$ for 32-bit datasets.

The resulting offset q into the data array can be computed for any x, y, z triple with the expression:

$$
\begin{aligned}
q \;=\;\; & ((x \div n) \div m)n^3 m^3 ((N_z \div n) \div m)((N_y \div n) \div m)\\
+\;\; & ((y \div n) \div m)n^3 m^3 ((N_z \div n) \div m)\\
+\;\; & ((z \div n) \div m)n^3 m^3\\
+\;\; & ((x \div n) \bmod m)n^3 m^2\\
+\;\; & ((y \div n) \bmod m)n^3 m\\
+\;\; & ((z \div n) \bmod m)n^3\\
+\;\; & (x \bmod n \times n)n^2\\
+\;\; & (y \bmod n) \times n\\
+\;\; & (z \bmod n),
\end{aligned}
$$

where N_x, N_y and N_z are the respective sizes of the dataset.

This expression contains many integer multiplication, divide, and modulus operations. On modern processors, these operations are extremely costly (32+ cycles for the MIPS R10000). Where n and m are powers of two, these operations can be converted to bit-shifts and bitwise logical operations. However, the ideal size is rarely a power of two, thus a method that addresses arbitrary sizes is needed. Some of the multiplications can be converted to shift/add operations, but the divide and modulus operations are more problematic. The indices could be computed incrementally, but this would require tracking nine counters, with numerous comparisons and poor branch prediction performance.

Note that this expression can be written as:

$$q = F_x(x) + F_y(y) + F_z(z)$$

where

$$
\begin{aligned}
F_x(x) &= ((x \div n) \div m)n^3 m^3 ((N_z \div n) \div m)((N_y \div n) \div m) \\
&+ ((x \div n) \bmod m)n^3 m^2 \\
&+ (x \bmod n \times n)n^2 \\
F_y(y) &= ((y \div n) \div m)n^3 m^3 ((N_z \div n) \div m) \\
&+ ((y \div n) \bmod m)n^3 m \\
&+ (y \bmod n) \times n \\
F_z(z) &= ((z \div n) \div m)n^3 m^3 \\
&+ ((z \div n) \bmod m)n^3 \\
&+ (z \bmod n).
\end{aligned}
$$

We tabulate F_x, F_y, and F_z and use x, y, and z respectively to find three offsets in the array. These three values are summed to compute the index into the data array. These tables will consist of N_x, N_y, and N_z elements, respectively. The total sizes of the tables will fit in the primary data cache of the processor even for very large data set sizes. Using this technique, we note that one could produce mappings which are much more complex than the two-level bricking described here, although it is not at all obvious which of these mappings would achieve the highest cache utilization.

For many algorithms, each iteration through the loop examines the eight corners of a cell. In order to find these eight values, we need to only look up $F_x(x)$, $F_x(x+1)$, $F_y(y)$, $F_y(y+1)$, $F_z(z)$, and $F_z(z+1)$. This consists of six index table look-ups for each eight data value look-ups.

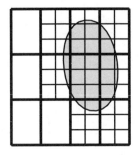

Figure 6.13.   With a two-level hierarchy, rays can skip empty space by traversing larger cells. A three-level hierarchy is used for most of the examples in
this chapter.

Multilevel grid

The other basic optimization we use is a multilevel spatial hierarchy to
accelerate the traversal of empty cells as is shown in Figure 6.13. Cells
are grouped into equal portions, and then a "macro-cell" is created which
contains the minimum and maximum data value for its children. This is a
common variant of standard ray-grid techniques [17] and is especially similar to previous multilevel grids [147, 157]. The use of minimum/maximum
caching has been shown to be useful [320, 321, 92]. The ray-iso-surface traversal algorithm examines the minimum and maximum at each macro-cell
before deciding whether to recursively examine a deeper level or to proceed
to the next cell. The typical complexity of this search will be $O(\sqrt[3]{n})$ for a
three-level hierarchy [147]. While the worst case complexity is still $O(n)$, it
is difficult to imagine an iso-surface occurring in practice approaching this
worst case. Using a deeper hierarchy can theoretically reduce the average
case complexity slightly, but also dramatically increases the storage cost
of intermediate levels. We have experimented with modifying the number of levels in the hierarchy and empirically determined that a tri-level
hierarchy (one top-level cell, two intermediate macro-cell levels, and the
data cells) is highly efficient. This optimum may be data-dependent and
is modifiable at program startup. Using a tri-level hierarchy, the storage
overhead is negligible ($< 0.5\%$ of the data size). The cell sizes used in the
hierarchy are independent of the brick sizes used for cache locality in the
first optimization.

Macro-cells can be indexed with the same approach as used for memory
bricking of the data values. However, in this case, there will be three table
look-ups for each macro-cell. This, combined with the significantly smaller

memory footprint of the macro-cells made the effect of bricking the macro-cells negligible.

6.2.3 Algorithms

This section describes three types of volume visualization that use ray tracing:

- Iso-surfacing on rectilinear grids.

- Iso-surfacing on unstructured meshes.

- Maximum-intensity projection on rectilinear grids.

The first two require an operation of the form: Find a specific scalar value along a ray. The third asks: What is the maximum value along a ray? All of these are searches that can benefit from the hierarchical data representations described in the previous section.

Rectilinear iso-surfacing

Our algorithm has three phases: traversing a ray through cells which do not contain an iso-surface, analytically computing the iso-surface when intersecting a voxel containing the iso-surface, shading the resulting intersection point. This process is repeated for each pixel on the screen. A benefit is that adding incremental features to the rendering has only incremental cost. For example, if one is visualizing multiple iso-surfaces with some of them rendered transparently, the correct compositing order is guaranteed since we traverse the volume in a front-to-back order along the rays. Additional shading techniques, such as shadows and specular reflection, can easily be incorporated for enhanced visual cues. Another benefit is the ability to exploit texture maps which are much larger than physical texture memory which is currently available up to 64 MB. However, newer architectures that use main memory for textures eliminate this issue.

For a regular volume, there is a one-to-one correspondence with the cells forming bricks and the voxels. This leads to a large branching factor for the shallow hierarchy which we have empirically found to yield the best results.

If we assume a regular volume with even grid point spacing arranged in a rectilinear array, then ray-isosurface intersection is straightforward. Analogous simple schemes exist for intersection of tetrahedral cells as described below.

To find an intersection (Figure 6.14), the ray $\vec{a} + t\vec{b}$ traverses cells in the volume checking each cell to see if its data range bounds an iso-value. If it

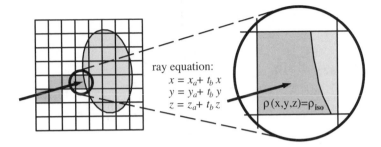

Figure 6.14.   The ray traverses each cell (left), and when a cell is encountered that has an iso-surface in it (right), an analytic ray-isosurface intersection computation is performed.

does, an analytic computation is performed to solve for the ray parameter t at the intersection with the iso-surface:

$$\rho(x_a + tx_b, y_a + ty_b, z_a + tz_b) - \rho_{\mathrm{iso}} = 0.$$

When approximating ρ with a tri-linear interpolation between discrete grid points, this equation will expand to a cubic polynomial in t. This cubic can then be solved in closed form to find the intersections of the ray with the iso-surface in that cell. We use the closed form solution for convenience since its stability and efficiency have not proven to be major issues for the data we have used in our tests. Only the roots of the polynomial which are contained in the cell are examined. There may be multiple roots, corresponding to multiple intersection points. In this case, the smallest t (closest to the eye) is used. There may also be no roots of the polynomial, in which case the ray misses the iso-surface in the cell. Note that using tri-linear interpolation directly will produce more complex iso-surfaces than is possible with a marching cubes algorithm. An example of this is shown in Figure 6.15 which illustrates case 4 from Lorensen and Cline's paper [180]. Techniques such as the Asymptotic Decider [210] could disambiguate such cases but they would still miss the correct topology due to the iso-surface interpolation scheme.

Unstructured iso-surfacing

For unstructured meshes, the same memory hierarchy is used as is used in the rectilinear case. However, we can control the resolution of the cell size at the finest level. We chose a resolution which uses approximately the same number of leaf nodes as there are tetrahedral elements. At the leaf nodes,

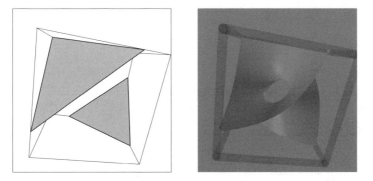

Figure 6.15. Left: The iso-surface from the marching cubes algorithm. Right: The iso-surface resulting from the true cubic behavior inside the cell.

a list of references to overlapping tetrahedra is stored (Figure 6.16). For efficiency, we store these lists as integer indices in an array of all tetrahedra.

Rays traverse the cell hierarchy in a manner identical to the rectilinear case. However, when a cell is detected that might contain an iso-surface for the current iso-value, each of the tetrahedra in that cell are tested for intersection. No connectivity information is used for the tetrahedra; instead, they are treated as independent items, just as in a traditional surface-based ray tracer.

The iso-surface for a tetrahedron is computed implicitly using barycentric coordinates. The intersection of the parameterized ray and the iso-plane is computed directly, using the implicit equations for the plane and the parametric equation for the ray. The intersection point is checked to

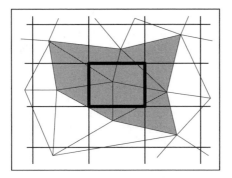

Figure 6.16. For a given leaf cell in the rectilinear grid, indices to the shaded elements of the unstructured mesh are stored.

see if it is still within the bounds of the tetrahedron by making sure the barycentric coordinates are all positive.

Maximum-intensity projection

The maximum-intensity projection (MIP) algorithm seeks the largest data value that intersects a particular ray. It utilizes the same shallow spatial hierarchy described above for iso-surface extraction. In addition, a priority queue is used to track the cells or macro-cells with the maximal values. For each ray, the priority queue is first initialized with a single top level macro-cell. The maximum data value for the dataset is used as the priority value for this entry in the priority queue. The algorithm repeatedly pulls the largest entry from the priority queue and breaks it into smaller (lower level) macro-cells. Each of these cells are inserted into the priority queue with the pre-computed maximum data value for that region of space. When the lowest-level cells are pulled from the priority queue, the algorithm traverses the segment of the ray which intersects the macro-cell. Bilinear interpolation is used at the intersection of the ray with cell faces since these are the extremal values of the ray-cell intersection in a linear interpolation scheme. For each data cell face which intersects the ray, a bilinear interpolation of the data values is computed, and the maximum of these values in stored again in the priority queue. Finally, when one of these data maximums appears at the head of the priority queue, the algorithm has found the maximum data value for the entire ray.

To reduce the average length of the priority queue, the algorithm performs a single tri-linear interpolation of the data at one point to establish a lower bound for the maximum value of the ray. Macro-cells and data-cells which do not exceed this lower-bound are not entered into the priority queue. To obtain this value, we perform the tri-linear interpolation using the t corresponding to the maximum value from whatever previous ray a particular processor has computed. Typically, this will be a value within the same block of pixels and exploits image-space coherence. If not, it still provides a bound on the maximum along the ray. If this t value is unavailable (due to program startup, or a ray missing the data volume), we choose the midpoint of the ray segment which intersects the data volume. This is a simple heuristic which improves the performance for many datasets.

Similar to the iso-surface extraction algorithm, the MIP algorithm uses the three-dimensional bricking memory layout for efficient cache utilization when traversing the data values. Since each processor will be using a different priority queue as it processes each ray, an efficient implementation of a priority queue which does not perform dynamic memory allocation is essential for performance of the algorithm.

6.2.4 Results

We applied ray tracing iso-surface extraction to interactively visualize the Visible Woman dataset. The Visible Woman dataset is available through the National Library of Medicine as part of its Visible Human Project [208]. We used the *Computed Tomography* (CT) data which was acquired in 1mm slices with varying in-slice resolution. This rectilinear data is composed of 1,734 slices of 512 x 512 images at 16 bits. The complete dataset is 910 MB. Rather than down-sample the data with a loss of resolution, we utilize the full resolution data in our experiments. As previously described, our algorithm has three phases: traversing a ray through cells which do not contain an iso-surface, analytically computing the iso-surface when intersecting a voxel containing the iso-surface, and shading the resulting intersection point.

Figure 6.17 shows a ray tracing for two iso-surface values. Figure 6.18 illustrates how shadows can improve the accuracy of our geometric perception. Figure 6.19 shows a transparent skin iso-surface over a bone iso-surface. Table 6.1 shows the percentage of time spent in each of these phases, as obtained through the cycle hardware counter in Silicon Graphics' Speedshop.[1] As can be seen, we achieve about 10 *Frames Per Second* (FPS) interactive rates while rendering the full, nearly 1 GB, dataset.

Table 6.2 shows the scalability of the algorithm from 1 to 128 processors. View 2 uses a zoomed-out viewpoint with approximately 75% pixel coverage whereas view 1 has nearly 100% pixel coverage. We chose to examine both cases since view 2 achieves higher frame rates. The higher frame rates cause lower parallel efficiency due to synchronization and load balancing. Of course, maximum interaction is obtained with 128 processors, but reasonable interaction can be achieved with fewer processors. If a smaller number of processors were available, one could reduce the image size in order to restore the interactive rates. Efficiencies are 91% and 80% for view 1 and 2, respectively, on 128 processors. The reduced efficiency

Iso-surface	Traversal	Intersec.	Shading	FPS
Skin ($\rho = 600.5$)	55%	22%	23%	7-15
Bone ($\rho = 1224.5$)	66%	21%	13%	6-15

Table 6.1. Data From Ray Tracing the Visible Woman. The *Frames Per Second* (FPS) gives the observed range for the interactively generated viewpoints on 64 CPUs.

---

[1]Speedshop is the vendor-provided performance analysis environment for the SGI IRIX operating system.

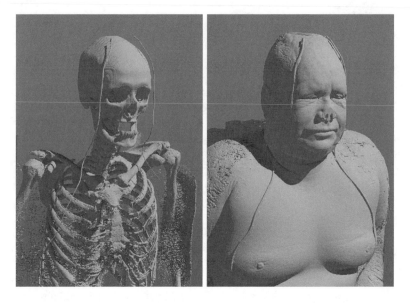

Figure 6.17.   Ray tracings of the bone and skin iso-surfaces of the Visible Woman. See also Color Plate 3.

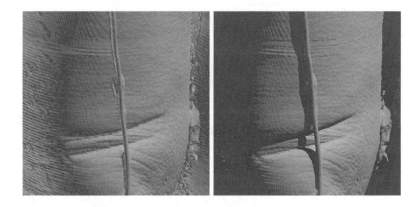

Figure 6.18. Ray tracing with and without shadows. See also Color Plate 2.

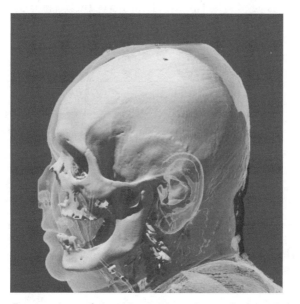

Figure 6.19. Ray tracings of the skin and bone iso-surfaces with transparency. See also Color Plate 4.

| | View 1 | | View 2 | |
# CPUs	FPS	Speed-up	FPS	Speed-up
1	0.18	1.0	0.39	1.0
2	0.36	2.0	0.79	2.0
4	0.72	4.0	1.58	4.1
8	1.44	8.0	3.16	8.1
12	2.17	12.1	4.73	12.1
16	2.89	16.1	6.31	16.2
24	4.33	24.1	9.47	24.3
32	5.55	30.8	11.34	29.1
48	8.50	47.2	16.96	43.5
64	10.40	57.8	22.14	56.8
96	16.10	89.4	33.34	85.5
128	20.49	113.8	39.98	102.5

Table 6.2. Scalability results for ray tracing the bone iso-surface in the visible human. A 512x512 image was generated using a single view of the bone iso-surface.

View	Initial	Bricking	Hierarchy+Bricking
Skin: front	1.41	1.27	0.53
Bone: front	2.35	2.07	0.52
Bone: close	3.61	3.52	0.76
Bone: from feet	26.1	5.8	0.62

Table 6.3. Times in seconds for optimizations for ray tracing the visible human. A 512x512 image was generated on 16 processors using a single view of an iso-surface.

with larger numbers of processors (> 64) can be explained by load imbalances and the time required to synchronize processors at the required frame rate. The efficiencies would be higher for a larger image.

Table 6.3 shows the improvements which were obtained through the data bricking and spatial hierarchy optimizations.

Using a ray tracing architecture, it is simple to map each iso-surface with an arbitrary texture map. The Visible Man dataset includes both CT data and photographic data. Using a texture mapping technique during the rendering phase allows us to add realism to the resultant iso-surface. The photographic cross section data which was acquired in 0.33mm slices, and can be registered with the CT data. This combined data can be used as a texture-mapped model to add realism to the resulting iso-surface. The size of the photographic dataset is approximately 13 GB which clearly is too large to fit into texture memory. When using texture mapping hardware, it is up to the user to implement intelligent texture memory management. This makes achieving effective texture performance nontrivial. In our implementation, we down-sampled this texture by a factor of 0.6 in two of the dimensions so that it occupied only 5.1 GB. The frame rates for this volume with and without shadows and texture are shown in Table 6.4. A sample image is shown in Figure 6.20. We can achieve interactive rates when applying the full resolution photographic cross sections to the full resolution CT data. We know of no other work which achieves these rates.

	Frame rate
No shadows, no texture	15.9
Shadows, no texture	8.7
No shadows, texture	12.6
Shadows, texture	7.5

Table 6.4. Frame rates for varying shadow and texture for the Visible Male dataset on 64 CPUs (FPS).

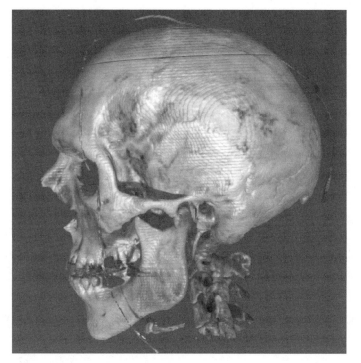

Figure 6.20. A three-dimensional texture applied to an iso-surface from the Visible Man dataset. See also Color Plate 4.

Figure 6.21 shows an iso-surface from an unstructured mesh made up of 1.08 million elements which contains adaptively refined tetrahedral elements. The heart and lungs shown are polygonal meshes that serve as landmarks. The rendering times for this data, rendered without the polygonal landmarks at 512 x 512-pixel resolution, is shown in Table 6.5. As would be expected, the frame rate decreases for structured data, but the method scales well. We make the number of lowest-level cells proportional to the number of tetrahedral elements, and the bottleneck is the intersection with individual tetrahedral elements. This dataset is composed of adaptively refined tetrahedra with volume differences of two orders of magnitude.

Figure 6.22 shows a maximum-intensity projection of the Visible Female dataset. This dataset runs in approximately 0.5 to 2 FPS on 16 processors. Using the "use last t" optimization saves approximately 15% of runtime. Generating such a frame rate using conventional graphics hardware would require approximately a 1.8 GPixel/second pixel fill rate and 900 Mbytes of texture memory.

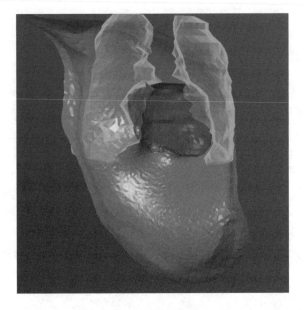

Figure 6.21.   Ray tracing of a 1.08 million element unstructured mesh from bio-electric field simulation. The heart and lungs are represented as landmark polygonal meshes and are not part of the iso-surface.

# CPUs	FPS	Speed-up
1	0.108	1.00
2	0.21	1.97
3	0.32	2.95
4	0.42	3.91
6	0.63	5.86
8	0.84	7.78
12	1.25	11.56
16	1.64	15.20
24	2.44	22.58
32	3.21	29.68
48	4.76	44.07
64	6.46	59.81
96	9.05	83.80
124	11.13	103.06

Table 6.5.   Data from ray tracing unstructured grids at 512 x 512 pixels on 1 to 124 processors. The adaptively refined dataset is from a bio-electric field problem.

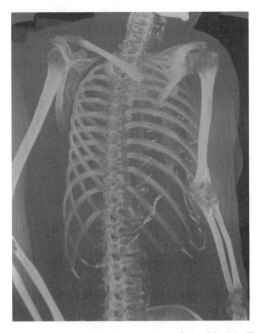

Figure 6.22. A maximum-intensity projection of the Visible Female dataset.

6.2.5   Discussion

We contrast the application of our algorithm to the explicit extraction of polygonal iso-surfaces from the Visible Woman data set. For the skin iso-surface, we generated 18,068,534 polygons. For the bone iso-surface, we generated 12,922,628 polygons. These numbers are consistent with those reported by Lorensen given that he was using a cropped version of the volume [179]. With this number of polygons, it would be challenging to achieve interactive rendering rates on conventional high-end graphics hardware. Our method can render a ray-traced iso-surface of this data at roughly ten frames per second using a 512 x 512 image on 64 processors. Table 6.6 shows the extraction time for the bone iso-surface using both NOISE [178] and marching cubes [180]. Note that because we are using static load balancing, these numbers would improve with a dynamic load balancing scheme. However, this would still not allow interactive modification of the iso-value while displaying the iso-surface. Although using a down-sampled or simplified detail volume would allow interaction at the cost of some resolution. Simplified, precomputed iso-surfaces could also yield interaction, but storage and precomputation time would be signifi-

# CPUs	NOISE build	NOISE extract	Marching cubes
1	4838	110	627
2	2109	81	324
4	1006	56	171
8	885	31	93
16	437	24	49
32	118	14	26
64	59	12	24

Table 6.6. Explicit bone iso-surface extraction times in seconds.

cant. Triangle stripping could improve display rates by up to a factor of three because iso-surface meshes are usually transform-bound. Note that we gain efficiency for both the extraction and rendering components by not explicitly extracting the geometry. Our algorithm is therefore not well-suited for applications that will use the geometry for nongraphics purposes.

The interactivity of our system allows exploration of both the data by interactively changing the iso-value or viewpoint. For example, one could view the entire skeleton and interactively zoom in and modify the iso-value to examine the detail in the toes, all at about 10 FPS. The variation in frame rate is shown in Figure 6.23.

Brady et al. [34] describe a system which allows, on a Pentium workstation with accelerated graphics, interactive navigation through the Visible Human data set. Their technique is two-fold: 1) combine frustum culling with intelligent paging from disk of the volume data; and 2) utilize a two-phase perspective volume rendering method which exploits coherence in adjacent frames. Their work differs from ours in that they are using incremental direct volume rendering while we are exploiting iso-surface or MIP rendering. This is evidenced by their incremental rendering times of about 2 seconds per frame for a 480 x 480 image. A full (nonincremental) rendering takes nearly 20 seconds using their technique. For a single CPU, our iso-surface rendering time is several seconds per frame (see Table 6.2) depending on viewpoint. While it is difficult to directly compare these techniques due to their differing application focus, our method allows for the entire data set to reside within the view frustum without severe performance penalties since we are exploiting parallelism.

The architecture of the parallel machine plays an important role in the success of this technique. Since any processor can randomly access the entire dataset, the dataset must be available to each processor. Nonetheless, there is fairly high locality in the dataset for any particular processor. As a result, a shared memory or distributed shared memory machine, such as

# processors	Frame rate /Speedup				
1	0.427 /1.00	0.304 /1.00	0.084 /1.00	0.155 /1.00	0.568 /1.00
2	0.84 /1.97	0.60 /1.98	0.17 /1.99	0.31 /2.00	1.13 /1.98
3	1.26 /2.94	0.89 /2.93	0.25 /2.95	0.46 /2.96	1.68 /2.96
4	1.67 /3.91	1.19 /3.92	0.33 /3.96	0.62 /3.97	2.24 /3.94
6	2.45 /5.73	1.76 /5.77	0.50 /5.97	0.93 /5.96	3.29 /5.80
8	3.20 /7.50	2.32 /7.61	0.67 /7.94	1.23 /7.93	4.36 /7.67
12	4.81 /11.26	3.44 /11.30	1.00 /11.89	1.84 /11.88	6.51 /11.47
16	6.38 /14.93	4.59 /15.08	1.33 /15.84	2.45 /15.80	8.64 /15.21
24	9.54 /22.33	6.84 /22.48	1.98 /23.54	3.65 /23.49	12.92 /22.76
32	12.65 /29.61	9.12 /29.96	2.63 /31.38	4.88 /31.47	17.09 /30.10
48	18.85 /44.13	13.52 /44.39	3.92 /46.72	7.30 /47.02	25.27 /44.50
64	24.73 /57.90	17.72 /58.19	5.18 /61.78	9.64 /62.14	32.25 /56.80
96	35.38 /82.82	25.04 /82.23	7.67 /91.38	14.28 /92.02	45.50 /80.14
124	43.06 /100.79	30.28 /99.45	9.73 /115.88	18.17 /117.08	57.70 /101.63

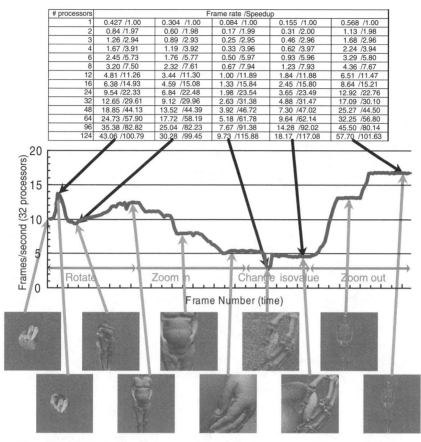

Figure 6.23. Variation in frame rate as the viewpoint and iso-value change.

the SGI Origin 2000, is ideally suited for this application. The load balancing mechanism also requires a fine-grained, low-latency communication mechanism for synchronizing work assignments and returning completed image tiles. With an attached Infinite Reality graphics engine, we can display images at high frame rates without network bottlenecks. We feel that implementing a similar technique on a distributed memory machine would be extraordinarily challenging, and would probably not achieve the same rates without duplicating the dataset on each processor.

We have shown that ray tracing can be a practical alternative to explicit iso-surface extraction for very large datasets. As data sets get larger, and as general purpose processing hardware becomes more powerful, we expect this to become a very attractive method for visualizing large scale scalar data both in terms of speed and rendering accuracy.

6.3   Ray Tracing for Terrain Visualization

Techniques similar to the volume visualization methods described above have applications in other domains as well. We have applied the memory bricking and shallow hierarchy to the traversal of height-field data for terrain visualization. Figure 6.24 shows example images from this system.

The traversal mechanism is very similar. A ray traversal is performed on a coarse resolution height-field that contains the range of heights for the underlying height-field data. When the ray intersects this bound, the algorithm recurses and examines the next finer resolution data. When we reach the finest resolution containing the actual data samples, we perform an intersection of the bilinear patch with the ray. In practice, a hierarchy of three to five levels has given optimal performance.

One particular advantage of ray tracing for this application is the ability to handle extremely large datasets with a sublinear performance degradation. Figure 6.25 shows the performance of the system on two large fractal terrains. The first is a height-field of resolution 8193 x 8193 (approximately 67 million quadrilaterals/bilinear patches), and the second is a height-field of resolution of 16385 x 16385 (approximately 268 million quadrilaterals/bilinear patches). Although the larger dataset is approximately four times as large, the frame rate decreases by only a few percent.

Figure 6.24.   Terrain visualization using the real-time ray tracer. This application achieves over 22 frames per second at 1024x1024 resolution on 256 processors. See also Color Plate 5.

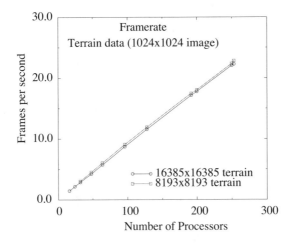

Figure 6.25. Performance of terrain visualization using two different terrain resolutions. Notice that even though the data is increased by a factor of 4, the performance decreases only slightly (3%).

This system has been utilized to visualize terrains of up to 17 billion quadrilaterals/bilinear patches.

6.4 Conclusions

We have demonstrated a parallel interactive ray tracing system. The system works on small to large shared-memory machines which are becoming increasingly available. The resulting system utilizes the inherent scaling properties of ray tracing in order to achieve interactive visualization of extremely large datasets and models.

7 | Interactive Ray Tracing on PCs

Philipp Slusallek

For almost two decades, researchers have argued that ray tracing will eventually become faster than the rasterization technique that completely dominates today's graphics hardware. However, this has not yet happened. Ray tracing is still almost exclusively being used for off-line rendering of photorealistic images. It is commonly believed that ray tracing is simply too costly to ever challenge rasterization-based algorithms for interactive use.

In this chapter, we show that interactive ray tracing is indeed possible on commodity PCs. We first present a *highly optimized ray tracer* that improves performance by more than an order of magnitude compared to currently available ray tracers. The new algorithm makes better use of computational resources such as caches and SIMD instructions, and better exploits image and object space coherence. Secondly, we show that this software implementation can challenge and even *outperform high-end graphics hardware* in interactive rendering performance for complex environments.

We also demonstrate how ray tracing can be made to work efficiently on a cluster of commodity PCs without shared memory. The same techniques that increased the speed of the ray tracing algorithms also helps to hide latency and reduce bandwidth for network communication in a distributed setup. Finally we show that the distributed ray tracing algorithm can handle highly complex models of tens of millions of polygons while still achieving interactive frame rates of up to ten frames per second on a small cluster of seven PCs.

7.1 Introduction

Ray tracing is famous for its ability to generate high-quality images, but is also well-known for long rendering times due to its high computational cost. This cost is due to the need to traverse a scene with many rays, intersecting each with the geometric objects, shading the visible surface samples, and finally sending the resulting pixels to the screen. Due to the cost associated with ray tracing the technique is viewed almost exclusively as an off-line technique for cases where image quality matters more than rendering speed. Only recently has interactive ray tracing been shown on large supercomputers, as presented in Chapter 6.

Ray tracing offers a considerable number of advantages over other rendering techniques. Basic ray casting, i.e., sampling the scene with individual rays, is a fundamental task that is the core of a large number of algorithms not only in computer graphics. Other disciplines use the same approach, for example, to simulate propagation of radio waves [65], neutron transport [5], and diffusion [228].

But even if we only concentrate on rendering applications, ray tracing offers a number of benefits over rasterization-based algorithms that dominate todays algorithms targeted at interactive three-dimensional graphics:

Occlusion culling and logarithmic complexity. Ray tracing enables efficient rendering of complex scenes through its built-in occlusion culling, as well as its logarithmic complexity in the number of scene primitives.

Flexibility. Ray tracing allows us to trace individual or unstructured groups of rays. This provides for efficient computation of just the required information, e.g., for sampling narrow glossy highlights; computing reflection without first computing a complete reflection map; for filling holes in image-based rendering; and importance sampling of illumination [310].

Efficient shading. With ray tracing, samples are only shaded after visibility has been determined. Given the trend towards more and more realistic and complex shading, this avoids redundant computations for invisible geometry.

Simpler shader programming. Programming shaders that create special lighting and appearance effects has been at the core of realistic rendering. While writing shaders (e.g., for the RenderMan standard [12]) is fairly straightforward, adopting these shaders to be used in the pipeline model of rasterization has been very difficult [224]. Since ray tracing is not limited to this pipeline model, it can make direct use of shaders [101, 275].

Correctness. By default, ray tracing computes physically correct reflections, refractions, and shading. This is contrary to rasterization, where approximations are the only option, and it is difficult to even come close to realistic effects. Every effect requires another rendering "trick" to fit it into the rendering pipeline, which makes it hard to combine different effects efficiently. Of course, ray tracing can make use of the same approximations such as reflection or environment maps.

Parallel scalability. Ray tracing is known for being "trivially parallel" as long as a high enough bandwidth to the scene data base is provided. Given the exponential growth of available hardware resources, ray tracing should be better able to utilize it than rasterization, which has been difficult to scale efficiently [68].

Coherence. The key to efficient rendering is coherence. Due to the low coherence between rays in traditional recursive ray tracing implementations, performance has been rather low. However, as we show in this chapter, ray tracing still offers considerable coherence that can be exploited to speed up rendering to interactive levels even on a standard PCs.

It is due to this long list of advantages that we believe ray tracing is an interesting alternative even in the field of interactive three-dimensional graphics. The challenge is to improve the speed of ray tracing to the extent that it can compete with rasterization-based algorithms as used in all three-dimensional graphics cards today. It seems that some hardware support will eventually be needed to reach this goal. However in this chapter we concentrate on a pure software implementation.

While it is certainly true that ray tracing has a high computational cost, its low performance on today's computers is also strongly affected by the structure of the basic algorithm. It is well-known that the recursive sampling of ray trees neither fits with the pipeline execution model of modern CPUs, or with the use of caching to hide low bandwidth and high latency when accessing main memory [222].

Many research projects have addressed the topic of speeding up ray tracing [76, 91] by various methods such as better acceleration structures, faster intersection algorithms, parallel computation [229, 41], approximate computations [23], etc. This research has resulted in a large number of improvements to the basic algorithm and is documented in the ray tracing literature of the past decades.

In our implementation we build on this previous work and combine it in a novel and optimized way, paying particular attention to caching, pipelining, and SIMD issues to achieve more than an order of magnitude improvement in ray tracing speed compared to other well-known ray tracers

Figure 7.1. Interactive ray tracing: The office, conference and Soda Hall models contain roughly 40 k, 680 k, and 8 million triangles, respectively. Using our software ray tracing implementation on a single PC (Dual Pentium-III, 800 MHz, 256 MB) at a resolution of 512^2 pixels, these scenes render at roughly 3.6, 3.2, and 1.6 frames per second using both processors.

such as Rayshade or POV-Ray. As a result, we are able achieve interactive frame rates even on standard PCs (see Figure 7.1).

7.1.1   Previous Work

Even though ray tracing dates to 1968 [13, 152, 318, 55], its use for interactive applications is relatively new. Recently Muus and Parker et al. [205, 206, 219, 220, 221] demonstrated that interactive frame rates could be achieved with a full-featured ray tracer on a large shared-memory supercomputer. Parker's work is presented in more detail in Chapter 6.

Their implementation offers all the usual ray tracing features, including parametric surfaces and volume objects, but is carefully optimized for cache performance and parallel execution in a nonuniform memory access environment. They have proven that ray tracing scales well in the number of processors in a shared memory environment, and that even complex scenes of several hundred thousand primitives could be rendered at almost real-time frame rates.

Pharr et al. [226] have shown that coherence can be exploited by completely reordering the ray tracing computation. They were able to render scenes with up to 46 million triangles. Their approach actively manages the scene geometry and rays through priority queues, instead of relying on simple caching as we do. However, their system was far from real time.

Hardware implementations of ray tracing are available [290], but are currently limited to accelerating off-line rendering applications, and do not target interactive frame rates. However, several research projects have recently started looking at hardware implementations for ray tracing. One such approach is presented in Chapter 9.

7.2 An Optimized Ray Tracing Implementation

The following four sections describe our implementation of a highly optimized ray tracing engine that outperforms currently available ray tracers by more than an order of magnitude (see Section 7.6).

We start with an overview of general optimization techniques and how they have been applied to our ray tracing engine, such as reducing code complexity, optimizing cache usage, reducing memory bandwidth, and prefetching data. A similar discussion of optimization issues—although on a higher level—can also be found in [276]. In the following sections we then discuss the use of SIMD instructions (commonly available on microprocessors today) to efficiently implement the main three components of a ray tracer: ray intersection computations, scene traversal, and shading.

7.2.1 Code Complexity

A modern processor has several hardware features such as branch prediction, instruction reordering, speculative execution, and other techniques [117, 133] in order to avoid expensive pipeline stalls. However, the success of these hardware approaches is fairly limited and depends to a large degree on the complexity of the input program code. Therefore, we prefer simple code that contains few conditionals, and organize it such that it can execute in tight inner loops. Such code is easier to maintain and can be well-optimized by the programmer as well as the compiler. These optimizations become more and more important as processor pipelines get longer, and the gap between processor speed, memory bandwidth, and latency opens further.

For traversing the scene, we use an axis-aligned BSP tree [285]. Its ray traversal algorithm is shorter and simpler compared to octrees, *Bounding Volume Hierarchies* (BVH), and grids. Even though most easily formulated recursively, it can be transformed to a compact iterative algorithm [154].

We have also chosen to support only triangles as geometric primitives. As a result, the inner loop that performs intersection computations on lists of objects does not have to branch to a different function for each type of primitive. By limiting the code to triangles we lose little flexibility as all surface geometry can be converted. The same approach is being used by most commercial ray tracers (according to information from their developers). While the number of primitives increases, this is more than compensated for by the better performance of the ray tracing engine.

For shading, we need the flexibility to support arbitrary shaders and thus allow for dynamic loading of shaders. Advanced shading features like multitexturing, bump mapping or reflections could be added without changing the core of the ray tracing engine. Flexibility in the shading stage is much less problematic than for intersection computations, as it is only called once for each shading ray, while we perform an average of 40–50 traversal steps and 5–10 intersection tests per ray.

7.2.2 Caching

Contrary to general opinion, our careful profiling reveals that a ray tracer is not bound by CPU speed, but is in fact bandwidth-bound by access to main memory. Shooting rays incoherently (as done in many global illumination algorithms) results in almost random memory accesses and bad cache performance. On current PC systems, bandwidth to main memory is typically up to 8–10 times smaller than to primary caches. Even more importantly, memory latency increases by similar factors as we go down the memory hierarchy. Memory issues become even more important for BSP traversal, where the ratio of computation to memory bandwidth is lower, thus making it more difficult to hide memory latencies.

Since data transfer between memory and cache is always performed in entire cache lines of 32 bytes, the *effective* cost when accessing memory is not directly related to the number of bytes read, but rather the number of cache line transfers. As a general result, we need to carefully lay out data such that it makes best use of the available caches, and design our algorithms so that we can efficiently hide latency by prefetching data such that it is already available in a cache when it is needed for computations.

We carefully align data to cache lines: This minimizes the additional bandwidth required to load two cache lines simply because some data happen to straddle a cache line boundary. However, there are often trade-offs. For instance, our triangle data structure requires about 37 bytes. By padding it to 48 bytes we trade off memory efficiency and cache line alignment.

We keep data together if and only if it is used together: e.g., only data necessary for a triangle intersection test (plane equation, etc.) are stored in our geometry structures, while data that is only necessary for shading (such as vertex colors and normals, shader parameters, etc.) is stored separately. Because we intersect on average several triangles before we find an intersection, we avoid loading data that will not be used.

Given the increased latency of accessing main memory, it becomes necessary to load data into the cache before it will be used in computations and not fetch it on demand. This way the memory latency can be completely hidden. Most of todays microprocessors offer instructions to explicitly prefetch data into certain caches. However, in order to use prefetching effectively, algorithms must be simple enough that it is easy to predict which data will be needed in the near future.

7.2.3 Coherence through Packets of Rays

The most important aspect of accelerating ray tracing is to exploit coherence as far as possible. Our main approach is to exploit coherence of primary and shadow rays by traversing, intersecting, and shading *packets of rays* in parallel. Using this approach, we can reduce the computation time of the algorithm by using SIMD instructions on multiple rays in parallel; reduce memory bandwidth by requesting data only once per packet; and increase cache utilization at the same time.

7.2.4 Parallelism through SIMD Extensions

Several modern microprocessor architectures offer SIMD extensions, which allow them to execute the same floating point instructions in parallel on several (typically two to four) data values, thereby yielding a significant speed-up for floating-point intensive applications, including three-dimensional graphics. Such extensions also contain instructions for explicit cache management like prefetching. Examples of such extensions are Intel's SSE [134], AMD's 3dNow! [4], and IBM/Motorola's AltiVec [200].

In the following three sections we discuss in more detail how coherent computations with packets of rays and SIMD operations can be used together to speed up the core of a ray tracer—namely triangle intersection, ray traversal, and shading.

7.3 Ray Triangle Intersection Computation

Optimal ray triangle intersection code has long been an active field of research in computer graphics, and has led to a large variety of algorithms, e.g., Moeller-Trumbore [196], Glassner [89], Badouel [19], Pluecker [69], and many others [195]. Before discussing SIMD implementations, we first describe the triangle test used in our C code without using assembler or SSE optimizations. This forms the base for our later discussions.

7.3.1 Optimized Barycentric Coordinate Test

The triangle test used in our implementation is a modification of Badouel's algorithm [19]. It first computes the distance to the point where the ray pierces the plane defined by the triangle, and checks that distance for validity. Only if the distance falls within the interval where the ray is searching for intersections, is the actual hit point H computed and projected onto one of the x-y, x-z, or y-z planes.

In order to prevent numerical instabilities, the plane with the largest angle to the triangle normal is chosen for the projection. This results in three cases for the intersection computation. The barycentric coordinates of the hit point H can then be calculated efficiently in two dimensions. Based on the signs of the barycentric coordinates, it can be decided whether the ray pierces the triangle or not.

For the implementation, we need only the properly scaled two-dimensional edge equations for two of the triangle edges, together with the plane equation for the distance calculation and a tag to mark the projection axis. By preprocessing and proper scaling of these equations, this information can be expressed by nine floats plus the projection flag. For cache alignment purposes, we pad that data to a total of 48 bytes.

7.3.2 Evaluating Instruction Level Parallelism

The implementation of the barycentric triangle test requires only few instructions, and offers almost no potential for exploiting instruction-level parallelism. Optimizing the algorithms using the Intel SSE extensions results in a speed-up of about 20%. It is clear that this speed-up is not sufficient for interactive ray tracing.

As another alternative, we also evaluated a SIMD implementation of the Pluecker triangle test (see [266, 69]). Due to a linear control flow and a somewhat higher computational cost, this triangle test offers much more potential for instruction-level parallelism. The SSE implementation is straightforward and showed good speed-ups compared to a C implementation of the Pluecker test. However, due to its higher computational cost, and particularly, its higher bandwidth requirements, the instruction-parallel Pluecker code is effectively not significantly faster than the original barycentric C code (see Table 7.1).

7.3.3 SIMD Barycentric Coordinate Test

The speed-up achieved with the instruction-level parallel implementations is too small to be of significant impact on rendering time. We therefore went back to the already fast barycentric code, and used data parallelism by performing four-ray triangle tests in parallel: This means to either intersect one ray with four triangles, or to intersect a packet of four rays with a single triangle. The latter case requires a change to the overall architecture of the ray tracing engine.

Intersecting one ray with four triangles would require us to always have four triangles available for intersection to achieve optimal performance. However, voxels of acceleration data structures should contain only few triangles on average (typically 2–3). More importantly, triangles fall into three different projection cases, each with slightly different code, which precludes the use of this approach.

In contrast, it is much simpler to bundle four rays together and intersect them with a single triangle. However, this approach requires us to always have a bundle of four rays available, which requires a completely new scene-traversal algorithm, which we discuss in the next section.

The data-parallel implementation of the intersection code corresponds almost exactly to the original algorithm, and is straightforward to implement in SSE. A potential source of overhead is that even though some rays may have terminated early, all four rays have to be intersected with a triangle. Information on which of the four rays is still active is kept in a bit-field, which can be used to mask out invalid rays in a conditional move instruction when the hit point information is stored. In practice, we obtain almost perfect parallelism for primary rays, and to a somewhat lesser degree for shadow rays.

In our implementation, the SSE code for intersecting four rays with a single triangle requires 86–163 CPU cycles. Amortizing this cost over the four rays results in only 22 to 41 cycles per intersection, which corresponds to roughly 20 to 36 million ray triangle intersection tests per second on a 800 MHz Pentium-III CPU. The observed speed-up is 3.5–3.7 (see Table 7.1), and is close to the maximum expected value.

It is interesting to compare the performance of this code over a number of different CPUs. We have seen a perfectly linear speed-up of the code from

	Bary. C code	Pluecker SSE	Bary. SSE 4-1	Speed-up
min	78	77	22	3.5
max	148	123	41	3.7

Table 7.1. Cost (in CPU cycles) for the different intersection algorithms. 41 cycles correspond to roughly 20 million intersections per second on a 800 MHz Pentium-III. Measured by using the internal Pentium-III CPU counters. The performance scales linearly with the clock speed of the processors (tested up to up to 1.5 GHz on an Intel Pentium 4) indicating nondependencies on external memory speed.

the original tests on Pentium-III with 800 MHz to the different architecture of Pentium 4 with up to 1.5 GHz. This indicates that there have been few architectural changes with respect to the SSE units and that we execute almost exclusively with the CPU caches, as there is no dependency on access to slow external memory.

7.4 BSP Traversal

Even before accelerating the triangle test, traversal of the acceleration structure was typically 2–3 times as costly as ray triangle intersection. As the SSE triangle intersection code reduces the intersection cost by more than a factor of three, traversal is the limiting factor in our ray tracing engine. Since our SSE intersection procedure requires us to always have four rays available this suggests a data-parallel traversal of a bundle of at least four rays.

A wide variety of ray tracing acceleration schemes have been developed, such as octrees, general BSP trees, axis-aligned BSP trees, regular and hierarchical grids, ray classification, bounding volume hierarchies, and even hybrids of several of these methods. See [271, 89] for an overview and further references. Our main reason for using a BSP tree in our implementation is the simplicity of the traversal code. Traversing a node is based on only two binary decisions, one for each child, which can efficiently be done for several rays in parallel using SSE. If any ray traverses a child, the entire packet will traverse it in parallel.

This is in contrast to algorithms like octrees or hierarchical grids, where each of the rays might take a different decision of which voxel to traverse next. Keeping track of these states is nontrivial, and was judged to be too complicated to be implemented efficiently. Bounding volume hierarchies have a traversal algorithm that comes close in simplicity to BSP trees. However, BVHs do not implicitly order their child nodes, which is another reason for our choice of axis-aligned BSP trees.

7.4.1 Traversal Algorithm

Before describing our algorithm for traversal of four rays in parallel, we first take a look at the traversal of a single ray, as presented in [285]. In each traversal step, we maintain the *current ray segment* [*near*, *far*], which is the part of the ray that actually intersects the current voxel. This ray segment is first initialized to $[0, \infty)$, then clipped to the bounding box of the scene, and is updated incrementally during traversal. For each traversed

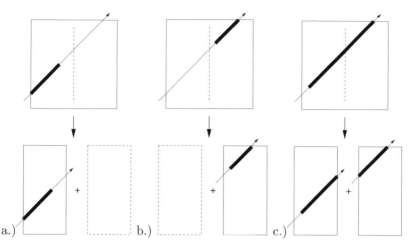

Figure 7.2. The three traversal cases in a BSP tree: (a) a ray segment completely in front of the splitting plane; (b) completely behind it; (c) intersecting both sides.

node, we calculate the distance d to the splitting plane defined by that node, and compare that distance to the current ray segment.

If the ray segment lies completely on one side of the splitting plane ($far < d$ or $d < near$), we immediately proceed to the corresponding child voxel. Otherwise, we traverse both children in turn, with the ray segment clipped to the respective child voxel. This avoids problems for rays that are forced by another ray from the same packet to traverse a voxel they would not otherwise traverse. For those rays, the ray segment will be the empty interval. It is also important to properly update the ray segments after traversal from child nodes, if intersections did occur there. See also Figure 7.2.

The algorithm for tracing four different rays is essentially the same: For each node, we use SSE operations to compute the four distances to the splitting plane and to compare these to the four respective ray segments, all in parallel. If all rays require traversal of the same child, we immediately proceed to that child without having to change the ray segments. Otherwise, we traverse both children, with each ray segment updated to $[near, min(far, d)]$ for the closer, and $[max(near, d), far]$ for the distant child.

When traversing several rays at the same time, the order of traversal can be ambiguous, since different rays might require a different traversal order. Since the order is based only on the sign of the respective direction, this can happen only if the signs of the four direction vectors do not match—which is a rare case if we assume the rays to be coherent. Additionally, it can be shown that no two rays with the same origin can require different traversal orders, which completely resolves this problem for pinhole cameras and point light sources. If rays are allowed to start in different locations, a straightforward solution is to only allow rays with matching direction signs in the same packet, tracing the few special cases separately.

7.4.2   Memory Layout for Better Caching

As mentioned above, the ratio of computation to the amount of accessed memory is very low for scene traversal. This requires us to carefully design the data structure for efficient caching and prefetching. Memory bandwidths and cache utilization have been improved with a compact, unified node layout. For inner nodes in a BSP node we have to store:

- Pointers to the two child nodes. By implicitly storing the right child immediately after the left child, this can be represented with a single pointer.

- A flag on whether it is a leaf node or the type of inner node (splitting axis), which requires two bits.

- The split coordinate, which is the coordinate where the plane intersects its perpendicular axis.

For best performance we use one float for the split coordinate and squeeze the two flag bits into the two low order bits of the pointer, which results in 8 bytes per node or four nodes per cache line. By aligning the two children of a node on half a cache line, we make sure that both children are fetched together since they are likely to be traversed together. The additional computations to extract these two bits from the pointer are negligible, as the traversal code performs very few computations compared to the amount of memory it accesses.

For leaf nodes the pointer addresses the list of objects, and the other fields can be used to store the number of objects in the list. Using the same pointer for both node types allows us to reduce memory latencies and pipeline stalls by prefetching, as the next data (either a node or the list of triangles) can be prefetched before even processing the current node. Even though prefetching can only be used with SSE cache control operations, the reduced bandwidth and improved cache utilization also affect the pure C implementation.

	2×2	4×4	8×8	256^2	1024^2
Shirley 6	1.4%	4.4%	11.8%	5.8%	1.4%
MGF office	2.6%	8.2%	21.6%	10.4%	2.6%
MGF conf.	3.2%	10.6%	28.2%	12.2%	3.2%

Table 7.2. Overhead (measured in number of additional node traversals) of tracing entire packets of rays at an image resolution of 1024^2 in the first three columns. As expected, overhead increases with scene complexity (800, 34 k, and 280 k triangles, respectively) and packet size, but is tolerable for small packet sizes. The two columns on the right show the overhead for 2×2 packets at different screen resolutions.

7.4.3 Traversal Overhead

Traversing packets of rays through the acceleration structure generates some overhead: Even if only a single ray requires traversal of a subtree or intersection with a triangle, the operation is always performed on all four rays. Our experiments have shown that this overhead is relatively small as long as the rays are coherent. Table 7.2 shows the overhead in additional BSP node traversals for different packet sizes.

The overhead is in the order of a few percent for 2×2 packets of rays, but goes up for larger packets. On the other hand, increasing screen resolution also increases coherence between primary rays. Most important is the fact that the effective memory bandwidth has been reduced essentially by a factor of four through the new SIMD traversal and intersection algorithms, as triangles and BSP nodes need not be loaded separately for each ray. This effect is particularly important for ray traversal as the computation-to-bandwidth ratio in relatively low.

Of course, one could operate on even larger packets of rays to enhance the effect: however, our results show that we are running almost completely within the processor caches even with only four rays. We have therefore chosen not to use more rays per ray packet, as it would additionally increase the overhead due to redundant traversal and intersection computations.

7.5 SIMD Phong Shading

As data-parallel intersection and traversal has proven to be very effective, the same benefits should also apply for shading computations. Similar to the traversal and intersection code, we can shade four rays in parallel. Since the four hit points may have different materials, data has to be rearranged. Although this setup results in some overhead, the following shading operations can be very efficiently implemented in SSE, yielding almost perfect utilization of the SSE units.

Light sources are processed in turn. For each light source, we first determine its visibility by shooting shadow rays by using the traversal and intersection algorithms described above. If a light source is visible from at least one pixel, its contribution to all four hit points is computed in parallel. This contribution is then added to the visible hit points only, by masking out shadowed points. This procedure computes information that may get discarded later and thus has some overhead. However, this happens only in the case that the visibility of a light source is different between the set of hit points. For a coherent set of rays this rarely happens.

Special care has to be taken when shooting the shadow rays. Since shadow rays typically make up the largest fraction of all rays in a ray tracer, shooting them with the fast SSE traversal code is desirable. Yet this is only efficient as long as the rays are coherent, which is not automatically true for shadow rays, since all shadow rays from a single hit point typically go in very different directions. However, coherent primary rays are also likely to hit similar locations in the scene, yielding coherent shadow rays if they are all connected to a single light source. In the worst case (i.e., if the rays

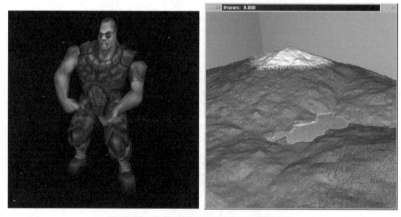

Scene	Flat	Textured
Quake	4.22 fps	3.85 fps
Terrain	1.05 fps	0.96 fps

Figure 7.3. Texturing comes rather cheaply: Even for a complex scene with incoherent texture access, texturing only slightly reduces the frame rate, rendering even a scene of one million triangles interactively. Image resolution is 512^2. See also Color Plate 6.

are incoherent), performance degrades to the performance achieved when tracing each ray individually.

Implementing shading in SSE operations gives a speed-up of 2 to 2.5 as compared to the C implementation on top of the speed-up obtained by the general optimizations discussed above. Texturing has shown to be relatively cheap. Even an unoptimized version has reduced frame rates by less than 10 percent, as can be seen in Figure 7.3. This cost could probably be reduced even more due to a large potential for prefetching and parallel computations that we currently do not utilize. As shading typically makes up for less than 10 percent of total rendering time in our examples, more complex shading operations could easily be added without a major performance hit.

We have implemented a shader interface that allows us to dynamically load shading code into the ray tracer. Using this interface we can easily switch between different shaders.

7.6 Performance of the Ray Tracing Engine

Now that all the parts of a full ray tracer are together, we can evaluate the overall performance of our system (*Real-Time Ray Tracer* (RTRT)). We start by evaluating the performance for primary rays, as this will allow us to compare the ray tracing algorithm directly to rasterization-based algorithms that do not directly support shadows, reflection, and refraction effects.

On a single 800 MHz Pentium-III, we achieve a rendering performance from about 200,000 to almost 1.5 million primary rays per second for the SSE version of our algorithm. If we compare the performance of this version to our optimized C code we see an overall speed-up between 1.8 and 2.5. This is a bit less than that for ray triangle intersection, but is due to the worse ratio of memory accesses to computations in the traversal stage and the strict sequential traversal order that does not allow for better prefetching.

7.6.1 Comparison to Other Ray Tracers

In order to evaluate the performance of our optimized ray tracing engine we tested it against a number of freely available ray tracers, including POV-Ray [225] and Rayshade [162]. We have chosen the set of test scenes so that they span a wide range regarding the number of triangles and the overall occlusion within the scene. Unfortunately, both other systems failed to

	Tris	Rayshade	POV-Ray	RTRT
MGF office	40k	29	22.9	2.1
MGF conf.	256k	36.1	29.6	2.3
MGF theater	680k	56.0	57.2	3.6
Library	907k	72.1	50.5	3.4
Soda Floor 5	2.5m	OOM	OOM	2.9
Soda Hall	8m	OOM	OOM	4.5

Table 7.3.   Performance comparison of our ray tracer against Rayshade and POV-Ray. All rendering times are given in microseconds per primary ray including all rendering operations for the same view of each scene at a resolution of 512^2 (OOM = out of memory).

render some of the more complex test scenes due to memory limitations even with 1 GB of main memory.

The numbers of the performance comparison for the case of primary rays are given in Table 7.3, clearly demonstrating that our new ray tracing implementation improves performance consistently by a factor between 11 and 15 (!) compared to both POV-Ray and Rayshade. The numbers show that paying careful attention to caching and coherence issues can have a tremendous effect on the overall performance, even for such well-analyzed algorithms as ray tracing.

The numbers also seem to indicate that the performance gap widens slightly for more complex scenes, which indicates that the caching effect is even more pronounced in these cases. Our implementation was tested on a machine with only 256 MB of main memory, while we had to use a machine with 1 GB of memory for the other ray tracers.

Some comments on these results are necessary. Rayshade is using a uniform grid as an acceleration structure and we had to determine the best grid size for each scene by trial and error. No such manual optimizations were necessary for POV-Ray and our implementation. Both other ray tracers also seem to make inefficient use of memory and require significantly more memory to even load the scene. They were never designed to handle scenes of this size.

Of course, POV-Ray and Rayshade offer considerably more features than our ray tracing engine. However, most of these features are related to shading and could easily be added to our engine using dynamically loadable shaders. This would have little effect on the performance of the core engine unless those features are used. The other ray tracers are also not limited to use only triangles to represent objects: however, we believe this is actually an advantage for us and is partly the reason for the good performance.

Finally, these other ray tracers are not written with highest optimization in mind but are more targeted towards a large feature set. We believe that we will be able to show in the future that these two goals do not contradict each other.

7.6.2 Reflection and Shadow Rays

A ray tracing engine would not be complete if it could not handle shadows, reflection, and refraction. These effects also challenge our overall approach as ray coherence can be considerably less for shadow or even reflection rays. Although the handling of secondary rays is not yet fully optimized in our implementation, we were surprised by the good performance we observed even for extreme cases of reflectivity.

We have tested a walkthrough of the MGF conference scene, where most of the materials are at least slightly reflective. Even the doors, wall panels with fixtures, and metal frames of the seats generate reflection rays; often resulting in multiple reflections, which is clearly visible when zooming towards the fire extinguisher, which reflects the entire scene (see Figure 7.4).

Sphere-like objects such as the fire extinguisher are potential hot spots in scenes like these, as they can trigger large numbers of reflection rays that sample the entire visible environment and are likely to have an adverse ef-

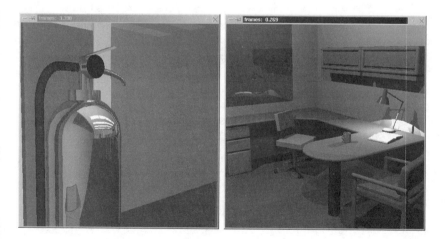

Figure 7.4.   Frames from a video showing the entire conference room being reflected in the fire extinguisher (left). Performance only drops slightly even when a large fraction of the scene is reflective. The office has been rendered with many reflective materials (window, lamp, mug, and others) and three point light sources. See also Color Plate 7.

fect on caching. It is interesting to see that the effect is hardly noticeable as long as these objects cover only moderate parts of the image. In this case, only a few rays are reflected almost randomly into the environment. Those rays potentially sample the entire scene but our acceleration structure successfully limits the data being accessed to only a few BSP cells and triangles along the paths of those few rays. As a result, the impact on performance remains low.

Performance degrades significantly only if zooming in on a reflective object such that it fills the field of view. In this case, almost all visible geometry will actually be sampled, and caching will no longer be effective for large scenes. However, this is an unavoidable consequence of dealing with a working set much larger than the cache (our largest scenes occupy close to 2 GB of memory but usually render fine with 256 MB of main memory).

An example image rendered with reflections and shadows can be seen on the right in Figure 7.4. Many objects are reflective and generate reflection rays. Also, three shadow rays are sent for each intersection. The performance is mainly influenced by the number of shadow rays.

7.6.3   Comparison with Rasterization Hardware

We started this chapter with the claim made by researchers in the past that ray tracing would eventually become faster than rasterization hardware. However, it was unclear at which point that crossover would happen, if at all. With the ray tracing system described above we are now in a position to answer these questions: We have already reached the crossover point and can now even outperform rasterization hardware with a software ray tracer—at least for complex scenes and moderate screen resolutions.

For this demonstration, we compared the performance of our ray tracing implementation with the rendering performance of the OpenGL-based hardware. In order to get the highest possible performance on this hardware we chose to render the scenes with SGI Performer [254], which is well-known for its highly optimized rendering engine that takes advantage of most available hardware resources including multiprocessing on our multiprocessor machines. We have used the default parameters of Performer when importing the scene data via the NFF format and while rendering. The 32-bit version of Performer that we used was unable to handle the largest scene (Soda Hall) because it ran out of memory. We used simple constant shading in all cases.

The rasterization measurements of our experiments were conducted on three different machines in order to get a representative sample of todays hardware performance. On our PCs (dual Pentium-III, 800 MHz, 256 MB), we used an Nvidia GeForce II GTS graphics card running under Linux.

Scene	Tris	Octane	Onyx	PC	RTRT
MGF office	40k	>24	> 36	12.7	1.8
MGF conf.	256k	>5	> 10	5.4	1.6
MGF theater	680k	0.4	6–12	1.5	1.1
Library	907k	1.5	4	1.6	1.1
Soda Floor	2.5m	0.5	1.5	0.6	1.5
Soda Hall	8m	OOM	OOM	OOM	0.8

Table 7.4. OpenGL rendering performance in frames per second with SGI Performer on three different graphics hardware platforms compared with our software ray tracer at a resolution of 512^2 pixels on a dual processor PC. The ray tracer uses only a single processor, while SGI Performer actually uses all available.

Additionally, we used an SGI Octane (300 MHz R12k, 4 GB) with the V8 graphics subsystem as well as a SGI Onyx-3 graphics supercomputer (8x 400 MHz R12k, 8 GB) with InfiniteReality3 graphics and four raster managers. The results are shown in Table 7.4.

The results clearly show that the software ray tracer already outperforms the best hardware rasterization engines for scenes with a complexity of roughly 1 million triangles or more, and is already competitive for scenes of about half the size. The ray tracing numbers can be scaled easily by adding more processors—simply enabling the second CPU on our machines doubles our RTRT numbers given in Table 7.4.

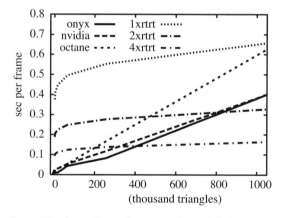

Figure 7.5. Logarithmic scaling of ray tracing with input complexity. We also show the linear scaling of different rasterization hardware and compare the performance to ray tracing on one, two, and four CPUs. The test scenes were obtained by subsampling high resolution terrain from Figure 7.3 with more than one million triangles. Other scenes show even better results due to more occlusion.

In order to visualize the scaling behavior of rasterization and ray tracing-based renderers, we used the large terrain scene shown in Figure 7.3 and subsampled the geometry. The results are shown in Figure 7.5. Even though SGI Performer uses a number of techniques to reduce rendering times, we see the typical linear scaling of rasterization. Even occlusion culling would not help in this kind of scene. Ray tracing benefits from the fact that each ray visits roughly a constant number of triangles but needs to traverse a BSP tree with logarithmically increasing depth. Ray tracing also subsamples the geometry for the higher resolution terrain, as the number of pixels is less than the number of triangles.

For scenes with low complexity, rasterization hardware benefits from the large initial cost per ray for traversal and intersection required by a ray tracer. However, we believe that for these cases there is still room for performance improvements. The large initial cost per ray also favors rasterization for higher image resolutions. However, this effect is linear in the number of pixels and can be compensated by adding more processors, for instance in the form of a distributed ray tracer.

7.7   Interactive Ray Tracing on PC Clusters

So far we have concentrated on simple ray tracing with primary rays only. As we add special ray tracing effects such as shadows, reflections, or even global illumination, we are confronted with the need to trace an increasing number of rays. Due to the "embarrassingly parallel" nature of ray tracing the results achievable on a single processor scale well with the use of multiple processors as long as they all get the necessary bandwidth to the scene database.

Both the system realized by Muuss, and the Utah system have proven that this is easily realized for shared-memory multiprocessor supercomputer systems (see [204, 206, 222] as well as Chapter 6). In this case, all processors have the same high-speed access to the single scene database. However, on commodity PCs shared-memory is not available, which has made large distributed ray tracing systems difficult to implement efficiently in the past.

In addition to achieving high performance ray tracing through parallelization, we also target the handling of very complex scenes. Because ray tracing can easily be run in a mode that loads data on demand as a ray traverses the scene, it becomes feasible to render huge data sets as long as the data accessed by a single frame remains small enough.

Fortunately, there are a large number of applications that fall into this category. Examples include large engineering applications (e.g., construction of whole airplanes, cars, or power plants), visualization of large data

sets such as urban environments, realistic rendering with detailed displacement maps, and many more. Scenes often contain tens of millions of triangles that cannot be handled interactively by today's graphics hardware.

Splitting the scene into small pieces is laborious if at any point in time
only a small fraction is accessible. Another approach is to approximate
the complex model with fewer polygons. In the car industry several man
months are usually spent on remodeling a car with a low polygon count in
order to visualize it in a Virtual Reality environment.

For testing high performance through distributed rendering, as well as
the handling of large data sets, we have chosen a well-known reference
model, which has been used for similar purposes before by Aliaga et al. [6].
This "UNC power plant" model contains 12.5 million individual triangles
(see Figure 7.6).

We have chosen this model since it has already been used to demonstrate
interactive walkthroughs using rasterization hardware [6]. However, this
approach required excessive preprocessing that was estimated to take up

Figure 7.6.   Four copies of the UNC power plant reference model with a total of
50 million triangles. In this view, a large fraction of the geometry is visible. At
640 x 480 pixels, the frame rate is 3.4 fps using seven networked dual Pentium-III
PCs. See also Color Plate 10.

to three weeks for the entire power plant model. Advanced preprocessing algorithms were required in order to reduce the number of polygons that had to be rendered per frame. The techniques included textured depth-meshes, triangle decimation, level-of-detail rendering, and occlusion culling.

Ray tracing can render the same scene without any of these advanced, but still only semiautomatic, techniques. It only requires simple spatial indexing of the scene database. For stress testing the ray tracing algorithm, we also created a larger model by replicating the power plant four times, generating a model with 50 million triangles total (see Figure 7.6).

7.7.1 Overview

We use the classic setup for distributed ray tracing with a single master machine responsible for display and scheduling together with many working clients that trace, intersect, and shade rays (see Chapter 3).

The idea is to use our already fast ray tracing engine, replicate it across a number of machines, and keep them busy all the time. If successful, we would obtain a very simple, highly efficient, and scalable distributed ray tracer. All clients would essentially execute the exact same highly optimized ray tracing algorithm as a stand alone machine. The key issue here is to intervene only if the basic algorithm stops due to missing scene data. We must then fetch the data as quickly as possible, and keep the ray tracer busy tracing other rays in order to hide the latency of the data transfer.

Another cause of idle time of a client is load imbalances. A client might have to wait for other clients that have not yet finished their processing before starting a new frame. We solve all these issues with a novel approach that exploits coherence using the same basic ideas as described above but on a coarser level:

- *Explicit management of the scene cache.* In a preprocessing step, a high-level BSP tree is built while adaptively subdividing the scene into small, self-contained voxels. Since preprocessing is only based on the spatial location of primitives, it is simple and relatively fast. Each voxel contains the complete intersection and shading data for all of its triangles, as well as a low-level BSP for this voxel. The complete preprocessed scene is stored only once on a scene master server and all clients request voxels on demand. Each client explicitly manages a local cache of voxels.

- *Latency hiding.* By reordering the computations, we hide some of the latencies involved in demand loading of scene data across the network by continuing computations on other rays while waiting for missing data to arrive. This approach can easily be extended by trying to prefetch data for future frames based on rays coarsely sampling a predicted new view.

- *Load balancing.* We use the usual task queue approach based on image tiles for load balancing. Instead of randomly assigning image tiles to clients, we try to assign tiles to clients that have traced similar rays in previous frames, thus improving cache hit rates and lowering network bandwidth. Reordering of computations and buffering of work tiles is used to bridge communication and voxel loading latencies, thus achieving almost perfect CPU utilization.

7.8 Distributed Data Management

In the original implementation of coherent ray tracing, as described above [307], we created a single binary file containing the model. We used the main memory layout for storing data in the file such that we could directly map the entire file into our address space using the Unix memory mapping facilities. However this is no longer possible with huge models that generate files larger than the supported address space.

On the other hand, we did not want to replicate the entire model of several GB on each of our client machines. This means that demand loading of mapped data would be performed across the network with its low bandwidth and large latency. While this approach is technically possible and simple to implement by memory mapping a file across an NFS-mounted file system, it drastically reduces performance for large models. For each access to missing data, the whole ray tracing process on the client is stalled while the operating system reads a single memory page across the network.

Even only a few milliseconds of stalling due to network latency are very costly for an interactive ray tracer: Because tracing a single ray costs roughly one thousand cycles [307], we would lose several thousand rays for each network access. Instead, we would like to suspend work on only those rays that require access to missing data. The client can then continue working on other rays while the missing data is being fetched asynchronously.

7.8.1 Explicit Data Management

Instead of relying on the operating system, we had to explicitly manage the scene cache ourselves. For this purpose we decompose the models into small voxels. Each voxel is self-contained and has its own local BSP tree.

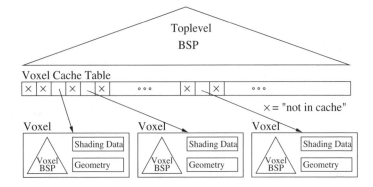

Figure 7.7. The data structure used to organize the model data. Voxels are the smallest entity for caching purposes. Their average compressed size is roughly 75 KB.

In addition, all voxels are organized in a high-level BSP tree starting from the root node of the entire model (see Figure 7.7).

This high-level BSP tree is used both for accelerating ray traversal and for the cache index structure. The leaf nodes of the high-level BSP tree contain additional flags indicating whether the particular voxel is in the cache or not.

If a missing voxel is accessed by a ray during traversal of the high-level BSP tree, reordering of computations if performed: The current ray is suspended and an asynchronous loader thread is notified about the missing voxel. Once the data of the voxel has been loaded into memory by the loader thread, the ray tracing thread is notified, which resumes tracing of rays waiting for this voxel. During asynchronous loading, ray tracing can continue on all nonsuspended rays currently being processed by the client. More latency could still be hidden by deferring shading operations until all rays are stalled or a complete tile has been traced. We use a simple *Least-Recently-Used* (LRU) strategy to manage a fixed size geometry cache.

The time to load a voxel is strongly dominated by the time to transfer a voxel over the network. To reduce the volume of transferred data, we use compression. For compression, we use the LZO compression library [216], which allows fast and efficient (de)compression of voxels. Though this compression is more optimized towards speed, its compression ratio is approximately 3:1 for our voxel data. Decompression performance is significantly higher than the network bandwidth, taking at most a few hundred microseconds, thus making the decompression cost negligible compared to the transmission time even for compressed voxels.

7.8.2 Preprocessing

The total size of a single copy of our reference power plant model is roughly 2.5 GB after preprocessing, including the BSP trees and all triangle and shading data. Due to this large data size, an out-of-core algorithm is required to spatially sort and decompose the initial model.

This algorithm needs to read the entire data set once in order to determine the bounding box. It then recursively determines the best splitting plane for the current BSP node, and sorts all triangles into the two child nodes. Triangles that span both nodes are replicated. Note that the adaptive decomposition is able to subdivide the model finely in highly populated areas (see Figure 7.8), and generates large voxels for empty spaces.

Once the size of a BSP node is below a given threshold we create a voxel and store it in a file that contains all its data (triangles, BSP, shading data, etc.). At this stage, each node is a separate file on disk in a special format that is suitable for streaming the data through the preprocessing programs.

The cost of preprocessing algorithms has a complexity of $O(n \log n)$ in the model size. Preprocessing is mainly I/O bound, as the computation per triangle is minimal. We are currently using a serial implementation, where each step in the recursive decomposition is a separate invocation of a single program. The resulting files are all located on a single machine acting as the model server.

7.9 Load Balancing

The efficiency of distributed/parallel rendering depends to a large degree on the amount of parallelism that can be extracted from the algorithm (see

Figure 7.8.   Two images showing the structure of the high-level BSP tree by color coding geometry to each voxel in the image at the bottom. Voxels are relatively large for the walls but become really small in regions with lots of details. See also Color Plate 8.

Figure 7.9. Two complex views of the power plant. Both still render at about 8 to 10 frames per second. See also Color Plate 9.

Chapter 3). We are using demand driven load balancing by subdividing the image into tiles of a fixed size (usually 32 x 32 pixels). As the rendering time for different tiles can vary significantly (e.g., the large variations in model complexity in Figures 7.6 and 7.9), we must distribute the load evenly across all client CPUs. This has to be done dynamically, as frequent camera changes during an interactive walkthrough make static load balancing inefficient.

We employ the usual dynamic load balancing approach where the display server distributes tiles on demand to clients. The tiles are taken from a pool of yet unassigned tiles, but care is taken to maintain good cache locality in the clients. Currently, the scheduler tries to give clients tiles they have rendered before in order to efficiently reuse the data in their geometry caches. This approach is effective for small camera movements but fails to make good use of caches for larger movements.

7.10   Implementation

Our current setup uses two servers—one for display and one for storing and distributing the preprocessed models. Both machines are connected via Gigabit Ethernet to a Gigabit switch. These fast links help in avoiding network bottlenecks. In particular, we require a high bandwidth connection for the display server in order to deal with the pixel data at higher resolutions and frame rates. The bottleneck for the model data could be avoided by distributing it over a set of machines.

For our experiments we have used seven dual P-III 800–866 MHz machines as ray tracing clients. These clients are normal desktop machines in our lab but were mostly unused while the tests were performed. The client machines are connected to a 100 Mbit FastEthernet switch that has a Gigabit uplink to the model and display server.

We have tested our setup with the power plant model from UNC [6] to allow for a direct comparison with previous work. This also provides for a comparison of algorithms based on rasterization versus ray tracing. The power plant test model consists of roughly 12.5 million triangles mostly distributed over the main building that is 80 meters high and has a floor plan of 40 x 50 meters (Figure 7.6).

Preprocessing, including conversion from the original PLY-files into our format as well as voxel decomposition, took roughly 2.5 hours with our unoptimized, sequential implementation. This already is significantly faster than the preprocessing required for [6]: This approach required 17 hours for a partial preprocessing that only allowed for interactive movements in a small fraction of the overall model. Their preprocessing time for the whole model was estimated to take three weeks [6]. We estimate that once parallel preprocessing is fully implemented, our preprocessing time could be reduced to less than an hour.

7.11 Results

Figure 7.10 gives a compact summary of our overall results. It shows the frame rate achieved by our system as well as the amount of geometry fetched over the course of a walk through the model. The total time of the walkthrough is 92 seconds using all seven clients. Note that we only trace primary rays for this test in order to allow direct comparison with the results from [6]. We only show the results of a single walk through, as they closely match those from other tests.

With seven dual CPU machines, we achieve an almost constant frame rate of 3–5 fps (Figure 7.10). However, all numbers are computed with plain C++ code. We have currently disabled the optimized SIMD version of our ray tracing engine because it had not yet been converted to use the new two-level BSP tree. Our latest experiments with the updated SSE version of the ray tracer have indeed shown the expected speedup by a factor of two and increased the frame rate to roughly 8–10 fps, which is about the same frame rate achieved in [6]. Note that we still render the original model with all details and not a simplified version of it.

Figure 7.8 visualizes the BSP structure that is built by our preprocessing algorithm. The voxel size decreases significantly for areas that have more geometric detail.

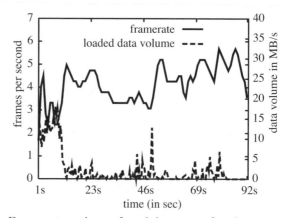

Figure 7.10. Frame rate and transferred data rate after decompression during a walkthrough heading from the outside to the inside of the power plant building. The frame rate is relatively constant around 4–5 fps unless large amounts of data are transferred (as in the beginning where the whole building is visible). The frame rates have been measured without the SIMD optimizations. The newest version includes SSE optimization and runs about twice as fast at about 8–10 fps.

In order to test some of the advanced features of ray tracing, we added a distant light source to the model and made some of the geometry reflective (see Figure 7.11). Of course, we see a drop in performance due to additional rays being traced for shadows and reflections. However, the drop is mostly proportional to the number of traced rays, and shows little effect due to the reduced coherence of the highly diverging rays that are reflected off the large pipe in the front, as well as all the tiny pipes in the background.

We also tested the scalability of our implementation by using one to seven clients for rendering exactly the same frames as in the recorded walk-through used for the tests above and measured the total runtime. The experiment was performed twice—once with empty client caches and once again with the caches filled by the previous run. The difference between the two would show network bottlenecks and any latencies that could not be hidden. As expected, we achieved almost perfect scalability with filled caches (see Figure 7.12), but the graph also shows some network contention effects with four clients and we start saturating the network link to the model server beyond six or seven clients. Note that perfect scalability is larger than seven because of variations in CPU clock rates.

Because we did not have more clients available, scalability could not be tested beyond seven clients. However, our results show that performance is mainly limited by the network bandwidth to the model server, which

Figure 7.11. Shadow and reflection effects created with ray tracing using one light source. The performance drops roughly proportional to the number of total rays traced, but the size of the working set increases. Note the reflections off all the small pipes near the ground. Diffuse case: 1 ray per pixel, 4.9 fps, with shadow and reflection (multiple of 2 rays): 1.4 fps. See also Color Plate 10.

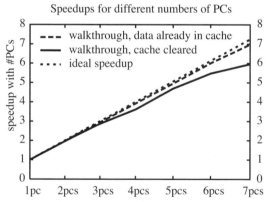

Figure 7.12. Our implementation shows almost perfect scalability for one to seven dual CPU PCs if the caches are already filled. With empty caches, we see some network contention effects with four clients, but scalability is still very good. Beyond six or seven clients we start saturating the network link to the model server.

suggests that a distributed model data base would allow scalability well beyond the above numbers.

Figure 7.9 provides some other views of the power plant, showing some of the complexity hidden in this test model.

For a stress test of our system, we have placed four copies of the power plant model next to each other, resulting in a total model complexity of roughly 50 million triangles (see Figure 7.6), as explained previously. Preprocessing time increases as expected, but the frame rates remain almost identical compared to the single model. Essentially, the depth of the higher-level BSP tree was increased by two, which has hardly any effect on inside views.

However, for outside views we suffer somewhat from the relatively large voxel granularity, which results in an increased working set and corresponding longer loading times that can no longer be completely hidden during camera movements. When standing still, the frame rates quickly approach the numbers measured for a single copy of the model.

7.12   Conclusions

The computational cost of ray tracing is known to be logarithmic on average, in terms of the number of triangles. In contrast, the rendering cost using a rasterization pipeline appears linear in the number of triangles, even with optimizations such as view frustum culling. Therefore, a break-even point in model complexity was expected, above which ray tracing would be preferred over rasterization hardware. We have shown that ray tracing has already passed this break-even point, even if comparing a software implementation of ray tracing with highly optimized rasterization hardware.

Our ray tracing implementation exploits a number of novel techniques that make it more than an order of magnitude faster compared to other ray tracers. These techniques include the following:

- Careful attention is paid to exploiting coherence in the ray tracing algorithms in order to achieve good caching behavior such that the algorithms can essentially run within the first and second level data caches of the processors. Our experiments indicate that this results in a speed-up of roughly half an order of magnitude.

- Several strategies have been investigated for utilizing SIMD instructions found on commodity processors. In our implementation, we used Intel's SSE extensions on a Pentium-III processor. A significant speed-up can only be obtained by reordering the ray tracing algorithm so that rays are traced in packets of four coherent rays. This reduces the memory bandwidth by a factor of four and gives an additional speed-up of about two.

We have compared rendering speeds of our ray tracing implementation on an 800 MHz Pentium-III based Linux PC with those obtained on a high-end commercial visualization package (SGI Performer) using three different graphics accelerators (NVidia GeForce II GTS, SGI Octane with V8 graphics board, SGI Onyx-3 with InfiniteReality 3 graphics).

Experiments with a variety of models (Table 7.4), suggest that the break-even point is reached for models of the order of magnitude of 1 million triangles at a screen resolution of 512×512. For larger models, ray tracing wins.

Ray tracing also offers a significant number of benefits over rasterization based approaches. Most important is its flexibility to efficiently trace single or small groups of rays.

However, both ray tracing and the Z-buffer algorithm have a cost component that is linear in the number of screen pixels. In hardware implementations of the rasterization pipeline, this cost component is almost negligible, while it is a major factor for software ray tracing (see constant offset in Figure 7.12). The break-even point therefore shifts towards more complex models, proportional to screen resolution. Moreover, more sophisticated occlusion culling algorithms currently being developed may reduce the cost of a rasterization pipeline to be sublinear.

On the other hand, by paying careful attention to caching issues, ray tracing is not limited by memory bandwidth, but runs within the processor caches and performance scales linearly with the image resolution, the speed of the processor, and with the number of processors.

We were able to maintain the high performance and the scalability of the ray tracing algorithm for a distributed implementation using a small cluster of commodity PCs. On a higher level, we exploited essentially the same caching, reordering, and prefetching techniques that made the stand-alone ray tracer so fast. Our distributed implementation is very simple, highly efficient, and should scale to significantly more clients than we could test if the current network bottleneck at the scene server is solved as proposed earlier.

We also tested our ray tracing implementation on a 4-CPU shared-memory system with no performance degradation. We estimate a gradual bottleneck due to limited memory bandwidth only at around 6–8 CPUs with current PC technology. The memory bandwidth of current PC systems is rather poor and measures at about 200 MB per second to main memory. A hardware implementation would allow for memory bandwidth in the order of several GB per second—enough to keep a large number of parallel ray tracing units busy. This would allow for real-time visualization for a very wide range of models. We are actively investigating suitable hardware architectures for this approach.

We conclude that, unlike widely believed, the ray tracing algorithm is a viable alternative for a Z-buffer based rasterization pipeline especially when it comes to visualizing large polygonal datasets.

Acknowledgements

We would like to thank Anselmo Lastra for providing the power plant model, and Philippe Bekaert for helping out with models and the hardware comparisons. Many thanks go to Markus Wagner, Andreas Pomi, and Georg Demme, who have helped with the system infrastructure. The research in parallel rendering was supported by a donation from AMD.

8

Toshiaki Kato

The "Kilauea" Massively Parallel Ray Tracer

By taking advantage of the increased performance and decreased cost of personal computers today, and by making use of the massive computational resources gained from parallelizing such machines, we can create images of complexity and quality that have never before been possible. However, overcoming inherent difficulties of parallel processing requires various techniques and efforts, especially when developing a parallel renderer. In this chapter, we describe our rendering research and development project, and explain the different approaches we attempted in order to solve these problems. This information should be useful when constructing a similar system in a similar environment. We hope this chapter will serve as an aid to correctly understand the possibilities of parallel processing on PC clusters, and make parallel processing a more realistic and feasible option for attacking new challenges.

8.1 What Is the Kilauea Project?

The Kilauea project, currently taking place within the R&D division of Square USA's Honolulu Studio, is a project intended to develop a renderer that is completely different from the currently available renderers focusing on local illumination. The renderer is called Kilauea, named after an active volcano on the island of Hawaii. Kilauea is clearly distinguished from other renderers mainly due to two of its ultimate goals:

1. **Global illumination.** Demand for global illumination is increasing day by day. However, the amount of computation required for global illumination is much greater than that of a local illumination renderer.

2. **Support for extremely complex scenes.** The scenes being rendered are also becoming more complex, and rendering performance

naturally decreases as scene complexity increases. In addition to increasing the required computation power, complex scenes also severely impact the memory requirements.

These two goals are fundamentally the ultimate goals of any photorealistic renderer, and achieving them clearly requires many innovative ideas different from the conventional methodology. With these goals in mind, the Kilauea project was started in order to create a testbed designed for conducting many technical experiments. Currently, the development team consists of six members. Code is entirely in C++ and the total source code size is more than 700,000 lines, including test programs for all components.

8.2   Basic Idea

The global illumination solution of Kilauea is based on the photon map method (including final gathering), instead of other approaches such as radiosity. As a result, ray tracing was absolutely necessary as the underlying algorithm in the rendering engine. These decisions are based on the fact that the ability to render effects such as motion blur and global illumination from both specular and diffuse components was mandatory. The photon map method allows a straightforward implementation of these requirements. As for the computational power, the Kilauea project's basic premise is to use parallel processing as a solution.

Parallel processing is also the Kilauea project's solution to the problem with the large memory space required for rendering complex scenes. In other words, if a single machine cannot store the entire scene data, it is distributed among two machines. If two is not enough, then three. In this manner, the entire scene is contained in memory using as many machines as necessary.

The Kilauea project took this approach because storing the entire scene data in memory is much more convenient from a ray tracing standpoint. The ray tracing optimization in terms of memory usage is implemented based on the assumption that the scene is distributed among multiple machines. Being able to render the same scene with less memory is important, since this means that more complex scenes can be rendered with the same amount of memory. Furthermore, the ability to distribute the scene across multiple machines is more important in eliminating the constraint of maximum memory size of one machine. Because Kilauea can distribute the scene data across multiple machines, there is no software upper limit to the supported scene size, despite using a simple ray tracing algorithm. The upper limit is determined by the sum of the memories of the multiple machines to which Kilauea has access. It provides an environment where users can just throw in more machines as they become necessary.

The initial goals of this project implied that we had to seriously devote ourselves to parallel processing. We ended up using two different levels of parallel processing. One is a shared memory type of parallel processing within a multi-CPU environment, and another is message passing-based parallel processing over a cluster of PCs. The current implementation of Kilauea is able to perform almost all of its computation in parallel.

8.3 System Design

8.3.1 Hardware Environment

Kilauea is implemented with two levels of parallel processing. The first is parallel processing within a multi-CPU machine, and the other is parallel processing across multiple machines. These mechanisms are designed with a hardware environment in mind that incorporates multi-CPU Linux machines, a PC cluster, and 100Base-T connections via a switching hub.

PCs have become extremely inexpensive recently. A 1 GHz dual processor machine with 1 gigabyte of RAM can be bought for around $1,500 (as of January 2001) if building from parts. Prices are dropping every month, so the same $1,500 will buy a much more powerful machine today. The machines run Linux, and individual machines are connected with 100Base-T connection via a switching hub (Figure 8.1).

Figure 8.2 shows the photographs of the render farm that the Kilauea team uses for experimentation. We are using machines ranging from Pen-

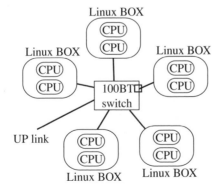

Figure 8.1. Kilauea hardware environment.

Figure 8.2. Left: Kilauea render farm A. Right: Kilauea render farm B.

tium III 450MHz single CPU with 512 megabyte of RAM, to a Pentium III 1 GHz dual CPU with 1 gigabyte of RAM in our experiments. In total, we have 37 machines with 60 CPUs available for development.

8.3.2 Pthreads

Building a dual-CPU Linux box is very inexpensive these days. To take advantage of this, Kilauea is designed for parallel processing on a multi-CPU machine. The Pthread library is used in the actual implementation. Parallel processing within a single machine is a shared memory implementation.

8.3.3 Message Passing

Pthreads allows parallel processing implementation within a single machine, but some form of data transmission will be necessary for parallel processing between individual machines. We have considered several methodologies, with the emphasis on adopting the most widely accepted standard. We considered PVM and others at one time, but since the general trend seemed to be converging towards MPI [1], we adopted MPI without hesitation and started developing with it. We actually ended up doing a

---

[1] http://www-unix.mcs.anl.gov/mpi/

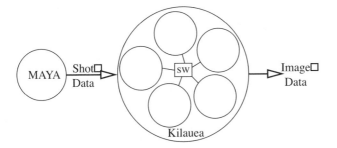

Figure 8.3. Maya and Kilauea interaction.

variety of experimentation on the MPI implementation itself. This will be described in detail in Section 8.6.2.

8.3.4   Front-End Process

Kilauea is a rendering engine. It has no GUI of any sort. It also has no features for animation or model data creation. Normally Maya[2] serves as a front-end to Kilauea. Animation, modeling, and other scene data are created/edited within Maya. This information is then sent to Kilauea for rendering. Kilauea is a collection of processes running on multiple machines, but to a Maya user, it appears to be a single external rendering process (Figure 8.3).

A file format called ShotData is used for sending data from Maya to Kilauea. This is the equivalent of rib files for RenderMan. All the scene data is converted to this ShotData format before being sent to Kilauea. The important features of the ShotData format include multiple frame storage, incremental data storage, and a binary format. Details on the ShotData format are discussed in Section 8.4.

8.3.5   Launching Kilauea

Kilauea is a system in which processes running on multiple machines communicate with each other in order to generate the final image. The boot process of Kilauea needs to be controlled between multiple machines in some standardized way. Kilauea daemons manage this by residing in Kilauea server machines and launching processes as requested, while communicating with each other (Figure 8.4). This Kilauea daemon also handles

---

[2]http://www.aliaswavefront.com/

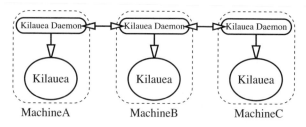

Figure 8.4. Booting Kilauea through Kilauea daemon.

the termination of the Kilauea processes and plays a role in the fail-safe mechanism. The fail-safe mechanism is discussed further in Section 8.6.9.

8.3.6   Single Executable Binary

Kilauea runs across multiple machines, but the executable binary which runs on all machines is exactly the same. One of the benefits in doing so is the simplicity of maintenance in freezing a specific version of the binary by just copying a single file.

8.3.7   Multiframe Rendering

The Kilauea system is designed to render multiple frames at a time. This design has the advantage of reducing the time required to construct the data for the next frame by loading only the changes between the current frame and the next. For example, the scene construction time is greatly reduced if a very complex background scene is read in once and shared among multiple frames, rather than reading it in every frame. This becomes more advantageous as the amount and the complexity of static data in the animation increase.

Not having to reread data is even more useful when recomputing the same scene. Consider the situation where the user is experimenting with the shading parameter of some object's surface. Kilauea only needs to receive the modified shading parameter from outside (from Maya, for example) and immediately restart a rendering. In this case, all the geometry data in the scene can be reused, reducing the time required for communication and rendering preprocessing to almost zero. To take advantage of these traits, Kilauea is designed to stay resident as a process until it is explicitly shut down from outside.

8.3.8   Global Illumination Renderer

Kilauea has the following remarkable characteristics derived from its design as a global illumination renderer.

Parallel ray tracer.   Kilauea generates images by performing ray tracing in parallel. Kilauea executes two types of parallel processing depending on the scene size. If the scene data fits completely within a single Kilauea process, each process will contain a complete copy of the scene. In this case, parallelizing ray tracing is very simple. If the scene is too large to fit within a single Kilauea process, then multiple Kilauea processes are used to store the entire scene. Ray tracing is not so straightforward in this case. This will be discussed in detail in Section 8.5. Currently, Kilauea does not perform optimizations such as the ones specific to primary rays from the screen space. This is because the time spent on primary ray computation is only a very small percentage of the global illumination rendering. This type of optimization is one of the planned enhancements in the future.

Antialiasing.   Aliasing problems in screen space and along the time axis are all handled by supersampling. Because Kilauea uses ray tracing as its underlying algorithm, supersampling is the simplest method that can handle all cases.

Global illumination.   Kilauea renders global illumination with the combination of final gathering and photon maps [142, 144]. This allows global illumination effects such as caustics and color bleeding. The photon map method also has other benefits such as the relative ease of implementing motion blur with acceptable quality.

Volume shading.   Kilauea allows the user to define a volume container within the scene. When a ray enters the volume container, ray marching is used to perform volume rendering. Global illumination may be performed on volume elements by using volume photon maps [143].

Subsurface scattering.   Kilauea supports subsurface scattering, which is necessary for special types of shading like a human skin. Subsurface scattering also uses volume photon maps [63].

8.4   The ShotData File Format

Kilauea uses the ShotData format to receive data from a front-end such
as Maya.

Binary data format.   ShotData is a binary data format. This makes the file
size smaller and increases the read/write performance of the file. ShotData
absorbs the byte order issues between different CPU architectures, allowing
Intel Linux executables to read data from an SGI.

Version-free file format.   File format specifications frequently undergo
changes or additions as a result of debugging or the addition of new features. This is an annoying problem in an ordinary binary format. Because
ShotData has a version-free data structure, it can adapt to these changes
in a very flexible way.

ShotData is composed of various commands. For example, a command
specifying a vertex is then followed by the values of the (x, y, z) coordinates.
Every element of the scene can be described by these combinations of commands. There are two main problems with this approach alone. The first
problem occurs when the number of parameters for a command needs to be
modified for some reason. In this case, new executables must still be able
to read any previous data that was previously dumped. The other problem
occurs when adding new commands. Especially because this is a binary
format, special mechanisms are necessary for skipping commands that the
parser does not know about. To solve these problems, ShotData embeds
information about commands and their parameter within itself. The first
problem is circumvented by not allowing a previously defined command to
be redefined. Whenever a command's parameters need to be changed,
a new command is added instead and new data is dumped using the
new command. Because command definition information is written
into the ShotData, the second problem can be dealt with by skipping.
The parser looks at the command definition block and parse only the
commands which it can understand. By using this mechanism, ShotData
that was dumped a long time ago can be read by the latest Kilauea
executable and vise versa.

Multiframe format.   ShotData contains data spanning multiple frames.
ShotData can just contain a single frame, but generally an animation sequence of some length is recorded. The advantage of using this will become
clearer after introducing the incremental data format described below.

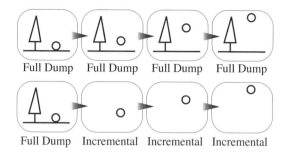

Figure 8.5. ShotData construction by incremental algorithm.

Incremental data format. When recording multiple frames, ShotData defines the scene as incremental data between the frames. The current frame contains only the difference from the previous frame. Since the first frame obviously does not have a previous frame, it contains full information for the frame. When there is an object in the scene that neither moves nor deforms, the description for that object is only contained in the first frame. This tremendously compresses the data size for a sequence of animation.

A frame that contains all the data for the frame is referred to as a full dump frame. Thus the first frame of ShotData is always a full dump frame. Because ShotData takes the form of incremental data, it can very efficiently handle the reading of frames in a sequence. When rendering only a specific frame in the middle of a sequence, having to read the incremental data from the top to the target frame is inefficient. Such requests probably will happen frequently. In order to handle these situations, full dump frames can be embedded at user-specified intervals (Figure 8.5).

Frame boundaries. Inside Kilauea, frame numbers take on a real number value, and frame N actually specifies a range between frame $N - 0.5$ and

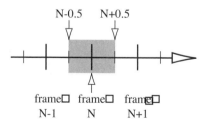

Figure 8.6. Frame number within Kilauea.

frame $N + 0.5$. All frame numbers in ShotData are specified in this way. Motion blur shutter timing is specified by a moment value which is normalized to be between 0.0 and 1.0. 0.0 is equivalent to $N - 0.5$, and 1.0 is equivalent to $N + 0.5$. When motion blur is turned off, the image generated uses the values of frame N, in other words, shutter timing 0.5 (Figure 8.6).

Motion blur information. To allow Kilauea to more correctly compute motion blur, incremental data for every subframe is written out to the ShotData. Kilauea interpolates the subframe data internally to generate a motion blurred image. Motion blur precision can be increased by increasing the number of these subframes, which can be user-specified. Around three subframes is sufficient for most cases.

For example, when the number of subframes is one (motion blur off), a single frame is composed of one subframe. In this case, the subframes will fall exactly at integer frame numbers. For example, when outputting the frame data between frame one and three, data at frames 1.0, 2.0, and 3.0 is the output.

If three subframes are specified, each frame will generate three subframes of data. When processing frames one to three, frame one generates data at 0.5, 1.0, and 1.5. Frame two generates data at 1.5, 2.0, and 2.5. Finally, frame three generates data at 2.5, 3.0, and 3.5. This data is finally represented as seven subframes at 0.5, 1.0, 1.5, 2.0, 2.5, 3.0, and 3.5.

Users may only specify an odd number of subframes, i.e., 1,3,5,7,9 ... This way, the subframes always come to the center of the frame. Turning motion blur off is equivalent to simply rendering the subframe in the middle. This ensures the generation of consistent images between when motion blur is turned on/off.

Interpolation between subframes is done by using Catmull-Rom splines. This ensures that interpolated data go through the control points and the values at the subframes are always used. Linear interpolation of subframes is also available, if desired.

String table. Scene data usually contain a lot of string data. Strings are frequently used for object and light source names, shader names attached to the object surfaces, etc. The representation of these strings has a large impact on the file size because they are almost always reused between multiple frames. ShotData creates a look-up table of strings used in the scene. These strings are internally represented as indices to the string table. ShotData contains a string table block, which is also represented as incremental data between frames. By using this method, every string is represented as an ID in the string table, contributing significantly to file size reduction. Any processing that occurs within or after the parsing of the ShotData can check for identical strings by simply comparing this ID. This speeds up string search operations, which frequently occur.

Multiple ShotData files. Essentially, the upper bound of the scene complexity Kilauea can handle only depends on the total number of machines that Kilauea has access to. Therefore, a scene which is difficult to handle on a single machine can be rendered as long as Kilauea can read the data into multiple machines. However, Kilauea depends completely on the front-end environment (Maya) for the scene creation and therefore, the scene size is practically limited to the size of memory available to the front-end. In order to work around this issue, Kilauea can read multiple ShotData simultaneously. The scene is divided according to some convention and converted into multiple ShotData. Each ShotData can be created independently, using the maximum memory allowed by the front-end environment, and multiple ShotData are finally combined in three dimensions. In the actual rendering stage, Kilauea does not care whether a scene is composed of single or multiple ShotData, and simply renders it as one large scene. Figure 8.7 shows the three typical ways in which shot data is created and used between Maya and Kilauea.

The multiple ShotData idea was originally designed as a way to load such complex scenes into Kilauea, but there are three properties which turned out to be useful when we actually started testing the system. The first property is that since the scene can be converted to ShotData in pieces, more than one person can work on a single scene on different machines. The second property is that ShotData can be created incrementally as work progresses, which means that there is no need to regenerate a ShotData for completed parts of the scene when doing test rendering. Once a part of a scene with director's approval is converted into ShotData, the ShotData can be reused. This makes it easier to think about caching ShotData. The third property is that by managing special-case data as separate ShotData, implementation can be made easier.

For example, consider the case of creating a special geometry data for an object which undergoes deformation using cyclic animation. This can be done by adding a new framework to describe this object within the ShotData, but by taking advantage of how ShotData works, implementation can be made simpler than that. An object which undergoes deformation using cyclic animation itself is represented as a sequential data of subframes which can be described as incremental data. The only missing piece is the length of the animation within the scene; all the other elements can share almost all the existing mechanisms of the ShotData format. By taking

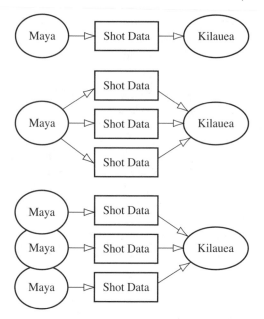

Figure 8.7. Multiple ShotData files.

advantage of the ShotData format and interpreting the data differently, implementation can be made easier

Rendering multiple ShotData combined within Kilauea does not suffer from any of the problems associated with rendering a large scene in separate layers. Objects casting shadows onto each other and color bleeding between objects naturally work perfectly fine. The human labor of dividing the scene into layers can be completely offloaded to machines.

ShotData can describe every element of the scene. This offers a great freedom in how the scene is divided and converted into ShotData. Users have complete freedom over dividing the scene on the basis of the elements composing the scene (such as light sources, objects, and shading information), or the progress of work (every ShotData has its own lights, objects, and shading information).

Overwrite rule. When rendering with multiple ShotData and there happens to be the same data with different contents, a decision has to be made on which one to use. For example, an inconsistency occurs if there are two ShotData files and an object called A with different attributes exists in both files. Kilauea handles this problem by following an overwrite rule. When combining multiple ShotData within Kilauea, whether the existing object A will be overwritten by the new object A, or vice versa, is user-specified. By using this functionality, it is possible to create a ShotData that only contains the update information of a preexisting ShotData, applying a patch to the scene at loading time. This further broadened the beneficial aspects of the ShotData caching which was mentioned in Section 8.4. This can be a very powerful feature in a production pipeline where every second counts.

8.5 Parallel Ray Tracing

Kilauea performs all hidden surface removal by pure ray tracing. Ray tracing fundamentally needs to reference all the geometry data in the scene. The algorithm simply consumes as much memory as the scene size, thus it poorly handles extremely large scenes. Kilauea overcomes this weakness in the ray tracing algorithm by sharing data among multiple machines. This is a brute-force approach, but it is a reasonable decision considering the price drops of PCs today.

In a simple scene where the entire scene data can be contained within a single process, each node computes ray tracing completely independent of each other, resulting in a direct linear speedup (Figure 8.8).

The parallel ray tracing methodology when the entire scene is too complex to be stored in one machine is a highly debatable subject with various suggested algorithms. Assume that a certain scene is too large that two machines are required to store it. Several possible methods to execute ray tracing in this situation basically boil down to either the transfer of object data among machines or the transfer of ray data among machines.

In the first approach, as machine A computes the ray's path, it will eventually need to retrieve scene information from other machines (Figure 8.9).

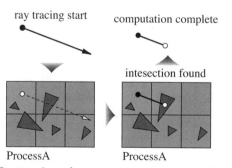

ray tracing start   computation complete

intesection found

ProcessA   ProcessA

Figure 8.8. Ray tracing where one process contains the entire scene.

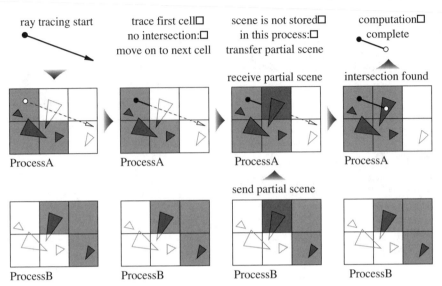

Figure 8.9. Ray tracing by transferring partial scene data.

This transmitted scene information must be stored in memory efficiently. There should be no extra memory to waste in the system since that is the reason why the scene was distributed to multiple machines in the first place. For the efficiency, geometry data should probably be separated into the one that stays resident and the one that is managed by some clever memory cache considering certain geometry size.

There have been several proposals on clever techniques to strategically distribute the scene data among multiple machines [239]. Nevertheless, performance of this approach essentially depends on how fast the geometry data can be transmitted between machines.

The second approach is the completely opposite approach. Instead of geometry information, ray information is exchanged between machines. If ray tracing cannot be resolved within the partial scene managed by one machine, the ray information is sent to another machine. The receiver of the ray then continues the computation (Figure 8.10).

Generally speaking, the ray data is much simpler than the geometry data, making ray transmission a much more attractive solution. The disadvantage of exchanging ray data is that the amount of transmitted data depends on the quality of the image being rendered, the properties of the scene each machine is handling, and the paths of the rays. In a two-machine configuration, if ray tracing cannot be resolved in one, the other must have

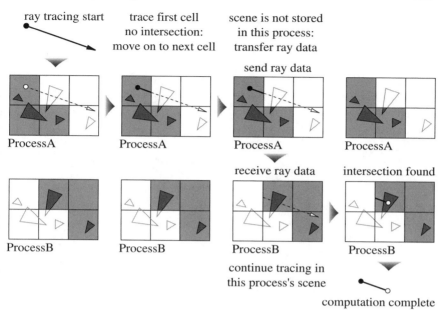

ray tracing start | trace first cell | scene is not stored
 | no intersection: | in this process:
 | move on to next cell | transfer ray data

send ray data

ProcessA | ProcessA | ProcessA | ProcessA

receive ray data | intersection found

ProcessB | ProcessB | ProcessB | ProcessB

continue tracing in
this process's scene

computation complete

Figure 8.10. Ray tracing by transferring ray data.

the solution. If the scene is distributed to more than two machines, the ray tracing may have to be performed over multiple levels (Figure 8.11).

Kilauea ended up adopting the method which transfers the ray data instead of the geometry data. We created a prototype using the first method earlier in our development, but in the end, we were unable to suppress the geometry transmission overhead to an acceptable level.

This geometry transmission overhead is due to the way Kilauea stores the geometry information. Kilauea restricts the type of primitive that can be rendered only to triangles. Any other primitive is internally converted to triangles. This geometry data is stored in a data structure called accel grid (Section 8.6.5) to speed up ray tracing. As scenes become more complex, required memory size increases. The maximum scene data size that one machine can hold is closely related to the accel grid data size. Kilauea manages all the vertices of triangles separately from the triangle itself, allowing sharing of vertices and thus conserving memory as much as possible.

This is an excellent idea to save memory, but it becomes a problem when trying to send only a portion of the scene. Vertices are shared on a per object basis and do not pay much attention to dividing the scene into parts. Shared vertex data in this form perform inefficiently in exchanging the scene partially. On the other hand, exchanging rays between machines is a lot simpler than exchanging geometry data. This is clear from the fact

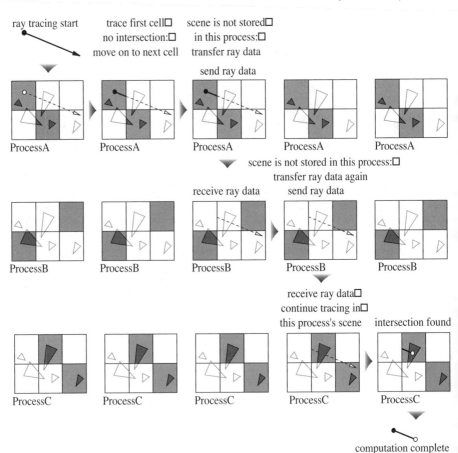

Figure 8.11. Ray tracing over multiple processes.

that rays are basically independent of each other. The problem is then reduced to the speed of sending a large amount of ray data.

Kilauea's approach distributes geometry data statically across the different machines, and only the ray data is exchanged. However, this does not solve all the problems. If the scene data is distributed among a very large number of machines, the ray may have to be transmitted from machine to machine. This is especially apparent when there is a larger number of machines. The situation also depends on how the geometry data is distributed across the machines.

These situations depend on the state of the ray itself. Certain rays may be able to get a result on the first machine, while others may have to go though all the machines before finding a solution. By dynamically assigning what route the ray should take at runtime, this overhead might be minimized. This can be done by making a table of scenes that each machine has, and sending the rays using the table as a guide. Even if this portion can be optimized enough, however, the load may still be concentrated on one machine in situations where space traversal requests concentrate on a certain area in space.

The discussions above lead to the conclusion that an ideal method is the one which statically distribute geometry data across the machines, require no complex routing of rays, and ensure that the load does not concentrate on a single machine. The stability was the top agenda in coming up with such a method. That is, an algorithm which only works efficiently for certain scene types, but raises fatal problems in others is avoided. Instead, we prefer a robust algorithm that works decently on all scenes.

Once again, consider the case where the scene is distributed across the two machines in a completely random manner on a per-primitive basis. Ideally, each machine has close to half the scene's geometry data, and the spatial density in the machines is almost identical. The ray tracing performance characteristics on the two machines are statistically close to being equal, given enough rays (Figure 8.12).

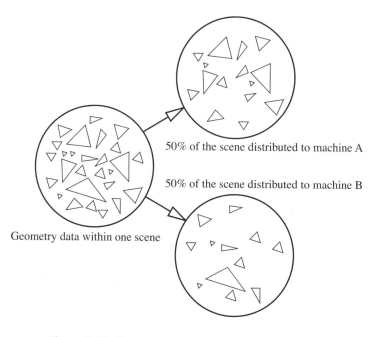

50% of the scene distributed to machine A

50% of the scene distributed to machine B

Geometry data within one scene

Figure 8.12. Scene data distributed to two machines.

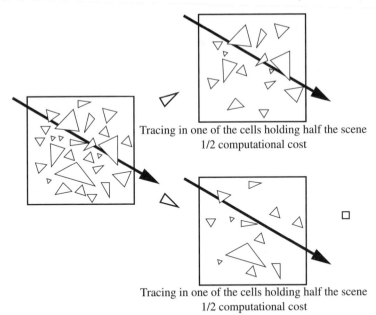

Tracing in one of the cells holding half the scene
1/2 computational cost

Tracing in one of the cells holding half the scene
1/2 computational cost

Figure 8.13. Performance of parallel intersection calculation to multiple objects within one cell.

Ray tracing computation on scenes divided in this fashion is executed as follows (Figure 8.13). First, the two machines perform the ray tracing on the exact same ray. Each machine independently performs the space traversal computation. Each of the ray tracing operations can be completely parallelized. Because the two machines share no scene data, the ray tracing results are obviously different. The results are compared on one of the machines and the closer intersection point is determined as the final result, discarding the other result.

The comparison of the space traversal requests can be performed in parallel as well. Two machines first get two completely different ray tracing requests. These rays are duplicated to two equivalent requests in both machines. Each machine sends one request to itself, the other to the other machine, and each machine performs the ray tracing independently. The computed result is sent back to the sender if the request originated on the other machine, and the returned result is compared with the result of the originating machine. The comparison finds out the closest intersection point as the final result, and one ray tracing is complete. As described in Figure 8.14, the distribution of rays, the ray tracing, and the comparison of the results can all be executed in parallel.

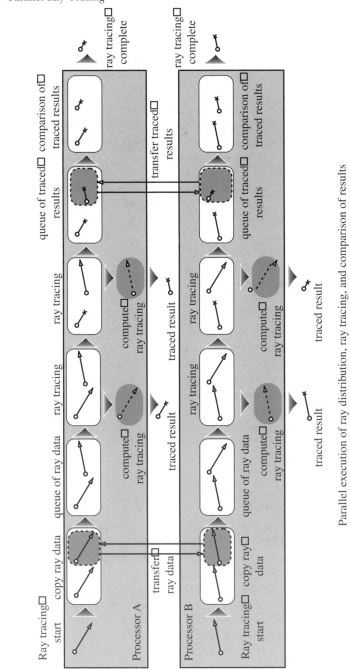

Figure 8.14. Parallel execution of ray distribution, ray tracing, and comparison of results.

This method appears to be performing unnecessary computation, but has the advantage of being extremely stable under any pattern and/or size of scene data. Even if the objects are distributed across a very large number of machines, it can be executed in the exact same manner. At the moment, experiments show this method works reliably with up to 75 million triangle scene data, and there is no reason why it shouldn't work for larger scenes.

A structure called accel grid is used to speed up the space traversal in each machine. This method accelerates the space traversal by dividing the entire scene into uniform cells. Ray tracing traverses these cells, narrowing down the objects to perform the final intersection calculation. This method performs intersection calculation on each primitive in a cell and returns the closest one as the result. The parallel space traversal in Kilauea is equivalent to performing this in-cell intersection detection in parallel.

Each ray goes through a space traversal on multiple machines, including the originating machine. This process is performed in almost the same computation time across all machines. Every ray trace request resolves in one level of ray transmission and computation. This characteristic indicates that the method is far more reliable and tractable than the one where a ray must be transmitted over unpredictable number of levels to resolve. Experiments show that the load average using this method across multiple machines turns out to be almost equal, meaning that complex processing for load balancing is not required.

There are problems, on the other hand. The method may perform lots of wasteful computation that gets discarded eventually. Consider a scene in which the geometry is divided into spaces A and B. Inside A's accel grid, one triangle is placed directly in front of the camera. The scene is uniformly distributed (no data is shared), so this triangle does not exist in B's accel grid. In such a case, space traversal in A hits this big triangle and finishes immediately. B, however, has no way of knowing this. B must continue its space traversal further, until it resolves somehow. B performs far more computation than A in order to find an intersection point that gets thrown away. Clearly, reducing this wasteful calculation will be the key improvement to this parallel ray tracing. We are currently experimenting several ways to improve the algorithm, but unfortunately, we have not implemented them in Kilauea yet.

8.6 Implementation

8.6.1 Low-Level Data Structure

Kilauea is a multilevel pipeline engine with large amounts of computation. Computation at each pipeline stage is implemented as an independent

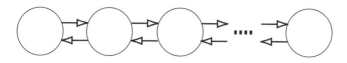

Figure 8.15. Simple doubly linked list.

thread, and the engine is designed to let data flow through these threads. Low-level data structures which form the core part of this engine, and their programming policy, are discussed below.

Queue data structure

One of the most frequently used and extremely important data structures in Kilauea is the queue. Kilauea has several special purpose low-level queue classes to simplify coding for specific needs. These queues are closely tied to the memory management scheme which is explained in Section 8.6.1. Some techniques to solve the problems often encountered when developing specialized queues are provided in this section as well.

Simple doubly linked list. A linked list data structure is the basis of all queue structures. The Kilauea library defines a generic doubly linked list base class. In most cases, the lists need to be doubly linked, though for some cases, a separate single-linked list class is prepared for full optimization (Figure 8.15).

Multithread safe linked list. Whenever data needs to be exchanged between different threads using a queue, a mutual exclusion lock mechanism is necessary to insert or remove items to/from a queue. Multithread safety is basically achieved by just locking the queue every time insertion or removal operations to the queue occurs. This, however, can hurt the performance by causing frequent lock collisions between threads. In order to deal with this situation, the Kilauea library provides several multithread safe linked lists optimized with attention to these special cases (Figure 8.16):

1. Both insertion and removal can be restricted to a single thread.

2. Insertion is done from multiple threads, but removal is restricted to a single thread.

3. Insertion is restricted to a single thread, but removal is done from multiple threads.

4. Insertion and removal are both done from multiple threads.

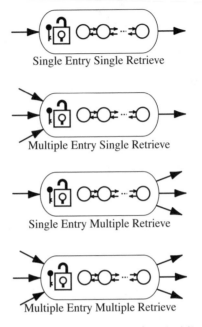

Single Entry Single Retrieve

Multiple Entry Single Retrieve

Single Entry Multiple Retrieve

Multiple Entry Multiple Retrieve

Figure 8.16. Multithread safe linked list.

The development stance of Kilauea is to first derive a queue class from the most appropriate one of the existing base classes. If further performance increase is desired in certain situations, they are individually optimized. However, the generic multithread safe list classes are optimized well enough that, in most cases, they can be used without any modification.

Lock problem. If accesses to the queue from multiple threads occur relatively infrequently, mutual exclusion locks do not cause too many problems. However, frequent collision of blocking locks have undesirable effects such as imposing a burden on thread scheduling and causing race conditions when acquiring the lock. One possible solution for getting around this problem is the use of a non-blocking lock (try-lock).

Figure 8.17 illustrates how this try-lock mechanism avoids lock collisions. Before inserting data to a queue, a thread first try-locks to check if it can acquire the lock. If try-lock is successful, the thread continues the insertion as in the case of an ordinary blocking lock. If try-lock fails, i.e. some other thread already owns the lock, then the thread gives up and inserts the data into a local list, hoping that it will be inserted in the following attempts. If try-lock succeeds in the next attempt, the thread

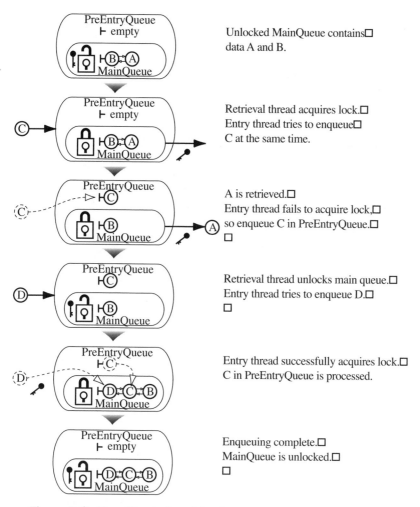

Figure 8.17. Use of try-lock and local queue to avoid lock collisions.

first inserts the data from this thread-local list, and then inserts the new data. The thread-local list continues to grow if the attempt fails again.

This mechanism allows increased independency of the thread execution by avoiding blocking when the lock cannot be obtained. Taking this idea further, the frequency of try-lock failures can be greatly reduced by not attempting try-lock every time.

However, queues using such mechanisms are essentially more complex than a simple thread-safe list structure, leading to a performance disadvantage. Storing data into a thread-local list in order to reduce the number of try-locks causes a latency in the data exchange between threads. Excessive use of this mechanism results in a serious degradation of performance.

The use of this mechanism should be restricted only to the case where a normal multithread safe linked list structure fails to perform well. It offers a very powerful optimization solution for some special purposes, however.

Condition wait.   If a thread attempts to take data out of the queue, but the queue is empty, the thread sleeps in Pthread's condition wait mechanism. The sleeping thread wakes up when another thread inserts new data into the queue. Figure 8.18 shows this mechanism in action. Condition wait allows the CPU resource to be used more efficiently. However, frequent sleeps and wake-ups inflict a major performance overhead. The key to maximum performance is to keep the threads running at all times as much as possible and to sleep and wake up threads at appropriate times.

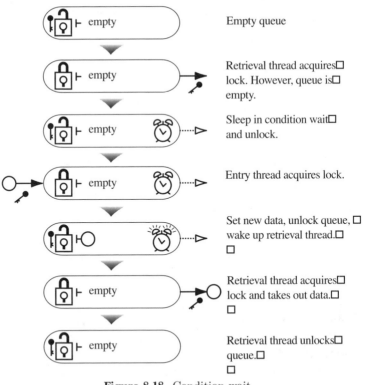

Figure 8.18. Condition wait.

More information on how to manage threads and queues can be found in the literature [209].

Memory management

Special attention to memory management is vital when programming in a multithreaded environment. Kilauea has a built-in memory manager to cope with issues such as multithread safety and fragmentation.

Multithread safety. `malloc()` is normally used when dynamically allocating memory, but this causes serious problems in a multithreaded environment. Kilauea has its own multithread safe `malloc()` with automatic locking. The C++ `new` operator is also overloaded to use this `malloc()`, so all normal construction using `new` is executed in a multithread safe manner.

Dynamic memory allocation. Implementing original memory allocation routines instead of using the existing ones is very effective when the memory allocation pattern is predictable. In Kilauea, the memory allocation request size is usually extremely small, mostly under 16 kilobytes. Kilauea's own memory manager is optimized with the focus on such small memory allocations. Every memory request is first categorized as either over 16 kilobytes or under 16 kilobytes. Requests under 16 kilobytes are then grouped into requests of predetermined size. Requests over 16 kilobytes are considered to be a request of continuous 16 kilobyte blocks. Figure 8.19 explains how the Kilauea memory manager handles requests under 16 kilobytes.

For every memory request, the very first one reserves the entire 16 kilobytes, which is then broken down into series of equally sized memory blocks. The next request is allocated from within the stock of memory that has just been created. The memory manager does not allocate any new memory area until all memory in the stock is used up.

Consider the case where an allocation of 30 bytes takes place. According to a predefined table for memory allocation size, this request is internally processed as a request for 32 bytes. When the first 32-byte request comes in, the memory allocation library allocates 16 kilobytes from the system. The 16-kilobyte block is then used as 512 units of 32-byte blocks. The first block from this 512 blocks is returned as the result of the memory request.

Assume that the next allocation request is 29 bytes. Internally this request is again treated as a request for 32 bytes. Since the memory manager already has 511 units of 32 bytes blocks internally, no new memory is allocated from the system, and the next available block is simply returned.

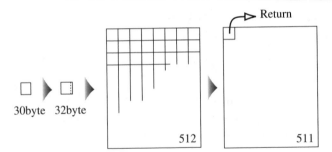

A request for 30 bytes is treated as a 32 byte request. First
512 units of 32 byte memory block are allocated. The top one in
the stock is returned. 511 units remain in the stock.

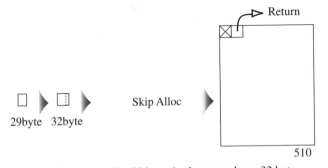

Next request for 29 bytes is also treated as a 32 byte
request. Stock of 511 memory units already exists so a memory
allocation does not take place. The topmost memory unit of the stock
is returned. 510 units remain in the stock.

Figure 8.19. Memory management.

Whenever memory is freed, the freed memory is returned to the internal
stock of memory.

If the stock is exhausted, a new memory space of 16 kilobytes is allocated
and used in the same way. When every element of this 16 kilobyte block
is freed, the entire 16-kilobyte block is freed in such a way that it can
be used for memory requests of a different size. In conjunction with the
previously mentioned lock mechanism for multithread safety, threads can
independently manipulate memory in 16-kilobyte units, allowing a finer
management of heap memory.

Thread local memory control.   Frequent allocation of numerous equal-sized
blocks of data occurs inside Kilauea. These memory requests repeatedly

create a data structure of a certain size and then free it, so in most cases, objects do not really have to be newed and deleted. Once an object that has been allocated by new is no longer necessary, it is linked to an internal stock list and completely recycled. If correctly implemented, this recycling mechanism not only reduces the cost of construction and destruction, but also eliminates or significantly reduces the number of locks necessary in a multithread environment, thus increasing the independency and efficiency of each thread.

In some cases, an object that is newed by one thread is deleted by another thread. Returning the object to the original thread and having the thread which newed the object delete it solves the complications most of the time, as illustrated in Figure 8.20.

The Kilauea library has a thread local memory management for random-sized memory requests in the same way as our implementation of malloc(). Using this memory management, developers do not need to pay special attention to make sure that memory is local to the thread. They can, instead, concentrate on the essence of the algorithm itself.

Memory verification mechanism. Even when writing a sequential program, memory-related problems cause a lot of headaches at times. When writing a multithread program, the problem is even more serious. Such bugs are often very difficult to locate. Kilauea's memory manager has an integrated memory verification mechanism in order to easily spot memory problems. This is possible only because Kilauea has its own implementation of dynamic memory management routines such as malloc().

When the memory verification function is called, tables constructed and managed internally are checked from various aspects for any inconsistency. This is done in a mutually exclusive way to all memory requests, thus changing the various timings such as thread scheduling. Therefore, it is not effective in all situations. However, the verification failure most surely indicates the existence of a critical problem in the program. Problems such as mismatched new(malloc) and delete(free), accidental reuse of memory that is currently being used, and freeing of memory that has already been freed, are relatively easy to spot using this memory verification.

In some cases, developers want to find out the details about the types of memory usage patterns. To satisfy such demand, the memory manager can log the memory management history to a file for later analysis. Doing so obviously puts a heavy load on the system and the thread scheduling and performance are significantly affected. Nevertheless, by carefully using this logging facility, developers were able to obtain valuable memory usage information and figure out the optimal memory management scheme.

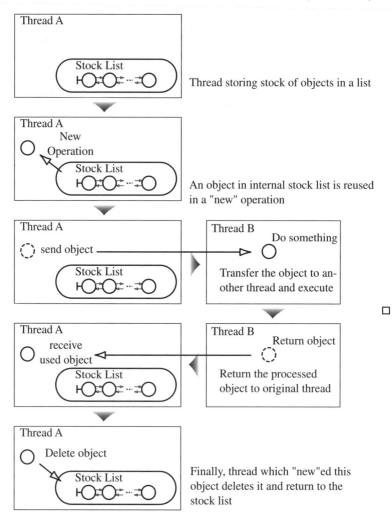

Thread storing stock of objects in a list

An object in internal stock list is reused in a "new" operation

Transfer the object to another thread and execute

Return the processed object to original thread

Finally, thread which "new"ed this object deletes it and return to the stock list

Figure 8.20. Thread-local memory control.

Thread tree structure

Kilauea uses the Pthread library for multithreaded execution. The Kilauea library has a C++ wrapper class for starting and stopping threads. This class maintains every thread created by a process in a tree structure, and this tree can handle such operations as stopping all the threads that are subtrees of a certain node, or checking the execution status of a certain thread. Programmers are able to very easily create and control threads

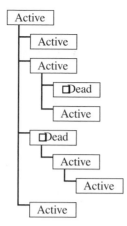

Figure 8.21. Thread tree structure.

without knowing about the actual Pthread functions. Also, the program is able to monitor the status of a thread at any time in the program execution, based on this tree structure information. Monitoring of threads such as whether a thread has started executing or already completed executing can be done all by using this thread tree structure (Figure 8.21).

8.6.2 MPI (Message Passing Interface) Layer

The MPI layer handles the exchange of data between multiple machines. This layer defines the message passing information description and actually performs the message passing. In the initial stage of development, we adopted MPI which was starting to become widely used at the time. At that point (around 1999), we were developing on the assumption that an external library will be used for this portion, but there were two problems: reliability and multithread safety.

At the time, we were using an MPI implementation which was available from SGI for SGI machines. With this MPI implementation, messages frequently did not arrive at the recipient or were lost in transit when a large number of machines were involved. In most cases, it was a problem in our application, but we still had tough time dealing with the program dying suddenly with a broken pipe. Also, the maximum number of nodes were restricted to around 100 nodes at the time, which did not meet our requirements.

The MPI implementation at the time was not multithread safe. This was a serious restriction for our application, since the renderer was initially designed to be multithreaded with messages flying all over the place from each thread independently of each other.

After considering these issues, we have decided to implement a subset of MPI on our own. We based this decision on the following discussions inside the team:

1. MPI's spec covers a wide area, but our application only uses a small subset of it.

2. There is a specific pattern to the data size of messages being used inside Kilauea, and we want to specifically optimize for that.

3. We need a multithread safe MPI implementation.

4. We want to do a dynamic node configuration.

Kilauea's MPI implementation currently partially supports item 4, but it has complete support for 1, 2, and 3. In implementing our own MPI subset, we took care not to change the MPI API whenever possible. This is to leave open the possibility of returning to a standard MPI distribution at some point in the future. Message creation uses the same methodology as in standard MPI. Message tags, ranks, etc. all follow MPI's philosophy. Our implementation has the following characteristics:

1. Point-to-point communication only. Broadcast is not used.

2. Designed with multithreaded environment in mind, and is implemented in a multithread safe manner.

3. Socket send and recv within the MPI layer is a multithreaded implementation. Also, socket communication uses TCP instead of UDP.

4. Based on the analysis of message sizes required for Kilauea, the memory management is optimized for a specific data size, resulting in a speed up.

5. Simplified implementation based on the assumption that the byte order will be consistent within a single running system.

6. If the recipient of a message is the same process as the sender, then socket communication is bypassed for speed.

Kilauea currently performs all message passing using our implementation of MPI. The portability of this layer is extremely high, and we have been able to easily port this code to all our target hardware environments.

8.6.3   Tcl Command Interface

Kilauea is just a renderer, but it is far more complex than other renderers designed as a sequential program, in that it runs on a cluster of PCs communicating with each other. It is designed as a testbed for experimenting new features designed for very ambitious goals. Developers needed to be able to implement different features and easily test them individually. Also, since Kilauea stays resident like a daemon process once launched, having a way to control it from something like a console was useful. Users also wanted to be able to control the various features of Kilauea from a command, and be able to combine these commands together. For these reasons, Kilauea has a Tcl command interface. Tcl was preferred over other interpreters for its ease of integration.

Changes to Tcl

All Kilauea controls are processed through the Tcl interpreter. Kilauea opens a console displaying a command prompt, constantly waiting for Tcl command input. The Tcl command interpreter was implemented as one of the threads inside Kilauea. Tcl is not intended to be used from threads this way and Kilauea needed to work around this problem.

Thread-safe Tcl.   Thread safety here refers to using Tcl from inside Kilauea. From Kilauea's point of view, the Tcl interpreter is just one thread out of many running inside the entire Kilauea system. All threads inside Kilauea are managed in a tree structure, so any thread that the Tcl interpreter spawns needs to be put into this thread management tree. In the actual implementation, Tcl's thread initialization mechanism is modified to support this.

Sharing data such as variables between multiple Tcl interpreters.   Spawning another instance of Tcl interpreter from the main Tcl interpreter can be very useful at times. The original Tcl interpreter had problems with data sharing in this case. For example, imagine the case of opening up a socket port to connect Kilauea and other programs such as Maya or telnet (we refer to this kind of connection as a back door). For such cases, the Tcl interpreter had to be modified to share the Tcl internal data in a thread-safe manner.

Kilauea command

Every Kilauea command is accessible as a Tcl command. Most commands are for fine-tuning specific functions inside Kilauea. Kilauea developers add new Tcl commands to test new features. By doing this, specific functions can be tested quickly and individually, rather than performing complete rendering tests in the entire Kilauea. This increases the development productivity by conducting series of tests and perfecting each component faster. After an individual feature has been tested thoroughly, this Tcl command is then used in the final rendering sequence.

General rendering sequences are represented by a combination of Tcl commands. A group of functions called the script library combines the individual low-level Kilauea commands, allowing users to manage Kilauea at a more abstract level. This system may seem very strange compared to other renderers. However, this is a very reasonable and flexible solution considering the architecture of Kilauea.

There are multiple units of computation inside Kilauea which are referred to as tasks (explained in the next section). For example, STask is responsible for shading and ATask is responsible for ray tracing. Kilauea can control which task to be launched on which machine with what kind of parameters, all from a Tcl script. Trying out all the combinations and various adjustments as many times as desired from a Tcl script is far more productive than modifying C++ source files and recompiling every time to conduct a test. Once a desirable configuration is found from these tests and decided to be adopted for general rendering, this configuration is embedded in a function inside a Tcl script. This allows flexibility in modifying settings on the fly and enhancing features.

Kilauea's front-end process composes and sends these Tcl commands to the Kilauea Tcl interpreter through a socket connection. Therefore, users do not need to worry about Tcl scripting at all under normal circumstances. Power users may prefer to directly create Tcl scripts for full control. Tcl scripts can also provide a temporary workaround for a bug.

Kilauea usually reads in a scene from ShotData, but it is also possible to describe a scene completely from within Tcl scripts. This is clearly not a normal way to create a scene, and is very difficult to do. However, this is effective as an emergency procedure at times.

Incremental rendering

Since the Tcl interpreter is implemented as one independent thread within Kilauea, Tcl commands may be issued while Kilauea is running some rendering task. This mechanism is used to stop Kilauea's rendering task in the middle. Being able to enter a command through the Tcl interpreter and dump the internal state of Kilauea is very useful for debugging at times.

Users are not only limited to viewing internal values. Changing values in the middle of rendering can be used for purposes outside of debugging.

For example, users may change the material parameters or light sources dynamically. We are currently implementing a GUI for fine-tuning of material parameters and incremental rendering without rereading the scene.

Command interface to C++ objects

Kilauea handles almost everything in parallel by using threads, and each thread is implemented as a group of objects of a specific class. Being able to send commands to these objects at run time will be effective for adding new features and debugging. To support this, we have implemented a unified interface for sending text command strings to a specified object. For commands such as passing parameters at initialization which are not executed often and small in data transmission size, raw text messages are directly sent to individual objects, where the messages are parsed and interpreted. This allowed us to implement new commands quickly without writing complex code for MPI style message passing.

8.6.4   Rank and Task

The concept of "rank" and "task" needs to be explained first when describing the structure of Kilauea. Kilauea's message passing basically follows the MPI standard. The meaning of rank is equivalent to that of MPIs. When Kilauea is using three machines and one Kilauea process is running on each machine, there is a total of three Kilauea processes running within the entire Kilauea system. Kilauea assigns rank IDs to these processes using a convention. In this case, the ID takes a value of zero to two. Rank ID can be viewed as a unique ID for specifying a process which reside within the Kilauea system. Rank also has a one-to-one correspondence with a Unix process (Figure 8.22).

Inside Kilauea, there is a concept of multiple "tasks" which are units of some computation classified according to their function. Basically, a task is a set of computation which has been classified and grouped together.

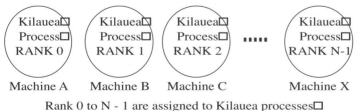

Rank 0 to N - 1 are assigned to Kilauea processes☐
running on N individual machines

Figure 8.22. Rank ID.

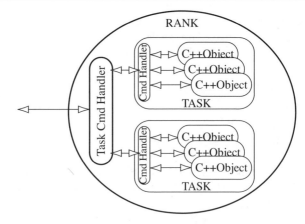

Figure 8.23. Task handler and text command interface.

Section 8.6.4 explains the roles of different tasks in Kilauea. For example, WTask is a task that reads ShotData, expanding the incremental data and building the scene data necessary for rendering. ATask performs ray tracing on a scene. STask processes the shading.

The task assignment to ranks can be defined in a very flexible manner in Kilauea. A task handler which is running inside each rank controls the execution of multiple tasks in parallel, using multiple threads. This means that multiple tasks can be assigned to a single rank.

The task configuration inside Kilauea can be separated from the correct execution of individual tasks. This property is very effective for moving development along flexibly. An optimal task configuration for a certain scene complexity can be adjusted just by modifying a Tcl script, which means that Kilauea can be easily adapted to the needs of a specific scene in a movie production.

A task handler running on each rank provides a general method for controlling a specific task by message passing of text command data, as shown in Figure 8.23. Control commands can be sent to and results received from specific tasks without writing new code (Section 8.6.3). The ability to stop and diagnose a specific task is also available within this general framework (Section 8.6.1).

Task types

The following tasks currently exist inside Kilauea: MTask (Master Task), BTask (Binary Task), WTask (World Task), TTask (Tile Task), STask (Shading Task), RTask (Ray Task), ATask (Accel grid Task), ETask (Emit

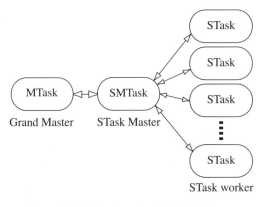

Figure 8.24. Task control inside Kilauea.

Task), LTask (look-up Task), PTask (Photon Task) and OTask (Output Task). Multiple instances of each task may exist within a Kilauea system, and one task master is required for each kind of task.

Figure 8.24 shows the case where there are N STasks managed by one SMTask, which is the task master for STasks, inside the Kilauea system. All management of STasks are done through this SMTask, and individual STasks may not be controlled directly from other tasks. Other tasks will not even be able to find out how many STasks currently exist within the Kilauea system unless they query the SMTask. In the actual rendering, STask configuration details are queried ahead of time; data transmission destination is determined based on this information and directly processed for each STask. There is one exception to the task master rule. This is MTask (Master Task). This task bundles all the task masters and controls them. There is no equivalent of an MMTask because only one instance of MTask can exist within the Kilauea system.

All task controls begin with the MTask. MTask sends control data to each task master, which then sends the data to the corresponding tasks. This data path is for the task control only. In the actual rendering, data will be exchanged directly. The role of each task in Kilauea is explained below.

MTask (Master Task). MTask manages the information of all the task masters within the Kilauea system. MTask has an integrated Tcl interpreter, and is able to open a command console. Direct control of everything inside Kilauea is possible by entering Tcl commands through this console. All control of tasks are executed with this MTask as a starting point. Only one instance of MTask exists within a Kilauea system.

BTask (Binary Task). This task reads in external data files. Inside Kilauea, other tasks do not open and read from a file directly. All file I/O goes through this BTask, and data is then sent to the appropriate tasks via message passing. In most normal production work, the scene data is managed by a central server. When the Kilauea system is running and multiple machines are running in parallel, having every machine access the central server is not desirable. Restricting access to one machine and thus narrowing problems down to that machine and the central server is safer. When a very large number of file I/O occurs, creating problems between the central server and the machine running the BTask, augmenting the file I/O and network hardware performance of that machine solves the problem. BTask may be preferentially assigned to a machine customized for I/O performance to minimize the problem in communication with the outside network.

Data that is read in will eventually be sent to the appropriate tasks. This transmission is necessary for Kilauea system to render an image, and nothing can be done about the amount of data being sent here. However, transmission efficiency is easily improved by intelligently compressing data within the BTask. Also, because the network packets generated for this transmission do not need to go outside the Kilauea system, we can control the network congestion appropriately by working out the physical machine connections via a switching hub.

There are instances where data reading efficiency can be increased without generating actual file I/O by controlling the data caching inside BTask. Take the case of reading in the ShotData. Many file pointer seeks will be necessary to read in a ShotData. By cleverly using cached data to handle these seeks, it is possible to read data without generating an actual file I/O.

It is also possible to launch multiple BTasks within the Kilauea system. This allows file I/O to be handled by multiple BTasks instead of a single BTask, allowing them to be processed in parallel. For these reasons, Kilauea has adopted the design of using this BTask for all file I/O.

WTask (World Task). ShotData is represented as incremental data. WTask handles the computation necessary to interpret this data correctly and construct the scene data for the specified frame. WTask handles the reading of multiple ShotData, as well as controlling the data overwrite management. The built scene is then sent to ATask. WTask is also responsible for distributing the scene across multiple ATasks. Because WTask is in charge of building the scene data, it is idle during the actual rendering stage until the scene data for the next frame needs to be built.

It is also possible to launch multiple WTasks. In this case, each instance is in charge of building a part of the scene data. When multiple WTasks are launched, all the processing beginning from the incremental data analysis through the building of scene data and finally the transmission of data to ATasks, will be executed in parallel.

TTask (Tile Task). TTask creates the schedule for pixel sampling in screen space, and shoots rays accordingly. Even though the task is named "tile," the scheduling is not restricted to just rectangular tiles. The scheduling unit is represented as an abstract data and implementation of a new scheduling algorithm is relatively simple. TTask also handles the adaptive sampling in screen space. This is very effective in normal ray tracing. TTask also performs adaptive sampling along the time axis, which is necessary for motion blur. Multiple TTasks are usually executed to shoot primary rays and collect their result in parallel.

STask (Shading Task). STask performs the shading computation on an object surface. Kilauea uses a method called SPOTEngine (Section 8.6.6) for shading computation, and STasks control this SPOTEngine. This task only handles the computation on the object surface, and does not perform further ray tracing from the surface. In addition, STask handles the texture data sampling and filtering for shading. STask is not just limited to surface shaders. Every shader implemented in Kilauea is executed in this STask. Details about the various shaders are explained in Section 8.6.6. Multiple STasks are usually launched to handle shading computation in parallel.

RTask (Ray Task). RTask compares the ray tracing results returned from ATasks. A single ray trace is complete after RTask returns the result of the comparison.

ATask (Accel grid Task). ATask is the ray tracing engine. This task performs ray tracing, using a data structure called accel grid for optimization (Section 8.6.5). ATask contains the geometry data of the scene, needed for ray tracing. Ray tracing is computed in parallel by executing multiple ATasks.

ETask (Emit Task). Kilauea uses photon maps for global illumination. This task handles the photon shooting from light sources used in the photon map method. By launching multiple ETasks, photon shooting is executed in parallel.

LTask (Look-Up Task). LTask handles the photon look-up operation during the shading computation of object surface. Photon maps can be distributed over multiple machines, and this task also handles the look-up of distributed photon maps (Section 8.6.7). By executing multiple LTasks, photon look-up can be processed in parallel.

PTask (Photon Task). PTask contains the photon map data. This task stores photons, preprocesses them before rendering, and performs photon searching at rendering time (Section 8.6.7). By executing multiple PTasks, these operations can be processed in parallel. This task performs the equivalent of ATask for photon maps.

OTask (Output Task). OTask handles the final output processing of an image. All results of sampling operations for images are eventually sent to this OTask, where they are collected, filtered, and output to an external image viewer or to an image file.

Because Kilauea executes all sampling operations in parallel, there is no guarantee that the sampling results will return to OTask in the order that they were requested in TTask. OTask efficiently collects the sampling data coming back in an unpredictable order, applying pixel filters appropriately.

Holding the entire image in memory may not be possible when rendering a large image. OTask processes the samples as soon as they are ready to be filtered, outputs the results, and discards any unnecessary samples to conserve memory. This task itself does not have the ability to display an image. It can, however, send the data via a socket to an external image viewer.

Currently, only one OTask can exist within a Kilauea system. Only one OTask is sufficient because collection of samples and pixel filtering are relatively light operations compared to other tasks. If a problem with performance comes up in the future, parallel processing with multiple OTasks may be implemented.

Task configuration

The only task existing in the system after Kilauea boots up is MTask. From this state, Kilauea launches specific tasks and task masters for each rank. How the tasks are launched on the ranks is fully controllable from the Tcl script.

Kilauea starts rendering as soon as the task configuration is determined. Currently, task configuration cannot be modified during the rendering phase. Runtime modification of the task configuration has not yet been discussed since there has not been any situation where this feature was necessary. This is listed as one of the enhancements for the future, however.

Many serious problems occur if dynamic configuration of tasks takes place at runtime. There are many dependencies between tasks while rendering, so an appropriate mechanism will have to be implemented in order to handle the dynamic modification of these dependencies. A flexible modification mechanism of inter-task dependencies is required in order to handle dynamic task configuration.

Task grouping

The scene data which is too large to fit in the memory of one machine is shared across multiple machines. This is implemented by grouping several ATasks together. For example, if the memories of three machines are needed to store one scene, three ATasks are registered as one ATaskGroup. Kilauea uses all ATasks in one ATaskGroup as a unit to store the entire scene data.

During ray tracing, one ray sent to an ATaskGroup is internally duplicated to N rays, where N is the number of ATasks in the ATaskGroup. Each ATask then processes the ray independently. Results are compared in each ATaskGroup to compute the final ray tracing result.

Creating multiple ATaskGroups is possible if enough machines are available. Ray tracing speed will increase in direct proportion to the number of ATaskGroups. Multiple ATaskGroups can process ray tracing completely independent of each other, without any data exchange.

Such task grouping can be applied to PTask as well. PTask is responsible for storing and searching photons. Photon look-up operation can be parallelized in almost exactly the same way as ray tracing in ATask. A photon map which is too large to fit in the memory of one machine can be distributed to multiple PTasks grouped as one PTaskGroup, allowing them to be looked up in parallel. Parallel processing of the photon map is discussed in Section 8.6.7.

Data flow between tasks

Rendering within Kilauea is handled by passing data between tasks. Within each task, data is repeatedly fetched from an input queue, processed, and then the result is written out to the output queue. Figure 8.25 shows how the data flows between the tasks.

Instead of sending individual data separately between tasks, they are often packeted and sent out in one shot to reduce the communication overhead if the tasks reside in different processes. The decision on what data to packet is solely dependent on the type of inter-task message passing.

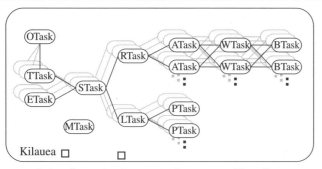

A data flow exists between tasks connected by a line.
Multiple instances of tasks other than OTask and MTask may exist.

Figure 8.25. Kilauea internal data flow.

8.6.5   Details of Ray Tracing

Engine design policy

Currently all hidden surface removal inside Kilauea is done by ray tracing. No optimization such as screen space scan line algorithm for primary rays is implemented. In a global illumination renderer, the percentage cost of primary ray computation is very small and optimizing this does not contribute much to the final performance. It is on the list of things to develop, but its priority is very low.

All rays of all generations are processed with exactly the same algorithm. In addition to the direct illumination rays, Kilauea also has photon tracing and final gather rays. These special rays are treated in the same way. Kilauea's ray tracing engine requires a uniform performance regardless of the position or the direction of the ray. Optimizing just for a particular position or direction causes other computations to become more complex, especially shading.

Primitives

There is a lot of discussion regarding optimal primitive types for ray tracing. In Kilauea, every primitive is converted to triangles in order to simplify the internal computation and use a unified algorithm. The ray tracing computation only considers intersection with triangles. Restricting primitives in this way puts less stress on developers for feature enhancements and maintenance.

The data structure of triangles changes depending on whether rendering with motion blur or not. If there is no motion blur, i.e., triangles exist statically in the scene, then triangles are simply stored in the accel grid, which is explained in Section 8.6.5. Intersection with the ray is simply an intersection with the stored triangle.

If there is motion blur, the path of the motion is computed and the data is stored in all accel grids where the motion passes. The path of motion blur is computed by sampling the coordinates of the triangle vertices at some intervals while the shutter is open, and connecting the points with Catmull-Rom splines. The volume constructed in this way is divided into parts along the time axis while the shutter is open, and the partial volumes of each part are stored in the accel grid. When computing the actual intersection with the triangle, it is moved to the position at the moment (time) of the ray. The triangle is moved by simply moving the vertices along the spline. After the triangle is moved to that moment, the intersection point is computed. In the case of motion blur, primitives are inside the accel grid as small blocks of space over the time axis of when the shutter is open, so it is possible to remove objects which will obviously not intersect at that moment.

Accel grid

Kilauea uses a hierarchical uniform grid to optimize the space traversal of the ray. As Figure 8.26 shows, it is a data structure of space divided into equal parts, where each element (cell) is further subdivided recursively. If the division size is two, then the data structure is equivalent to an octree. The reason why Kilauea uses a hierarchical grid instead of an octree is that the cost for space traversal is smaller than an octree, with the sacrifice of using extra memory.

Accel grid does not need to be modified dynamically while rendering a specific frame, but is completely reconstructed when rendering the next frame. Accel grid does its own memory management in order to avoid problems like memory fragmentation when reconstructing a large accel grid.

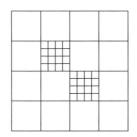

Figure 8.26. Hierarchical uniform grid.

When the scene data is small enough to fit completely within a single machine, the accel grids in each machine are identical when performing parallel ray tracing in multiple ranks. In this case, each rank independently performs the exact same computation to generate the same accel grid. Ideally, performing the same computation should be avoided to speed up the accel grid construction using parallel processing. But in that case, partial accel grids must be transmitted to other ranks as they are being computed. Since accel grids internally reference data using pointers in a complex way, this is not simple. In any case, the time required to construct the accel grid is only a small part of the entire rendering computation, so we do not think this is a very critical issue for now.

If the scene does not fit in a single rank, then the scene is distributed over multiple ranks (Section 8.5). Each rank independently generates accel grids in parallel. There is a high level of parallelization here, and we can expect a speed-up directly proportional to the number of machines. This is because no data is exchanged between ranks in the creation of accel grid. However there are two problems.

The first problem is space correspondence. Independently creating accel grids for scenes divided in multiple ranks implies that there can be almost no correspondence between the created grids. Each accel grid should generate an optimized accel grid for its particular data. This causes problems when accel grids generated this way need some sort of correspondence (Figure 8.27).

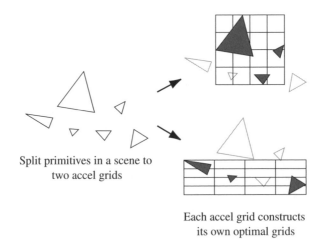

Split primitives in a scene to
two accel grids

Each accel grid constructs
its own optimal grids

Figure 8.27. Problem with parallel accel grid construction.

As mentioned in Section 8.5, Kilauea currently exchanges no geometry data whatsoever between the ranks. Therefore, specifying some part of space, removing that part, or inserting that part will never take place. But if we ever want to do this, having differently structured accel grids in two different ranks is a problem.

The second problem is in the precision of space traversal. This is a problem in the precision of the accel grid. For example, the precision of values used to describe the size and position of the grids is an issue. We construct accel grids as a hierarchical uniform grid, but traversing inside the grids is done using incremental computation whenever possible. The precision of the traversal is related closely to the precision of the incremental computation, and ultimately the precision of the size and position of the grids. This implies that ray tracing results could differ for the exact same data, depending on how the accel grids were constructed.

Because our ray tracing algorithm executes the traversal of the exact same ray on multiple accel grids, discrepancies in the space traversal results could be fatal. We must somehow ensure that the results are computed at the same precision.

We handle this problem as follows. The size and position of accel grids are specified using an IEEE single precision floating point number (32 bits). We precompute the space that can be represented by this number into a table, and make sure that grid boundaries only fall on values in this table. By doing this, we have made it possible to keep the size and position information of accel grids completely consistent no matter what kind of data is created in what order. By doing this, we have ensured that the final ray tracing result is always done at the same precision (Figure 8.28).

8.6.6   Shading Computation

Shading computation inside Kilauea is separated from the rest of the system such as parallel ray tracing. This allows the shading computation implementation to be improved independently. Kilauea's shading engine handles the various issues of parallel processing all "under the hood"; shader writers do not need to think about parallel processing and can write their shaders as if Kilauea was an ordinary sequential ray tracer.

Issues with parallel shading computation

Inside Kilauea, shading computation on the object surface and space traversal using ray tracing are processed separately in different threads. They may even be processed by different machines (depending on the configuration of tasks). This raises situations where something that can easily be done on a sequential shader is extremely difficult.

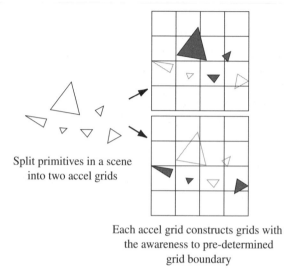

Split primitives in a scene
into two accel grids

Each accel grid constructs grids with
the awareness to pre-determined
grid boundary

Figure 8.28. Avoiding problems with parallel accel grid construction.

Say that some shading computation is being done on some object surface. This object has a specular reflection, so the color of reflected ray must be taken into account for computing the final color of this surface.

In a normal sequential ray tracer, shading computation is done on the object surface. The reflection ray is then computed, and a new ray is shot. The new ray is processed recursively, before any other computation takes

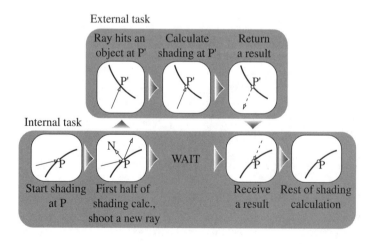

Figure 8.29. Problem in parallel shading calculation.

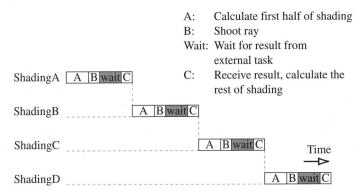

Figure 8.30. Apparently wasteful CPU processing.

place. This result is then used in the surface computation, and the final color of the object is determined. However, this cannot be done easily in Kilauea.

Ray tracing must be done in order to compute reflection. Since the computation on the surface and the ray tracing are done in different tasks within Kilauea, ray data must be exchanged between the tasks in some way. In the worst case, the desired task may be on a different rank, so data must be transmitted using message passing.

Ray tracing is then executed on the transmitted ray, performing a new shading computation which intersects another object. The computed color is then returned to the original object surface and added to the surface color, determining the final color of the surface. The problem here is that since the ray tracing is being done in a different task, computation on the object surface cannot proceed until the ray tracing resolves. If the surface computation stops until the color of the ray comes back, CPU cycles are wasted, seriously degrading parallel processing performance (Figures 8.29 and 8.30).

Overview of solving the parallel shading problem

There are mainly two solutions to this problem: Do not allow shaders to depend on ray colors and somehow keep the CPU busy. The first solution gets around the problem by changing the way in which shaders are written. For example, by restricting shaders to not perform a computation based on the color of the returned ray. However, we have given up on this approach because being able to easily write shaders is extremely important for a production renderer. The second method allows users to write a shader in the same way as a sequential ray tracer without having to use a special way of thinking. There are several ideas for accomplishing this.

One idea is to send the intermediate results attached to the ray whenever a new ray needs to be cast. Computation proceeds as the required elements become available, and the solution can be found when all the elements are available. This appears to avoid making the CPU idle.

This idea may seem to work, but there are problems with implementing it. The information added to the ray will most likely grow very large, especially for complex shaders. This is not desirable for Kilauea, since Kilauea is designed to frequently exchange rays between ranks.

Also, in some cases the distributed computation must be collected in one place. One example is when computing the shadow contributions by collecting multiple shadow rays shot from the object surface. To do this computation using this method, multiple shadow rays must be sequentially evaluated. Multiple shadow rays are independent, so the computation should be parallelized. Because of these reasons, we have adopted the following method (Figure 8.31).

1. If a new ray needs to be shot while computing a surface, shoot the ray and wait until the result comes back.

2. But this will cause the CPU to be idle, so start a new shading computation.

3. Usually, there are a large number of shading computations going on inside Kilauea, so execute whatever shading computations that can be processed in turn, in order to keep the CPU from being idle.

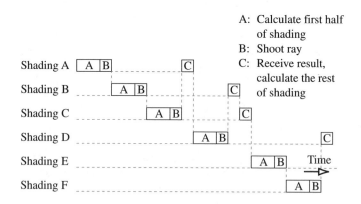

Figure 8.31. Keep CPU busy by optimally scheduling the shading.

4. Some shading computations will shoot a ray and wait.

5. The first ray comes back while doing all this.

6. The returned result is used in the original computation, and the computation continues.

7. Finally all the computation completes, and the colors are finalized.

This method takes advantage of the fact that there are many independent shading computations going on, and controls them so that the CPU does not become idle. While the previous method tries to solve the problem by adding more information to the rays, i.e., send more messages; this idea does not change the amount and the size of the messages. Instead, the execution order of the computations is changed. On the other hand, this method requires much more memory in order to manage the execution sequence. We have designed a shading engine based on this idea that is general enough. Memory management has been optimized as much as possible by writing special-purpose mechanisms. Currently, all shaders run on top of this engine. We call this engine the SPOTEngine (Shading Parallel Object Task Engine).

SPOTEngine

The SPOTEngine is explained here in terms of shader creation and computation.

Decomposition of shading computation. When implementing a shader, the shader writer breaks down the shader computation into functions performed by an external task and functions performed by the shader itself. There are only two kinds of computation performed by an external task: ray tracing and photon look-up. The shader computation is in a wait state whenever these two tasks are being processed. Once the shader computation is decomposed into these two elements, any part of the computation which does not depend on outside tasks can be performed sequentially. We refer to these parts as SPOT (Shading Parallel Object Task, pronounced es-pot).

Computation to be performed after receiving data from outside tasks can also be considered SPOTs for the same reason. Therefore, computation before and after external tasks can always be combined into a SPOT. A SPOT that receives data from an outside task and acts on it is referred to as receiving SPOT. Dividing shader computation into SPOT execution units easily allows the SPOTEngine to determine under what condition some

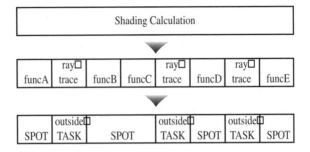

Figure 8.32. Decomposing shading computation.

computation can proceed with its execution (Figure 8.32). Ultimately, one shader is composed of multiple SPOTs where the data flows through to perform a shading computation.

SPOT network. SPOTEngine internally treats a SPOT as some unit of execution that cannot be decomposed further. SPOTs can define data along with computation (method). This represents exactly what an object is in an object-oriented philosophy (Figure 8.33).

Actual shaders are represented as a network structure of SPOTs that pass data to each other and perform the computation defined for each SPOT. The network can be structured in a very flexible way, and all shaders are described with this network. In other words, Kilauea executes shader computation by passing data in sequence along this SPOT network (Figure 8.34).

At actual rendering time, there are as many SPOTs waiting for data from outside tasks, or sending data to outside tasks (i.e., ray tracing requests or photon look-up requests) as there are a number of shading computations being performed inside the SPOTEngine. SPOTEngine's job is to appropriately pick out a SPOT that can be executed and process it. Shading computation inside Kilauea proceeds by processing massive amounts

Figure 8.33. SPOT.

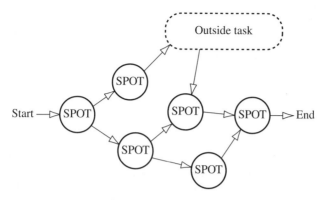

Figure 8.34. SPOT network.

of SPOTS quickly. SPOTEngine's performance determines the speed of shader computation and required memory.

SPOT (Shading Parallel Object Task). As previously mentioned, SPOT is the smallest execution unit inside the SPOTEngine. The characteristics of SPOTs which are required to build the SPOT network will now be described.

SPOT can define data entry points called "slots" (Figure 8.35). These slots are used to get data from other SPOTs, or receive data from outside tasks. These slots are basically used to describe the network structure of SPOTs. Most SPOTs exist somewhere on the network, so they usually have at least one or more slots, but it is possible in special cases to define a SPOT with zero slots.

A SPOT also has an execution status. Currently, there are four kinds of execution status (Figure 8.36): waiting, active, dead, and static. A waiting condition means that the SPOT is waiting for values to be inserted to its

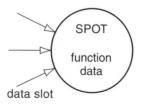

Figure 8.35. SPOT slot.

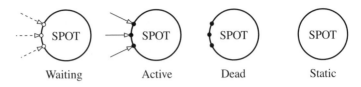

Waiting   Active   Dead   Static

Figure 8.36. SPOT Condition.

slots. The method defined in the SPOT cannot be executed yet. An active condition means that all the slots are filled, and that the method defined in the SPOT can be executed. Dead means that the SPOT has finished its execution. Static is a special case, used for defining a SPOT that exist regardless of the other conditions mentioned above.

In the network that uses slots, it is easy to determine which SPOTs can be executed by monitoring the SPOT's status. SPOTEngine tracks the condition of every SPOT that it manages, and executes the methods defined in the SPOTs as they become Active.

In an actual shader implementation, SPOTs derive from the basic SPOT class, implementing the required computation as a method defined in the subclass. Computation such as sending data to other SPOTs, sending data to external tasks, and receiving data from other tasks, are all performed by calling the various methods implemented in the basic SPOT class. Programmers need not worry about these details when implementing a new SPOT.

SPOTSpace. Inside the SPOTEngine, multiple SPOTs exist connected in a network structure. SPOTEngine's main job is to execute the SPOTs that are ready to run. To handle this more efficiently, SPOTs related to each other are grouped into a SPOTSpace.

Specifically, one shading computation unit (all computation on a particular surface) composes one SPOTSpace, and all SPOTs required for that surface are constructed within that SPOTSpace. When this shading computation is complete, SPOTSpace ends its purpose and is destroyed (Figure 8.37).

Shading computations inside Kilauea are basically independent of each other. Some shading computations cannot refer to an intermediate result of another. For example, shading computations on two different pixels on screen are processed as completely independent computations, and one cannot refer to the results of other while computing. The sequence in which shading computation is performed depends on the particular state of parallel processing at the time, and for this reason, it is not possible to guarantee the availability of data (Figure 8.38).

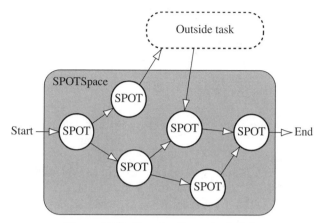

Figure 8.37. One shading calculation.

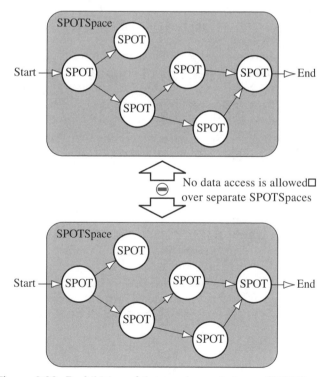

Figure 8.38. Prohibition of data exchange between SPOTSpace.

SPOTEngine uses SPOTSpaces to make one shading computation completely independent, and to help handle the memory management of one shading request appropriately. At rendering time, multiple SPOTSpaces exist inside the SPOTEngine, and a network of SPOTs exist within the SPOTSpace. SPOTs in the network that are ready to be executed are processed as they become ready.

PSA (Pot Space Address). Consider the case in which one SPOT shoots a ray and another SPOT is waiting for its result. The shot ray goes through an appropriate path and is sent to the accel grid for space traversal. If some intersection point is found as a result, then a new shading computation begins at that point. The color at that point is then determined, returned to the original SPOT, and computation proceeds according to the SPOT network inside that SPOTSpace.

To make this work, one important mechanism needs to be implemented. That is the mechanism for correctly returning the result to the original SPOT that requested the color information. In order to meet this requirement, we need an address information that uniquely points to a single SPOT within the Kilauea system.

We call this address the PSA (Pot Space Address). All data going to an outside task use PSA to specify the destination SPOT where the result of computation should be sent. Usually inside, Kilauea system, there are multiple STasks in multiple ranks. Inside a STask is a SPOTEngine. Inside a SPOTEngine are a large number of SPOTSpaces. Inside an SPOTSpace are a large number of SPOTs. PSA is an address that can uniquely specify a single SPOT out of the very large number of SPOTs, from when the Kilauea system is launched to when it is shut down. By using the PSA one can guarantee that data will be sent without errors. PSA information forms the root of Kilauea's shading computation scheme.

Multithreaded implementation. SPOTEngine itself, like other parts of Kilauea, is a multithreaded implementation. SPOTSpaces do not need to communicate with each other, and it is simple to find parallelism in the evaluation of the SPOT network in SPOTSpace. So there is no reason why we shouldn't try a multithreaded implementation. We have divided the computation inside SPOTEngine across several threads.

SPOT garbage collection. The massive number of shading computations is represented inside SPOTEngine by a large number of SPOTSpaces and the network of SPOTs inside the SPOTSpace. Memory used by SPOTs must be freed as soon as they perform their computation and become dead.

Otherwise, the available memory will be exhausted. However, freeing of memory must be done carefully in a multithreaded SPOTEngine. If the thread which allocated the memory is different from the thread freeing it, memory management must be coded to expect accesses from two different threads, and be coded in a thread-safe manner. This makes coding more complicated, and is bug-prone. This also makes optimization and modification more difficult. One solution is to always return memory to the thread that allocated the memory, and let the allocating thread handle the release. SPOTEngine manages memory in this way, and increases efficiency by performing thread-local memory management.

Detection of dead SPOTs is one of the features implemented in the SPOT class itself, and subclasses of SPOT used for writing shaders do not need to handle this. Similarly, SPOTEngine directly controls the freeing of dead SPOTs, optimally handling memory release automatically.

Thus, shader writers do not need to take into consideration the small details of multithreaded memory management—the SPOTEngine handles everything automatically.

Shader types

The functionality required for shading computation is classified into several types of shaders in Kilauea. Currently, Kilauea has the following shaders: emit shader, surface shader, light shader, background shader, and volume shader. All of these shaders are implemented as SPOT networks, and SPOTEngine executes them. All shader types are described below.

Emit shader. Any kind of computation involving the shooting of rays is classified as an emit shader. Inside Kilauea, there are two main cases where this shader is necessary. The first case is when controlling the rays being shot from the camera in normal ray tracing. Each camera has one emit shader. By writing an emit shader that takes into account the characteristics of the camera, it is simple to implement features such as a lens distortion. Separate emit shaders will be created for different lens characteristics (Figure 8.39).

The other case is the controlling of photon tracing. In order to create a photon map, photon tracing must be done. This shoots photons of appropriate number and intensity from light sources in the scene, tracing how these photons spread in the scene. Emit shaders control this basic framework. However, the photon emit function implemented in each of the light sources is in charge of taking into consideration the emission characteristics of each light source and shooting the photons appropriately. This

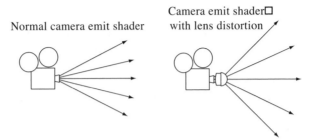

Figure 8.39. Camera emit shader.

function exists inside the light shader. Therefore, emit shaders in the photon tracing only control the higher levels of how multiple light sources in the scene shoot the photons, and are not directly involved in the shooting of the photons. Currently, one kind of emit shader for photon shooting suits all our needs, and there is no need to develop new emit shaders for photon tracing.

Surface shader. Surface shaders describe how shading computation should be done on an object surface. When a ray hits some object surface as a result of space traversal, a new surface shader is called at that point. A surface shader only describes the computation that will be done on the surface. If necessary, it will shoot shadow rays, reflection rays, refraction/transparent rays, etc. SPOT already implements the necessary functions for shooting these rays, so new shaders simply call these functions.

When creating a surface shader that takes global illumination into account, final gathering and photon map searching must be done on the object surface. It is also simply a matter of calling the functions that SPOT already implements.

Whether global illumination is considered in the shading computation of object surface depends on the kind of surface shader assigned to that object. This means that in order to correctly perform global illumination on the entire scene, every object in the scene must be assigned a surface shader that takes global illumination into account.

Surface shaders also define a function that decides how the shader will behave at the time of photon tracing. This function describes how a photon will behave on the object surface when photon tracing is done. New photons may have to be shot from the object surface inside this function. This is also performed by calling functions already implemented in SPOT.

Basically, surface shaders independently define the following two computations: direct illumination on the object surface and photon tracing

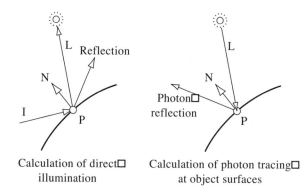

Calculation of direct□   Calculation of photon tracing□
illumination   at object surfaces

Figure 8.40. Two roles of surface shader.

computation on the object surface. These are closely related, and correct computation cannot be done if there are any inconsistencies here. However, the two functions can be defined independently in order to allow more freedom in shading description even at the cost of unnatural computation (Figure 8.40).

Light shader. Light shaders define the computation for light sources. Basically they define the following: light source computation for direct illumination and behavior of photon emission for photon tracing. These two elements may be described independently, but the simulation of light will not be physically correct unless its attributes are consistent. For the same reason as in the surface shader, we allow them to be defined independently for more freedom in lighting description (Figure 8.41).

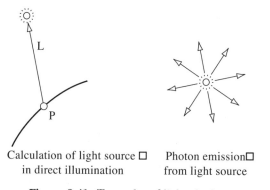

Calculation of light source □   Photon emission□
in direct illumination   from light source

Figure 8.41. Two roles of light shader.

When tracing photons, the emit shader calls the second mechanism of the light shader. Photon emission from this light source is controlled according to the definition of the emission characteristics, light intensity, color, etc. In the direct illumination computation, the surface shader calls the first mechanism. The color on the surface is computed based on the relationship between the surface shader and the light.

Light shaders also take care of the shadow computation. The light shaders are called from the object surface, and first shoot a shadow ray onto itself to see if it is a shadow. If not, the light color computation is executed. Shader writers do not have to think about these details when writing new light shaders because this mechanism is implemented in the shader template described below.

Light shaders can describe many different variations of light. Currently, area lights are described in addition to the common point, directional, and spot lights. Sky lights are also implemented as a light shader denoting a special kind of light source. This light source computes the light coming from the sky, and it is used when shooting photons that take into account light from the sky. This is necessary when the image takes such light into account.

Background shader. This shader is called whenever the ray performs space traversal, but fails to hit anything. Currently background shaders are used only when computing direct illumination. Photons that do not hit anything at photon tracing time disappear into infinity.

Volume shader. This is called when a ray performs space traversal and enters a volume container. Kilauea uses ray marching for volume computation, and volume shaders define what kind of computation will be performed for each step of ray marching.

Volume shaders, just like the surface shaders, have two roles in computation: direct illumination in the volume and photon tracing in the volume. The second computation defines the behavior of photons for volume photon map creation. (Figure 8.42)

Figure 8.43 illustrates how the data flows between each shader in a general shading computation.

Implementation-level techniques used for Kilauea shader development are described next.

Shader template. If the shading computation on an object surface can be processed by a local illumination model, each shader simply performs independent computation. Each shader simply determines the color. When

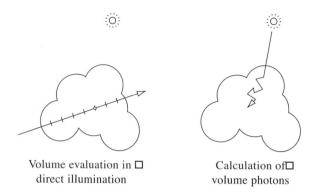

Volume evaluation in □
direct illumination

Calculation of□
volume photons

Figure 8.42. Two roles of volume shader.

writing a shader that takes global illumination into consideration, however, shaders must perform the various global illumination computations.

In the case of Kilauea, final gathering and photon look-up is necessary for global illumination. Final gathering must be executed in the surface shader of the object surface taking into account global illumination. Basically, the same algorithm can be applied to all surface shaders that take global illumination into account.

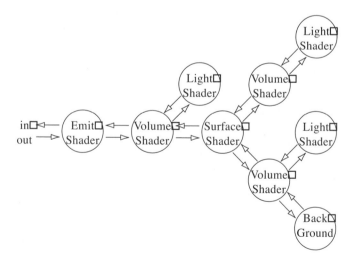

Figure 8.43. Relationship of shaders.

8.6.7   Photon Map Method

All surface shaders are implemented using SPOT, so final gathering and photon look-up are treated as computation on the SPOTs. Therefore, every surface shader which takes global illumination into account must have final gathering and photon look-up implemented.

The shader template is prepared to simplify the task of writing shaders supporting global illumination. The shader template basically bundles everything that does not depend on the surface characteristics, and includes controls for final gather and photon maps. By using this shader template to write new surface shaders, it is possible to easily write a global illumination shader simply by writing the parts which depend on the object surface characteristics.

It's possible to write a global illumination surface shader without using this shader template. In this case, the new shader simply has to control everything itself. Implementation-wise, this shader template is also composed using SPOT. One shader template exists for each shader type.

Texture sampling. Texture data sampling can be done from every SPOT. The actual sampling operation is managed separately within the SPOTEngine, and things like the partial caching of texture data when

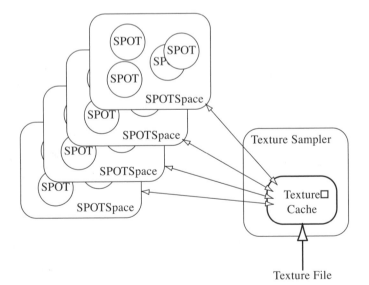

Figure 8.44. Texture sampling function.

multiple sampling operations are done on the same texture is automated. It is also possible to appropriately control the memory required for sampling multiple separate textures. Basically, it takes the approach of caching part of an image in memory, so users are able to have complete control over how much memory will be used for the texture cache. Because this functionality is implemented in the base SPOT class, all SPOT classes which inherit the base SPOT class can perform texture sampling. (Figure 8.44)

Kilauea uses the photon map method (including final gathering) for global illumination computation [140, 141]. The photon map method generates global illumination images in two passes. The first pass is called photon tracing, where photons are emitted from light sources, traced through the scene, and stored in photon maps. The second pass performs the actual rendering, where the photon maps are looked up to compute the global illumination component. Kilauea's implementation simply adopts the general photon map method. The only difference is that our implementation takes advantage of parallel processing, performing parallel photon tracing and parallel photon look-ups.

Parallel photon tracing

Parallelizing photon tracing is extremely simple in an environment where ray tracing is already parallelized. Photon tracing is purely ray tracing from an algorithmic standpoint. In our case, ray tracing is already parallelized, so there is no problem in the parallelizing of the photon tracing.

The strategy for saving photon data in multiple photon maps needs careful consideration. When there are multiple PTasks in different ranks, each PTask stores photon map data. There are two cases to be considered here depending on how photons are stored in each photon map. The photon map either fits in the memory of one machine, or it does not. The first case is simple. The same photon data is stored in every photon map and every photon map ends up with the exact same data. The second case is similar to the idea of parallel ray tracing. The distribution strategy of photons across multiple machines follows the method used for distribution of the accel grids.

If two machines share the memory to store the photon map, each machine will contain approximately 50% of the total photons. The distribution and density of the photons in two machines should be almost equivalent. If there are more than two machines, the photons are distributed uniformly among photon maps, with a similar distribution and density (Figure 8.45).

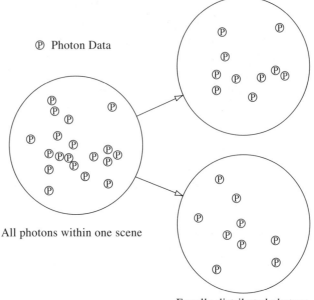

Figure 8.45. Distribution of photon data.

Parallel photon look-up

The processing of each photon in photon tracing is completely independent from other photons, so the parallel processing performance of this portion has the same characteristics as Kilauea's parallel ray tracing performance. However, there are some different characteristics from the final ray tracing. Ray tracing is called from within a shading computation, and it resolves when color values are returned at the end. In the case of photon tracing, there is no need to return a value once the data is stored in the photon map. Because this is essentially a one-way operation, it has an even higher degree of parallelism, very suitable for multi-CPU or PC cluster environment.

To speed up the rendering stage, the irradiance estimate at the location of each photon is precalculated after the photon tracing [47]. This precomputation phase can be processed in parallel for each distributed photon map.

Kilauea looks up photons during shading computation to take global illumination components into account. This look-up operation searches the already constructed photon maps and retrieves the necessary values.

Photon look-up is handled in a task outside of SPOTEngine, just like ray tracing is handled outside of SPOTEngine. Photon look-up requests are sent to a photon map inside the PTask, and the look-ups are performed there. The results are returned to the SPOTSpace that requested the look-ups, and the shading computation continues from there.

If all the photons in the scene can be handled in a single photon map, then it is just a matter of doing the look-up in that photon map. If the photon map for the entire scene is distributed across several photon maps, the same kind of strategy as parallel ray tracing is used (Figure 8.46).

First, an identical photon look-up request is created and sent to each of the distributed photon maps. Each request executes the look-up operation for each photon map, and and returns the precomputed irradiance. Based on the results, the final photon look-up result is computed.

Each photon look-up is handled in the PTask, and computing the final result from the returned results is done in LTask. Photon look-ups in multiple photon maps basically have the exact same properties as ray tracing in multiple accel grids. Implementation and multithreading can be done using the exact same ideas. In the case of Kilauea, parallel ray tracing implementation and parallel photon look-up implementation have a one-to-one correspondence.

There are fundamental differences as well. In the case of ray tracing, only the closest intersection point is used and others are thrown out. In the case of photon look-ups, results from every photon map are used in the computation of the final photon look-up result. Please refer to the SIGGRAPH 2001 course notes on photon maps (course 38), particularly the note "A few photon map tricks," for further details on parallel photon maps.

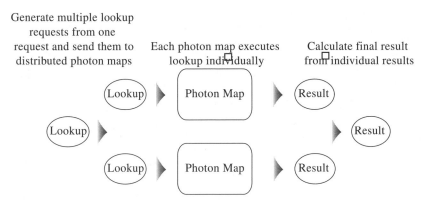

Figure 8.46. Parallel photon look-up.

8.6.8   Things to Note in Shading Computation

Auto-cruise control of queues

All shading computation is done using the SPOTEngine. SPOTEngine can be abstracted as an extremely deep pipeline. The queue data structure which handles this pipeline could exhaust all the available memory at times. The problem manifests itself when the execution speed of two stages in the pipeline becomes excessively unbalanced for some reason. If a later pipeline stage becomes too slow, the data stored in the queue will accumulate.

Most of these problems can be predicted at the initial design phase of the algorithm, and can be circumvented by evenly distributing the computational load among multiple threads. There is still a possibility that memory will be wasted due to some external cause, however. In extreme cases, CPU power is used to allocate more memory for the queue data, which further aggravates the situation. If the socket connection is hindered for some reason, even for a short amount of time, data that was supposed to leave for outside ranks quickly can no longer do so, eventually causing the kinds of problems mentioned above.

Another cause of dramatic changing in the data flow through the pipeline is that the computation of each SPOT is completely dependent on the shader. SPOTEngine constantly faces the above danger because the computational load of some SPOT is unknown until it is actually executed.

The current implementation of SPOTEngine is able to resist the worst situation of explosive use of memory by the pipeline queue for almost every SPOT. SPOTEngine also has a built-in "auto-cruise" control of queues to avoid such situation.

When some method is inserting its computed result into the queue to be handled by the next stage in the pipeline, the insertion operation is blocked if the queue is longer than a certain length. The next stage in the pipeline will process items from the queue while the previous stage is blocked, eventually allowing the value to be added to the queue (Figure 8.47).

Ideally, the program logic should be constructed in such a way that this kind of mechanism is unnecessary, but this is an effective technique for avoiding the worst possible situation.

Thread priority boost

One solution to the problem mentioned above is to change the execution priority of the threads. This is generally referred to as the priority boost of the thread. This sounds like an appealing idea, though experiments show that controlling thread scheduling with priority does not work as expected. First of all, the Pthread library that Kilauea currently uses

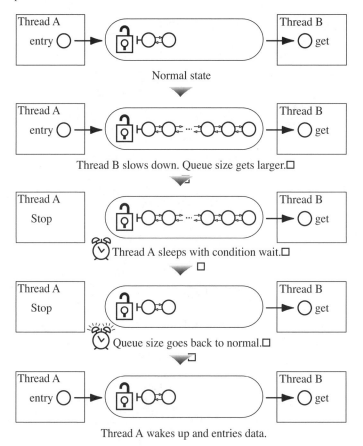

Normal state

Thread B slows down. Queue size gets larger.□

Thread A sleeps with condition wait.□

Queue size goes back to normal.□

Thread A wakes up and entries data.

Figure 8.47. Auto-cruising queue data flow.

does not allow changing individual thread's priority. In our experiments on an SGI, controlling the thread scheduling was very difficult even with full control over the individual thread's priority. For these reasons, Kilauea does not use any thread priority boosting.

Passing rule inside the queue

In a similar problem as the one mentioned above, there are times when the memory in SPOTEngine is excessively used, and SPOTEngine cannot continue its job because it is too busy trying to allocate memory. The engine easily encounters this situation if all shading requests are processed with equal priority.

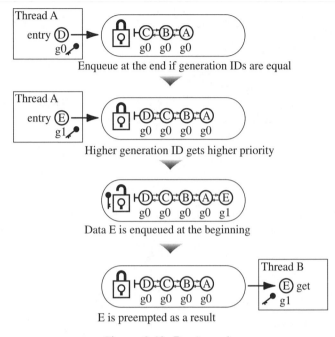

Figure 8.48. Passing rule.

Consider shooting a new ray from the object surface when shading. This ray hits another object, shoots another ray, and so on at multiple levels. Normally, SPOTEngine handles shading requests as they enter the queue. All requests actually start from primary rays shot from the camera. SPOTEngine executes these requests as they go in the queue, and these requests generate new rays, which request new shading computation at their intersection points. If the new shading request is inserted to the end of the queue, and it cannot execute until the requests earlier in the queue have been completed, SPOTEngine will have to store all in-progress SPOTs by using an extremely large amount of memory. In other words, once all primary ray computations are complete, the secondary ray computation begins, then the tertiary ray computation begins. This is often referred to as a breadth-first strategy. To get around this problem, we take the approach of adding generation IDs to all data that goes through the SPOTs. A computation with a larger generation ID unconditionally preempts (has a higher priority than) a computation with a lower generation ID, as illustrated in Figure 8.48. This method, often referred to as a depth-first strategy, avoids the problem of an explosive increase of the queue length inside the SPOTEngine.

Latency and dynamic adaptive sampling

As mentioned previously, the shading computation inside Kilauea is a pipeline with a very large number of stages. Compared with a sequential implementation, this parallel shading engine suffers from a much longer latency in computing the shading results.

Dynamic adaptive sampling has trouble dealing with this latency in the shading engine. Dynamic adaptive sampling determines the next action based on the previous sampling results. In the initial stage of rendering, there are enough sampling requests to keep the pipeline busy all the time. However, the CPU gradually becomes more and more idle as the computation gets near the end. Currently, the only solution is to shorten the time required to process one request. This problem is alleviated to some extent by improving the latency of SPOTEngine, but a fundamental solution has not been discovered yet.

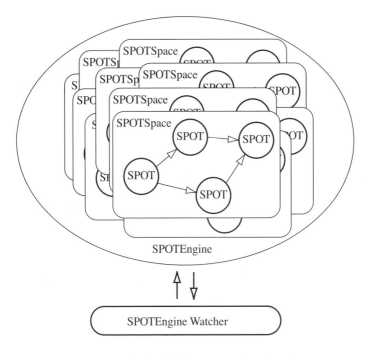

Figure 8.49. SPOTEngine watcher thread.

Profiling

Being able to learn how the shading computation is processed within the
SPOTEngine and pinpointing the bottleneck is very vital ro improving the
system. However, in the case of our SPOTEngine which is implemented in
a multithreaded manner, we were unable to find effective tools for analyzing
the performance. SPOTEngine performs self-analysis and self-diagnosis as
it executes its shading computations. The self-diagnosis/analysis mechanism is a separate thread, collecting various statistical information from
the internals of the SPOTEngine. This information is very helpful in determining whether the SPOTEngine is running soundly or some potential
problem is disturbing the performance (Figure 8.49). This mechanism can
be started and stopped as necessary from the Tcl script.

8.6.9   Development in General

Kilauea is the result of cooperative effort of multiple developers. This
section discusses our development environment and policy.

Debugging, debuggers, and development style

Debugging is a very difficult process. We have not found any debuggers
or debugging methods that perfectly match our requirements. Our main
debugger is gdb, and it is only a tool for debugging within one process, down
to threads. When debugging something related to message passing between
multiple ranks, we cannot use any debugger whatsoever. Launching two
Kilauea processes on two machines with gdb in most cases is not effective
either.

In order to avoid such situations as much as possible, our development
style first focuses on perfecting each module independently. Kilauea has
several mechanisms for helping this. Kilauea is an extremely large system
as a renderer, but all computation is divided into tasks, making individual
testing of tasks simpler. In some cases, parts of rendering computation
can be simulated inside Kilauea, or simple scene data can be created inside
Kilauea. Each task has a general way of sending text commands through
the master task in a unified way, thereby making implementation of debugging and testing methods simple. Multiple developers are currently
involved in the project, and in most cases, development effort is divided on
a per-task basis. Individual programmers can perform tests individually
and check code into the master source tree when it is relatively bug-free.
This development style is working very well.

Message passing protocol

Kilauea adopted MPI's philosophy for message passing between multiple ranks, but someone must determine how and what data is transmitted. One idea is to standardize the details of binary data transmission protocol for specific tasks, documenting and implementing them after the programmers have agreed on it. This is not the approach we take because we want to avoid the overhead of having to communicate all the time in order to decide on transmission protocols that may change every day. We only define a class for transmission and its API methods, completely leaving actual transmission method and protocol to the programmer in charge of implementing that class. The programmer may change and/or improve the transmission protocol as often as he desires, but under the rule that the class API does not change. In this way, we have tried to allow each other's development to proceed smoothly by removing as many dependencies on each other as possible.

Inherent difficulty of debugging parallel computation

Debugging parallel programs is unquestionably much more difficult than debugging sequential programs. Bugs in parallel processing are often not reproducible. Most reproducible bugs are not likely to be bugs related to the parallel processing, but rather very simple errors in logic.

When development gets to a certain stage, most of the simple bugs are fixed, leaving only the complex and difficult bugs that are deeply rooted in the parallel processing. Sometimes bugs may be difficult to reproduce if they only occur after ten hours of continuous rendering. Cores dumped by Kilauea often do not have any useful information, or are very difficult to analyze. Even worse, Kilauea may just hang up in a thread deadlock. Tracking down this sort of bug is a very tedious process.

Instability is a fatal flaw in applications such as a renderer. In an ordinary sequential renderer, we should improve stability by fixing all the bugs as they appear, but in the case of our parallel renderer, this kind of policy may just put a hopeless load on the developers without improving the situation at all. Of course, bugs should be located and fixed, so we can't just leave them alone. For Kilauea, we have decided to come up with a fault-tolerant mechanism for getting around fatal bugs. We ended up with this conclusion after facing the reality that we cannot keep the code 100% bug-free, even though we should definitely fix bugs.

Consider the case where Kilauea is rendering multiple frames over many hours. Some potential bug is lurking in the system, and it is extremely difficult to fix because it is deeply rooted in the parallel processing logic.

The worst symptom of this bug is that it stops the rendering. Imagine that one starts a rendering job at night, only to find out the next morning that it has frozen in the middle of the first frame. Kilauea observes this phenomenon as some sample requests never returning the results for some reason. Kilauea has the mechanism to monitor this problem by setting a time-out for every sampling computation. For samples that time out, Kilauea determines that fatal errors which lock up the computation occurred and attempts to reschedule those samples.

If, after several attempts, they keep timing out, then Kilauea finally gives up and shuts down all Kilauea processes. At this time, Kilauea returns a status code saying that it shut down due to some internal trouble. The Kilauea daemons which monitor the Kilauea system analyze the status code, and understand that Kilauea shut itself down due to internal troubles. In this case, the Kilauea daemons reboot all Kilauea processes, and instruct them to restart the computation starting from the frame with the problem. The restarted Kilauea may be able to compute the frame correctly this time. The more the bug is based on some complex timing issues of parallel processing, the more likely rendering would succeed on the second try.

This fault-tolerant mechanism is rarely triggered now because Kilauea is becoming more stable day by day. However, this kind of mechanism should exist considering the difficulty of debugging a parallel program. Apparently, the mechanism is of no use against simple bugs which are easily reproduced. It is only effective for getting around bugs whose cause is difficult to find and fix.

8.7 Rendering Results

This section presents Kilauea rendering results and analyzes its performance. All renderings used the following hardware configuration: maximum 18 Pentium III machines running at 1 GHz with 512 MB memory connected with 100BaseT Ethernet and a 100BaseT switching hub.

8.7.1 Sample 1: Quatro

Quatro (Figure 8.50) has 700,233 triangles and is lit by two light sources: one directional light and one skylight. Using 18 machines, the computation took 7 minutes, 19 seconds. This scene data is small enough to fit in the memory of one machine. There is no need for distributing the scene data to multiple machines and each ATask on each machine can compute ray tracing individually. In this case, all ATasks in all machines will hold identical copies of the geometry data. Let us examine how the rendering

Figure 8.50. Quatro (700,233 triangles). See also Color Plate 11.

time changes as more machines are added. Table 8.1 shows the rendering time of Quatro as the number of machines is increased. Figure 8.51 shows the graph of the ratio of the rendering time compared to the result using one machine. Triangular plots represent the total rendering time, from the very initial boot-up stage of Kilauea to the shutdown of Kilauea. Square plots represent timing results only for the actual rendering stage, which mostly consists of ray tracing and surface shading. Square plots do not include the time for reading in the scene, distributing it to multiple machines, and constructing the accel grid.

The plot of the total rendering time falls off from the optimal linear performance as the number of machines increases. This performance loss is mostly due to the stages such as reading in the scene and constructing the accel grid, which are not suitable for parallel processing or not thoroughly parallelized yet. Excluding these stages, the actual rendering stage (ray tracing and shading) is developed with full attention to the parallel performance. The super-linear property illustrated by the graph proves this.

We have not yet been able to profile Kilauea to the full extent to determine the cause of this super-linear behavior. Caching at various levels is perhaps effectively boosting the parallel performance, but detailed analysis is necessary to verify this. Unfortunately, we were only able to prepare 18 machines with the same spec as written at the beginning of this section, and could not conduct further tests. Theoretically, the network bandwidth will be the bottleneck at some point. However, with this single ATask

# of Machines	All (hr:min:sec)	Ray Trace (hr:min:sec)
1	1:30:23	1:13:15
2	0:45:23	0:35:40
3	0:30:59	0:23:42
4	0:23:48	0:17:42
5	0:19:37	0:14:10
6	0:16:48	0:11:47
7	0:15:05	0:10:05
8	0:13:32	0:08:49
9	0:12:03	0:07:52
10	0:11:04	0:07:01
11	0:10:15	0:06:19
12	0:09:33	0:05:45
13	0:09:03	0:05:17
14	0:08:41	0:04:53
15	0:08:23	0:04:32
16	0:07:52	0:04:14
17	0:07:35	0:03:59
18	0:07:19	0:03:45

Table 8.1. Quatro rendering time.

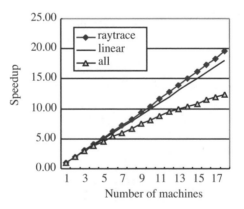

Figure 8.51. Number of machines versus speed-up ratio in single ATask case.

configuration used in this experiment, the only communication involved is transferring final pixel data and the same optimal performance is still expected even at around 100 machines.

8.7.2 Sample 2: Jeep

Jeep1 (Figure 8.52) has 715,059 triangles, and as in the first sample, is lit by two light sources: directional and skylight. The rendering took 8 minutes, 27 seconds using 18 machines. Just like in the first example, this scene is small enough to fit in the memory of one machine and there is no reason to share the data across several machines. In the next sample, a large scene which cannot fit in the memory of one machine is intentionally created using the same model data. Jeep4 (Figure 8.53) contains four identical copies of the Jeep data. For the experimental purpose, Jeeps are not instantiated. The entire scene contains 2,859,636 triangles: four times the original. This scene uses the same light settings, and the rendering time was 12 minutes, 38 seconds using 18 machines. 512MB of memory is not enough to store this scene data, so the scene needs to be distributed to at least two ATasks in two machines to render. If more than two machines are available, further speed-up is achievable by adding more pairs of machines. Let us have a look at how the performance increases as the number of machines increases in this case.

Table 8.2 is the rendering time of Jeep4 as the number of ATask groups is increased. Figure 8.54 shows the graph of the ratio of the rendering time

© 2001 Square USA Rendered by Kilauea

Figure 8.52. Jeep1 (715,059 triangles). See also Color Plate 11.

Figure 8.53. Jeep4 (2,859,636 triangles).

compared to the result using one machine. The graph has two plots, just like in the case of Quatro. Actually, the *x*-axis of this graph represents the number of ATask groups, not the number of machines. In this experiment, there are two machines in one ATask group, so the actual number of machines is twice the value of the *x*-axis.

The results show almost identical parallel performance as in the case of Quatro. As the number of ATask groups increases, the total rendering time gradually falls off from the optimal value. This is due to the same reason as in Quatro: Some stages are simply unsuitable for parallel processing. If only the actual rendering stage is observed, the graph shows a super-linear performance.

# of ATask groups	All (hr:min:sec)	Ray Trace (hr:min:sec)
1	1:35:45	1:23:26
2	0:47:46	0:41:19
3	0:34:08	0:27:32
4	0:25:38	0:20:37
5	0:21:00	0:16:25
6	0:17:50	0:13:29
7	0:15:30	0:11:26
8	0:13:50	0:09:55
9	0:12:38	0:08:47

Table 8.2. Jeep4 rendering time.

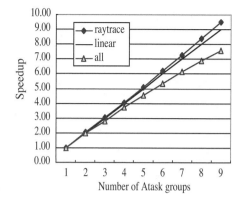

Figure 8.54. Number of ATask groups versus speed-up ratio in multi-ATask case.

8.7.3 Sample 3: Jeep 8

Jeep8 (Figure 8.55) has even more uninstantiated full copies of Jeeps in it to increase the total number of triangles. The scene contains 5,719,072 triangles, and there is no change to the light sources. Two ATasks in two machines do not have enough memory to hold this many triangles, so instead four ATasks in four machines are used to store the entire scene. In other words, the minimum number of machines in one ATask group is four. The scene took 18 minutes, 43 seconds to render with four sets of

Figure 8.55. Jeep8 (5,719,072 triangles).

these ATask groups, which totals to 16 machines. Again, in this example, the scalability obtained by increasing the number of ATask groups behaves the same way as in the previous samples: the total rendering time falls off gradually from the optimal value as the number of ATask groups increases, but when only the actual rendering stages are considered, it shows a super-linear performance.

8.7.4   Consideration of Rendering Results

As previously explained, Kilauea stays in the system even after the rendering completes and waits for further instructions from the user. This enables users to modify the shading parameters and restart a rendering without going through initialization processes such as reading in the scene and constructing accel grid again. Such characteristic is very important in a production pipeline, where most of the hours are spent on the repetition of tweaking a few shading parameters and rendering to see its outcome. Independent from the number of machines in one ATask group, Kilauea exhibits super-linear scalability in the ray tracing computation. Rendering is one of the most heavily repeated processes in the production, and thus, this super-linear property is a huge benefit. Simply put, when using Kilauea, the more machines one invests, the more productivity one gets.

This is how one would work with Kilauea. First, prepare N machines, where N is the minimum number of ATasks required to hold the scene. Then prepare M sets of N machines to achieve more than M times of the rendering performance. However, in reality, the performance gain is capped by the network bandwidth. Even if there is no communication between ATask groups, there will always be communication for gathering final pixel results. When this communication fills up the network bandwidth, the performance curve is expected to saturate. However, in a typical global illumination rendering with $N = 1$ (no communication between ATasks), the saturation does not happen even at more than 100 machines. We haven't conducted experiments on a larger scale due to physical limitations.

When $N >= 2$, there is no communication between individual ATask groups, but within each ATask group, ray data is heavily sent back and forth. The bandwidth consumed by this ray data is far more than that of the pixel data. The network saturation is reached more easily in this case, causing CPUs to perform less. In the case of Jeep8 ($N = 4$), the network traffic within one ATask group currently reaches 5 MB/sec, which is approaching close to the real bandwidth limit of a 100 BaseT network. When N is larger, the network will surely become the bottleneck. In the current Kilauea implementation, many data fields in the ray packets exchanged within one ATask group are relatively experimental in nature, and the packet size can be reduced in the future. By combining this packet size optimization and streaming compression, the network traffic is estimated to be halved. This will allow N to be about 8 to 10, even when using 100 BaseT network. Additionally, by moving onto Gigabit Ethernet, whose price is dropping rapidly lately, the saturation point can be pushed away even further.

The memory required to render a certain scene depends mostly on the implementation of the accel grid. Improvement in the memory efficiency of the accel grid is under way to allow more data to be stored in one machine, which leads to lesser N. Nevertheless, there will always be demand for rendering scenes larger than the memory size of one machine. Using multiple machines to enhance the productivity will surely be an essential part of the future production work. The scalability of the Kilauea architecture achieves satisfactory performance to fulfill such demands.

Other sample renderings by Kilauea are given in Figures 8.56–8.57. Figure 8.56 shows, in reading order, the Cornell box with Stanford bunnies (208,389 triangles and 1 area light); Running Phantom (55,336 triangles, skylight and 1 point light); Gondola (72,637 triangles, skylight and 1 point light); Phantom Crowd (25,340,322 triangles and 1 point light); and two images of the Spiritual Plant Control Room (899,720 triangles and 1 point light). Figure 8.57 depicts the Lab (1,007,508 triangles and 1 spot light (bounce light)) and Mr. Kilauea (33,493 triangles and 1 spot light (bounce light)). Finally, Figure 8.58 shows the Escape POD (468,321 triangles, skylight and 1 point light); SCN101 (787.255 triangles and 1 area light); ANS Gun (20,279 triangles and 1 point light); and a Japanese Tea Room (37,669 triangles, 8 area lights and 1 directional light).

8.8 Conclusion

At the moment, Kilauea has achieved its original goals in two ways: linear scalability and extensible architecture. As analyzed in Section 8.7.4, Kilauea achieved a satisfactory result in the linear scalability when the number of Atask groups is increased. The more investment in the number of machines, the more performance increase in the actual rendering stage (i.e., ray tracing and shading), independent of the scene size.

Kilauea can be thought as an extremely extensible testbed to conduct experiments on parallel processing of the rendering technology in general, including global illumination. In the future, Kilauea will aid in verifying various ideas to augment the speed and the image quality of the rendering algorithms.

Figure 8.56. Example images from the Kilauea renderer (see text for details as well as Color Plate 12).

Figure 8.57. Example images from the Kilauea renderer (see text for details).

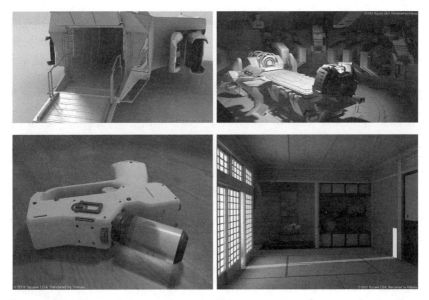

Figure 8.58. Example images from the Kilauea renderer (see text for details as well as Color Plates 13 and 14).

8.9 Future Plans and Tasks

Here is a brief list of planned additions and enhancements to Kilauea in the near future.

Optimization. Kilauea has distinguishing features such as message passing and SPOTEngine that do not exist in ordinary sequential ray tracers. Thus, we must admit that when running on a single machine, Kilauea has a speed disadvantage against a simple ray tracer. One technical goal is to make this penalty as small as possible. Optimization is being done from two perspectives. One is the optimization of SPOTEngine internals, and the other is the optimization of parallel ray tracing. These two both form the root of all computation in Kilauea, so they are constantly being improved to be more efficient. As far as SPOTEngine goes, the first implementation was very experimental, leaving lots of room for improvement. We are currently implementing a new version based on the problems and characteristics discovered through experimentation. We are also conducting some experiments on improving the parallel ray tracing algorithm, looking for an efficient implementation with more parallelism. Another future topic is improving the efficiency of final gathering and photon mapping.

Stability. We are currently stabilizing Kilauea. Specifically, these include improvements to the Kilauea daemon and modifying the internal computation to safer logics.

User interface. Kilauea is completely controlled by Maya which serves as the front-end, and all GUI is created with Mel or Maya plug-ins. We are working to provide a more comfortable environment. Another topic for the future is to create an interactive environment for determining the material properties of objects, taking advantage of Kilauea's ability to change elements of the scene while rendering.

Other plans for the future. Additionally, we intend to implement a shading compiler, allow dynamic reconfiguration of tasks at runtime and support for more primitives.

Acknowledgments

Our sincere thanks go to Kazuyuki Hashimoto, Kaveh Kardan, Shiro Kawai, and to the entire Square USA R&D team for their advice and ideas concerning the Kilauea Project. We also thank Jack Liao for his great assistance for the creation of the test images, and Junichi Kimura for his assistance with the translation of this document.

Contributors

The following Kilauea R&D team members contributed to this section:

- Toshi Kato (Project leader): Overall system architecture design, SPOTEngine design and implementation, MPI layer, ray tracing engine, and global illumination speed-up.

- Hitoshi Nishimura: Overall system architecture design, prototype renderer, surface and volume shader implementation, and GUI design.

- Tadashi Endo: Maya interactive/batch tools for Kilauea and test scene creation and rendering.

- Tamotsu Maruyama: Scene data read and distribution, shader base layer using SPOTEngine, Tcl script interface, subdivision surface, and NURBS and displacement mapping.

- Jun Saito: Pixel scheduling, sampling and filter, image viewer, Kilauea daemon, render farm administration system, and Ruby script interface.

- Motohisa Adachi: Kilauea job control system and shader GUI design.

- Per H. Christensen: Design and implementation of global illumination using photon mapping.

Additionally, Sergio Garcia Abad, Takuya Hada, Takashi Kubota, Jack Liao, Tatsuro Maruyama, Takao Noguchi, and Moto Sakakibara contributed to the creation of the test scenes.

9

Parallel Ray Tracing on a Chip

Tim Purcell

In previous chapters, we discussed the general principles and constraints of parallel processing applied to ray tracing. We have also seen several examples of parallel ray tracing in action on both large supercomputers and clusters of PCs. We now consider parallel ray tracing on a single chip. There are many types of chips we could consider: a custom designed chip like the AR250 [290], a stream processing chip like Imagine [155], or a multiprocessor on a single chip solution like Smart Memories [184].

The AR250 is designed primarily to accelerate off-line rendering. Custom hardware design for an interactive ray tracer is beyond the scope of our discussion. Streaming processors like Imagine are an interesting alternative to multithreaded architectures and are currently being investigated. We will focus our discussion on the Smart Memories chip. Smart Memories provides multiple processors on a single chip, much like shrinking an entire supercomputer or cluster onto a single chip. The principles we saw for parallel ray tracing in more traditional environments still apply, but we now have on-chip communication and on-chip shared memory access.

We will investigate the strengths of a multiprocessor on a single chip solution for parallel ray tracing. First, we describe the Smart Memories chip. We will then discuss SHARP, a multithreaded ray tracer we have studied on the Smart Memories chip. Finally, we will present results from our simulations for both caching and the overall system performance of SHARP running on Smart Memories.

9.1 The Smart Memories Chip

Smart Memories is a multiprocessor on a single chip computing substrate. It is a reconfigurable architecture. The memory system, computation, and communication systems are all reconfigurable. Smart Memories was designed to be a universal computing element, running efficiently for a wide variety of applications. Reconfigurability allows the Smart Memories chip

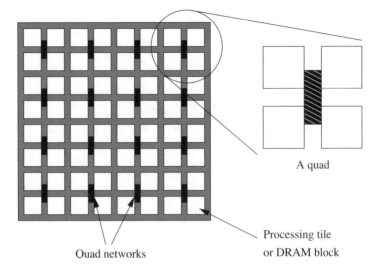

A quad

Processing tile
or DRAM block

Quad networks

Figure 9.1. A Smart Memories chip. A single chip consists of 64 processing tiles or DRAM blocks. A fast interconnect clusters groups of four tiles into quads. Quads are connected together by a dynamically routed global network.

to efficiently emulate architectures as different as the streaming Imagine processor [155] and the speculative multithreaded Hydra [108] processor. The chip is designed to be a replacement for custom designed chips.

A Smart Memories chip is shown in Figure 9.1. A single chip is composed of 64 independent processing tiles connected by a packet-based dynamically routed network. Processing tiles are grouped together in groups of four called *quads*. Quads are then connected together over the globally routed network.

A processing tile is shown in detail in Figure 9.2. Each tile devotes an equal amount of area to a processor core, network interconnect, and 128 kB of SRAM. The processor core is a 64-bit 1 GHz RISC-style processor. Each core contains two integer clusters and one floating point cluster. The floating point cluster has two adders, a multiplier, and a divide/square root unit. The available compute resources are similar to that found in a MIPS R10000 processor. The memory system and interconnect are designed to deliver 64 GB/s of memory bandwidth to any processing tile within the same quad. The global bandwidth available between quads is targeted to be 8 GB/s. See Mai et al. [184] for further architectural details on the Smart Memories chip.

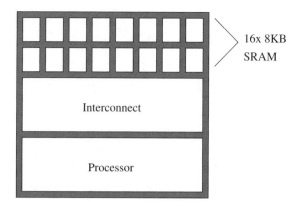

Figure 9.2. A Smart Memories processing tile. Tile area is split evenly between interconnect, a 64-bit RISC processor, and 128 kB of SRAM.

9.2 The SHARP Ray Tracer

We use a multithreaded ray tracer called SHARP for evaluating ray tracing on Smart Memories. Before discussing the mapping of SHARP to Smart Memories, we must enumerate the design decisions made for the ray tracer. First, the only primitive the ray tracer can intersect is triangles. This simplifies the intersection routines and regularizes scene database storage. Second, triangles are intersected using the Möller-Trombore [196] method for triangle intersection. Third, dynamic scenes are a challenge to all ray tracing implementations and are an active area or research [246]; therefore, we will not address dynamic scenes in this context. Finally, we choose to use a uniform grid acceleration structure. Like all acceleration structures, the uniform grid has its strengths and weaknesses (see Havran [114] for a nice study of several acceleration structures). We chose the uniform grid because it performs well in general, is simple to implement, and looks to map well to hardware.

We have decomposed the ray tracing problem into several independent threads, as shown in Figure 9.3. The eye ray generator generates eye rays from the camera and scene information. Rays are then passed to the traversal thread. This thread initializes the rays into the scene grid, and steps them through empty voxels. When a voxel containing geometry is found, the ray and voxel ID are passed to the triangle intersector thread. The intersector fetches and intersects against all the triangles associated with the voxel ID. If a successful intersection (or hit) is found, the hit is passed along to the shading thread. If no hit is found, the ray is instead passed

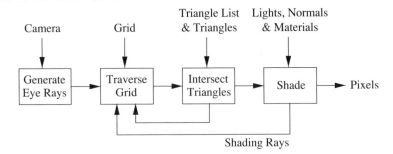

Figure 9.3. Data flow diagram for the SHARP ray tracer. Each box represents a separate computation thread, and the arrows represent data passed between threads.

back to the traversal thread for further traversal through the grid. The shading thread evaluates the color contribution for the given hit, and generates any shadow, reflection, or refraction rays. These rays are sent back to the traversal thread and flow through the same processing sequence as eye rays.

One way we exploit the parallelism inherent in ray tracing is to replicate the individual threads according to the workload for the scene. Figure 9.4 shows some example configurations of SHARP. Configuration (a) is biased towards shading. Since all hits can be shaded independently, we simply replicate the shading thread. Configuration (b) is more typical of what the system we analyze looks like. Here, we have replicated the traversal and intersection threads. We take advantage of distributed hardware FIFOs on Smart Memories for communication between the threads.

As mentioned previously, Smart Memories is a reconfigurable architecture. The SHARP ray tracer is also reconfigurable. The space for configuration options when mapping SHARP onto Smart Memories is huge. We will focus on just one situation: Smart Memories configured as a threaded multiprocessor with a single thread running on each processing tile. Each thread described for the SHARP ray tracer then maps to a processing tile. Our simulations show that for simple shading models, about half the total execution cycles to render a scene are spent performing ray-triangle intersection tests, and the other half is spent performing traversals. In other words, only about 5% of the total cycles were spent in ray generation or shading. Thus, we chose to use half the chip (30 tiles) to run triangle intersection threads, and nearly all the other half (28 tiles) for traversal threads.

There are several possible ways to arrange the placement of intersection and traversal threads on the chip. The overall goal is to minimize the global

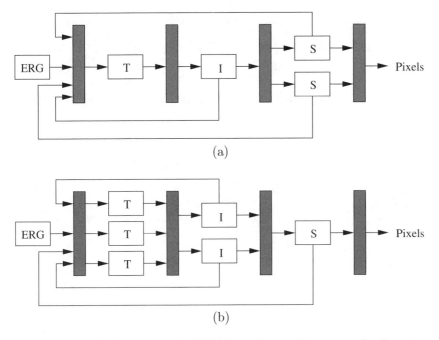

Figure 9.4. Configurations for SHARP on Smart Memories. Configuration (a) is biased towards shading computations, and configuration (b) is biased towards traversal and intersection. Each stage has a distributed FIFO for reading and writing.

communication that must occur between the different units. Rather than focus on the exact layout, we chose to simulate worst case communication behavior. Any time a tile needs to communicate with another tile, we assume it takes place with the maximum latency. Our system turns out to be computationally-limited in this worst case scenario, and thus the exact thread to tile mapping is a secondary concern.

9.3   Simulation Results

We now show some results we have obtained from running SHARP on Smart Memories. Because the Smart Memories design is still being finalized, cycle-accurate simulations for the entire chip are unavailable. Instead, we use high-level simulations and cycle-accurate tile simulation results. These simulations allow us to derive reasonable estimates for system performance, and are subject to final chip specifications.

| Bunny | MGF Conf. Room | Soda Hall Outside | Soda Hall Inside |
| 69K | 282K | 1.5M | 1.5M |

| Low Res Terrain | High Res Terrain | Quake | SPD Rings |
| 32K | 2.1M | 35K | 1.7M |

Figure 9.5. Test scenes and their triangle counts. See also Color Plate 15.

We test our system on several test scenes, with varying geometric complexity and depth complexity. These scenes in no way represent a benchmark, but do span a large spectrum of interesting scenes to render. They are shown in Figure 9.5 with their triangle count for reference during the rest of our discussion.

9.3.1   Caching

We evaluate the caching performance of our system for triangle intersection tiles. Triangles are represented as 9 floating point values plus a geometry ID and material ID. We chose to map different cache levels to the memory hierarchy present in Smart Memories. We define a tile's L1 cache to be the memory associated with the given tile. Technically, this should apply to any tile in the quad, but our simulations do not take advantage of quad efficiencies. Smart Memories has a globally addressable memory space, so our L2 cache is composed of all L1 caches on the chip. Finally, data not found on chip is brought in from off chip. When a miss occurs, the found data is brought directly to the local cache of the requester, replacing something else. If multiple tiles request the same data, we will have multiple tiles with redundant information.

The caching behavior of Smart Memories is configurable. We tested caches ranging in associativity from direct mapped to fully associative. We

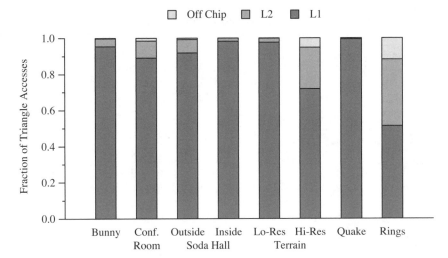

Figure 9.6. Caching rates for our test scenes. The total number of cache accesses is normalized to 1 for each scene. The bars for each scene show the fraction of triangle requests satisfied by each level of the memory hierarchy. All scenes were rendered at 1024×1024 pixels.

settled on a four-way set associative cache as having the best hit rate to implementation cost ratio. Each intersection tile dedicates 44 kB to triangle data. We configure the cache line size to equal a single triangle, resulting in 1,024 triangles cached per tile. The results for our test scenes are shown in Figure 9.6. For most of our test scenes, more than 93% of triangle requests are satisfied on chip, the notable exceptions being the high-res terrain model and the SPD rings model. The on-chip triangle cache only holds around 5% of the working set size of these scenes. Overall, our results indicate that a small simple triangle cache works remarkably well for our system.

9.3.2 Estimated Performance

Our simulations indicate the performance of SHARP on Smart Memories to be nearly an order of magnitude higher than the fastest single processor ray tracers today [307]. We estimate that 32 intersection tiles can perform 150 M ray-triangle intersections/s and 30 tiles can perform 500 M ray-voxel traversals/s. These translate to between 1 and 5 frames per second for our test scenes at 1024 × 1024 pixels.

We can suggest several enhancements to the Smart Memories design to enhance this performance. It turns out that SHARP is compute limited on Smart Memories. If we split the 64-bit floating point units into two 32-bit floating point units, we can double our performance immediately. If we had specialized or SSE-like instructions tuned for graphics operations, we expect to increase the performance between 2 and 5 fold. Combining these enhancements leads to nearly another order of magnitude performance increase.

9.4   Conclusions

Intuitively, highly parallel code requires a highly parallel compute substrate to take advantage of the available parallelism. Ray tracing is one example of a highly parallel algorithm that maps naturally to parallel machines. Chips that are inherently parallel, such as the Smart Memories chip, will be available in the near future. We have shown that ray tracing works very well on these chips, with performance surpassing that possible on conventional parallel machines or clusters of computers.

Bibliography

[1] W. B. Ackerman. Data flow languages. In N. Gehani and A. D. McGettrick, editors, *Concurrent Programming*, chapter 3, pages 163–181. Addison-Wesley, 1988.

[2] S. J. Adelson and L. F. Hodges. Stereoscopic ray-tracing. *The Visual Computer*, 10(3):127–144, 1993.

[3] S. J. Adelson and L. F. Hodges. Generating exact ray-traced animation frames by reprojection. *IEEE Computer Graphics and Applications*, 15(3):43–52, 1995.

[4] Advanced Micro Devices. *Inside 3DNow! Technology*. http://www.amd.com/products/cpg/k623d/inside3d.html.

[5] G. Albert. A general theory of stochastic estimates of the neumann series for solution of certain fredholm integral equations and related series. In *Symposium on Monte-Carlo Methods*, pages 37–46. John Wiley & Sons, New York, 1956.

[6] D. Aliaga, J. Cohen, A. Wilson, E. Baker, H. Zhang, C. Erikson, K. Hoff, T. Hudson, W. St rzlinger, R. Bastos, M. Whitton, F. Brooks, and D. Manocha. MMR: An interactive massive model rendering system using geometric and image-based acceleration. In *1999 ACM Symposium on Interactive 3D Graphics*, pages 199–206, Atlanta, USA, April 1999.

[7] G. S. Almasi and A. Gottleib. *Highly Parallel Computing*. Benjamin Cummings, Redwood City, California, 2nd edition, 1994.

[8] L. Alonso, X. Cavin, J.-C. Ulysse, and J.-C. Paul. Fast and accurate wavelet radiosity computations using high-end platforms. In *Proceedings of the third Eurographics workshop on parallel graphics and visualisation*, pages 25–38, 2000.

[9] J. Amanatides and A. Woo. A fast voxel traversal algorithm for ray tracing. In *Eurographics '87*, pages 3–10. Elsevier Science Publishers, Amsterdam, North-Holland, August 1987.

[10] G. M. Amdahl. Validity of the single-processor approach to achieving large scale computing capabilities. In *AFIPS*, volume 30, Atlantic City, April 1967. AFIPS Press, Reston, Va.

[11] M. Annaratone et al. Warp architecture and implementation. In *13th Annual International Symposium on Computer Architecture*, pages 346–356, Tokyo, June 1986.

[12] A. Apodaka and L. Gritz. *Advanced RenderMan*. Morgan Kaufmann, 2000.

[13] A. Appel. Some techniques for shading machine renderings of solids. *SJCC*, pages 27–45, 1968.

[14] B. Arnaldi, T. Priol, and K. Bouatouch. A new space subdivision method for ray tracing csg modeled scenes. *The Visual Computer*, 3:98–108, 1987.

[15] B. Arnaldi, T. Priol, L. Renambot, and X. Pueyo. Visibility masks for solving complex radiosity computations on multiprocessors. *Parallel Computing*, 23(7):887–897, July 1997. Special Issue on Parallel Graphics and Visualisation.

[16] B. Arnaldi, X. Pueyo, and J. Vilaplana. On the division of environments by virtual walls for radiosity computation. In *Photorealism in Computer Graphics*, pages 198–205, 1991. Proceedings 2nd EG Rendering Workshop.

[17] J. Arvo and D. Kirk. A survey of ray tracing acceleration techniques. In A. S. Glassner, editor, *An Introduction to Ray Tracing*. Academic Press, San Diego, CA, 1989.

[18] J. Backus. Can programming be liberated from the von Neumann style functional style and its algebra of programs. *Communications of the ACM*, 21(8):613–641, 1978.

[19] D. Badouel. An efficient ray polygon intersection. *Graphics Gems III*, 1992.

[20] D. Badouel, K. Bouatouch, and T. Priol. Distributing data and control for ray tracing in parallel. *IEEE Computer Graphics and Applications*, 14(4):69–77, 1994.

[21] S. Badt. Two algorithms for taking advantage of temporal coherence in ray tracing. *The Visual Computer*, 4:55–64, 1988.

[22] H. Bal. *Programming Distributed Systems*. Silicon Press, Summit, New Jersey, 1990.

[23] K. Bala, J. Dorsey, and S. Teller. Radiance interpolants for accelerated bounded-error ray tracing. *ACM Transactions on Graphics*, July 1999.

[24] A. Basu. A classification of parallel processing systems. In *ICCD*, 1984.

[25] K. Batcher. Design of a massively parallel processor. *IEEE Transactions on Computers*, 29(9):836–840, September 1980.

[26] A. Beguelin, J. Dongarra, A. Geist, R. Manchek, K. Moore, and V. Sunderam. PVM and HeNCE: Tools for heterogeneous network computing. In J. J. Dongarra and B. Tourancheau, editors, *Environments and Tools for Parallel Scientific Computing*, pages 139–153, North Holland, 1993. Elsevier Science Publishers B. V.

[27] M. Ben-Ari. *Principles of Concurrent and Distributed Programming*. Addison-Wesley, Wokingham, England, 1990.

[28] J. I. Benavides, G. Cerruela, P. P. Trabado, and E. L. Zapata. Fast scalable solution for the parallel hierarchical radiosity problem in distributed memory architectures. In K. Bouatouch, A. Chalmers, and T. Priol, editors, *Proceedings of the second Eurographics workshop on parallel graphics and visualisation*, pages 49–57, 1998.

[29] G. Bishop, H. Fuchs, L. McMillan, and E. J. Scher Zagier. Frameless rendering: Double buffering considered harmful. In A. Glassner, editor, *Proceedings of SIGGRAPH '94 (Orlando, Florida, July 24–29, 1994)*, Computer Graphics Proceedings, Annual Conference Series, pages 175–176. ACM SIGGRAPH, ACM Press, July 1994.

[30] J. F. Blinn and M. E. Newell. Texture and reflection in computer generated images. *Communications of the ACM*, 19(10):542–547, October 1976.

[31] K. Bouatouch, D. Menard, and T. Priol. Parallel radiosity using a shared virtual memory. In *First Bilkent Computer Graphics Conference, ATARV-93*, pages 71–83, Ankara, Turkey, July 1993.

[32] K. Bouatouch and T. Priol. Parallel space tracing: An experience on an iPSC hypercube. In N. Magnenat-Thalmann and D. Thalmann, editors, *New Trends in Computer Graphics (Proceedings of CG International '88)*, pages 170–187, New York, 1988. Springer-Verlag.

[33] K. Bouatouch and T. Priol. Data management scheme for parallel radiosity. *Computer-Aided Design*, 26(12):876–882, December 1994.

[34] M. Brady, K. Jung, H. Nguyen, and T. Nguyen. Interactive Volume Navigation. *IEEE Transactions on Visualization and Computer Graphics*, 4(3):243–256, July 1998.

[35] A. W. Burks. Programming and structural changes in parallel computers. In W. Händler, editor, *Conpar*, pages 1–24, Berlin, 1981. Springer.

[36] N. Carriero and D. Gelernter. *How to Write Parallel Programs*. MIT Press, Cambridge, Massachusetts, 1990.

[37] M. B. Carter and K. A. Teague. The hypercube ray tracer. In D. Walker and Q. Stout, editors, *The 5th Distributed Memory Computing Conference Vol. I*, pages 212–216. IEEE Computer Society Press, April 1990.

[38] X. Cavin, L. Alonso, and J.-C. Paul. Parallel wavelet radiosity. In *Proceedings of the second Eurographics workshop on parallel graphics and visualisation*, pages 61–75, 1998.

[39] X. Cavin, L. Alonso, and J.-C. Paul. Overlapping multi-processing and graphics hardware acceleration: performance evaluation. In *IEEE Parallel visualization and graphics symposium*, pages 79–88, 1999.

[40] D. Chaiken, J. Kubiatowicz, and A. Agarwal. LimitLESS directories: A scalable cache coherence scheme. In *Proceedings of the 4th International Conference on Architectural Support for Programming Languages and Operating Systems, ASPLOS-IV*, pages 224–234, April 1991.

[41] A. Chalmers and E. Reinhard. Parallel and distributed photo-realistic rendering. In *Course notes for SIGGRAPH 98*, pages 425–432. ACM SIGGRAPH, Orlando, USA, July 1998.

[42] A. G. Chalmers. Occam - the language for educating future parallel programmers? *Microprocessing and Microprogramming*, 24:757–760, 1988.

[43] A. G. Chalmers and D. J. Paddon. Communication efficient MIMD configurations. In *4th SIAM Conference on Parallel Processing for Scientific Computing*, Chicago, 1989.

[44] A. G. Chalmers and D. J. Paddon. Parallel processing of progressive refinement radiosity methods. In *2nd EG Workshop on Rendering*, pages 1–11, Barcelona, Spain, May 1991.

[45] J. Chapman, T. W. Calvert, and J. Dill. Exploiting temporal coherence in ray tracing. In *Proceedings of Computer Graphics Interface '90*, pages 196–204, Halifax, Nova Scotia, 1990.

[46] P. Chaudhuri. *Parallel Algorithms: Design and analysis*. Prentice-Hall, Australia, 1992.

[47] P. H. Christensen. Faster photon map global illumination. *Journal of Graphics Tools: JGT*, 4(3):1–10, 1999.

[48] J. H. Clark. Hierarchical geometric models for visible surface algorithms. *Communications of the ACM*, 19(10):547–554, 1976.

[49] J. G. Cleary, B. M. Wyvill, G. M. Birtwistle, and R. Vatti. Multiprocessor ray tracing. *Computer Graphics Forum*, 5(1):3–12, March 1986.

[50] B. Codenotti and M. Leonici. *Introduction to parallel processing*. Addison-Wesley, Wokingham, England, 1993.

[51] D. Cohen. Voxel traversal along a 3d line. In P. S. Heckbert, editor, *Graphics Gems IV*, pages 366–369. Academic Press, Inc. 1994.

[52] M. F. Cohen, S. E. Chen, J. R. Wallace, and D. P. Greenberg. A progressive refinement approach to fast radiosity image generation. In J. Dill, editor, *Computer Graphics (SIGGRAPH '88 Proceedings)*, volume 22, pages 75–84, August 1988.

[53] M. F. Cohen and D. P. Greenberg. The hemi-cube: A radiosity solution for complex environments. In B. A. Barsky, editor, *Computer Graphics (SIGGRAPH '85 Proceedings)*, volume 19, pages 31–40, July 1985.

[54] M. F. Cohen and J. R. Wallace. *Radiosity and Realistic Image Synthesis*. Academic Press, Inc., Cambridge, MA, 1993.

[55] R. L. Cook, T. Porter, and L. Carpenter. Distributed ray tracing. *Computer Graphics*, 18(3):137–145, 1984.

[56] M. B. Cox and D. Ellsworth. Application-controlled demand paging for Out-of-Core visualization. In *Proceedings of Visualization '97*, pages 235–244, October 1997.

[57] R. A. Cross. Interactive realism for visualization using ray tracing. In *Proceedings Visualization '95*, pages 19–25, 1995.

[58] J. Danskin and P. Hanrahan. Fast algorithms for volume ray tracing. *1992 Workshop on Volume Visualization*, pages 91–98, 1992.

[59] T. A. Davis and E. W. Davis. A parallel frame coherence algorithm for ray traced animations. In K. Bouatouch, A. Chalmers, and T. Priol, editors, *Proceedings of the Second Eurographics Workshop on Parallel Graphics and Visualisation*, pages 105–113, September 1998.

[60] T. A. Davis and E. W. Davis. Exploiting frame coherence with the temporal depth buffer in a distributed computing environment. In *IEEE Parallel Visualization and Graphics Symposium*, pages 29–37, 1999.

[61] A. L. DeCegama. *The Technology of Parallel Processing: Parallel Processing Architectures and VLSI Design*. Prentice-Hall International Inc., 1989.

[62] M. A. Z. Dippé and J. Swensen. An adaptive subdivision algorithm and parallel architecture for realistic image synthesis. In *Computer Graphics (SIGGRAPH '84 Proceedings)*, pages 149–158, July 1984.

[63] J. Dorsey, A. Edelman, J. Legakis, H. W. Jensen, and H. K. Pedersen. Modeling and rendering of weathered stone. In A. Rockwood, editor, *Siggraph 1999, Computer Graphics Proceedings*, Annual Conference Series, pages 225–234, Los Angeles, 1999. Addison Wesley Longman.

[64] R. A. Drebin, L. Carpenter, and P. Hanrahan. Volume rendering. *Computer Graphics*, 22(4):65–74, July 1988. ACM Siggraph '88 Conference Proceedings.

[65] G. Durgin, N. Patwari, and T. Rappaport. An advanced 3D ray launching method for wireless propagation prediction. In *IEEE 47th Vehicular Technology Conference*, volume 2, May 1997.

[66] P. Dutré. *Mathematical Frameworks and Monte Carlo Algorithms for Global Illumination in Computer Graphics*. PhD thesis, Katholieke Universiteit Leuven, Belgium, September 1996.

[67] D. L. Eager, J. Zahorjan, and E. D. Lazowska. Speedup versus efficiency in parallel systems. *IEEE Transactions on Computers*, 38(3):408–423, March 1989.

[68] M. Eldridge, H. Igehy, and P. Hanrahan. Pomegranate: A fully scalable graphics architecture. *Computer Graphics*, pages 443–454, July 2000.

[69] J. Erickson. Pluecker coordinates. *Ray Tracing News*, 1997. http://www.acm.org/tog/resources/RTNews/html/rtnv10n3.html#art11.

[70] V. Faber, O. M. Lubeck, and A. B. White Jr. Super-linear speedup of an efficient sequential algorithm is not possible. *Parallel Computing*, 3:259–260, 1986.

[71] M. Feda. Parallel radiosity on transputers with low communication overhead. In S. Ferenczi and P. Kacsuk, editors, *Proceedings of the 2nd Austrian-Hungarian Workshop on Transputer Applications*, pages 62–70, Budapest, Hungaria, September–October 1994. Hungarian Transputer Users Group and Austrian Centre for Parallel Computing. Report KFKI-1995-2/M, N.

[72] M. Feda and W. Purgathofer. Progressive refinement radiosity on a transputer network. In *2nd EG Workshop on Rendering*, Barcelona, Spain, May 1991. held in Barcelona, Spain; 13-15 May 1991.

[73] C.-C. Feng and S.-N. Yang. A parallel hierarchical radiosity algorithm for complex scenes. In *1997 Symposium on Parallel Rendering*, pages 71–77. ACM SIGGRAPH, October 1997.

[74] H. P. Flatt and K. Kennedy. Performance of parallel processors. *Parallel Computing*, 12:1–20, 1989.

[75] M. J. Flynn. Some computer organisations and their effectiveness. *IEEE Transactions on Computers*, 21(9):948–960, 1972.

[76] Foley, van Dam, Feiner, and Hughes. *Computer Graphics – Principles and Practice, second edition in C.* Addison Wesley, 1997.

[77] H. Fuchs, Z. M. Kedem, and B. F. Naylor. On visible surface generation by a priori tree structures. In *ACM Computer Graphics*, volume 14, pages 124–133, July 1980.

[78] H. Fuchs, J. Poulton, J. Eyles, T. Greer, J. Goldfeature, D. Ellsworth, S. Molnar, G. Turk, B. Tebbs, and L. Israel. Pixel-plane 5: A heteregeneous multiprocessor graphics system using processor-enhanced memories. In *Siggraph conference*, pages 79–88, 1989.

[79] A. Fujimoto, T. Tanaka, and K. Iwata. ARTS: Accelerated ray tracing system. *IEEE Computer Graphics and Applications*, 6(4):16–26, 1986.

[80] T. A. Funkhouser. Coarse-grained parallelism for hierarchical radiosity using group iterative methods. In H. Rushmeier, editor, *SIGGRAPH 96 Conference Proceedings*, Annual Conference Series, pages 343–352. ACM SIGGRAPH, Addison Wesley, August 1996. held in New Orleans, Louisiana.

[81] T. A. Funkhouser and C. H. Séquin. Adaptive display algorithm for interactive frame rates during visualization of complex virtual environments. In J. T. Kajiya, editor, *Computer Graphics (SIGGRAPH '93 Proceedings)*, volume 27, pages 247–254, August 1993.

[82] B. W. G. Wyvill, C. McPheeters. Data structures for soft objects. *The Visual Computer*, 2:227–234, 1986.

[83] M. Garland and P. S. Heckbert. Surface simplification using quadric error metrics. In T. Whitted, editor, *SIGGRAPH 97 Conference Proceedings*, pages 209–216. ACM SIGGRAPH, Addison Wesley, August 1997.

[84] R. Garmann. On the partionability of hierarchical radiosity. In *IEEE Parallel visualization and graphics symposium*, pages 69–78, 1999.

[85] R. Garmann. Spatial partitioning for parallel hierarchical radiosity on distributed memory architectures. In *Proceedings of the third Eurographics workshop on parallel graphics and visualisation*, pages 13–23, 2000.

[86] M. Garrity. Ray Tracing Irregular Volume Data. In *1990 Workshop on Volume Visualization*, pages 35–40, 1990. San Diego.

[87] A. Geist, A. Beguelin, J. Dongarra, W. Jiang, R. Manchek, and V. Sunderam. *PVM: Parallel Virtual Machine:A Users' Guide and Tutorial for Network Parallel Computing*. MIT Press, Cambridge, MA, 1994.

[88] C. F. Gerald and P. O. Wheatley. *Applied numerical analysis*. World Student Series. Addison-Wesley, Reading, MA, 5th edition, 1994.

[89] A. Glassner. *An Introduction to Raytracing*. Academic Press, 1989.

[90] A. S. Glassner. Space subdivision for fast ray tracing. *IEEE Computer Graphics and Applications*, 4(10):15–22, October 1984.

[91] A. S. Glassner, editor. *An Introduction to Ray Tracing*. Academic Press, San Diego, 1989.

[92] A. Globus. Octree optimization. Technical Report RNR-90-011, NASA Ames Research Center, July 1990.

[93] C. M. Goral, K. E. Torrance, D. P. Greenberg, and B. Battaile. Modeling the interaction of light between diffuse surfaces. In *Computer Graphics (SIGGRAPH '84 Proceedings)*, volume 18, pages 213–222, July 1984.

[94] S. J. Gortler, P. Schröder, M. F. Cohen, and P. Hanrahan. Wavelet radiosity. In *Computer Graphics Proceedings, Annual Conference Series, 1993*, pages 221–230, 1993.

[95] P. Green and E. Morgan. Parallelisation schemes for the progressive refinement radiosity method for the synthesis of realistic images. In P. Nixon, editor, *Transputer and Occam Developments (Proceedings of the 18th World Occam and Transputer User Group Technical Meeting*, pages 97–112, Amsterdam, April 1995. IOS Press.

[96] S. A. Green and D. J. Paddon. A non-shared memory multiprocessor architecture for large database problems. In M. Cosnard, M. H. Barton, and M. Vanneschi, editors, *Proceedings of the IFIP WG 10.3 Working Conference on Parallel Processing*, Pisa, 1988.

[97] S. A. Green and D. J. Paddon. Exploiting coherence for multiprocessor ray tracing. *IEEE Computer Graphics and Applications*, 9(6):12–26, November 1989.

[98] S. A. Green and D. J. Paddon. A highly flexible multiprocessor solution for ray tracing. Technical Report TR-89-02, Computer Science Department, University of Bristol, Merchant Venturers Building, Woodland Road, Bristol BS8 1UB, March 1989.

[99] S. A. Green and D. J. Paddon. A highly flexible multiprocessor solution for ray tracing. *The Visual Computer*, 6(2):62–73, March 1990.

[100] N. Greene. Environment mapping and other applications of world projections. *IEEE Computer Graphics and Applications*, pages 21–29, November 1986.

[101] L. Gritz and J. K. Hahn. BMRT: A global illumination implementation of the renderman standard. *Journal of Graphics Tools*, 1(3):29–47, 1996.

[102] E. Groëller and W. Purgathofer. Using temporal and spatial coherence for accelerating the calculation of animation sequences. In F. H. Post and W. Barth, editors, *Proceedings of Eurographics '91*, pages 103–113, 1991.

[103] H. A. Grosch. High speed arithmetic: The digital computer as a research tool. *Journal of the Optical Society of America*, 43(4):306–310, April 1953.

[104] H. A. Grosch. Grosch's law revisited. *Computerworld*, 8(16):24, April 1975.

[105] P. Guitton, J. Roman, and C. Schlick. Two parallel approaches for a progressive radiosity. In *2nd EG Workshop on Rendering*, pages 1–11, Barcelona, Spain, May 1991.

[106] P. Guitton, J. Roman, and G. Subrenat. Implementation results and analysis of a parallel progressive radiosity. In *1995 Parallel Rendering Symposium*, pages 31–38. ACM SIGGRAPH, October 1995.

[107] J. L. Gustafson. Re-evaluating Amdahl's law. *Communications of the ACM*, 31(5):532–533, May 1988.

[108] L. Hammond, B. A. Nayfeh, and K. Olukotun. A single-chip multiprocessor. *Computer*, 30(9):79–85, September 1997.

[109] P. Hanrahan and D. Saltzman. A rapid hierarchical radiosity algorithm for unoccluded environments. In C. Bouville and K. Bouatouch, editors, *Photorealism in Computer Graphics*, Eurographics Seminar Series, New York, 1992. Springer Verlag.

[110] P. Hanrahan, D. Saltzman, and L. Aupperle. A rapid hierarchical radiosity algorithm. *Computer Graphics*, 25(4):197–206, August 1991.

[111] P. Hanrahan and D. Salzman. A rapid hierarchical radiosity algorithm for unoccluded environments. Technical Report CS-TR-281-90, Department of Computer Science, Princeton University, August 1990.

[112] D. R. Hartree. The ENIAC, an electronic computing machine. *Nature*, 158:500–506, 1946.

[113] V. Havran. *Heuristic Ray Shooting Algorithms*. Ph.d. thesis, Department of Computer Science and Engineering, Faculty of Electrical Engineering, Czech Technical University in Prague, November 2000.

[114] V. Havran, J. Prikryl, and W. Purgathofer. Statistical comparison of ray-shooting efficiency schemes. *Technical Report/TR-186-2-00-14, Institute of Computer Graphics, Vienna University of Technology*, July 2000.

[115] A. Heirich and J. Arvo. Scalable monte carlo image synthesis. *Parallel Computing*, 23(7):845–859, July 1997.

[116] M. Henne, H. Hickel, E. Johnson, and S. Konishi. The making of toy story. In *IEEE COMPCON '96 Digest of Papers*, pages 463–468, Los Alamitos, CA, 1996. IEEE Computer Society Press.

[117] J. L. Hennessy and D. A. Patterson. *Computer Architecture: A quantitative approach*. Morgan Kaufmann, San Mateo, CA, 1990.

[118] T. Hey. Scientific applications. In G. Harp, editor, *Transputer Applications*, chapter 8, pages 170–203. Pitman Publishing, 1989.

[119] D. W. Hillis. *The Connection Machine*. The MIT Press, 1985.

[120] R. W. Hockney and C. R. Jesshope. *Parallel Computers 2: Architecture, Programming and Algorithms*. Adam Hilger, Bristol, 1988.

[121] M. Homewood, M. D. May, D. Shepherd, and R. Shepherd. The IMS T800 transputer. *IEEE Micro*, pages 10–26, 1987.

[122] H. Hoppe. Progressive meshes. In H. Rushmeier, editor, *SIGGRAPH 96 Conference Proceedings*, Annual Conference Series, pages 99–108. ACM SIGGRAPH, Addison Wesley, August 1996.

[123] H. Hoppe. View-dependent refinement of progressive meshes. In T. Whitted, editor, *SIGGRAPH 97 Conference Proceedings*, Annual Conference Series, pages 189–198. ACM SIGGRAPH, Addison Wesley, August 1997.

[124] H. Hoppe, T. DeRose, T. Duchamp, J. McDonald, and W. Stuetzle. Mesh optimization. In J. T. Kajiya, editor, *Computer Graphics (SIGGRAPH '93 Proceedings)*, volume 27, pages 19–26, August 1993.

[125] R. M. Hord. *Parallel Supercomputing in MIMD Architectures*. CRC Press, Boca Raton, 1993.

[126] S. Horiguchi, M. Katahira, and T. Nakada. Parallel processing of incremental ray tracing on a shared-memory multiprocessor. *The Visual Computer*, 9(7):371–380, 1993.

[127] R. J. Hosking, D. C. Joyce, and J. C. Turner. *First steps in numerical analysis*. Hodder and Stoughton, London, 1978.

[128] HPF Forum. High Performance Fortran language specification. *Scientific Programming*, 2(1), June 1993.

[129] http://www.3dlabs.com/.

[130] H. Hubschman and S. W. Zucker. Frame-to-frame coherence and the hidden surface computation: Constraints for a convex world. *Proceedings of SIGGRAPH '81 in ACM Computer Graphics*, 15(3):45–54, 1981.

[131] K. Hwang. *Advanced Computer Architecture: Parallelism, Scalability, Programmability*. McGraw-Hill Series in Computer Engineering. McGraw-Hill, Inc., New York, 1993.

[132] S. E. Hyeon-Ju Yoon and J. W. Cho. Image parallel ray tracing using static load balancing and data prefetching. *Parallel Computing*, 23(7):861–872, July 1997.

[133] Intel Corp. *Intel Computer Based Tutorial*. http://developer.intel.com/vtune/cbts/cbts.htm.

[134] Intel Corp. *Intel Pentium III Streaming SIMD Extensions*. http://developer.intel.com/vtune/cbts/simd.htm.

[135] V. İşler, C. Aykanat, and B. Özgüç. Subdivision of 3D space based on the graph partitioning for parallel ray tracing. In *Proceedings of the Second Eurographics Workshop on Rendering*, Barcelona, Spain, May 1991.

[136] E. J., S. Molnar, J. Poulton, T. Geer, A. Lastra, N. England, and L. Westover. Pixelflow: The realization. In *1997 Siggraph/Eurographics Workshop on Graphics Hardware*, pages 57–68, August 1997.

[137] F. W. Jansen. Data structures for ray tracing. In L. R. A. Kessener, F. J. Peters, and M. L. P. Lierop, editors, *Data Structures for Raster Graphics*, pages 57–73, Berlin, 1985. Springer-Verlag.

[138] F. W. Jansen and A. Chalmers. Realism in real time? In M. F. Cohen, C. Puech, and F. Sillion, editors, *4th EG Workshop on Rendering*, pages 27–46. Eurographics, June 1993. held in Paris, France, 14–16 June 1993.

[139] F. W. Jansen and E. Reinhard. Data locality in parallel rendering. In K. Bouatouch, A. Chalmers, and T. Priol, editors, *Proceeding of the Second Eurographics Workshop on Parallel Graphics and Visualisation*, pages 1–15, September 1998.

[140] H. W. Jensen. Global illumination using photon maps. In *7th EG Workshop on Rendering*, pages 21–30, Porto, Portugal, June 1996.

[141] H. W. Jensen. *Realistic Image Synthesis Using Photon Mapping*. A K Peters, 2001.

[142] H. W. Jensen and N. J. Christensen. Siggraph course 8: A practical guide to global illumination using photon maps, 2000.

[143] H. W. Jensen and P. H. Christensen. Efficient simulation of light transport in scenes with participating media using photon maps. In M. Cohen, editor, *SIGGRAPH 98 Conference Proceedings*, Annual Conference Series, pages 311–320. ACM SIGGRAPH, Addison Wesley, July 1998.

[144] H. W. Jensen, P. H. Christensen, and F. Suykens. Siggraph course 38: A practical guide to global illumination using photon mapping, 2001.

[145] J. P. Jessel, M. Paulin, and R. Caubet. An extended radiosity using parallel ray-traced specular transfers. In *2nd Eurographics Workshop on Rendering*, pages 1–12, Barcelona, Spain, May 1991. held in Barcelona, Spain; 13-15 May 1991.

[146] D. Jevans. Object-based temporal coherence. In *Proceedings of Computer Graphics Interface '92*, Vancouver, 1992.

[147] D. Jevans and B. Wyvill. Adaptive voxel subdivision for ray tracing. In *Proceedings of Graphics Interface '89*, pages 164–172, June 1989.

[148] D. A. J. Jevans. Optimistic multi-processor ray tracing. In R. A. Earnshaw and B. Wyvill, editors, *New Advances in Computer Graphics (Proceedings of CG International '89)*, pages 507–522, New York, 1989. Springer-Verlag.

[149] J. T. Kajiya. The rendering equation. In D. C. Evans and R. J. Athay, editors, *Computer Graphics (SIGGRAPH '86 Proceedings)*, volume 20, pages 143–150, August 1986. held in Dallas, Texas, August 18–22, 1986.

[150] J. T. Kajiya. An overview and comparison of rendering methods. *A Consumer's and Developer's Guide to Image Synthesis*, pages 259–263, 1988. ACM Siggraph '88 Course 12 Notes.

[151] A. Kaufman. *Volume Visualization*. IEEE CS Press, 1991.

[152] T. L. Kay and J. T. Kajiya. Ray tracing complex scenes. *Computer Graphics*, 20(4):269–278, August 1986. ACM Siggraph '86 Conference Proceedings.

[153] M. J. Keates and R. J. Hubbold. Accelerated ray tracing on the KSR1 virtual shared-memory parallel computer. Technical Report UMCS-94-2-2, Department of Computer Science, University of Manchester, Oxford Road, Manchester, UK, February 1994.

[154] A. Keller. *Quasi-Monte Carlo Methods for Realistic Image Synthesis*. PhD thesis, University of Kaiserslautern, 1998.

[155] B. Khailany, W. J. Dally, S. Rixner, U. J. Kapasi, P. Mattson, J. Namkoong, J. D. Owens, and B. Towles. IMAGINE: Signal and image processing using streams. In IEEE, editor, *Hot Chips 12: Stanford*

University, Stanford, California, August 13–15, 2000, 1109 Spring Street, Suite 300, Silver Spring, MD 20910, USA, 2000. IEEE Computer Society Press.

[156] H.-J. Kim and C.-M. Kyung. A new parallel ray-tracing system based on object decomposition. *The Visual Computer*, 12(5):244–253, 1996. ISSN 0178-2789.

[157] K. S. Klimansezewski and T. W. Sederberg. Faster ray tracing using adaptive grids. *IEEE Computer Graphics & Applications*, 17(1):42–51, January-February 1997. ISSN 0272-1716.

[158] H. Kobayashi, T. Nakamura, and Y. Shigei. Parallel processing of an object space for image synthesis using ray tracing. *The Visual Computer*, 3(1):13–22, February 1987.

[159] H. Kobayashi, T. Nakamura, and Y. Shigei. A strategy for mapping parallel ray-tracing into a hypercube multiprocessor system. In N. Magnenat-Thalmann and D. Thalmann, editors, *New Trends in Computer Graphics (Proceedings of CG International '88)*, pages 160–169, New York, 1988. Springer-Verlag.

[160] A. J. F. Kok. Grouping of patches in progressive radiosity. In M. Cohen, C. Puech, and F. Sillion, editors, *Fourth Eurographics Workshop on Rendering*, pages 221–231, Paris, France, June 1993.

[161] A. J. F. Kok. *Ray Tracing and Radiosity Algorithms for Photorealistic Image Synthesis*. PhD thesis, Delft University of Technology, The Netherlands, May 1994. Delft University Press.

[162] C. Kolb. Rayshade home-page.
http://graphics.stanford.edu/~cek/rayshade/rayshade.html.

[163] KSR. *KSR Technical Summary*. Kendall Square Research, Waltham, MA, 1992.

[164] V. Kumar, A. Grama, A. Gupta, and G. Karyps. *Introduction to Parallel Computing*. Benjamin/Cummings, Redwood City, California, 1994.

[165] H. T. Kung. *VLSI array processors*. Prentice-Hall, Englewood Cliffs, NJ, 1988.

[166] H. T. Kung and C. E. Leiserson. Systolic arrays (for VLSI). In Duff and Stewart, editors, *Sparse Matrix proceedings*, Philadelphia, 1978. SIAM.

[167] T. M. Kurç, C. Aykanat, and B. Özgüç. A parallel scaled conjugate-gradient algorithm for the solution phase of gathering radiosity on hypercubes. *The Visual Computer*, 13(1):1–19, 1997.

[168] Z. Lahjomri and T. Priol. KOAN: A shared virtual memory for the iPSC/2 hypercube. Technical Report Report 597, IRISA, Campus de Beaulieu, 35042 Rennes Cedex, France, July 1991.

[169] Lambert. Photometria sive de mensura et gradibus luminis, colorum et umbrae, 1760.

[170] C. Lazou. *Supercomputers and Their Use.* Claredon Press, Oxford, revised edition, 1988.

[171] D. Lenoski, J. Laudon, T. Joe, D. Nakahira, L. Stevens, A. Gupta, and J. Hennessy. The DASH prototype: Logic overhead and performance. *IEEE Transactions on Parallel and Distributed Systems*, 4(1):41–61, January 1993.

[172] M. Levoy. Display of surfaces from volume data. *IEEE Computer Graphics & Applications*, 8(3):29–37, 1988.

[173] M. Levoy. Efficient ray tracing of volume data. *ACM Transactions on Graphics*, 9(3):245–261, July 1990.

[174] T. Lewis and H. El-Rewini. *Introduction to parallel computing.* Prentice-Hall, 1992.

[175] K. Li. Ivy: A shared virtual memory system for parallel computing. *Proceedings of the 1988 International Conference on Parallel P Processing*, 2:94–101, August 1988.

[176] C. Lin and Y. Ching. An efficient volume-rendering algorithm with an analytic approach. *The Visual Computer*, 12(10):515–526, 1996.

[177] G. J. Lipovski and M. Malek. *Parallel Computing: Theory and comparisons.* John Wiley, New York, 1987.

[178] Y. Livnat, H. Shen, and C. R. Johnson. A near optimal isosurface extraction algorithm using the span space. *IEEE Trans. Vis. Comp. Graphics*, 2(1):73–84, 1996.

[179] B. Lorensen. Marching through the visible woman. http://www.crd.ge.com/cgi-bin/vw.pl, 1997.

[180] W. E. Lorensen and H. E. Cline. Marching cubes: A high resolution 3d surface construction algorithm. *Computer Graphics*, 21(4):163–169, July 1987. ACM Siggraph '87 Conference Proceedings.

[181] K. Ma, J. Painter, C. Hansen, and M. Krogh. Parallel Volume Rendering using Binary-Swap Compositing. *IEEE Comput. Graphics and Appl.*, 14(4):59–68, July 1993.

[182] J. D. MacDonald and K. S. Booth. Heuristics for ray tracing using space subdivision. *The Visual Computer*, (6):153–166, 1990.

[183] P. W. C. Maciel and P. Shirley. Visual navigation of large environments using textured clusters. In P. Hanrahan and J. Winget, editors, *1995 Symposium on Interactive 3D Graphics*, pages 95–102. ACM SIGGRAPH, April 1995.

[184] K. Mai, T. Paaske, N. Jayasena, R. Ho, W. J. Dally, and M. Horowitz. Smart memories: A modular reconfigurable architecture. In *The 27th International Symposium on Computer Arcitecture*, pages 161–171. ACM ISCA, June 2000.

[185] S. Marschner and R. Lobb. An evaluation of reconstruction filters for volume rendering. In *Proceedings of Visualization '94*, pages 100–107, October 1994.

[186] P. H. Matthew Eldridge, Homan Igehy. Pomegranate: a fully scalable graphics architecture. In *Siggraph conference*, pages 443 – 454, 2000.

[187] H. Maurel, Y. Duthen, and R. Caubet. A 4d ray tracing. *Computer Graphics Forum*, 12(3):285–294, 1993.

[188] M. D. May and R. Shepherd. Communicating process computers. Inmos technical note 22, Inmos Ltd., Bristol, 1987.

[189] L. F. Menabrea and A. Augusta(translator). Sketch of the Analytical Engine invented by Charles Babbage. In P. Morrison and E. Morrison, editors, *Charles Babbage and his Calculating Engines*. Dover Publications, 1961.

[190] D. Meneveaux and K. Bouatouch. Memory management schemes for radiosity computation in complex environments. Technical report, INRIA, 1997. To appear in Computer Graphics International, 1998.

[191] D. Meneveaux, E. Maisel, and K. Bouatouch. A new partitioning method for architectural environments. Technical Report TR 3148, INRIA, April 1997. To appear in Journal of Visualization and Computer Animation, 1998.

[192] K. Menzel. Parallel rendering techniques for multiprocessor systems. In *Proceedings of Spring School on Computer Graphics*, pages 91–103. Comenius University Bratislava, June 1994. Held June 6–9 in Bratislava, Slovakia.

[193] Message Passing Interface Forum. Document for a standard message-passing interface. Technical report, University of Tennessee, Knoxville, 1993.

[194] S. Michelin, G. Maffeis, D. Arquès, and J. C. Grossetie. Form factor calculation: a new expression with implementations on a parallel t.node computer. *Computer Graphics Forum*, 12(3):C421–C432, 1993. Eurographics '93.

[195] T. Moeller. Practical analysis of optimized ray-triangle intersection. http://www.ce.chalmers.se/staff/tomasm/raytri/.

[196] T. Möller and B. Trumbore. Fast, minimum storage ray-triangle intersection. *Journal of Graphics Tools*, 2(1), 1997. ISSN 1086-7651.

[197] S. Molnar, M. Cox, and H. Fuchs. A sorting classification for prallel rendering. *IEEE Computer Graphics and Applications*, 14(4):23–32, 1994.

[198] J. S. Montrym, D. R. Baum, D. L. Dignam, and C. J. Migdal. Infinitereality: a real-time graphics system. In *Siggraph conference*, pages 293–302. ACM, 1997.

[199] P. Morer, A. M. García-Alonso, and J. Flaquer. Optimization of a priority list algorithm for 3-D rendering of buildings. *Computer Graphics Forum*, 14(4):217–227, October 1995.

[200] Motorola Inc. *AltiVec Technology Facts*. available at http://www.motorola.com/AltiVec/facts.html.

[201] T. Muller and E. Haines. *Real-Time Rendering*. A K Peters, 1999.

[202] K. Murakami and K. Hirota. Incremental ray tracing. In *Proceedings of the Eurographics Workshop on Photosimulation, Realism, and Physics in Computer Graphics*, pages 15–29, 1990.

[203] M. J. Muuss. Rt and remrt - shared memory parllel and network distributed ray-tracing programs. In *USENIX: Proceedings of the Fourth Computer Graphics Workshop*, October 1987.

[204] M. J. Muuss. Towards real-time ray-tracing of combinatorial solid geometric models. In *Proceedings of BRL-CAD Symposium*, June 1995.

[205] M. J. Muuss. Towards real-time ray-tracing of combinatorial solid geometric models. In *Proceedings of BRL-CAD Symposium '95*, June 1995.

[206] M. J. Muuss and M. Lorenzo. High-resolution interactive multispectral missile sensor simulation for atr and dis. In *Proceedings of BRL-CAD Symposium '95*, June 1995.

[207] K. Nakamaru and Y. Ohno. Breadth-first ray tracing utilizing uniform spatial subdivision. *IEEE Transactions on Visualization and Computer Graphics*, 3(4):316–328, 1997.

[208] National Library of Medicine (U.S.) Board of Regents. Electronic imaging: Report of the board of regents. u.s. department of health and human services, public health service, national institutes of health. NIH Publication 90-2197, 1990.

[209] B. Nichols, B. Buttlar, and J. P. Farrell. *Pthreads Programming*. O'Reilly & Associates, Inc., 1996.

[210] G. Nielson and B. Hamann. The asymptotic decider: Resolving the ambiguity in marching cubes. In *Proceedings of Visualization '91*, pages 83–91, October 1991.

[211] J. Nimeroff, J. Dorsey, and H. Rushmeier. Implementation and analysis of an image-based global illumination framework for animated environments. *IEEE Transactions on Visualization and Computer Graphics*, 2(4):283–298, 1996.

[212] R. van Liere. Divide and conquer radiosity. In *Photorealism in Computer Graphics*, pages 191–197, 1991. Proceedings 2nd EG Rendering Workshop.

[213] I. Notkin and C. Gotsman. Parallel adaptive ray-tracing. In V. Skala, editor, *Proceedings of the Third International Conference in Central Europe on Computer Graphics and Visualisation 95*, volume 1, pages 218–226, Plzeň, Czech Republic, February 1995. University of West Bohemia. WSCG 95.

[214] I. Notkin and C. Gotsman. Parallel progressive ray-tracing. *Computer Graphics Forum*, 16(1):43–56, March 1997.

[215] D. Nussbaum and A. Argarwal. Scalability of parallel machines. *Communications of the ACM*, 34(3):56–61, March 1991.

[216] M. Oberhume. LZO-compression library. available at http://www.dogma.net/DataCompression/LZO.shtml.

[217] D. E. Orcutt. Implementation of ray tracing on the hypercube. In G. Fox, editor, *Third Conference on Hypercube Concurrent Computers and Applications*, pages 1207–1210, 1988. vol. 2.

[218] D. Paddon and A. Chalmers. Parallel processing of the radiosity method. *Computer-Aided Design*, 26(12):917–927, December 1994. ISSN 0010-4485.

[219] S. Parker, W. Martin, P.-P. Sloan, P. Shirley, B. Smits, and C. Hansen. Interactive ray tracing. In *Symposium on Interactive 3D Computer Graphics*, April 1999.

[220] S. Parker, M. Parker, Y. Livnat, P.-P. Sloan, C. Hansen, and P. Shirley. Interactive ray tracing for volume visualization. In *IEEE Transactions on Visualization and Computer Graphics*, July-September 1999.

[221] S. Parker, P. Shirley, Y. Livnat, C. Hansen, and P.-P. Sloan. Interactive ray tracing for isosurface rendering. In *Proceedings Visualization '98*, 1998.

[222] S. Parker, P. Shirley, Y. Livnat, C. Hansen, and P. P. Sloan. Interactive ray tracing. In *Interactive 3D Graphics (I3D)*, pages 119–126, April 1999.

[223] S. N. Pattanaik. *Computational Methods for Global Illumination and Visualisation of Complex 3D Environments*. PhD thesis, National Centre for Software Technology, Bombay, India, February 1993.

[224] M. S. Peercy, M. Olano, J. Airey, and P. J. Ungar. *Interactive Multi-Pass Programmable Shading*. ACM Siggraph, New Orleans, USA, July 2000.

[225] Persistence of Vision Development Team. Pov-ray home-page. http://www.povray.org/.

[226] M. Pharr, C. Kolb, R. Gershbein, and P. Hanrahan. Rendering complex scenes with memory-coherent ray tracing. In T. Whitted, editor, *SIGGRAPH 97 Conference Proceedings*, Annual Conference Series, pages 101–108. ACM SIGGRAPH, Addison Wesley, August 1997.

[227] P. Pitot. The voxar project. *IEEE Computer Graphics and Applications*, 13(1):27–33, January 1993.

[228] P. Plasi, B. L. Saëc, and G. Vignoles. Application of rendering techniques to monte-carlo physical simulation of gas diffusion. In J. Dorsey and P. Slusallek, editors, *Rendering Techniques '97*, pages 297–308. Springer, 1997.

[229] D. J. Plunkett and M. J. Bailey. The Vectorization of a Ray Tracing Algorithm for Improved Execution Speed. *IEEE Computer Graphics and Applications*, 6(8):52–60, August 1985.

[230] M. Potmesil and E. M. Hoffert. The pixel machine: A parallel image computer. In *Computer Graphics (SIGGRAPH '89 Proceedings)*, volume 23, pages 69–78, July 1989.

[231] C. E. Prakash and S. Manohar. Volume rendering of unstructured grids–a voxelization approach. *Computers & Graphics*, 19(5):711–726, September 1995. ISSN 0097-8493.

[232] T. Priol and K. Bouatouch. Static load balancing for a parallel ray tracing on a MIMD hypercube. *The Visual Computer*, 5(1/2):109–119, March 1989.

[233] W. Purgathofer and M. Zeiller. Fast radiosity by parallelization. In *Proceedings Eurographics Workshop on Photosimulation, Realism and Physics in Computer Graphics*, pages 173–183, Rennes, France, June 1990.

[234] B. Purvis. Programming the Intel i860. *Parallelogram International*, pages 6–9, October 1990.

[235] M. J. Quinn. *Parallel Computing: Theory and practice.* McGraw-Hill, New York, 1994.

[236] V. Rajaraman. *Elements of parallel computing.* Prentice-Hall of India, New Dehli, 1990.

[237] R. J. Recker, D. W. George, and D. P. Greenberg. Acceleration techniques for progressive refinement radiosity. In R. Riesenfeld and C. Sequin, editors, *Computer Graphics (1990 Symposium on Interactive 3D Graphics)*, pages 59–66, March 1990. held in Snowbird, Utah; 25-28 March 1990.

[238] S. F. Reddaway. DAP - a Distributed Array Processor. In 1st *Annual Symposium on Computer Architecture*, 1973.

[239] E. Reinhard. *Scheduling and Data Management for Parallel Ray Tracing.* PhD thesis, Bristol, 1999.

[240] E. Reinhard and A. Chalmers. Message handling in parallel radiance. In M. Bubak, J. Dongarra, and J. Waśniewski, editors, *Proceedings EuroPVM-MPI'97*, pages 486–493. Springer - Verlag, November 1997.

[241] E. Reinhard, A. Chalmers, and F. W. Jansen. Overview of parallel photorealistic graphics. In *Eurographics STAR – State of the Art Report*, pages 1–25, August-September 1998.

[242] E. Reinhard, A. Chalmers, and F. W. Jansen. Hybrid scheduling for parallel rendering using coherent ray tasks. In *Proceedings Parallel Visualization and Graphics Symposium*, 1999.

[243] E. Reinhard, A. Chalmers, and F. W. Jansen. Hybrid scheduling for realistic image synthesis. In *Proceedings ParCo99*, 1999.

[244] E. Reinhard and F. W. Jansen. Pyramid clipping. Ray Tracing News, volume 8, number 2, May 1995.

[245] E. Reinhard and F. W. Jansen. Rendering large scenes using parallel ray tracing. *Parallel Computing*, 23(7):873–886, July 1997. Special issue on Parallel Graphics and Visualisation.

[246] E. Reinhard, A. J. F. Kok, and A. G. Chalmers. Cost distribution prediction for parallel ray tracing. In K. Bouatouch, A. Chalmers, and T. Priol, editors, *Proceedings of the Second International Workshop on Parallel Graphics and Visualisation*, pages 77–90, September 1998.

[247] E. Reinhard, A. J. F. Kok, and F. W. Jansen. Cost prediction in ray tracing. In X. Pueyo and P. Schroeder, editors, *Rendering Techniques '96*, pages 41–50, Porto, June 1996. Eurographics, Springer Wien.

[248] E. Reinhard, P. Shirley, and C. Hansen. Parallel point reprojection. Submitted to IEEE 2001 Symposium on Parallel and Large-Data Visualization and Graphics.

[249] E. Reinhard, L. U. Tijssen, and F. W. Jansen. Environment mapping for efficient sampling of the diffuse interreflection. In G. Sakas, P. Shirley, and S. Müller, editors, *Photorealistic Rendering Techniques*, pages 410–422, June 1994.

[250] L. Renambot, B. Arnaldi, T. Priol, and X. Pueyo. Towards efficient parallel radiosity for DSM-based parallel computers using virtual interfaces. Technical Report 3245, Institut National de Recherche en Informatique et en Automatique (INRIA), Campus Universitaire de Beaulieu, 35042 Rennes Cedex, France, September 1997.

[251] L. Renambot, B. Arnaldi, T. Priol, and X. Pueyo. Towards efficient parallel radiosity for DSM-based parallel computers using virtual interfaces. In *1997 Symposium on Parallel Rendering*, pages 79–86. ACM SIGGRAPH, October 1997.

[252] L. Renambot and D. Figuls. Convergence analysis in a parallel radiosity algorithm using virtual interfaces. In *Proceedings of the second Eurographics workshop on parallel graphics and visualisation*, pages 31–48, 1998.

[253] J. Richard and J. P. Singh. Parallel hierarchical computation of specular radiosity. In *1997 Symposium on Parallel Rendering*, pages 59–69. ACM SIGGRAPH, October 1997.

[254] J. Rohlf and J. Helman. IRIS Performer: A high performance multiprocessing toolkit for real-time 3D graphics. *Computer Graphics*, 28(Annual Conference Series):381–394, July 1994.

[255] H. E. Rushmeier, C. Patterson, and A. Veerasamy. Geometric simplification for indirect illumination calculations. In *Proceedings of Graphics Interface '93*, pages 227–236, Toronto, Ontario, May 1993. Canadian Information Processing Society.

[256] R. M. Russel. The CRAY-1 computer system. *Communications of the ACM*, 21:63–72, 1978.

[257] P. Sabella. A rendering algorithm for visualizing 3d scalar fields. *Computer Graphics*, 22(4):51–58, July 1988. ACM Siggraph '88 Conference Proceedings.

[258] G. Sakas, M. Grimm, and A. Savopoulos. Optimized maximum intensity projection (MIP). In *Eurographics Rendering Workshop 1995*. Eurographics, June 1995.

[259] J. Salmon and J. Goldsmith. A hypercube ray-tracer. In *Proceedings of the 3rd Conference on Hypercube Concurrent Computers and Applications Vol. II*, pages 1194–1206. ACM Press, 1988.

[260] I. D. Scherson and C. Caspary. Multiprocessing for ray tracing: A hierarchical self-balancing approach. *The Visual Computer*, 4(4):188–196, 1988.

[261] P. Schröder and G. Stoll. Data Parallel Volume Rendering as Line Drawing. In *1992 Workshop on volume Visualization*, pages 25–31, 1992. Boston, October 19-20.

[262] D. Scott, D. Olsen, and E. Gannett. An overview of the visualize fx graphics accelerator. *Hewlett-Packard*, pages 28–34, 1998. http://www.3dlabs.com/product/technology/parascal.htm.

[263] P. Shirley. *Physically Based Lighting Calculations for Computer Graphics*. PhD thesis, University of Illinois, Urbana-Champaign, November 1991.

[264] P. Shirley. *Realistic Ray Tracing*. A K Peters, Natick, Massachusetts, 2000.

[265] P. Shirley, B. Wade, D. Zareski, P. Hubbard, B. Walter, and D. P. Greenberg. Global illumination via density estimation. In *Proceedings of the Sixth Eurographics Workshop on Rendering*, pages 187–199. Springer-Verlag, June 1995.

[266] K. Shoemake. Pluecker coordinate tutorial. *Ray Tracing News*, 1998. http://www.acm.org/tog/resources/RTNews/ html/rtnv11n1.html#art3.

[267] J. E. Shore. Second thoughts on parallel processing. *Comput. Elect. Eng.*, 1:95–109, 1973.

[268] F. Sillion and J.-M. Hasenfratz. Efficient parallel refinement for hierarchical radiosity on a DSM computer. In *Proceedings of the third Eurographics workshop on parallel graphics and visualisation*, pages 61–74, 2000.

[269] F. X. Sillion and C. Puech. *Radiosity and Global Illumination*. Morgan Kaufmann Publishers, Inc., San Francisco, California, 1994.

[270] C. Silva, J. S. B. Mitchell, and A. E. Kaufman. Fast rendering of irregular grids. In *1996 Volume Visualization Symposium*, pages 15–22. IEEE, October 1996.

[271] G. Simiakakis. *Accelerating Ray Tracing with Directional Subdivision and Parallel Processing*. PhD thesis, University of East Anglia, 1995.

[272] M. Simmons and C. Séquin. Tapestry: A dynamic mesh-based display representation for interactive rendering. In *Proceedings of the 11th Eurographics Workshop on Rendering*, pages 329–340, Brno, Czech Republic, June 2000.

[273] J. S. Sing, A. Gupta, and M. Levoy. Parallel visualization algorithms: Performance and architectural implications. *IEEE Computer*, 27(7):45–55, July 1994.

[274] J. P. Singh, C. Holt, T. Totsuka, A. Gupta, and J. Hennessy. Load balancing and data locality in adaptive hierarchical N-body methods: Barnes-hut, fast multipole and radiosity. *Journal of Parallel and Distributed Computing*, 27(1):118–141, June 1995. ISSN 0743-7315.

[275] P. Slusallek, T. Pflaum, and H.-P. Seidel. Using procedural RenderMan shaders for global illumination. In *Computer Graphics Forum (Proc. of EUROGRAPHICS '95*, pages 311–324, 1995.

[276] B. Smits. Efficiency issues for ray tracing. *Journal of Graphics Tools*, 3(2):1–14, 1998.

[277] L. Sobierajski and A. Kaufman. Volumetric Ray Tracing. *1994 Workshop on Volume Visualization*, pages 11–18, October 1994.

[278] S. Spach and R. Pulleyblank. Parallel raytraced image generation. *Hewlett-Packard Journal*, 43(3):76–83, June 1992.

[279] D. Speray and S. Kennon. Volume probes: Interactive data exploration on arbitrary grids. In *1990 Workshop on Volume Visualization*, pages 5–12, 1990. San Diego.

[280] M. Sramek. Fast surface rendering from raster data by voxel traversal using chessboard distance. In *Proceedings of Visualization '94*, pages 188–195, October 1994.

[281] W. Stürzlinger, G. Schaufler, and J. Volkert. Load balancing for a parallel radiosity algorithm. In *1995 Parallel Rendering Symposium*, pages 39–45. ACM SIGGRAPH, October 1995.

[282] W. Stürzlinger and C. Wild. Parallel progressive radiosity with parallel visibility calculations. In V. Skala, editor, *Winter School of Computer Graphics and CAD Systems*, pages 66–74. University of West Bohemia, January 1994.

[283] W. Stürzlinger and C. Wild. Parallel visibility computations for parallel radiosity. In B. Buchberger and J. Volkert, editors, *Parallel Processing: CONPAR 94 - VAPP VI (Third Joint International Conference on Vector and Parallel Processing)*, volume 854 of *Lecture Notes in Computer Science*, pages 405–413, Berlin, September 1994. Springer-Verlag.

[284] D. Stuttard, A. Worral, D. Paddon, and C. Willis. A parallel radiosity system for large data sets. In V. Skala, editor, *The Third International Conference in Central Europe on Computer Graphics and Visualisation 95*,

volume 2, pages 421–429, Plzeň, Czech Republic, February 1995. University of West Bohemia.

[285] K. Sung and P. Shirley. Ray tracing with the BSP tree. *Graphics Gems III*, pages 271–274, 1992.

[286] I. E. Sutherland and G. W. Hodgman. Reentrant polygon clipping. *Communications of the ACM*, 17(1), January 1974.

[287] I. E. Sutherland, R. F. Sproull, and R. A. Schumacker. A characterization of ten hidden-surface algorithms. *Computing Surveys*, 6(1):1–55, March 1974.

[288] R. J. Swam, S. H. Fuller, and D. P. Siewiorek. 'Cm*—A Modular, Multi-Microprocessor'. In *Proc. AFIPS 1977 Fall Joint Computer Conference 46*, pages 637–644, 1977.

[289] L. Talbot and C. O'Sullivan. Analysis of visibility masks and resultant image quality. In *Proceedings of the third Eurographics workshop on parallel graphics and visualisation*, pages 75–80, 2000.

[290] A. R. Technologies. The AR250: A new architecture for ray traced rendering. In *Proceedings Of The Eurographics/SIGGRAPH Workshop On Graphics Hardware—Hot Topics Session*, pages 39–42, 1999.

[291] S. Teller and P. Hanrahan. Global visibility algorithms for illumination computations. In *SIGGRAPH 93 Conference Proceedings*, pages 239–246, 1993.

[292] S. Thakkar, P. Gifford, and G. Fiellamd. The Balance multiprocessor system. *IEEE Micro*, 8(1):57–69, February 1988.

[293] J. P. Tidmus. *Task and Data Management for Parallel Particle Tracing*. PhD thesis, University of the West of England, December 1997.

[294] J. P. Tidmus, A. G. Chalmers, and R. M. Miles. Distributed monte carlo techniques for interactive photo-realistic image synthesis. In R. Miles and A. Chalmers, editors, *17th World Occam and Transputer Users Group conference*, pages 139–147, Bristol, 1994. IOS Press.

[295] J. P. Tidmus, R. Miles, and A. Chalmers. Prefetch data management for parallel particle tracing. In A. Bakkers, editor, *Parallel Programming and Java, Proceedings of WoTUG-20*, volume 50 of *Concurrent Systems Engineering*, pages 130–137, University of Twente, Netherlands, 1997. World occam and Transputer User Group (WoTUG), IOS Press, Netherlands.

[296] P. C. Treleaven, D. R. Brownbridge, and R. P. Hopkins. Data driven and demand-driven computer architecture. *Communications of the ACM*, 14(1):95–143, March 1982.

[297] N. Trevett. Challenges and opportunities for 3d grpahics on the pc. In Eurographics/ACM, editor, *Eurographics/Siggraph Workshop on Graphics Hardware*, 1999.

[298] A. Trew and G. Wilson, editors. *Past, Present and Parallel: A survey of available parallel computer systems*. Springer-Verlag, London, 1991.

[299] C. Upson and M. Keeler. V-buffer: Visible volume rendering. *Computer Graphics*, 22(4):59–64, July 1988. ACM Siggraph '88 Conference Proceedings.

[300] L. G. Valiant. A bridging model for parallel computation. *Communications of the ACM*, 33(8):103–111, August 1990.

[301] I. Verdú, D. Giménez, and J. C. Torres. Ray tracing for natural scenes in parallel processors. In H. Liddell, A. Colbrook, B. Hertzberger, and P. Sloot, editors, *High-Performance Computing and Networking*, volume 1067 of *Lecture Notes in Computer Science*, pages 297–305. Springer-Verlag, April 1996.

[302] G. Vézina, P. A. Fletcher, and P. K. Robertson. Volume Rendering on the MasPar MP-1. In *1992 Workshop on volume Visualization*, pages 3–8, 1992. Boston, October 19-20.

[303] J. Žára, A. Holeček, and J. Přikryl. Parallelisation of the ray-tracing algorithm. In V. Skala, editor, *Winter School of Computer Graphics and CAD Systems 94*, volume 1, pages 113–117. University of West Bohemia, January 1994. WSCG 95.

[304] J. Žára, A. Holeček, and J. Přikryl. When the parallel ray-tracer starts to be efficient? In *Proceedings of Spring School on Computer Graphics*, pages 108–116. Comenius University Bratislava, June 1994. Held June 6–9 Bratislava, Slovakia.

[305] I. Wald and P. Slusallek. State of the art in interactive ray tracing. In *Eurographics STAR - State of the Art reports*, pages 21–42, 2001.

[306] I. Wald, P. Slusallek, and C. Benthin. Interactive distributed ray tracing of highly complex models. In S. J. Gortler and K. Myszkowski, editors, *Proceedings of the 12th Eurographics Workshop on Rendering*, pages 274–285, 2001.

[307] I. Wald, P. Slusallek, C. Benthin, and M. Wagner. Interactive rendering with coherent ray tracing. *Computer Graphics Forum*, 20(3):153–164, 2001.

[308] J. Wallace, K. Elmquist, and E. Haines. A ray tracing algorithm for progressive radiosity. In *Computer Graphics (ACM SIGGRAPH '89 Proceedings)*, volume 23, pages 315–324, July 1989.

[309] B. Walter, G. Drettakis, and S. Parker. Interactive rendering using the render cache. In D. Lischinski and G. W. Larson, editors, *Rendering Techniques '99*, Eurographics, pages 19–30. Springer-Verlag Wien New York, 1999.

[310] G. Ward. Adaptive shadow testing for ray tracing. In *Photorealistic Rendering in Computer Graphics (Proceedings of the Second Eurographics Workshop on Rendering*, pages 11–20. Springer Verlag, New York, 1994.

[311] G. J. Ward. The RADIANCE lighting simulation and rendering system. In A. Glassner, editor, *Proceedings of SIGGRAPH '94*, pages 459–472, July 1994.

[312] G. J. Ward, F. M. Rubinstein, and R. D. Clear. A ray tracing solution for diffuse interreflection. *ACM Computer Graphics*, 22(4):85–92, August 1988.

[313] G. Ward Larson and R. A. Shakespeare. *Rendering with Radiance*. Morgan Kaufmann Publ., 1998.

[314] D. H. D. Warren and S. Haridi. The Data Diffusion Machine—a scalable shared virtual memory multiprocessor. In *Proceedings of the 1988 International Conference on Fifth Generation Computer Systems*, pages 943–952, Tokyo, Japan, December 1988.

[315] H. Weghorst, G. Hooper, and D. P. Greenberg. Improved computations methods for ray tracing. *Transactions on Graphics*, 3(1):52–69, January 1984.

[316] R. P. Weicker. Dhrystone: A synthetic systems programming benchmark. *Communications of the ACM*, 27(10):1013–1030, 1984.

[317] S. Whitman. A Survey of Parallel Algorithms for Graphics and Visualization. In *High Performance Computing for Computer Graphics and Visualization*, pages 3–22, 1995. Swansea, July 3–4.

[318] T. Whitted. An improved illumination model for shaded display. *Communications of the ACM*, 23(6):343–349, June 1980.

[319] J. Wilhelms and J. Challinger. Direct volume rendering of curvilinear volumes. In *1990 Workshop on Volume Visualization*, pages 41–47, 1990. San Diego.

[320] J. Wilhelms and A. Van Gelder. Octrees for faster isosurface generation. In *1990 Workshop on Volume Visualization*, pages 57–62, 1990. San Diego.

[321] J. Wilhelms and A. Van Gelder. Octrees for faster isosurface generation. *ACM Transactions on Graphics*, 11(3):201–227, July 1992.

[322] H. Xu, Q. Peng, and Y. Liang. Accelerated radiosity method for complex environments. In *Eurographics '89*, pages 51–61, Amsterdam, September 1989. Elsevier Science Publishers. Eurographics '89.

[323] Y. Yu, O. H. Ibarra, and T. Yang. Parallel progressive radiosity with adaptive meshing. In A. Ferreira, J. Rolim, Y. Saad, and T. Yang, editors, *Parallel Algorithms for Irregularly Structured Problems (Third International Workshop, IRREGULAR '96)*, volume 1117 of *Lecture Notes in Computer Science*, pages 159–170. Springer-Verlag, August 1996.

[324] E. S. Zagier. Frameless antialiasing. Technical Report TR95-026, UNC-CS, May 1995.

[325] E. S. Zagier. Defining and refining frameless rendering. Technical Report TR97-008, UNC-CS, July 1997.

[326] D. Zareski. Parallel decomposition of view-independent global illumination algorithms. Master's thesis, Cornell University, Ithaca, NY, 1995.

[327] D. Zareski, B. Wade, P. Hubbard, and P. Shirley. Efficient parallel global illumination using density estimation. In *1995 Parallel Rendering Symposium*, pages 47–54. ACM SIGGRAPH, 1995.

[328] E. Zeghers, K. Bouatouch, E. Maisel, and C. Bouville. Faster image rendering in animation through motion compensated interpolation. In S. P. Mudur and S. N. Pattanaik, editors, *Proceedings of the IFIP TC5/WG5.2/WG5.10 CSI International Conference on Computer Graphics (ICCG '93) in Graphics, Design, and Visualization*, pages 49–62, Amsterdam, 1993. North-Holland.

[329] M. van der Zwaan, E. Reinhard, and F. W. Jansen. Pyramid clipping for efficient ray traversal. In P. Hanrahan and W. Purgathofer, editors, *Rendering Techniques '95*, pages 1–10. Springer - Vienna, June 1995.

Index

3DLABS, 133, 136

ADI, 34, 36, 47–49, 66, 69, 70, 73, 86
AGP bus, 135
algorithm, 14, 15, 32–34
    embarrassingly parallel, 100
algorithmic decomposition, 31, 32, 92
algorithmic dependency, 49, 85
Amdahl's law, 23, 25, 49
animation, 165–184
    Glass Bounce, 176
    Newton-Left, 176
    Soda Worship, 176
anti-aliasing, 95, 173
AP, 17, 19, 20, 53, 56–60, 62, 66, 67, 69, 70, 73, 74, 81
AR250, 329
architecture, 7, 8, 30
    Jetstream, 139
    ParaScale, 136
array processor, 11
ATI, 133
atomic element, 46–48

Babbage, 3
balanced data driven, 37, 38, 40, 73
barrier, *see* synchronization point
bottleneck, 4, 6, 7, 35, 62
bricking, 197

broadcast, 75
bus, 8, 13, 75

C, 69
cache, 21, 70, 79, 81, 135
    directional, 130
    hierarchy, 197
    scene, 238
cache hit, 65
cache memory, 21, 73
caching, 81, 85, 222, 334
chain, 56, 59
coherence, 65, 81, 103, 219
    data, 127
    frame, 166, 167, 169
    image, 103
    incidental frame, 169
    object, 103
    ray, 103, 223
    stereoscopic views, 167
communication, 4, 12, 16
compression, 240
computation reordering, 130
computation to communication ratio, 16, 19, 48, 56–58, 60, 62
computational complexity, 41, 46, 53, 58, 86
computational model, 36, 38, 64
computational variations, 41, 48
conceptual allocation, 64, 86
concurrent, 9, 20, 34

Author Biographies

Alan Chalmers is a Reader in the Department of Computer Science at the University of Bristol, UK. He has published over 80 papers in journals and international conferences on parallel photo-realistic graphics. He was co-chairman of the IEEE Parallel Visualization and Graphics Symposium and is chairman of the Eurographics workshop series on Parallel Graphics and Visualisation. Recently he and Professor F. W. Jansen were the guest editors of the journal Parallel Computing for its special edition on Parallel Graphics and Visualisation. He is also currently Vice President of ACM SIGGRAPH. His research interests include the application of parallel photo-realistic graphics to archaeological site visualization in order to provide a flexible tool for investigating site reconstruction and utilization.

Timothy A. Davis is an assistant professor in the Computer Science Department at Clemson University where he works within the newly established DPA (Digital Production Arts) group, which trains students to produce special effects for entertainment and commercial projects. His research involves exploiting spatio-temporal coherence in a parallel environment to reduce rendering times for ray-traced animations. He received his Ph.D. from North Carolina State University and has worked in technical positions for the Environmental Protection Agency and NASA Goddard Space Flight Center.

Erik Reinhard is a post-doctoral researcher at the University of Utah in the fields of parallel ray tracing and visual perception. He received a 'TWAIO' diploma in parallel computer graphics from Delft University of Technology in 1996 and a Ph.D. degree from the University of Bristol in 2000. His current research interests include algorithms and data structures for real-time ray tracing. This includes mechanisms to trade-off visual quality for interactivity and to add animation capabilities to real-time ray tracing.

Kadi Bouatouch is an electronics and automatic systems engineer (ENSEM 1974). He was awarded a Ph.D. in 1977 and a higher doctorate on computer science in the field of computer graphics in 1989. He is working on global illumination, lighting simulation for complex environments, parallel radiosity, computer architecture for image synthesis, virtual augmented reality, computer vision and visual comfort. He designed a VLSI chip for image synthesis. He is currently Professor at the University of Rennes 1 (France) and researcher at IRISA. He has published more than seventy papers.

Toshi Kato has devoted his time to the development of high-end production-level renderers for sixteen years. Currently he is the project leader of an ongoing project "Kilauea," a parallel ray tracer developed at Square USA's R&D department. From 1993 to 1998 he developed an in-house scanline-based renderer at Rhythm & Hues in LA and participated in the production of movies such as Mouse Hunt (1998), Kazaam (1996) and Babe (1995). He also developed a special stereoscopic renderer for IMAX's Omnimax Solido dome.

Steven Parker is a Research Assistant Professor in the Department of Computer Science at the University of Utah. His research focuses on problem solving environments, which tie together scientific computing, scientific visualization, and computer graphics. He was a recipient of the Computational Science Graduate Fellowship from the Dept. of Energy. He received a Ph.D. from the University of Utah (1999), and B.S. in Electrical Engineering from the University of Oklahoma (1992).

Tim Purcell is a third year Ph.D. student in the department of Computer Science at Stanford University. His research focuses on architectural design for hardware ray tracing. He was a recipient of the Graduate Research Fellowship from the National Science Foundation. He received a B.S. in Computer Science from the University of Utah in 1998.

Philipp Slusallek is a professor at the computer graphics lab at Saarland University. He was visiting assistant professor at the Stanford University graphics lab (1998–1999). He received a Diploma in physics from the University of Tuebingen (1990) and a Ph.D. in computer science from the University of Erlangen (1995). He leads the Vision project, a large object-oriented, physically-based rendering system. His current research activities focus on interactive ray-tracing on off-the-shelf computers and designing a hardware architecture for real-time ray tracing.